Lawyers and the American Dream

LAWYERS
and the
AMERICAN
DREAM

Stuart M. Speiser

BLACKSTONE
PRESS LIMITED

First published in Great Britain 1993 by Blackstone Press Limited,
9-15 Aldine Street, London W12 8AW. Telephone 081-740 1173

© Stuart M. Speiser, 1993

ISBN: 1 85431 121 2

Manufactured in the United States of America

British Library Cataloguing in Publication Data
A CIP catalogue record for this book is available from the British Library.

Dedicated to Alfred and Annette Gans

You gotta have a dream.
If you don't have a dream,
How you gonna have your dream come true?

   — **Richard Rodgers and Oscar Hammerstein II,**
   "Happy Talk," *South Pacific,* **1949.**

Contents

Lexicon

Following are the author's simplified definitions of legal terms used in this book.

Parties to a civil lawsuit are the plaintiff (the one bringing the suit) and the defendant (the one being sued). Parties can be individuals, corporations, government agencies, and large groups of people. There can be unlimited numbers of plaintiffs and defendants in the same lawsuit. In Scotland, the parties are called (more colorfully and perhaps more accurately) the pursuer and the defender.

Liability is the court finding that the defendant is responsible for damages inflicted on the plaintiff. In the United States, the plaintiff has the right to have a jury determine liability, except when the plaintiff claims the damages were caused by the government; in such "nonjury" cases a judge decides both liability and damages. In the United Kingdom, judges usually determine both liability and damages, except that juries are allowed in defamation cases (libel and slander). In most other nations juries are not used in civil cases.

Damages is the amount fixed by the jury (or by the judge in nonjury cases) for the defendant to pay to the plaintiff. In most cases, this consists of *compensatory damages* which are designed to restore the plaintiff to the position he would have been in if the injury inflicted by the defendant had not occurred. In some cases involving intentional or highly irresponsible conduct *punitive damages* are added to compensatory damages, in order to punish the defendant and to set an example which will deter the defendant and others from such conduct in the future. For this reason, punitive damages are also called *exemplary damages.*

Even though the jury fixes the amount of damages, the trial judge and judges of appellate courts have the power (called *remittitur*) to review the jury's award, and to throw it out and order a new trial if they feel it was excessive or was not based on the evidence introduced at the trial.

Torts is the catch-all name for the "wrongful" conduct that gives rise to most civil lawsuits. The most common tort cases are those involving personal injury or death arising out of accidents. The tort involved in accident cases is usually called **negligence,** although in cases involving injuries or deaths caused by defective products, the tort is called **product liability** rather than negligence. Other prominent torts are **defamation** (which is called **libel** if it involves written words and **slander** if based on spoken words); **fraud; wrongful firing of employees; pollution of the environment; assault; battery; false imprisonment** ; and **invasion of privacy.** Lawyers who specialize in representing plaintiffs in tort cases are usually called tort lawyers, negligence lawyers, personal injury lawyers, or contingent-fee lawyers. For those interested in etymology, the word "tort" derives from the Latin verb "torqueo" (to twist or to bend)—something twisted, not right, and therefore wrong. Tort cases are brought to right these wrongs. But tort law covers only certain specific wrongs, and does not extend to crimes or breaches of contract, which have their own sets of rules. There really is no satisfactory overall definition of **torts,** but it is useful as a buzzword, like "arts" or "humanities."

If these definitions leave you less than exhilarated, you may prefer some of those coined by Ambrose Bierce, a nonfan of lawyers, in his 1911 book **The Devil's Dictionary:**

> **Lawyer:** One skilled in circumvention of the law.
> **Liar:** A lawyer with a roving commission.
> **Litigant:** A person about to give up his skin for the hope of retaining his bones.
> **Litigation:** A machine which you go into as a pig and come out as a sausage.
> **Trial:** A formal inquiry designed to prove and put upon record the blameless character of judges, advocates, and jurors.

Unfortunately, Ambrose did not undertake to define **torts.**

Lawyers and the American Dream

CHAPTER 1

What Is The American Dream?

Defining the American Dream is—to coin a phrase—like trying to catch a moonbeam in a jar. Dreams, of course, are highly
personal to the individual dreamer. So it is not surprising that
you won't find a standard definition in the dictionaries or ency-
clopedias.

An exception is *Safire's Political Dictionary*, written by William
Safire, whom *The New York Times Book Review* called "the perfect
political lexicographer." While Safire says that the American
Dream "defies definition as much as it invites discussion" he
does take a stab at defining it as used in political speeches: "the
ideal of freedom and opportunity that motivated the Founding
Fathers; the spiritual strength of the nation."

Safire says that for minorities and the poor, the political use
of the phrase emphasizes equality. He concludes that most observers see it as a combination of freedom and opportunity "with
growing overtones of social justice." Safire's analysis is confirmed by the words of the Pledge of Allegiance to the Flag,
which originated in an 1892 edition of a weekly magazine, *Youth's
Companion*, and was later made official by act of Congress. The
Pledge ends with the description of the United States as a nation
"with liberty and justice for all."

But our sights are not limited to political use of the phrase
"American Dream." We want to explore its meaning throughout
our society, and there is no better starting point than the 1931
book in which it first appeared: *The Epic of America*, by James
Truslow Adams, the Pulitzer prize-winning historian. He first
uses the phrase in his preface, where he explains that he has
endeavored to trace the beginnings of such American concepts as
"bigger and better," and especially "that American dream of a
better, richer, and happier life for all our citizens of every rank
which is the greatest contribution we have as yet made to the
thought and welfare of the world."

In the epilogue, after a 400-page narration of the history of the United States, Adams makes it clear that the American Dream, although greatly concerned with money and material success, means something more:

> If we hastened after the pot of gold, we also saw the rainbow itself, and felt that it promised, as of old, a hope for mankind.
>
> It is not a dream of motor cars and high wages merely, but a dream of a social order in which each man and each woman shall be able to attain to the fullest stature of which they are innately capable, and be recognized by others for what they are, regardless of the fortuitous circumstances of birth or position.
>
> The very foundation of the American dream of a better and richer life for all is that all, in varying degrees, shall be capable of wanting to share in it.
>
> That dream was not the product of a solitary thinker. It evolved from the hearts and burdened souls of many millions, who have come to us from all nations.

The dream was so crucial to the Epic of America that Adams concluded:

> The epic loses all its glory without the dream. The statistics of size, population, and wealth would mean nothing to me unless I could still believe in the dream.

Another idealistic view of the American Dream has been stated by Professor James Guimond, chairman of the English Department at Rider College. While the main purpose of his 1991 book, *American Photography and the American Dream*, was to show how the Dream has been depicted in photographs, I found his explanatory text to be among the best available commentaries on the Dream. He covers many versions of the Dream, both optimistic and pessimistic. Of the optimistic versions, such as the original James Truslow Adams formulation quoted above, he says:

> What lies behind many versions of the Dream is the conception of America as a kind of magic environment or society that has the power to transform people's lives, the idea that the United States is not merely a new world, but a different kind of world, a unique place where the limitations, boundaries, and inequities that formerly confined the human race either do not exist or are about to disappear. This belief, often described as "exceptionalism," is based on the assumption that America can never be an ordinary nation or society. Instead, to use a much-quoted

phrase from John Winthrop's 1630 sermon on the Arbella, it is destined to be a "city set upon a hill," whose inhabitants will lead lives of exceptional virtue, free from most of the tribulations and tragedies that have afflicted past history.

But most of the photos in Professor Guimond's book tell a much more pessimistic story of how the Dream has worked out in reality.

Let's go now to another significant source of the Dream's meaning: the opinions of a cross-section of the American people. In 1990, another Pulitzer prize-winning author, Richard Reeves, was commisioned by *Money* magazine to travel the nation in search of the current definition of the American Dream. His article, "In Search of the American Dream," was published as the cover story in the 1990 special year-end edition of *Money*. Reeves covered 15,000 miles and interviewed more than 200 people.

Using the Reeves article as a reservoir, we can update the defintion of the American Dream to 1990. Reeves's own feelings about the meaning of the Dream crystallized in his interview with a Catholic priest at LaGrange, Texas. Many of the parents and grandparents of the priest's parishioners had immigrated from Czechoslovakia to Texas in the nineteenth century. In response to the question of why those people came to America, the priest thought for a moment, and then said, "For something better." That phrase, "for something better," made a deep impression on Reeves:

> Those words are a force of nature. Human nature. The American Dream is part of the weather of the world. A freshening wind that knows no season or time, touching the faces and quickening the steps of men and women in the Prague of 1890 or the Guatemala City, Taipei or Bombay of 1990. That could sound melodramatic or anachronistic, even ridiculous, at a time when some Americans sleep in the streets and others fear to walk them. Yet when I heard Monsignor Harry Mazurkiewicz's words again and again as I traveled this country last April and May, I felt the wind.

Despite the apparent statistical and spirirtual decline of the United States, Reeves had trouble finding individual Americans who had given up the Dream. It isn't solely American anymore—it's gone global. For every American who is stumbling, there are a hundred foreigners, like the Czechs who came to Texas for something better, who will take the American's place. Around the world, this is the common belief:

In America, if you work hard you can get anything you want. And "get" is the operative word, not "be." The dream may be spiritual, but its ends are not. Our individual aspirations are usually acquisitions: bigger homes, slicker cars, more TV channels, more profitable educations for our children; even better health is seen as something for sale, a blessing you can earn.

Reeves perceived other elements of the American Dream: our university system, which Reeves feels is a wonder of the world and vastly underrated by Americans; our individualism, which he sees as something of an obstacle to a national work ethic; and the power of most Americans to choose, which he calls "one of the great forces of human history." He continues:

> Our version of freedom is not the chance to succeed—you can succeed in many places, particularly if you choose your parents well. What makes our brand great is the freedom to fail, and to try again, to make another choice. Going to school at night to change your life or going to a 24-hour Safeway to buy groceries and hair spray at 4:30 a.m. is what "pursuit of happiness" means. That is liberty.

Reeves firmly believes what he was told by Kuo-hsiang Liou, an immigrant from Taiwan now living in Los Angeles (where he is known as Leo): "America lets you do the best you can. We'll always get the best men and women from the rest of the world."

Although the fact that he was writing for the *Money* magazine audience probably influenced Reeves to take a highly materialistic view of the American Dream, note this important conclusion, which matches the idealistic vision of James Truslow Adams:

> If you lose the dream, you lose everything. And the dream is based on individuals believing they have both the freedom and the power to make something better for themselves.

The same 1990 year-end issue of *Money* contained a round-table discussion among six black leaders about the progress of blacks toward realization of Martin Luther King's famous 1963 dream:

> I have a dream my four little children will one day live in a nation where they will not be judged by the color of their skin but by the content of their character...

The six black leaders expressed a variety of feelings, ranging from a mere hope of survival to the white American's dream of affluence. Sandra McDonald, president and founder of Outreach Inc., a non-profit self-help community development group in Atlanta, said:

> In 1990, if you are the mother of a black teenage male, your primary goal is to get him through high school alive and drug-free. The dream is: "Lord, let my child live to be 30."

Ms. McDonald's views are similar to those expressed by Drew T. Brown III in his 1991 book, *You Gotta Believe!* which is subtitled *Education + Hard Work - Drugs = The American Dream.* Brown, a black former Navy Pilot who now flies for Federal Express, has established The American Dream Foundation, which undertakes to motivate youth toward those goals.

Joseph Perkins, editorial writer for the *San Diego Union* and a former assistant to Vice President Dan Quayle, portrayed a more optimistic dream in *Money* magazine:

> I think the American dream for most blacks is like that of the whites: to get married and have a wonderful family, college for their kids, a satisfying career and ultimately the kind of amenities that make life a little more comfortable. Since 1982, there has been a doubling of the number of black households earning more than $50,000 per year. That's an indication to me that blacks are increasingly attaining the American dream.

A more eclectic vision than that of Money magazine will be found in Studs Terkel's 1980 bestseller, *American Dreams: Lost & Found.* Terkel, called "America's foremost oral historian" by the *Chicago Tribune,* tape-recorded interviews with hundreds of people from all walks of life during the late 1970s, amassing over a million words of comment on the American Dream. Most of this testimony is highly personal and anecdotal, which increases the difficulty of compiling a consensus. Nevertheless there are some nuggets in this fascinating book. Such as:

Ted Turner, owner of CNN and other cable television networks: "Being something big to yourself, that's important. Being a star. Everbody's a star in the movie of their life."

Norman MacLean, Professor emeritus, University of Chicago: "I don't know if we have an American Dream. We have American Dreams. One of [my father's] biggest dreams was the dream of great education in this country and the necessity of every person to be educated."

Arnold Schwarzenegger, Austrian-born champion body-builder and movie superstar: "When I came over here to America, I felt I was in heaven. In America, we don't have an obstacle.

Nobody's holding you back. I believe very strongly in the philosophy of staying hungry. If you have a dream and it becomes a reality, don't stay satisfied with it too long. Make up a new dream and hunt after that one and turn it into reality. I am a strong believer in Western philosophy, the philosophy of success, of progress, of getting rich."

Nicholas von Hoffman, journalist, author, and television commentator: "One of the things that makes America such an unusual place is that it is perhaps the only society in history in which a vast number of its members are living their private dreams. It is a world that teaches the primacy of the personal, of oneself, which ironically leaves people powerless. This country has always been saved by a new minority, who realize they've been robbed. In the process of righting their private wrongs, they have re-animated our public rights. You who thought of yourself, up to that moment, as simply being a number, suddenly spring to life. You have that intoxicating feeling that you can make your own history, that you really count."

Erma "Tiny" Mouton, a poor black woman from Caruthersville, Missouri, who worked all her life for starvation wages: "What the dream means to me is for my children to be able to live anywhere they want to, even be able to come back home where they were born and raised, and get a good job, hold their head high. Not given something because they're black and not something taken away from them because they're black. But given something because they're a man and they deserved it. That's my American Dream. I do believe something's stirring. I want to live a long time. I want to see the world really turn about-face and people get together. 'Cause it doesn't have to be like it is now."

Tom McCall, former Republican governor of Oregon, defeated in his quest for a third term: "Heroes are not giant statues framed against a red sky. They are people who say: This is my community and it's my responsbility to make it better. Interweave all these communities, and you really have an America that is back on its feet, a comfortable nation to live in again. I really think we're gonna have to reassess what constitutes a hero."

James Abourezk, of Lebanese descent, former senator from South Dakota who declined to run for reelection: "We were always told there was an American Dream, where people have a right to be treated equal. It can't be fulfilled as long as the few have the power to overwhelm the many. I'd like to see an America where so much power was not in the hands of the few. Where everbody'd get a fair shake."

Jesse Helms, senator from North Carolina and a leading conservative Republican: "I would like to see a restoration of those values [of his childhood days.] Personal responsbility is no longer number one as it was back then. The Founding Fathers were unique in their reliance upon God. I see a growing emphasis on personal faith that was there when I was a boy. This is becoming a more spiritual, more concerned nation than I've ever seen. I have great hope."

John McClaughry, then the leader of the Conservative Caucus (of Republicans and Democrats,) later a White House advisor to President Reagan, and now a Vermont state senator: "The ideal to me is where a sufficient number of individuals can control their destinies and say, if necessary: 'To hell with it, I'm not gonna do it.' I've always been big on community corporations, small businesses, cooperatives, small farmers, independent professionals. Anyone who understands Jefferson could understand me in an instant. There's not a dime's worth of difference."

Sam Lopez, Chicago West Side Latino, fourth oldest of ten children, in trouble and in jail as a youth, first in his family to earn a college degree, now director of the Uptown Center, an adjunct of Northeastern University: "I don't see my life as something of the American Dream. I didn't make it because of the American Dream. I don't think America helped me, if by America you mean the White House, the system, the elements. I made it because I was aggressive enough to fight the elements that say, 'No, you will never make it.' I made it because there were certain people in my life, ordinary people, who helped me."

William Gothard, a corporation lawyer in Los Angeles: "Very few people have found the American Dream. When you stop searching, you no longer have it. America became strong because people, out of their own initiative, have succeeded. Sons and daughters of fishmongers and tailors became lawyers, doctors, and corporate presidents. They drove themselves. We live in a socially mobile society where you can succeed if you have the drive. Los Angeles, where I work, typifies in one city the best and the worst of American life. The home of franchise foods, home of the automobile society, home of Hollywood, your fantasia, your ultimate American Dream. Without roots."

Jill Robinson, a writer who grew up in the Hollywood of the 1940s and 1950s as the daughter of film producer Dore Schary: "Hollywood—the American Dream—is a Jewish idea. It combines the Puritan ethic—there's no sex, no ultimate satisfaction—

with baroque magnificence. The happy ending was the invention of Russian Jews, [Goldwyn, Zukor, Lasky, Warner] designed to drive Americans crazy....What else are we gonna live by if not dreams? We need to believe in something. What would really drive us crazy is to believe this reality we run into every day is all there is. If I don't believe there's that happy ending out there—that will-you-marry-me in the sky—I can't keep working today. That's true, I think, for all of us."

Many famous Americans have lived the Dream. Historian Matthew Josephson wrote of Thomas Alva Edison: "The rise of the former trainboy and tramp telegrapher from rags to riches was an enactment of the American Dream." The life story of Herbert Hoover could have been written by Horatio Alger: orphaned at the age of nine, he worked his way through Stanford, becoming a successful mining engineer and a millionaire. He then devoted himself to public works, administering food and other aid to the impoverished countries of Europe after World War I, before becoming Secretary of Commerce and then President. And Alex Haley's epic saga of his family's rise from slavery, in both the book and television miniseries versions of *Roots*, ends in achievement of the American Dream for him as a renowned writer, and for his family, which enjoys freedom and dignity on its own land in Tennessee.

Historian Herbert Muller, in his book, *The Uses of the Past*, supplies another important perspective: "In the incessant din of the mediocre, mean, and fraudulent activities of a commercial mass society, we are apt to forget the genuine idealism of democracy, of the long and painful struggle for liberty and equality." And Professor James Guimond reminds us in *American Photography and the American Dream* that "the Dream has been one of the hardiest perennials in the mass media and American popular culture, and for two hundred years it has inspired editors, journalists, salespeople, and ordinary citizens, who have used the phrase (or the concept behind it) loosely and frequently as a synonym for success, prosperity, equality, economic expansion, and social mobility."

In the 1992 election campaigns, all the major candidates used the vision of the American Dream in their speeches. And General Colin Powell, chairman of the Joint Chiefs of Staff, delivering a commencement address at Fisk University shortly after the 1992 Los Angeles riots, said:

> The problem goes beyond Rodney King. The problem goes beyond Los Angeles. It goes beyond the trial of those four officers. The problem goes to the despair that still exists in the

black community over the inability of black Americans to share fully in the American Dream.

The American Dream in Novels

Novels are another source of definitions of the American Dream, for they often reflect the main lights of American culture. Early examples are Mark Twain's *The Adventures of Huckleberry Finn*, with the hero making his own way down the Mississippi on a raft, and the many nineteenth-century novels by Horatio Alger, invariably featuring young boys struggling on their own against poverty and adversity to achieve wealth and honor.

The American Dream and the Popular Novel, a 1985 book written by Rice University Sociology Professor Elizabeth Long, examines the American Dream as visualized in dozens of bestselling novels published between 1945 and 1975. Professor Long's conclusions confirm what we have learned from our survey of individual opinions:

> The story of America has been the story of success. From the time of *Poor Richard's Almanack*, individual enterprise has been our national anthem.

Reviewing the most popular novels of James Michener, Edna Ferber, John Steinbeck, John Updike, Saul Bellow, Harold Robbins, James Clavell, and other leading authors, she finds that their concepts of the American Dream are based on success, the good life, and getting ahead. Prior to the 1950s, the heroes of popular novels were most often individual enterpreneurs like Jett Rink in Edna Ferber's *Giant* (played by Rock Hudson in the movie version). Around the mid-1950s, Professor Long finds a shift to the Organization Man, the Tom Rath type in Sloan Wilson's *The Man in the Gray Flannel Suit* (played by Gregory Peck in the film). But whether the quest for affluence and success is undertaken as an individual entrepreneur or in the climb up the corporate executive ladder, the ultimate Dream is the same: material success.

Professor Long notes another important change in the mid-1950s. Until then, leading novels were often based on "the heroic entrepreneurial tale of conquest, uniting individual self-interest and social amelioration." Thus, while Jett Rink in Edna Ferber's *Giant* uses his entrepreneurial drive to develop the Texas oil industry and increase his own wealth, he thereby creates many jobs, breaks the stranglehold of the rancher-based power structure, fosters fair elections, and opens the way for unions and more social justice for Mexican-Americans. He does well by doing good, in the tradition of Adam Smith's invisible hand that supposedly guides ordinary selfish humans to help others while meaning only to help themselves. But we didn't see many such novels after the 1950s. As Professor Long notes, when affluence became more widespread and we realized that it would not produce the orderly moral and social universe visualized in the ultimate American Dream, novelists focused on "the failure of success."

Tom Wolfe's *The Bonfire of the Vanities* (1987) and the works of other leading contemporary novelists such as Joseph Heller and John Updike, confirm that the American Dream is still one of success, but they portray it as a failed dream. Novels now rarely have happy endings or realizations of the American Dream.

Professor Long's book relates to "popular" rather than "serious" novels, a distinction we can accept here for discussion purposes even though some of the "serious" writers were also popular successes and some of the "popular" writers dealt seriously with serious subjects. The point of interest to us is that while the popular novelists shifted away from happy endings in the 1950s, the serious American novelists were writing unhappy endings long before that. *American Dreams, American Nightmares*, edited by author and playwright David Madden, examines the works of earlier American giants, such as Herman Melville, Sinclair Lewis, Eugene O'Neill, F. Scott Fitzgerald, William Faulkner, and Thomas Wolfe, as well as contemporaries like Norman Mailer and Arthur Miller. Most of their plots culminate in a failure to achieve the Dream, or the Dream itself turning into a nightmare.

Most serious novelists take a pessimistic attitude, apparently reasoning that the future is hopeless or that happy endings are unworthy of serious literature. An apt example is F. Scott Fitzgerald's 1925 classic, *The Great Gatsby*. Fitzgerald himself was so conscious of the novel's focus on the American Dream that he wanted to title it *Under the Red, White and Blue*. He never liked the Gatsby title but his editor at Scribner's, Maxwell Perkins, finally talked him into accepting it.

In *American Dreams, American Nightmares*, U.C.L.A. Professor Richard Lehan contributed an essay on *Gatsby*, whom he calls "The Nowhere Hero." Lehan points out that Jay Gatsby accepted completely the old Benjamin Franklin American Dream of rags-to-riches, and he equated this ideal with a woman, Daisy Fay. He says that Gatsby became the grotesque embodiment of what the

American Dream offers to our ambitious young people: "Gatsby with his silver suits, golden ties, and pin-striped shirts; Gatsby in his phony feudal castle built by a wealthy brewer (be it noted) who wanted to thatch the roofs of surrounding houses; and Gatsby in his oversized yellow car embellished with chrome."

Lehan says that Fitzgerald extended the grotesque Gatsby qualities to America itself, particularly in his descriptions of New York, and that the sense of lost promise in Fitzgerald's characters duplicated the lost promises of America itself. Lehan concludes:

> At the very end of the novel, as Nick looks out into the dark of Long Island Sound, he realizes that both Gatsby's dream and that of the republic lie behind us, and his last sentence catches the rhythm of his previous words, "So we beat on, boats against the current, borne back ceaselessly into the past."
>
> Gatsby watches over nothing, and we beat on into the past. The two ideas merge on the level of style as well as on the level of narrative theme. We move from hope to despair, from the present to the past where the promises of a young country and a young man have given way to—"nothing."

I have read *Gatsby* at least half a dozen times. It always enthralls me, but it certainly doesn't inspire me to work for changes that might restore the dreams of the young Gatsby or the young country. Neither Fitzgerald nor any of our other great novelists who share this negative vision of the American Nightmare have provided any hope of resurrecting the Dream. We don't need to read their books to learn how frightful the American Nightmare has become. The six o'clock evening television newscasts in all of our cities remind us of that every day.

If we try to define the American Dream through the visions of our great novelists, we will miss a crucial point. As we saw in the works of James Truslow Adams, Richard Reeves, and Studs Terkel, the American Dream is important in itself as a goal, even if never to be fully attained. The evidence of the Reeves/Terkel odysseys tells us that the driving forces which gave birth to this country, and the resilient spirit of its people, assure the survival of the American Dream. Even a very negative book like *The Day America Told the Truth*, written by James Patterson and Peter Kim, two officials of the J. Walter Thompson advertising agency, bears out the need for the Dream. The authors surveyed thousands of Americans and found them generally to be greedy, amoral, and shallow. They concluded: "It's been said that an era comes to an end when its dreams are exhausted. America's dreams are wearing thin—at least the kind of dreams that can sustain a great nation."

In a world full of negative images, I suggest that there is great value in trying to retain and expand such a positive concept as the American Dream, even if it requires us to indulge in optimism and idealism. *Time* magazine, explaining the instant popularity of Ross Perot in the 1992 election campaign, said that "the hopeful sincerity of his newfound supporters is a reminder of the latent idealism in the American character." And, as the Rodgers and Hammerstein *South Pacific* character, Bloody Mary, sings, "If you don't have a dream, then how you gonna have your dream come true?"

More concretely, there is scientific evidence that the way we perceive ourselves and the way we react to adversity can strongly influence our performance as individuals and as a nation. Dr. Martin E.P. Seligman, the UPS Foundation Professor of Social Science and Director of Clinical Training in Psychology at the University of Pennsylvania, has spent over 20 years in development of *cognitive therapy*. Hundreds of studies of animal and human reactions, and the testing and treatment of thousands of individuals—many of them monitored by the National Institute of Mental Health—have shown that while "learned helplessness" leads to depression and worsening of performance, "learned optimism" can lead to reversal of helplessness and curing of depression. As Dr. Seligman says in his 1991 book, *Learned Optimism*:

> The optimistic moments of our lives contain the great plans, the dreams, and the hopes. Reality is benignly distorted to give the dreams room to flourish. Without these times we would never accomplish anything difficult and intimidating, we would never even attempt the just barely possible. Mount Everest would remain unscaled, the four-minute mile unrun; the jet plane and the computer would be blueprints sitting in some financial vice-president's wastebasket. Every successful company, every successful life for that matter, requires both accurate appreciation of reality and the ability to dream beyond the present reality.

Dr. Seligman presents government statistics showing that depression is ten times more prevalent than it was 50 years ago. He ascribes this to our society's focus on the self, to the exclusion of older values that taught belief in the nation, in the family, in God, or in a purpose that transcends our own lives. Unfortunately, erosion of belief in the nation, which was accelerated by such events as the Vietnam War, Watergate, and the assassinations of John F. Kennedy, Robert Kennedy, and Reverend Martin Luther King Jr., coincided with "the waxing of the self" in our society. Obviously, preoccupation with the self to the exclusion of belief in the nation, the family, and other collective institutions, should be halted and reversed if possible. I suggest that one way to restore belief in the nation is to preserve and revitalize the American Dream.

To do this, it is not necessary to disregard the reality that in many respects we are closer to the Nightmare than the Dream. This reality does not require us to limit the Dream to a purely selfish vision, even though we know that many Americans would settle for financial success alone, preferably achieved through honest business dealings, but acceptably by cutting corners, or even by pulling off one good bank heist. There is little that is positive or uplifting in that Dream. To be of any real use, the Dream must include the rainbow as well as the pot of gold, as Adams saw so clearly.

So, as we struggle to define the American Dream, we must discard the Nightmare scenarios of the Fitzgeralds, the Wolfes, and the Updikes. Let us leave them with their well-deserved laurels for spellbinding us, and look elsewhere for the inspiration to find something positive in the concept of the American Dream. It follows that our definition will portray the optimistic/idealistic version of the Dream—the only version that is of any real use.

At the same time, we can't be so impractically idealistic that we try to eliminate self-interest. We must be realistic enough to recognize that self-interest is probably the strongest human drive, and that it must be included in any practical definition of the American Dream. The trick is to enlighten self-interest by blending it with idealism.

If I had to define the American Dream in one sentence, I would put it this way:

> Achieving excellence on your own, and using it to do well financially and have a happy life, while doing good for others less fortunate.

Since there are so many American Dreams that fit the optimistic/idealistic version, what we really need is a smorgasbord table from which each of us can put together a personal Dream platter. Here are the dishes to choose from, based on our survey of previous attempts to define the Dream.

Elements of the American Dream

1. A BETTER LIFE FOR ALL. Richer, happier. Wealth, material success, recognition. Loving and being loved. Owning your home.

2. ACHIEVING THIS ON YOUR OWN. Excellence. Self-made success. Individualism. Self-reliance. Self-initiative. Self-esteem. Drive for self-betterment. Education. Personal responsibility. Independence. Entrepreneurship. Hard work. Know-how. No reliance on help from government or institutions. Control of your own destiny.

3. HUMANITARIAN CONCERN FOR OTHERS. Doing well by doing good. Seeking the rainbow as well as the pot of gold.

4. FREEDOM FOR ALL. Freedom of choice. Freedom to do your best. Freedom from prejudice. Freedom from obstacles. Spirit of the Founding Fathers.

5. LIBERTY AND JUSTICE FOR ALL. Equality. Social justice. Equal justice under law.

6. OPPORTUNITY FOR ALL. Rags to riches. Empowerment of the weak and the underdog.

7. MELTING POT. Fulfilling the dreams of people from all parts of the globe.

8. HAPPY ENDING.

You will note that this smorgasbord is politically neutral. The elements are based on values shared by most Americans, whether Democratic/liberal or Republican/conservative. The Democrat/liberals would argue that not enough Americans can achieve the Dream, but their platform principles endorse the values involved. The Republican/conservatives might say that the possibility of achieving the Dream should satisfy everyone, so that no further government intervention or taxation is needed. These political questions don't concern us at this point, although some of them will crop up later in our story.

You may wish to return to this list later. In the meantime, let's move on to the Dream Factory.

The American Dream in Movies and Television

In his essay for *American Dreams, American Nightmares*, Leslie Fiedler wrote that movies—and most perfectly of all, television shows—are the supreme products of the technological magic that nurtures the American Dream; for "only what flickers for a moment in the eye, in the ear and is gone, leaving us still laughing or with the tears we need still not dry on our cheeks" will sustain the Dream.

As many others have noted, movies and television both create and reflect the dreams of the nation. But we must be careful not to try to read too much into movies and television shows that are, for the most part, designed for entertainment rather than enlightenment. Thus, the classic American cowboy movie—the horse opera—is almost pure entertainment, but it does contain important elements of the American Dream: A better, happier life for the good guys; rugged individualism; freedom; justice; helping the underdog; and a happy ending.

As in popular novels of the time, movies of the l930s and l940s were inclined to idealize American life by showing attainment of the American Dream. For example, *Knute Rockne, All-American*, the 1940 film starring Pat O'Brien in the title role and Ronald Reagan as the legendary halfback George Gipp, emphasized important elements of the Dream: triumph of the underdog (tiny, unknown Notre Dame University) through hard work that achieved excellence; and equality of opportunity for immigrants through the melting pot (Rockne as an immigrant from Norway). But of all the Hollywood films, those directed by Frank Capra were most clearly identified with the Dream.

When he died in 1991 at the age of 94, many of Frank Capra's obituaries pointed out that he had both lived the American Dream himself and had put it on the screen in dozens of popular movies. He sailed in steerage from Sicily to Los Angeles at the age of 6, one of six children, and lived the oppressive life of the poor, illiterate, immigrant family until he worked his way through college. Trained as a chemical engineer, somehow he wound up as a gag writer for Mack Sennett's silent film comedies, and eventually built Columbia Pictures into a major studio by directing a series of hit movies in the l930s.

The Capra trademark was the nobility and eventual triumph of the "pushed-around little guy." As he put it in his autobiography:

> I would sing the songs of the working stiffs, of the short-changed Joes, the born poor, the afflicted. I would gamble with the long-shot players who light candles in the wind, and resent with the pushed-around because of race or birth. Above all, I would fight for their causes on the screens of the world. Oh, not as a bleeding-heart with an Olympian call to "free" the masses. Masses is a herd term—unacceptable, insulting, de-

grading. When I see a crowd, I see a collection of free individuals: each a unique person; each a king or a queen; each a story that would fill a book; each an island of human dignity.

In addition to screening those themes, Capra's films were usually love stories, complete with lived-happily-ever-after embraces in the final scenes.

Of his more than 40 films, three are most instructive for our purposes. *Mr. Deeds Goes to Town*, his 1936 movie, starred Gary Cooper in the role of Longfellow Deeds, an unsophisticated young tuba-playing poet from Mandrake Falls, Vermont, who inherits $20 million and a New York opera house in the midst of the Depression. He goes to the big city, where, in Capra's words, he is "driven into a corner by predatory sophisticates" who want him to devote his money to the opera and their other highbrow interests. But Deeds, using his simple weapons of honesty, wit, and courage, routs the predators and strikes a blow for the little pushed-around guys whom he wants to help, by spending his millions to buy small plots for destitute farmers. For this he is forced to prove his sanity in a hilarious courtroom scene, defending himself against crooked high-powered lawyers with the help of the girl he gets in the end (played by Jean Arthur).

In *Mr. Smith Goes to Washington* (1939), James Stewart plays Jefferson Smith, a naive, idealistic pet-shop owner and Boy Scout leader who is appointed to fill a vacancy caused by the death of a senator from Montana. He idolizes the courtly, silver-haired senior senator from Montana, Joseph Paine, played by Claude Raines. But when Smith takes his seat in the Senate, he discovers that Paine has sold out to the corrupters and that he is expected to rubber-stamp Paine's dishonesty. Smith refuses to go along, and for that he seems about to be crushed by the steam roller of machine politics. But Jefferson Smith hangs on, with the help of a hard-boiled Washington insider with a heart of gold (Jean Arthur again), plus the words inscribed on the Lincoln Memorial, his gutty ideals, and a one-man filibuster aimed at blocking the corrupt legislation. During his filibuster, he says things like this: "Get up there with that lady that's on top of this Capitol dome— the lady that stands for liberty—and you'll see the whole parade of what man's carved out for himself after centuries of fighting for something better than just jungle law!" Finally, on the brink of exhaustion and defeat, his cause is rescued by Senator Paine, who does an about-face because his conscience will not let him destroy Smith.

Capra's 1946 film, *It's a Wonderful Life*, also starred James Stewart, this time as George Bailey, a small-town building and loan banker who sacrificed his own ambitions to help the little pushed-around guys achieve the dream of home ownership. After a series of confrontations with the town's Scrooge-like business tycoon (played by Lionel Barrymore), Bailey concludes that his life is a failure and no longer worth living. He attempts suicide, but is rescued by a guardian angel who temporarily grants his wish that he had never been born. This fantasy sequence demonstrates how many other lives would have been poorer if there had been no George Bailey. In the happy ending, set during the first Christmas season after World War II, the little guys that he had helped now return the favor by coming up with the money needed to keep Bailey Building & Loan operating. Bailey is restored to his loving family and community, and his guardian angel, having thus earned his wings, returns to heaven. The *New Republic* said in its 1946 review, "Hollywood's Horatio Alger fights with more cinematic know-how and zeal than any other director to convince movie audiences that American life is exactly like the *Saturday Evening Post* covers of Norman Rockwell." *Time* magazine's 1991 obituary of Capra noted that his career had contributed a new term to the language of films: Capraesque, which "signifies almost any improbable but distinctly inspirational story in which an idealistic little guy, though his principles may briefly waver, ultimately triumphs first over self-doubt, then over the big, expedient guys determined to exploit him and his class. And to most people the movie that epitomizes all this is *It's a Wonderful Life*."

People magazine's 1991 Capra obituary also featured the George Bailey role: "In Capra's unrepentantly sentimental world, the Baileys always won. They were just too good—and too darn stubborn—to give up. Capra conjured that version of the American Dream in more than twoscore films over four decades."

Capra's heroes (e.g., Longfellow Deeds, Jefferson Smith, and George Bailey), do not seek to crush the wealthy and powerful. Instead, the heroes win them over to the right side by bringing out their innate goodness. Thus his films did not criticize the American social/economic system as much as they tried to show how it could be made to work better and more equitably.

According to Robert Sklar, author of *Movie-Made America: A Cultural History of American Movies*, only three filmmakers of the 1930s captured huge audiences that included both the popular and highbrow tastes: Charlie Chaplin, Walt Disney, and Frank Capra. It is generally assumed that Capra's sentimental style—called "Capra-corn" by some—went out of fashion soon after World War II. Capra made his last film in 1961, and spent the last

30 years of his life deploring most of the new movies as portrayals of an "ashcan" view of life. Yet, throughout the 1970s and 1980s, continuing into the 1990s, *It's a Wonderful Life* has served as the American equivalent of Dickens's *A Christmas Carol*. It is replayed on television stations throughout the country during the Christmas season.

A campy version of Capra-corn lives on in the immensely popular Indiana Jones adventures. Also, Sylvester Stallone's *Rocky* films are thought by many to reflect Capra's influence, at least in the triumph of the underdog. Even though Rocky, the broken-down Philadelphia boxer, first appears as an enforcer for loan sharks rather than a Capraesque Boy Scout leader, Capra himself said of the first *Rocky*, "Boy, that's a picture I wish I had made."

In the video culture of the 1990s, where television reaches audiences that dwarf those ever enjoyed by novels and even by movies, there are signs that the yearning for the American Dream survives. While the six o'clock news shows us that our society is crumbling, Americans don't want to be told that the Dream has failed. They will flock to programs that nurture the hope of the "something better" that Richard Reeves found in his nationwide quest for the meaning of the Dream.

This ongoing quest for the Dream may help to explain the popularity of movies and television programs that show lawyers fighting for justice and the underdog. As author Linda Wolfe said recently in *The New York Times Book Review*:

> One of the curious phenomena of the late 20th-century culture is the way lawyers have emerged as our pop heroes. On television, in movies and in novels they are everywhere, and for the most part they are like yesteryear's pop hero, the cowboy: macho figures who fight not Indians but injustice, and who risk love, limb and even life to do so.

Nowhere is Linda Wolfe's theory more strongly supported than in the most-watched lawyer TV series of its time, *L.A. Law*. This show is popular for many reasons: it is well written, superbly cast and directed, and it doesn't wear out its welcome by producing too many shows when there aren't enough good stories to support a new episode every week. It goes in heavily for re-runs, and its ratings are often nearly as high the second time around.

I have another theory to explain the popularity of *L.A. Law*. In many ways, it epitomizes the American Dream. Not in the outmoded fashion of the Horatio Alger stories, or the blatant idealism of Capra-corn, but in the more realistic symbolism of the 1990s. Look back to the list of elements defining the American Dream, and you'll find that every episode of *L.A. Law* contains a healthy selection from the Dream smorgasbord: material success, love, self-made excellence, empowerment of the weak and the underdog, melting pot, happy ending; and, sometimes, even justice. There are generous portions of the individualism, best expressed in Thomas Jefferson's "life, liberty, and the pursuit of happiness," that has become America's secular religion.

The make-believe lawyers in the *L.A. Law* firm of McKenzie Brackman personify the American Dream in three ways:

1. They achieve for themselves a better, richer, happier life, with material success and recognition. They do this on their own, through education, individualism, hard work, entrepreneurship, and excellence.

2. They help others to achieve better lives, as well as freedom, liberty, opportunity, and justice; they do well by doing good.

3. Through their own success and the lifting of their clients, they portray an image of America that is attractive to millions of viewers outside the United States—for *L.A. Law* is among the leading television shows in 30 other nations.

Now let's examine the phenomenon of *L.A. Law* and compare it to reality. Do lawyers really personify the American Dream? And if so, *which* lawyers?

CHAPTER 2

McKenzie Brackman and Reality

I enjoy *L.A. Law* more than any other television series, and many lawyers whom I have questioned feel the same way. I think we like it because it portrays lawyers as heroes even though it shows their problems and weaknesses. And many of the lawyer heroics are performed in life-like settings, with realistic treatment of the ways in which lawyers, clients, judges, and jurors respond to legal problems.

L.A. Law's realism is important because fantasy superheroes like Perry Mason and Ben Matlock—homicide defense lawyers who always represent innocent clients, always get them acquitted, and usually solve the murders themselves in the courtoom—don't really turn lawyers on. *L.A. Law* strikes a more responsive chord because its lawyers don't always win, they don't always do the right thing, and they are constantly confronted by grey areas in law, ethics, and life, unlike the black-or-white worlds of Mason and Matlock.

A related reason for the program's popularity among lawyers is that it covers the whole spectrum of litigation by dramatizing both civil and criminal cases. Since the conventional wisdom is that a dramatic television series cannot succeed unless the main characters have life-and-death jobs (police officer, doctor, criminal lawyer) the long-running popularity of *L.A. Law* is a great tribute to its creators and players. There are life-and-death situations sprinkled amongst the episodes, but most of the trials during the show's first five seasons were civil cases involving mere money or personal rights rather than life.

In my opinion, a major reason why the L.A. lawyers look good is that they embody much of the American Dream in what they do for themselves, for their clients, and for the image of America in the eyes of foreign viewers.

As a footnote, I must confess that my own favorite TV lawyer is the redoubtable Horace Rumpole, John Mortimer's Old

Bailey hack who, it seems, Leo McKern was born to play. Unlike Perry Mason and Ben Matlock, Rumpole's clients are nearly always guilty of something, but he plays the law like a slightly out-of-tune old piano to get them off or minimize their punishment, winning our sympathy for them in the process. I have often wished that Rumpole could somehow be transplanted to an American civil practice, where he might represent clients more worthy of his magic than the Timson family of petty thieves who habitually run afoul of overzealous police officers. But the Rumpole character would probably lose its appeal if burdened with financial success.

The McKenzie Brackman Lawyers and their Practice

Steven Bochco built his reputation as the master of television ensemble comedy-drama in his hit police series of the early 1980s, *Hill Street Blues*, which portrayed teams of cops working on three or four different cases each week. He and his collaborator, Terry Lee Fischer, used the same formula to create *L.A. Law*. From the start of the series in 1986, David E. Kelley, a lawyer, was a crucial part of its success. He began as a story editor, became a co-producer in the second season, then supervising producer in year three, and (with the departure of Bochco) became executive producer in season four (1989-1990). Kelley drew on his three years of experience as a Boston litigator to create a law firm that lives and breathes litigation. When he left after season five, *L.A. Law's* story lines moved closer to the cops-and-robbers format used by many other shows, and its credibility began to slip.

Most of the lawyer characters who have played important continuing roles in the history of McKenzie Brackman are litigation specialists. The senior partner, Leland McKenzie (played by Richard Dysart), was an active litigator in his early years. Now he functions as rainmaker (business-getter), client-stroker, strategist, father figure, and chaplain.

Douglas Brackman Jr. (Alan Rachins) is the son of the deceased partner of that name who serves as the penny-pinching managing partner and resident boor.

Michael Kuzak (Harry Hamlin), sometimes known as Mickey, is a former prosecutor who heads the litigation department, trying criminal and civil cases.

Grace Van Owen (Susan Dey) starts as a prosecutor and the live-in girlfriend of Mickey Kuzak. At the end of season four she joins the firm as a partner.

Arnold Becker (Corbin Bernsen) is the firm's glamorous high-powered divorce specialist, whose sexual athletics bring a new dimension to the already demanding occupation of litigator.

Ann Kelsey (Jill Eikenberry) is the tall trial lawyer who is more naive and less bottom-line oriented than the others, which often brings her into conflict with her partners, especially Douglas Brackman.

Stuart Markowitz (Michael Tucker) is the firm's tax specialist whose normal fare of tax returns and IRS regulations sometimes bores him sufficiently to make him take on trial work unrelated to taxes. After a rocky courtship, he marries Ann Kelsey, as in real life he is married to Jill Eikenberry.

Victor Sifuentes (Jimmy Smits) is the handsome Chicano who first appears as a public defender, and is soon recruited by Mickey Kuzak to take on some of the firm's important trial work, civil and criminal.

Abby Perkins (Michele Greene) is the young litigator who has a hard time gaining self-confidence and recognition until she leaves the firm. She succeeds in trial work on her own, and then comes back to greater responsibilities at McKenzie Brackman.

Jonathan Rollins (Blair Underwood) is the black Harvard-trained lawyer whose academic achievements command a high starting salary. He becomes one of the most innovative of the firm's trial lawyers.

Rosalind Shays (Diana Muldaur) is the barracuda corporate lawyer whom Leland McKenzie brings into the firm to rescue it from financial doom. She becomes the senior partner but soon blows herself out of the firm, only to be revealed later as Leland's bedmate.

In season five, new blood was added. C.J. Lamb (Amanda Donohoe) is an English hippie type whose style of practice is far less conventional than that of the other McKenzie Brackman lawyers. Tommy Mullaney (John Spencer) is even more non-establishment than C.J. Lamb.

The most important of the non-lawyer characters are Benny Stulwicz (Larry Drake), the mentally retarded mail clerk/gofer, and Roxanne Melman (Susan Ruttan), Arnie Becker's long-suffering secretary. Their personal probelms test the ingenuity of McKenzie Brackman's lawyers, who are called upon to counsel them in the office and defend them in court.

McKenzie Brackman is given the aura of a prestigious, if small, law firm. Their plush offices are in a high-rent downtown Los Angeles skyscraper, and they are shown eating at the best restaurants. The partners are much concerned about the firm's image, and this is reflected in their discussions about potential new clients, hiring and firing of staff, and tactics to be used in litigation. In one episode, Leland McKenzie is selected for a federal judgeship, which falls through only because he refuses a demand to compromise the rights of a client in order to get the appointment.

The partners enjoy a fast-track life style. In season one, Arnie Becker is shown living (albeit as a renter) in a Malibu mansion that would have to cost $5 million or more. Even Victor Cifuentes, a mere associate fresh out of the Public Defender's office, with his roots in the poverty of the Mexican-American barrio, buys a BMW sports car in his first year with the firm.

Life in the fast track includes the portrayal of lawyers having sex relations with clients (mostly Arnie Becker and his divorce practice) and with each other (Mickey Kuzak, and later Victor Cifuentes, with Grace van Owen; Stuart Markowitz with Ann Kelsey, before and after their marriage; and even the senior eminence, Leland McKenzie, with Rosalind Shays).

The firm's practice is never described in detail. From week to week, clients appear and their problems are dealt with, but we are not shown a panoramic view of the firm's revenue sources. This is understandable because such details would not interest anyone except lawyers. The corporate clients are mentioned as being very important to the firm's profitability, with billings in the hundred-thousands or millions per year, but they are largely invisible because corporation law is not dramatic enough to hold a mass television audience. Here the show takes some liberties, because McKenzie Brackman's 10 to 12 lawyers (mostly young) are not really equipped for the heavy duty corporate work that brings in such fat fees. From time to time the cast members mention corporate work, such as defending against stockholder fraud claims or fighting off unfriendly takeover bids, but typically those jobs are handled by firms of 100 or more lawyers. Even smaller corporations whose annual legal costs are less than $1 million would need a much larger and more diversified firm to handle their legal problems.

Despite these mentions of corporate practice, reality governs in the end because the invisible corporate work is not sufficient to make the firm profitable or even to meet its running expenses. And from our standpoint, helping corporations to fend off legal problems is not important because it is not the stuff that the American Dream is made of. McKenzie Brackman is not a "power" law firm of the type likely to be selected by large companies that want to bury the opposition under a mountain of legal paperwork. The McKenzie Brackman lawyers' image is more like the lone American hero, in the mold of Lindbergh and Hopalong Cassidy.

The aspects of McKenzie Brackman's practice that make the program so popular are best summarized in Jane Pauley's interview of Harry Hamlin for the 1991 television program commemorating the 100th episode of *L.A. Law*. In explaining how he tried to project the character of Mickey Kuzak, Hamlin said that his mind went back to a favorite cartoon character of his childhood, Crusader Rabbit, who was always seeking truth, righteousness, and the American Way. To Hamlin, *L.A. Law* is about "making the right moral choice." This is echoed in Pauley's interview of Amanda Donohoe, who said that her approach to the C.J. Lamb character was to keep in mind that the lawyers of McKenzie Brackman are "good souls, not evil or manipulative people."

The Crusader Rabbit factor, combined with the glittering lifestyles of the McKenzie Brackman lawyers, squares with one of our major definitions of the American Dream: Doing well by doing good, seeking the rainbow as well as the pot of gold. And lawyers, whether in practice for themselves or as partners in a firm, are entrepreneurs, especially when they represent individual clients rather than large corporations. In representing individuals (other than the very wealthy) the lawyers have to invest their own capital and services to build an organization that can balance the scales of justice against the weight of the state or powerful private opponents. In many cases they have to lay out lots of money to prepare and present the case—money that they get back only if they win. Thus the entrepreneur-lawyers who represent the underdogs are cast in the role of *equalizers*, boosting their weaker clients onto their shoulders so that they stand as tall in court as their establishment opponents.

Clearly, Mickey Kuzak does not feel like Crusader Rabbit when he represents a large corporation against an individual, as he did in a season-one episode about a cold remedy that paralyzed a schizophrenic woman because she was not warned that the combination of her regular medication with the cold remedy could cause a deadly side-effect. Kuzak works out of that spot by convincing his client, Northland Pharmaceuticals, to pay decent compensation through an out-of-court settlement.

Kuzak *was* Crusader Rabbit when he defended Earl Davis, a black college professor indicted for the murder of his white student lover. The jury convicted Davis and he was sentenced to death, but Hamlin-Kuzak won his freedom by finding a witness who cast some doubt on the prosecution's case, thereby getting the jury verdict reversed by the California Supreme Court. Clearly Kuzak and McKenzie Brackman did good in the Earl Davis case—but they did not do well. The final bill for the firm's services to Davis was $485,000, all of it unpaid.

There are many other episodes of McKenzie Brackman doing good or performing public services without getting paid—what lawyers call "pro bono" work (*pro bono publico*: for the good of the public). There are also some interesting cases in which the firm's lawyers defend their own partners or employees: Kuzak's suspension from practice for ethical violations; Brackman's acrimonious relations with his next-door neighbor, and his arrest for picking up a hooker in a Sushi restaurant; Benny's trial for rape; Roxanne Melman's trial on violations of the securities laws when she is exploited by her con-man boyfriend. All of these non-revenue cases, plus the firm's willingness to represent the underdog even when there is no pot of gold at the end of the rainbow, keep it in precarious financial condition. This is why they are forced to bring aboard the unprincipled Rosalind Shays, even though they know she represents everything that is morally abhorrent to the other partners. She also represents paying clients, which McKenzie Brackman desperately needs to offset its pro bono extravagances.

Soon after taking over, Rosalind Shays decrees that before any new pro bono or contingent fee clients are accepted, they will have to be approved by the executive committee, consisting of Shays, McKenzie, and Brackman. This move is designed to staunch the flow of red ink that threatens the firm's solvency.

Shays wants to increase the firm's corporate practice, as this is her area of expertise and rainmaking prowess. But as we have seen, McKenzie Brackman does not have the manpower to handle big corporate clients, despite the scenes in which the partners talk about representing corporate clients in mammoth struggles such as unfriendly takeovers. The profit factor in corporate litigation is an army of associates whose time can be billed for 3 to 5 times what the firm pays them in salaries. This is known as "associate leveraging." Clients can be billed for as much as $100 to $250 per hour for the time of associates who are on the payroll for $40 per hour ($80,000 for a 2,000 hour year).

To the credit of the show's producers, they do not attempt to portray McKenzie Brackman as successful corporate lawyers— only as aspiring to more corporate work. It is my theory that the *L.A. Law* writers deny the firm a successful corporate practice because their Crusader Rabbit/American Dream image would not be served by winning cases for well-paying clients. Corporate law practice is an important function that attracts many of the best and brightest of American lawyers, but nothing about it smacks of Crusader Rabbit or championing the underdog. It is not usually the function of the corporate lawyer to do good, except in the general sense of enhancing the financial strength (and sometimes protecting the public image) of companies that provide jobs for millions of Americans.

Stuart Markowitz's tax practice could produce a pretty good living for him, but it could not develop into a big profit center for the firm without having major corporate clients and backup forces such as those mustered by much larger law firms. Most of Stuart's successes are for people trying to shortchange the government or minimize tax assessments they could well afford to pay. Again, a job requiring considerable skill, but hardly the stuff of the American Dream.

Arnie Becker's divorce practice is profitable for him, but it could not sustain any other members of the firm in a fast-track life style. Matrimonial law specialists typically practice in small firms or as individuals. No contingent fees are allowed, and the practice does not lend itself to heavy billing of associates' hours. Most of the work is done by the principal lawyers, the most effective of whom are called "bombers." So, despite Arnie's statement in season two that he charges $350 an hour, rising to $400 an hour in season five, his practice is not the stuff that makes general practice law firms wealthy.

The criminal defense work that Mickey, Victor, and Grace do is not very profitable, since it mostly involves violent crimes committed by individuals who are not in a position to pay hefty fees. White collar crime—tax evasion, banking frauds, money-laundering, defense contractor fraud, insider trading, and other lucrative callings—often produces handsome fees for defense firms, since associates can clock long hours while checking voluminous accounting records. And of course, defending leaders of organized crime can be very lucrative. But because representing racketeers and financial swindlers is anti-American Dream, McKenzie Brackman usually doesn't defend that type of criminal, and their bottom line suffers accordingly.

When we analyze the firm's practice, we find that their financial success, as well as their only sustainable method of doing well by doing good, is in the practice of tort law—personal injury, wrongful death, libel and slander, and other civil cases in which they represent individuals (usually of modest means) who claim to have been wronged by relatively rich companies or individuals.

Contingent Fee Tort Cases

Throughout the series, virtually the only fat fees banked by McKenzie Brackman are in these tort cases, which lawyers traditionally handle for a percentage of the winnings. As plaintiff's tort lawyers they are on the side of the underdog. As we shall see, this stance is inconsistent with the firm's self-image as a member of the establishment and its hopes of atttracting lucrative corporate clients. In other respects, McKenzie Brackman has acceptable underdog credentials. It is a small firm that often takes on more powerful opponents, such as the State of California and influential companies that are represented by larger law firms. The partners are portrayed as caring people who happily assume the burdens of hiring the mentally retarded Benny Stulwicz. Some of their important cases are tried by a Chicano (Victor Sifuentes) and a black (Jonathan Rollins). This is one of the important ways in which *L.A. Law* fulfills the American Dream.

Thus, in the very first episode, Mickey Kuzak files a wrongful death case for a father whose son was killed by a drunken driver. And Ann Kelsey, a mere associate, locks horns with Douglas Brackman over her representation of a woman who lost an eye in an accident. She wins Brackman over when her unconventional strategy yields a $1.1 million settlement. The Scrooge-like Brackman is all smiles as he contemplates the firm's one-third share of the $1.1 million.

Early in season one, Mickey Kuzak wins a $1.3 million jury verdict for a TV anchorwoman who was tortiously (wrongfully) discharged. Victor Cifuentes wins a verdict for the family of an 11-year old boy who was killed by a car in sight of his young sister. The jury awards $200,000 to the parents for death of the son, and $150,000 to the girl for her mental anguish in witnessing the disaster. All through the series, there are victories in contingent fee tort cases that keep the firm going financially and uphold its tradition of fighting for the underdog.

Season two finds Leland McKenzie trying his first case in many years, representing an old client who was fired to make way for a younger, lower-salaried executive. This is a relatively new field of tort litigation, called wrongful discharge or age discrimination. Leland wins a verdict of $1.8 million from the jury, but convinces the client to settle for $900,000 to avoid the delay and uncertainty of waiting out appeals, a particularly distasteful prospect for a senior citizen. The settlement brings $300,000 into the McKenzie Brackman coffers.

Ann Kelsey represents a movie actress who was libeled by a magazine article that wrongfully accused her of driving her daughter to suicide by dating the daughter's boyfriend. Ann wins a $1.3 million jury verdict, and again Douglas Brackman beams at the prospect of collecting the one-third contingent fee, this time more than $400,000.

Disparagement of a product can do as much harm as attacking a person's reputation. In another tort action, Victor Cifuentes represents Oscar Montoya, a Mexican-American entrepreneur who has developed Montoya Beer into a successful product. A competitor tried to buy Montoya's company but was turned down. The competitor then spreads false rumors that the beer contains urine, a disparagement that gains credibility because of consumer prejudice against the Mexican image. The rumors all but destroy the market for Montoya beer. Cifuentes rides to the rescue, representing the nearly insolvent Montoya on a contingent fee. In his final jury speech, Victor says, "Mr. Montoya believed in the American Dream." He begs the jurors not to let these vicious rumors destroy the Dream. While the jury is deliberating, the defendant caves in and agrees to a settlement that will enable Montoya to rebuild his beer business, thus realizing the American Dream for the underdog immigrant entrepreneur and for the entrepreneur-lawyers who equalize the scales of justice by putting their weight on Montoya's side.

The downside of tort practice is the huge investment of time and money needed to perform this equalization act. Victor Sifuentes represents the widow of Charley Fitzpatrick, a construction worker killed on the job when watered concrete weakened the structure that he was working under, causing it to collapse and crush him. Victor is up against a ruthless builder whose secret partner is a crooked politician. The politician pulled strings to get the construction contract for a federal office building, and the builder cut corners wherever possible to increase the profit, finding it cheaper to bribe crooked inspectors than to comply with safety requirements. The concrete for the 8th floor was sitting longer than usual, so the builder watered it to make it usable. It was supposed to be checked by a city building inspector, but he took his testing sample from the truck rather than the 8th floor site where the watering took place. That's not all the inspector took, according to Victor's argument.

Victor cross-examines the inspector vigorously, and wrings an admission that the reinforcing steel rods were set 12 inches apart instead of 9 inches as shown in the blueprints. How did Victor learn this, and how did he become aware of its significance? How was he able to hold his own against the builder's technical witnesses on the effects of watering the concrete on the 8th floor? The preparation work was not shown on the screen, but you can bet that in a real-life construction injury case, the plaintiff's lawyer would have to lay out thousands of dollars for engineering and architectural fees to equalize the advantages of the defense lawyer whose client has such experts on the full-time payroll.

Victor's solid preparation puts the builder on the defensive during the trial, winning Charley Fitzpatrick's widow a $1 million settlement, and McKenzie Brackman gets back the thousands it risked for experts' fees. But underdog cases don't always have happy endings, even on television. In O'Brien against Lehigh Tobacco Company, Mike Kuzak takes on the ultimate windmill of tort practice: representing a smoker against a cigarette manufacturer. Patrick O'Brien has smoked two to three packs a day for 30 years. By the time he is diagnosed as having emphysema, it is too late for him to quit smoking. When he takes the stand, he carries along his oxygen tank, and can barely breathe even with that assistance.

Real-life tort cases against tobacco companies routinely require six-figure outlays by plaintiff's lawyers for investigation and scientific evidence. Since the cigarette package now contains mandatory warnings about cancer, emphysema, and heart disease that may result from smoking, it is more difficult than ever to win such a case. Mike Kuzak tries, and he does convince the jury to find for his client, but because they hold O'Brien partly responsible for continuing to smoke in the face of the warning, they award only $1,000. On this one, McKenzie Brackman is out more than half a million dollars in expenses and the value of Kuzak's time.

Even when McKenzie Brackman represents a defendant in a personal injury case, the Crusader Rabbit/American Dream scenario is maintained. Victor Cifuentes defends a pajama manufacturer that is sued by a young boy who was horribly burned when lighter fluid which had spilled on his pajama sleeve was ignited. Even though the manufacturer was not at fault, and the disfigured boy's lawyer overplays his hand, Victor persuades his manufacturer client to pay a $300,000 settlement so that the boy is not entirely shut out.

Ann Kelsey finds herself in an even tighter spot in Franklin v. Washington Pure Water Corporation. Ann represents the water company, which removes impurities from their bottled drinking water and deposits them in a toxic waste dump located near a trailer park. Some of the toxic waste finds its way into the well used by residents of the trailer park for drinking water. Mrs. Franklin, who lived at the trailer park and drank the water while pregnant, gives birth to a baby that is deaf and blind, and she sues the water company for causing these birth defects.

The mother's lawyer claims that nickel leached from the toxic waste dump into the trailer park's well at the rate of two parts per billion. The water company supplies Ann with authoritative studies (including Environmental Protection Agency reports) showing that anything under 13 parts per billion would have no toxic side-effects. She uses this argument to claim there is no liability and that the baby's deafness and blindness must have been caused by other factors having nothing to do with the waste dump. But later in the trial, the plaintiff's lawyer calls Ann aside and presents her with some shocking news: An engineer who formerly worked for Ann's client is now serving as the plaintiff's expert witness, and he has come up with documents showing that as little as one part of nickel per billion can cause birth defects and might even be fatal. What's more, the engineer is prepared to testify that the top management of Washington Pure Water has known about these later studies for a long time, but is hiding behind the older two-parts-per-billion EPA studies in order to avoid the $15 million expense of cleaning up the waste dump.

The plaintiff's lawyer gives Ann a copy of the "smoking gun" documents, and asks $3 million to settle the case. The settlement would include his agreement to keep the one-part-per-billion report confidential. Ann confronts him with the fact that hundreds of other residents of the trailer park are still drinking the polluted water, and that some of them may die. "I'm sorry about that," says the plaintiff's lawyer, "but I don't represent them." Ann registers shock, but the cruel fact is that the lawyer's first duty is to get compensation for his client, and if this requires him to keep silent, he must do so. If he refused to keep the report confidential, he would be unethically depriving his helpless client of vital compensation.

There are other ways that resourceful plaintiff's lawyers can resolve such ethical dilemmas, but *L.A.Law* puts in a dramatic twist: Ann Kelsey solves the problem even though she represents the defendant, who is insisting on secrecy. First, she confronts her client, the chief executive officer of Washington Water, who reads the one-part-per-billion report without showing any emotion. This convinces Kelsey that he knew about the report all along. He orders her to settle the case, telling her that it is cheaper to pay $3 million to the handicapped baby than to pay $15 million to clean up the dump. Kelsey angrily reminds him that there are 300 more people in the trailer park who are even now drinking the nickel-contaminated water. He tells her that even if some of them are crippled or killed, they are mostly older people who are not earning a lot of money, so again it would be cheaper to settle their cases if and when they sue and are able to wait years for their cases to come to trial. He insists that she settle the Franklin baby's case on the basis of keeping the secret of the deadly well.

At this point, Kelsey kicks over all the constraints of law practice and takes matters into her own hands. She walks into the CEO's office and presents him with the settlement agreement that he requested. He happily signs that, whereupon Ann hands him another piece of paper that makes his eyes pop: a separate agreement between Ann Kelsey and Washington Pure Water Corp. calling for the company to voluntarily spend the $15 million to clean up the toxic waste dump, in exchange for Ann *not* giving the story to the *Los Angeles Times*!

The CEO correctly identifies this as an attempt by Ann to blackmail her own client, which accusation she readily accepts. He is infuriated, and threatens to sue McKenzie Brackman for millions. She informs him that she resigned from the firm before attempting to blackmail him, so they would not be responsible. He then says he will have her disbarred for blackmailing a client. She says, "Go ahead—but if you take me down you'll make this whole story public yourself and you'll have to clean up the poisoned well anyway!" Playing hardball to the end, the CEO says, "I don't believe this—you're bluffing!" Ann smiles and strides toward the door. As she reaches for the doorknob, the CEO folds his cards, stops her, and signs the agreement to clean up the dump.

This unlikely bit of melodrama keeps McKenzie Brackman on the side of the angels—and the American Dream—even when forced to represent a client who would direct his lawyers to use the obstacle course of the legal system to put the lives of 300 innocent people in danger. Ann Kelsey becomes the champion of those 300 underdogs even though she is getting paid to represent the villain.

There is a touching final scene in which Leland McKenzie asks Ann to explain the cryptic letter of resignation she had put on his desk. When she tells him the story of how she successfully blackmailed their client, he is aghast, and thinks about accepting her resignation. "You can't do this, Ann. If every lawyer let his conscience or his own moral code get in the way of duty to a client, our legal system would be in chaos!" She replies, "In the abstract, I agree with you. But this wasn't in the abstract. This was real people who were going to die. Could you have let them die, Leland?" He looks at her thoughtfully, then tears up her letter of resignation and silently walks out of the room as the camera fades to black and the episode ends.

Even when its financial problems cause the firm to fragment, with Kuzak, Cifuentes, and Van Owen breaking away to form their own practice, the surviving McKenzie Brackman lawyers continue to rely on tort cases. In the episode that shows the firm in receivership, Douglas Brackman tries a wrongful discharge case based on sex discrimination, and Tommie Mullaney tries a wrongful death claim for the parents of a college football player who had been hooked on anabolic steroids.

So, as you watch *L.A. Law* and enjoy the drama and suspense of criminal, divorce, and civil rights cases along with the more mundane personal injury cases, bear in mind that only the contingent fees in the tort cases will pay the rent for McKenzie Brackman—and that representing plaintiffs in those tort cases is the only way they can surely pursue the American Dream without having to browbeat or blackmail their own clients.

Douglas Brackman's Image of the Personal Injury Lawyer

Despite the firm's heroics in tort cases, Douglas Brackman turns up his nose at the image of the personal injury lawyer. He is happy to accept the proceeds of accident claims, but obviously he prefers to play the tweedier role of the prestigious paid-by-the-hour corporate lawyer even though the firm can't succeed financially without contingent tort fees. In season five, Douglas is dismayed to find the firm's reception area, hallways, and conference rooms bulging with 20 bandaged, bruised, half-naked fat men. They were on their way to a fat farm in Palm Springs when their bus was involved in an accident, leading to minor but painful injuries. The flaky newcomer C.J. Lamb has brought them in as clients. Now she runs in teams of doctors and psychologists to examine them en masse, making the office resemble a hospital emergency ward. Brackman is visibly embarrassed and tells C.J. this is not the kind of clientele the firm wants. But when she shows him the check for a total settlement of $225,000, he gives her his $75,000 (one-third of $225,000) smile.

Previously on *L.A. Law*, Douglas's disdain for personal injury lawyers was the subject of several episodes that brought him into conflict with this own half-brother. In season two, Douglas accidently discovers that his late father (the firm's second name partner) had a long-running affair with a porno movie star named Rusty Farrell. Douglas visits Rusty out of morbid curiosity, and discovers that he likes her. He also learns that her illicit union with Douglas's father produced an offspring, Errol. ("I had a crush on Errol Flynn," explains Rusty.) Rusty proudly tells Douglas that Errol, now 35, is also practicing law in L.A. "and doing very well." So the stage is set for Douglas to seek out his newly discovered illegitimate half-brother.

Douglas arrives at Errol's second-floor walkup office in a seedy section of Los Angeles, and has to thread his way through what appears to be a first-aid station. There are at least a dozen people crowded into the small waiting room, overflowing into the corridor. All are wearing casts, braces, or bandages, to demonstrate that they are accident victims. Many are black or hispanic. Douglas does not disguise his distaste at coming into contact with such people. His facial expression (about what you would expect of one who had just encountered a skunk) makes it clear that he looks down on this type of practice and feels very superior to his wretched half-brother.

Errol turns out to resemble the bald Douglas, especially in the hairline. It is clear that the writers and directors of *L.A.Law* want Errol to come across as a sleazeball, an embarrassment to Douglas. This they do by dressing him like a racetrack tout, writing dialogue that shows he is out to blackmail his more fortunate half-brother at every opportunity—but most of all by showing his practice to be many rungs down the ladder of prestige from that of McKenzie Brackman. The viewer is invited to conclude that because Errol has an office full of injured people, he is not "doing very well" as Rusty had claimed, and that Douglas is bound to be repelled by this lowly clientele.

L.A. Law is accurate in its portrayal of Brackman's revulsion, because the stereotype of the personal injury lawyer as an ambulance chaser and seedy character is widely accepted. Errol is not shown soliciting cases, or faking evidence, or doing anything other than having an office full of injured clients. Indeed, his only conversation with a client shows Errol treating a heavily bandaged man sympathetically, taking the time to guide him through the crowded office and reminding him to be careful going down the staircase. But the mere presence of injured people in his office is enough to confirm the stereotype.

The clumsy Douglas Brackman is clearly embarrassed by being related to a lawyer with such a lowly-regarded practice. Yet Douglas himself is about as sleazy and immoral as any practicing lawyer can get. Professionally, he ignores everything but the profit that can be made from a client's plight. He talks freely about advising clients to hide assets, and he keeps a paper-shredder in his office to help clients destroy evidence. In his personal life he is a slumlord, and he abuses legal process, tying up the courts with his vendettas against neighbors. He is an extreme caricature of everything that is despicable about the worst of our lawyers, and yet he considers himself many levels above Errol's practice of helping injured people recover damages. He calls Errol an ambulance chaser but he revels in the fat contingent fees collected by his own partners in accident cases.

Later in season two, Errol is shown to be a worthy sibling to Douglas. He cuts corners, lies, cheats, and jumps into bed with Douglas's estranged wife—but even in that department, he finishes a distant second as we observe Douglas having a steamy affair with Rusty, Errol's mother. Yet, that first scene in Errol's office was all we needed to see to receive the message that he was not prestigious and did not fit the McKenzie Brackman image. It was the same message transmitted by C.J. Lamb's office full of fat men injured in the bus accident. And again this is an accurate portrayal of the personal injury lawyer's image in the eyes of much of the general public, and indeed in the eyes of many lawyers who do not handle accident cases. Some lawyers who consider their corporate clients to be the crown jewels of law practice look upon tort lawyers as "mud wrestlers."

Independence and Charlie Keating

Early in season one, McKenzie Brackman is approached by Marshall Taft, a large New York-based law firm that has taken over firms throughout the country in pursuit of a chainstore law practice. Marshall Taft appears to be patterned after the real-life Finley Kumble, which took over firms in California, Florida, and other states, only to self-destruct in the largest law firm bankruptcy to date. The offer from Marshall Taft is lucrative, but McKenzie Brackman turns it down on principle. As Mickey Kuzak puts it, McKenzie Brackman is independent enough to tell its clients to go to hell if any of them demand services that would compromise the law firm's integrity; but if they became part of a 400-lawyer megafirm, they would lose that independence and become captives of their clients.

Mickey's reaction is consistent with his Crusader Rabbit image, but his description of McKenzie Brackman's independence from its clients is an exercise in self-delusion. Operating under the clumsy bureaucracy and bottom-line orientation of a huge multi-state law firm would constrict the free-wheeling style of McKenzie Brackman, but their independence as a small firm is illusory. In practically every episode there is clear evidence that the partners consider themselves dependent upon wealthy individual or corporate clients. Some cases in point:

(1) The sensitive Stuart Markowitz, wealthy in his own right and so moralistic that he refuses a direct bequest from a client's will, defrauds the federal government by foisting a nonexistent precedent on an overworked alcoholic IRS auditor to help a wealthy client cheat on his taxes.

(2) Arnie Becker represents Bruce Wellman, owner of an Aston-Martin sports car, who is suing a young short-order cook. It seems that the unfortunate cook happened upon the scene when Bruce's sports car skidded to the edge of a cliff. The cook saved Bruce's life by pulling him out of the teetering car, but in the process the car tipped over the cliff and was destroyed. The ungrateful Bruce insists on suing his rescuer for the loss of his beloved Aston-Martin. At a firm meeting, Jonathan Rollins questions why Arnie has taken on such a ridiculous claim. The answer: Bruce Wellman is the son of Ross Wellman, chief executive officer of one of the firm's biggest corporate clients.

(3) The partners vote to turn down Ann Kelsey's pro-abortion client, because wealthy corporate and individual clients are polarized on this issue.

(4) Douglas Brackman's questionable tactics in managing the firm's finances shock and disgust the partners, but all his shifty dealings are approved without a dissenting vote when he demonstrates how they have bolstered the firm's anemic bottom line.

Any semblance of independence is tossed overboard when Rosalind Shays is brought in to shore up the firm's crumbling finances by corralling more well-paying corporate clients. Indeed, she sells out a client's trust and the integrity of the firm when she goes behind Victor Sifuentes's back to force a $350,000 settlement of an accident case in which Victor had been seeking $2.5 million. The payoff for cheating Victor's client widow is a promise from the company she was suing to direct future legal business to McKenzie Brackman.

To the partners' credit, this sellout helps to trigger the ouster of Rosalind Shays—but by a very close vote and only after a long debate that produces a head-on collision between the firm's desire for corporate clients and its honor. Unfortunately, this is very life-like. The successful lawyer's fear of losing "important" clients (those that pay well and steadily) is probably as intense as any worker's fear of losing a job. While the successful lawyer should be able to count on replacing a lost client more readily than the average worker can duplicate the lost job, human nature and the stress of life in the fast lane militate against this. Fear of falling from a high place is often more daunting than the prospect of seeking another routine job. When Arnie Becker has to vote on a proposal that might cost him his Malibu mansion, his natural tendency is to shut his eyes as tightly as possible to the moral issues involved. In Douglas Brackman's mind, there is no moral issue that can possibly be as important as the bottom line. Thus the fear of losing well-paying clients makes many lawyers captives of those clients, although this is not openly admitted among partners in such firms, or even between the lawyer and his own conscience.

The corporate capture of law firms has been accelerated by the rapid development of large in-house corporate legal departments, some of them with cadres of 300 or more lawyers on permanent staff. These highly developed house counsel staffs have watered down the influence formerly wielded by outside law firms. Today General Motors insists that their outside law firms install computer software systems linking them with the General Motors legal department, for closer control of their activities and their billings. A generation ago, many law firms had enough influence to make final decisions on close questions that were accepted at face value by corporate clients. Today, company officials often shop around until they find the opinion they are looking for, either in-house or by canvassing several outside law firms.

This fear of losing a large client who pays millions of dollars in annual fees is enough to color the moral and ethical choices of the outside lawyers. It is not done directly, of course. Many corporate lawyers are skillful enough to mask the moral issues by finding an apparently legal method of enabling the client do what he wants to do. A striking case in point is the savings and loan debacle, of which Charles Keating is one of the most outrageous perpetrators.

Keating—a lawyer himself, sad to say—built a $6 billion savings and loan empire through monumental frauds that eventually will cost American taxpayers over $2.6 billion. He perverted the federal guarantee of S&L deposits into a device to accommodate his self-dealings, principally through a holding company called American Continental Corp (ACC) which controlled California-based Lincoln Savings & Loan. ACC employed his son, daughter, and sons-in-law—people in their twenties—at salaries of $500,000 or more. Using the $100,000-per-account government guarantee of deposits in Lincoln, he funneled this protected money into projects controlled by ACC, so that the profits would flow to him and his family rather than the Lincoln depositors. When it came to the losses—running into the billions on speculative real estate and business ventures—he made sure Lincoln was cut in handsomely.

Deregulation of the S&Ls during the Reagan years sowed the seeds for many Charley Keatings. The total estimated cost of $500 billion to bail out the S&Ls will be paid for by American taxpayers well into the 21st century. What distinguishes Keating in this rogues' gallery is his extensive use of lawyers and accountants to paper over the sewer of corruption he created, and his gall in using government-guaranteed bank accounts to finance his attempts to influence at least five senators. Keating tried to enlist the senators in his battle against bank regulators who were on to his game years before they were permitted to do their jobs and put a stop to it. And when the regulators finally shut Lincoln down by overcoming years of resistance by Keating and his lawyers (which included withholding of bank records and threats of personal lawsuits against the regulators), Keating had the colossal gall to bring suit against the government regulators in an attempt to force the return of Lincoln to his control.

His lawsuit, *Lincoln Savings & Loan Assoc. v. Wall*, was heard by U.S. District Judge Stanley Sporkin, one of the most respected jurists in the District of Columbia federal court. Sporkin had spent many years as a watchdog official of the Securities & Exchange Commission, and so was better equipped than most judges to ferret out fraud. After hearing exhaustive evidence, Sporkin ruled that Keating and his family had systematically looted Lincoln, and were unfit to resume control. At the end of his long decision, Sporkin wrote:

> What has emerged is not a pretty picture. It is abundantly clear that ACC's officials abused their positions with respect to Lincoln. Bluntly speaking, their actions amounted to a looting of Lincoln. This was not done crudely. Indeed, it was done with a great deal of sophistication. The transactions were all made to have an aura of legality about them. They even entered into a so-called formal tax sharing agreement in order to claim they had the approval of the regulatory authorities for this phase of their illicit activities.
>
> Keating testified that he was so bent on doing the "right thing" that he surrounded himself with literally scores of accountants and lawyers to make sure all the transactions were legal. The questions that must be asked are:
>
> Where were these professionals, a number of whom are now asserting their rights under the Fifth Amendment, when these clearly improper transactions were being consummated?
>
> Why didn't any of them speak up or disassociate themselves from the transactions?
>
> Where also were the outside accountants and attorneys when these transactions were effectuated?
>
> What is difficult to understand is that with all the professional talent involved (both accounting and legal), why at least one professional would not have blown the whistle to stop the overreaching that took place in this case.

As Judge Sporkin noted, there was a gloss of legal complexity enveloping Keating's looting that made it difficult to detect and stop quickly. Experienced government bank examiners had difficulty penetrating the legal maze, and even when they did, they were not in a position to demonstrate to their own bosses, to Congress, or to the viewers of television news programs or even to readers of serious newspapers, that the public was being defrauded. For this massive camouflage operation, the prestigious law firms that received Keating fees totaling more than $70 million can take a bow.

Keating's $2.6 billion looting of Lincoln is the most publicized S&L case, but obviously there were many more that brought the total projected cost to $500 billion. Martin Mayer, in his 1990 book *The Greatest-Ever Bank Robbery*, documents the sorry role of lawyers and accountants in the Keating case and many other huge S&L ripoffs. As Mayer puts it:

> Who protected the thieves? The nation's great law firms, dozens of them, in New York and Chicago as well as in Washington, Texas, and Los Angeles, which bullied regulators, threatened suit against them personally as well as against their agencies, created mazes the regulators would have to wander through before they could stop the looting by clients of these firms who could pay anybody's fees because deposit insurance gave them the key to the U.S. Treasury.

Knowing Mayer to be learned in law as well as in finance, I'm sure his disdain for Keating's lawyers is confined to those who helped him to disguise his illegal transactions, rather than those who defended him after he was indicted for crimes. Under our system, everyone—even a Keating—is entitled to the strongest representation he or she can muster to defend against criminal charges.

Mayer calls the S&L disaster "the worst public scandal in U.S. history," surpassing by far the Teapot Dome scandal of Warren Harding's administration and Ulysses Grant's Credit Mobilier affair. From our standpoint, it is important to note that both Teapot Dome and Credit Mobilier involved outright bribery of public officials, without the participation of prominent lawyers such as those who disguised the S&L lootings and kept them going for years after government regulators first discovered them. These lawyers put their reputations to work for the Keatings, knowing full well that those reputations would awe banking regulators and members of Congress who received complaints about S&L losses.

When the history of the S&L mess and other financial excesses of the 1980s—such as junk bonds—is finally written, will there emerge a single real-life Mickey Kuzak who was independent enough to tell a Charley Keating to go to hell? So far, I haven't heard of any.

Lawyers and judges speak disdainfully of "the morals of the marketplace," insisting that law practice requires a much higher standard of ethics than business. There was some substance to this position when lawyers stood tall above their clients, who would take their advice and stay with one law firm for generations. But today well-paying clients change lawyers like advertisers shift agencies, and they are quick to shop for positive opinions if their outside law firm tells them that some financially atttractive step is illegal. Moreover, they know that it will not be difficult to get a positive opinion if they are willing to pay hefty fees. And in the 1990s, even the largest and most revered "name" law firms are taking on "marketing directors" and "executive financial directors"—non-lawyers whose job it is to make law practice more businesslike.

The lawyer's code of ethics is still there, and it sets standards much higher than those of business, politics, or any other calling except perhaps the clergy. For example, when Senator David Durenberger of Minnesota was found guilty of violations of the Senate ethics rules in 1990, he was merely reprimanded by his colleagues. But the same violations caused the Minnesota Supreme Court to suspend him from law practice indefinitely in 1991, even though he continued to represent the people of Minnesota in the Senate. In the business world, leaders are debating whether there should be a formal code of ethics, and if so, what it should say. The question of enforcement is not even discussed, for business is not likely to adopt a stringent code whose violators would face penalties akin to the disbarment of lawyers.

Now the law firm marketing directors and the demands of well-paying clients are watering down the effectiveness of the legal ethics codes. As law firms redesign themselves to become more businesslike, it can only become more difficult for lawyers to resist the profit motive that creates it own relentless momentum. Lawyers still cling to the image of rising above the morals of the marketplace, but the experiences of the prestigious McKenzie Brackman firm—reflected in real life by the S&L and junk bond fiascos—teach us otherwise. Lawyers now look upon juicy clients as their marketplace, and the financial pressures of penetrating that market and retaining market share make it likely that the Charley Keatings will always be able to find prestigious lawyers to do their bidding.

Thus, the lawyer representing business clients is hardly in a position to evoke the American Dream. The underdog, self-reliant, and entrepreneurial aspects are missing. And while they often achieve for themselves the financial success that is part of the American Dream, usually they cannot do well by doing good. Many firms that make their profits from corporate practice contribute substantial amounts of time and money to pro bono work, but this is not directly related to their doing well. As we have seen, the only sustainable part of McKenzie Brackman's practice that squares with the American Dream is their representation of the underdog plaintiffs in tort cases.

While the producers of *L.A. Law* have accurately portrayed the financial pressures on lawyers who represent business companies, they have let the beautiful people of McKenzie Brackman achieve much of the American Dream without explaining that their expensive lifestyle is paid for largely by tort cases. They have avoided any implication that the tort lawyer as such is a hero of the American Dream. Instead, they have given us the obnoxious Errol Farrell as the stereotype of the tort specialist.

This departure from reality is doubly unfortunate because in real life, the substantial tort cases are handled by specialists, particularly in large cities like Los Angeles. McKenzie Brackman wouldn't have much chance to attract lucrative business clients if its lawyers spent most of their time bashing the business establishment, which is what successful plaintiff's tort lawyers must do. Victor Sifuentes would not have had the know-how to recover $1 million for Charley Fitzpatrick's widow in the building construction death case unless he had devoted most of his career to tort cases. In fact, the case never would have come to him or his firm unless they were known as tort specialists.

Who are the real-life plaintiff's tort specialists? Does the illegitimate Errol Farrell present an accurate portrait of them and their role in American justice?

L.A. Law has used a combination of real-life conflicts and glamorized lawyer characters to produce a televised version of the American Dream fulfilled. But it has distorted the role of tort lawyers in achieving the Dream. To get the true picture, we'll have to leave the make-believe office of McKenzie Brackman and search out the real-life Equalizers.

CHAPTER 3

The Equalizers and the Master Ocean Pilots

We have seen that the lawyers of McKenzie Brackman fulfill the American Dream when they act as Equalizers in tort cases, representing underdogs against the establishment, using their education, skills, entrepreneurship, and self-initiative to right wrongs and get rich themselves, in the process. In turning to real life, we need to examine the credentials of other Equalizers before focusing on tort lawyers, for there are other types of lawyers who can lay claim to balancing the scales of justice that otherwise would be weighted against underdogs.

The first group that comes to mind is the civil rights lawyers. Thurgood Marshall, who fought racism for decades and finally won the famous school desegregration case, *Brown v. Board of Education of Topeka*, in the U.S. Supreme Court, certainly was an Equalizer. His efforts over 23 years as chief counsel for the National Association for the Advancement of Colored People's Legal Defense Fund probably lifted more underdogs than any lawyer in history. In the 1980s and 1990s, Morris Dees, founder of the Southern Poverty Law Center, won many landmark cases on behalf of minorities and the poor, including multi-million dollar damage awards against the Ku Klux Klan and the White Aryan Resistance. The heroism of Marshall, Dees, and other dedicated civil rights lawyers certainly makes them major Equalizers. Indeed, it is their brand of heroism that distinguishes them from the Equalizers of the American Dream. They did good but did not do well financially because they were not interested in making a lot of money. They worked for small salaries and their services to the underdogs were rendered free of charge, funded by contributions. They are entitled to greater admiration than the more mercenary tort lawyers—but not as symbols of the financially-oriented American Dream. They represent an upgrading of the American Dream to *doing good for its own sake*. Very few lawyers (or nonlawyers, for that matter) are willing or able to make that lofty ideal the focus of their life's work.

There are many criminal lawyers who help underdogs, including the thousands of public defenders who represent indigents accused of crimes. But the defense of criminal cases is not part of the mainstream American Dream. Even those criminal lawyers who command large fees and win spectacular cases don't qualify, since their financial successes are usually achieved on behalf of mobsters and other characters who do not fit into the American Dream. While some criminal lawyers are heroic figures who achieve part of the American Dream by enriching themselves, they cannot meet our stringent requirement of doing well by consistently doing the good that comes from representing underdogs, simply because there is not much money in representing underdogs accused of crimes.

Lawyers who represent shareholders and bondholders in suits against financial manipulators qualify as Equalizers, for many of their clients are pension funds or people of moderate means whose life savings are at stake. Since the wrongs that they seek to right are actually torts (usually fraud) and they operate on contingent fees while laying out large sums to finance the costs of litigation, we shall treat them as tort lawyers even though the profession would classify them as securities specialists, distinguishing them from the vast majority of tort lawyers who specialize in accident cases.

Is it fair to tailor our definition of the American Dream's Equalizers so that it fits only tort lawyers? Even lawyers who practice in the large firms that represent the wealthy can claim to be Equalizers because of their strong commitment to doing pro bono work for underdogs. Perhaps someone will write an article or book portraying other types of lawyers as Equalizers of the American Dream. But this book is about tort lawyers because they clearly fit the description of doing well by doing good through their own efforts, unsubsidized by government or other well-heeled supporters. This is not because tort lawyers are more public-spirited or less self-interested than other practitioners. Tort lawyers simply have no choice. If they want to do well, they must do good at the same time, because of their total community of interest with underdog clients.

L.A. Law showed us that tort lawyers in the 1990s have the power to equalize, as Cifuentes did for the widow of construction worker Charley Fitzpatrick and Kuzak did for the wrongfully discharged TV anchorwoman. But tort lawyers weren't always that strong. Their equalizing power developed in the second half of the twentieth century, as we shall see. This happened to coincide with the onset of commercial television, but there is no connection between these two developments.

The stories of actual cases furnish the best lens through which we can observe how the plaintiff's tort lawyers became Equalizers. This is the "case method" used by *L.A. Law* itself, and in academic settings by schools of law and business administration. Our cases, however, will not be dramatizations or hypotheticals, but the real thing.

Since the Equalizers first emerged during the 1950s, we begin with a case that straddles the 1940s and 1950s. The case is *Jane Froman v. Pan American Airways*, which arose out of the crash of the Pan Am flying boat *Yankee Clipper* in the River Tagus at Lisbon, Portugal, on February 22, 1943, with Master Ocean Pilot Captain R.O.D. Sullivan at the controls. The case came to trial in New York during March 1953, more than 10 years later. To appreciate the forces arrayed against each other in this case, it will be useful to sketch some of their history. We shall cover Pan American Airways here, and do the same for the other players in the following chapters.

Pan Am stopped flying on December 4, 1991. Its final years were marked by a painful descent to financial oblivion. But Pan Am was a very different airline in its earlier days. Indeed, the story of its first 60 years is part of the American Dream, for millions of people throughout the world looked upon Pan Am as the essence of America's greatness.

Juan Trippe's Master Ocean Pilots

When the *Yankee Clipper* crashed in 1943, and ten years later when the Froman case came to trial, Pan Am stood head and shoulders above its competitors. The advertising slogan, "The World's Most Experienced Airline," was justified by Pan Am's history. *The Chosen Instrument*, written in 1982 by the husband-and-wife team of financial analysts, Marilyn Bender and Selig Altschul, evaluates Pan Am's history from the business standpoint:

> In many ways, the history of the middle decades of the twentieth century is the history of America's rise to world pre-eminence. That ascendancy was sparked by the spectacular growth of the aviation industry, an industry which made it possible to cross the Atlantic or fly from New York to California in a few hours, and enabled American business travelers and

government officials and tourists to go anywhere on the globe. At the center of this amazing technological revolution stands Pan American World Airways.

In his 1987 book, *Pan Am: An Airline and its Aircraft*, R.E.G. Davies, Curator of Air Transport for the National Air and Space Museum, wrote:

> From its modest beginnings in 1927, when Juan Trippe obtained an exclusive contract to fly the mail on the 90-mile flight between Key West and Havana, the airline has grown to encompass the entire globe, always pioneering new routes, experimenting with the newest and best aircraft available, accumulating valuable experience in long-distance navigation and weather forecasting. Pan Am was led by one of the airline industry's giants, Juan Trippe, and advised by, among others, the immortal Charles Lindbergh. They created a world airline network by developing long range navigational and logistical techniques. These were later to assume such immense importance in World War II that Pan Am could be classified as a national asset. Juan Terry Trippe embarked on a career that was, within barely a single decade, to build on a 90-mile route to Cuba to fashion the largest and most influential airline in the world.

In that remarkable period from 1927 to 1939 (called "barely a decade" by Davies because the airline didn't really get under way until 1929) Pan Am's fleet grew from a borrowed single-engine four-passenger fabric covered floatplane to the world's largest collection of flying boats and land-based airliners, spanning Latin America and the Pacific and Atlantic Oceans with the first commercial air mail and passenger services. While Trippe was the master business manager of this epic, its popular heroes were the breed of airmen led by Lindbergh and patterned after him, who became known as the Master Ocean Pilots.

The Caribbean served as a flying laboratory for Pan Am's growth. In addition to carving its routes out of wildnerness and working with manufacturers to develop suitable aircraft, Pan Am had to pioneer the special techniques of over-ocean flying, training departmentalized flight crews, and developing its own weather reporting, communications, and navigation facilities. Lindbergh led the way by surveying the Caribbean, as he would do for all of Pan Am's major routes.

One of the stewards on Pan Am's early Caribbean flights was Charles B. ("Bebe") Rebozo, later to become a Florida banker and the closest friend of President Richard Nixon. During the 1930s, as Bender and Altschul put it, "The Pan American Clippers were a shining symbol of popular culture in America. In Miami, visitors flocked to the terminal at Dinner Key to watch the flying boats come in over palm-fringed Biscayne Bay." That striking art deco terminal serves today as Miami's City Hall.

During the 1930s, Pan Am became the dominant factor in Latin American air transport, which put Trippe in position to be of great service to his country by forcing Axis-controlled airlines out of business before they could strike at the Panama Canal. But that's another story. The saga of the Master Ocean Pilots really began in 1935, when Trippe decided that Pan Am was ready to conquer the Pacific. The Sikorsky S-42, his longest-range flying boat, required five refueling stops between California and China. Pearl Harbor, Guam, and Manila were available, but to fill in the missing dots on the map, Pan Am had to build from scratch airport and living facilites on two islands that were practically unknown in 1935: Midway and Wake. This Trippe accomplished in four months by chartering a freighter, the *S.S. North Haven*, and transporting to the Pacific 74 construction workers, most of whom were college boys so imbued with the spirit of adventure that they signed on for backbreaking work at wages lower than those of ordinary laborers.

Early in 1935, preparations for conquest of the Pacific began in the Caribbean laboratory. Normally the Clipper crews would be headed by a captain, assisted by a younger co-pilot, called the first officer. But the handpicked crew of the Sikorsky S-42 *Pan Am Clipper* was headed by two of the airline's most experienced captains, Edwin C. Musick and Robert O'D (Rod) Sullivan. Musick and Sullivan were not mere captains. Both held the exalted rank of Master Ocean Pilot, which Pan Am had invented to distinguish its super-skippers from the ordinary run of airline captains.

Musick, then 41, was Pan Am's senior captain, having flown the airline's first commercial route (Key West to Havana) in 1927. He was the strong, silent type, who might have been portrayed on the screen by Gary Cooper. He was intent upon turning the barnstorming pilot's image into that of a scientist, even though he had been a barnstormer himself. He would not undertake a flight until he was personally satisfied that the airplane, the crew, and the ground facilities were up to his exacting standards. He insisted that Pan Am establish tougher pilot training and experience requirements than those used by the domestic airlines.

Sullivan, then 43, had joined Pan Am in 1928 after a long career in Naval Aviation dating back to World War I. Sullivan was the equal of Musick in skill and flying boat experience, but he was not the contemplative scientist type. Given to salty language and machismo tactics, he was known to have squeezed the arm of an inattentive co-pilot until it was bruised. Since he maintained the image of the swashbuckling pilot, he would have to be played by Jimmy Cagney.

Musick and Sullivan conducted practice flights out of Miami in the Sikorsky S-42 *Pan Am Clipper* to simulate the long distances that faced them in the Pacific. Then they flew to California and made simulated long-distance flights out of Pan Am's new base at Alameda, just across the bay from San Francisco. Finally on April 16, 1935, Musick and Sullivan flew the *Pan Am Clipper* from Alameda to Honolulu, an 18-hour trip that was the first airline flight from the mainland to Hawaii. They could go no further east since the bases at Midway and Wake were still only dreams on Juan Trippe's globe in his Chrysler Building office in New York.

Musick and Sullivan made a second survey flight in June 1935, this time pushing west from Hawaii to the newly constructed base at Midway. But Musick was needed elsewhere, since Pan Am was to introduce a very special new flying boat for the inauguration of commercial Pacific air service. Musick cut away from the survey flights to work on final preparation of the new Martin M-130 flying boat, the *China Clipper*, at the Martin factory in Baltimore. Sullivan took charge of the last two S-42 survey flights, making the first trips to Wake Island in August and to Guam in October.

The Martin M-130 could carry 41 passengers and had a range of 3,200 miles without ripping out passenger seats for extra gas tanks. It was the ocean liner that Trippe needed to establish commercial service across the Pacific. The majestic *China Clipper* captured the public's imagination as few airplanes have ever done. Its graceful beauty stirred even those who would never want to fly. It became a legend on the scale of the Orient Express, inspiring many a dream of escaping the Depression doldrums in romantic flights to exotic fantasy-lands.

The first revenue flight of the *China Clipper* was scheduled for November 22, 1935, over the new Pacific route, Alameda/Honolulu/Midway/Wake/Guam/Manila, with the Master Ocean Pilots Musick and Sullivan at the controls. The ceremonies surrounding this flight were more elaborate than any since Lindbergh's 1927 solo crossing of the Atlantic. Although it was a only

a non-passenger airmail flight over a route that had been surveyed for months in an S-42, the romantic image of the *China
Clipper* and the actual start of the shrinking of the globe by airline service made the 1935 Thanksgiving week flight an aviation
milestone.

It began with the launching ceremonies at Alameda. 150,000
people were on hand at the Pan Am base and across the bay in
San Francisco, crowding onto docks, rooftops and ferry decks for
a view of the historic takeoff. Millions more throughout the
United States and in other nations listened on the radio as Post-
master General James A. Farley read a message from President
Roosevelt.

Juan Trippe followed Farley to the microphones and put on a
show, first telling Captain Musick to stand by for takeoff instructions, then getting static-broken radio reports from the Pan Am
stations at all five stops (the last one in Manila, 8,000 miles
away). Then Farley officially ordered inauguration of Foreign Air
Mail Route No. 14, launching "a new era in world transportation,
a new and binding bond that will link, for the first time in history, the peoples of the East and the West." As the Navy band
played "The Star-Spangled Banner," millions of listeners around
the world heard the mighty engines of the *China Clipper* roar as
she headed into San Francisco Bay and started her takeoff run.
She was joined in the air by a convoy of Army planes that escorted her over the horizon.

Seven days later, after all the layovers and celebrations were
completed on schedule, another squadron of Army pursuit
planes picked up the *China Clipper* at the western tip of the Phil-
ippines and escorted her to a landing in Manila Bay. The historic
flight was completed in the record-setting flying time of 59 hours
and 48 minutes. By that time Captain Eddie Musick's name was
known to every red-blooded American boy, and his picture
landed on the cover of *Time* magazine's next edition. In the
depression year of 1935, Roosevelt and the country badly needed
a winner, and they had a big one in the perfectly-performed
China Clipper expedition. Millions of people throughout the
world heard the names of Midway Island and Wake Island for
the first time, and would later learn of their strategic importance
when they became the sites of monumental battles during World
War II.

The *China Clippers* carried their passengers in great luxury
and roominess. They were 41 passenger seats, but because so
much extra fuel had to be carried on the long San Fran-
cisco/Honolulu leg, they rarely carried more than eight passen-

gers. The extra cabin space was devoted to private suites, sleeping berths, paneled lounges, and gourmet dining arrangements. The central lounge was wider than a Pullman club car.

Musick continued his pioneering, surveying a new southerly route to New Zealand by way of Honolulu, Kingman Reef (another tiny dot in the Pacific), and Pago Pago in American Samoa. On his second survey flight in the *Samoan Clipper*, a long-range S-42, he landed at Pago Pago on January 10, 1938. The next morning he took off for Auckland, New Zealand, but after an hour in the air, the *Samoan Clipper* radioed that it was turning back to Pago Pago because of an engine oil leak. Fifty minutes later, with the plane within 12 miles of Pago Pago, another radio message said that Musick was jettisoning fuel in preparation for landing (since the fuel load required for the 12-hour Pago Pago/Auckland flight would have made the plane too heavy for a safe landing after having flown for only about two hours).

That was the last word ever heard from the Master Ocean Pilot and airline pioneer, Eddie Musick. When the *Samoan Clipper* did not turn up at Pago Pago, a U.S. Navy tender searched the area and found a large oil slick 12 miles west of Pago Pago, about the position of the last radio message. There were no witnesses to the crash and no wreckage was ever found, but investigators concluded that the plane exploded during fuel jettisoning. It was known that the S-42 had a design deficiency in that the fuel ejection vents were positioned close to the exhausts, and many an S-42 pilot had opted to land overweight rather than chance a fuel-dumping explosion. The state of the art of fuel jettisoning was not very high in 1938.

The loss of its number one pilot, who was also a worldwide symbol of airline safety and reliability, was a heavy blow to Pan Am. There was harsh criticism of Trippe for pushing ahead with the New Zealand service, for the harbor at Pago Pago made every landing a nightmare. The small bay had a narrow mouth that opened directly into the path of the prevailing trade winds, which built up huge ocean swells that threatened to swamp and destroy any flying boat that entered those stormy waters. To avoid running out of the bay into the swells, the approach to the bay had to be made at a steep angle over high hills. Musick himself described it as "landing in a teacup." These hazards forced Musick to use the dangerous S-42 fuel-jettisoning procedure. In a safer harbor he could have made a longer landing run and obviated the need for fuel dumping.

A great public outcry followed the demise of Musick and his crew in the first Pan Am Clipper to be lost at sea. Pan Am was forced to abandon the Pago Pago route, and when the Clippers returned to New Zealand it was by way of new bases at Canton Island and Noumea. This was one of the few times that Trippe had to backtrack despite the fact that he had pushed Pan Am's expansion beyond the limits of existing technology at virtually every opportunity. He had committed huge sums for construction of flying boats and ground bases long before the necessary radio and navigation implements were even invented, and he had forced manufacturers to skip whole generations of trial-and-error aircraft development in order to meet his visionary specifications. He had led a charmed life while driving his technical staff nearly to distraction. But the charm did not work at Pago Pago, and the great Eddie Musick was lost.

Musick was honored by memorial services at sea near Pago Pago, and later in the rotunda of the San Francisco City Hall. A World War II Liberty Ship was named in his honor and christened by his widow, Cleo, at the Kaiser Shipyard in Richmond, California.

Trippe had hoped to open the Altantic route before turning to the Pacific, but he was thwarted for years by international politics and the limited range of his flying boats, which could not cross the Atlantic without a refueling stop at Bermuda, a British Crown Colony. Britain would not allow such stops, nor would they grant U.K. landing rights to Pan Am, until their own airlines could operate such routes. They limited their airlines to purchase of British-made aircraft, which were not up to ocean flying. The same was true of other European countries, and so Trippe's Atlantic visions had to be put on hold from 1935 to 1939.

By 1939, Trippe's drive and foresight had forced into being a flying boat that was light years beyond its predecessors: the Boeing 314, which was 50 percent larger than the *China Clippers* and could carry twice the payload for longer range at greater speed. Each of its four engines developed 1,500 horsepower, compared to 830 horsepower in each of the *China Clipper's* engines.

The immediate advantage of the Boeing 314 was that it would enable Pan Am to bypass Bermuda and fly non-stop all the way from the United States to the Azores, which Portugal was willing to provide as a refueling stop. From there, Pan Am could enter Europe at Lisbon and push on to France through an agreement for landing rights at Marseilles. Thus the B-314 would allow Trippe to serve Europe without having to deal with Britain.

Faced with these new realities, and sensing the need for transatlantic air service due to the approaching conflict with

Hitler, the British finally relented and permitted Pan Am to begin regular transatlantic service to Southampton in 1939. Captain Harold E. Gray, whom Pan Am was grooming to replace Musick, commanded the first B-314 airmail flight to Southampton on June 24, 1939. Four days later, Captain Rod Sullivan was in charge of the first passenger flight, carrying 22 paying passengers from New York to Southampton.

Oliver E. Allen described the B-314 in his 1981 book, *The Airline Builders*:

> From the outside, the Boeing B-314, the largest airplane of its day, had the appearance of a giant blue whale with rigid wings on its back. Yet the interior of this airborne colossus, used by Pan American for both its Atlantic and Pacific Clipper services, was fitted out like a suite at the Ritz.
>
> Built to carry 74 passengers and a crew of eight, the 314 was equipped with sleeping berths for 40, separate dressing rooms for men and women and a well-stocked bar amidships. It also had a lounge that doubled as a dining room, and a deluxe cabin in the tail section that converted into a bridal suite. The 109-foot-long fuselage was divided into two levels connected by a spiral staircase. Passengers sat below in groups of 10 in soundproof compartments while the crew inhabited the upper level, where the baggage and freight were stowed. The plane was constructed of aluminum alloy on a central frame of steel. A walkway inside each wing allowed flight engineers to reach all four engines in case in-flight repairs were needed.

This flying hotel reached heights of luxury that would never again be achieved in an airliner, not even in the jet age. In addition, it was to compile an unprecedented safety record. It sold the public on the safety and convenience of long-distance air travel as no plane had done before. And it certainly was the greatest flying boat ever to serve the airlines. Ken Follett's best-selling 1991 novel, *Night Over Water*, uses a September 1939 Pan Am B-314 *Clipper* flight as its setting. Follett's first line is, "It was the most romantic plane ever made." (He justifies this appraisal by putting his characters through enough sexual acrobatics to have sent Boeing's engineers back to the drawing board to reinforce the airplane's structure.)

The crew accommodations of the B-314 were also special. The control cabin resembled that of an ocean liner, and was more spacious than the cockpit of any airplane before or since. There were desks and comfortable chairs for the navigators and flight engineers as well as the pilots, and a large "master's desk" conference table at the rear of the cabin. Since the ocean-going Clippers were required to carry double crews because of their long flights, there were comfortable sleeping quarters on the top deck for all crew members to use between tours of duty. The crew complements ranged from eight to twelve, depending on how many stewards were needed for various passenger loads.

Trippe ordered six of the B-314s, four of which were assigned to the Atlantic and two of which went into the Pacific service. The first B-314, the *Yankee Clipper*, was christened by First Lady Eleanor Roosevelt in Washington on March 3, 1939. She used a bottle of water gathered from the seven seas.

The B-314s gave the Master Ocean Pilots greater prestige and responsibility than ever before. They were truly masters of ocean-going ships of the air. While Rod Sullivan was senior to Harold Gray in age and Pan Am flight experience, Gray forged ahead in authority because he was clearly top management material. Besides being a skilled pilot, he was an aeronautical engineer with a good head for business management. Unlike the cocky Sullivan, Gray had the demeanor of a business executive whether he was in the office or in the cockpit. Gray and Sullivan, after making the inaugural Atlantic mail and passenger flights in 1939, continued to set the pace for their fellow Master Ocean Pilots. Then Gray began to move up into management, while Sullivan continued his role of the old sea dog, becoming the first pilot in history to rack up 100 Atlantic crossings.

The advent of World War II made Pan Am's Atlantic and Pacific routes more important than ever. From the start of war in September 1939, the B-314s carried VIPs all over the world—people like Queen Wilhelmina of the Netherlands; King George of Greece; Harry Hopkins, the top advisor to President Roosevelt; and hundreds of other officials and celebrities whose customary ship travel was precluded by hostile submarines. When the United States entered the war, the Clippers were quickly pressed into military service. The Navy assumed ownership of the Boeing 314s, leasing them back to Pan Am, which continued to operate them with its regular crews.

On December 18, 1941, Harold Gray took off from New York for China in a B-314 Clipper that was loaded with spare tires for the Flying Tigers' P-40 fighters, dozens of which had been grounded for lack of tires. Gray's precious cargo reached the Flying Tigers in time to help them win a crucial air battle that might otherwise have been lost to the Japanese.

There were to be thousands of such vital wartime missions for the Master Ocean Pilots. Despite the rapid development of the military's Air Transport Command, with thousands of four-engine Douglas C-54s (military versions of the DC-4) crossing the oceans, the Clippers were the preferred mode of travel for the most important passengers and cargo. Generals and admirals were ferried to and from their posts by the B-314s, and in January 1943 President Roosevelt himself made his historic trip to the Casablanca Conference aboard the *Dixie Clipper*, a B-314 manned by a Pan Am crew.

General Dwight Eisenhower shuttled between Washington and his European headquarters by B-314 Clipper. He became friendly with Captain Rod Sullivan during several such trips, and when the general became president in 1953, Sullivan attended the inauguration as his guest.

This brief history of Pan Am from its Caribbean inception to World War II is necessarily a salute to Juan Trippe. Clearly he was the driving force in Pan Am's remarkable growth and accomplishments, which made it the leading international airline, serving 62 countries or colonies on five continents. This great success was not achieved without creating enmity, for Trippe was, in the eyes of many government officials, would-be competitors, and even his own associates and employees, something of a martinet and robber baron. But unlike many robber barons, he brought the benefits of progress to millions of people.

It is worth noting that Trippe's success was not achieved in the underdog style of the American Dream. He was the scion of a wealthy investment banking family, and he chose as his wife Elizabeth Stettinius, daughter of a J.P. Morgan partner and sister of Edward Stettinius, who was to succeed Cordell Hull as Secretary of State in 1944. From the beginning of Pan Am he surrounded himself with Yale classmates and other sons of wealth, including Cornelius Vanderbilt (Sonny) Whitney, long-time Pan Am chairman and principal shareholder, and members of such families as the Rockefellers, Harrimans, Vanderbilts, and Lehmans. He used money, power, Wall Street muscle, and influence in government to rig the game in his favor. He swallowed up would-be competitors or cut off their life blood by cornering the airmail contracts that were vital to survival of the early airlines. Usually he was able to get these contracts without competitive bidding, by having the specifications framed so that no other company could possibly qualify. In fact, if not in name, Pan Am was the "chosen instrument" of the United States in international airline service during Trippe's heyday.

Trippe was at the height of his powers when the *Yankee Clipper* prepared for departure from the Marine Terminal of New

York's LaGuardia Airport on February 21, 1943. It was to be operated as Pan Am Flight 9035, New York/Bermuda/Horta (Azores)/Lisbon, with Master Ocean Pilot Rod Sullivan in command. In keeping with its unique mission, it would carry passengers whose wartime roles gave them the high priority needed to sit in the world's most coveted airline seats.

CHAPTER 4

The Yankee Clipper Goes Down

The United Service Organizations (USO) was organized in 1941 by a group of nonprofit organizations (including the YMCA, YWCA, National Catholic Community Service, Jewish Welfare Board, and the Salvation Army) to provide social, recreational, and spiritual facilities to members of the armed forces. One of its branches, USO Camp Shows, Inc. supplied troupes of professional performers to entertain service men and women. In New York, Saul Abraham was one of the USO Camp Shows coordinators who booked the performers and took care of their travel arrangements. Organizing troupes to visit bases in the United States was complicated enough, given the difficulties of domestic travel during wartime. But the shows for overseas bases were an even bigger headache for Saul and the USO, mainly because the War Department's secrecy policy required him to deliver whole troupes to airports without telling the performers where they were going.

On February 19, 1943, Saul received a phone call from the Army's Special Services Division in Washington, asking him to supply a troupe of seven performers for overseas entertainment. In the usual cloak-and-dagger style, he was told to pick up their tickets at the Pan Am office in New York, and was warned not to show the tickets to the performers or disclose their destination until they were at the airport ready to board the plane. He was ordered to report to LaGuardia Airport with the seven entertainers by 7:30 a.m. on February 21st. They were to be packed for a three-month trip, but nothing was to be said to them about where they were going.

Saul had dozens of entertainers on his standby list, established professionals who were willing to fly anywhere in the world at a moment's notice, without pay other than $10 per day for expenses. From the list he chose singers Jane Froman, Yvette Harris, and Tamara Swann; the husband-and-wife comedy/dance team of Lorraine and Roy Rognan, known professionally as Lorraine and Rognan; accordionist Gypsy Markoff; and puppeteer Grace Drysdale.

Saul was very happy with the troupe, as each member had performed to enthusiastic applause in past USO shows. It was a well-rounded group with emphasis on music, which was the easiest entertainment to provide at military bases and had the ingredient most likely to please the audiences: the popular songs that reminded them of home and the Dream they were fighting to preserve.

Tamara Swann, the Russian-born wife of a New York advertising executive, was brought to New York as a child after her family had been forced to flee from the 1917 revolution. She began her career singing Russian songs in night clubs and on radio. Later, known simply as Tamara, she was to star on the Broadway stage and popularize such songs as "Smoke Gets in Your Eyes," "Love for Sale," and "Get Out of Town." She also appeared in films.

Gypsy Markoff, of Russian-Egyptian parentage, was a world-class accordionist who had performed for several heads of state. She appeared regularly at the Waldorf-Astoria Hotel in New York, Shepheard's Hotel in Cairo, and many vaudeville theatres and nightclubs. She had made several stateside USO tours and was eagerly looking forward to this trip with her close friend Tamara.

Grace Drysdale was an accomplished puppeteer who performed mainly in the New York City area. Her credits included such diverse bookings as the Roxy Theatre, the Waldorf-Astoria Hotel, and Leon & Eddie's, the sophisticated nightclub.

Yvette Harris was a fetching blonde singer who was only 17 when she began her nightclub and radio career in 1941. Raised in New Orleans, she was an exponent of the "Ooh-la-la" school of singing, performing both in French and English. In the style of that day, she was billed simply as Yvette.

Lorraine and Roy Rognan were one of the great ongoing love stories of show business. Roy had been a circus acrobat and clown before turning to vaudeville, and Lorraine was a comedienne/dancer when they met in 1936. They quickly decided to put their acts together in 1937, and six months later were married. They had performed together in vaudeville, nightclubs, and films since then. One of their most popular dancing acts was described in *Variety* as "a burlesque ballroom routine that would make the good citizens of Vienna gasp with horror." Their marriage endured despite the demands of performing together, and even in their sixth year as husband and wife they were known to openly show affection for each other. They had been offered a paid engagement with another camp show in 1942, but chose to await a call for unpaid performers. They were delighted when Saul Abraham called and told them he would pick them up on February 21st. They were looking forward eagerly to their first overseas USO show.

Jane Froman, the brightest star of the troupe, was recognized as one of the leading female vocalists of her time. Her rich contralto voice had been trained for the classics at the Cincinnati Conservatory of Music, but she preferred popular songs. She started her professional career on radio stations in Cincinnati and Chicago. In 1931, she was discovered by Paul Whiteman, then America's most prominent band leader. She sang with Whiteman's band on tour and on radio, and made her Broadway debut as the singing star of the "Ziegfield Follies of 1933." She appeared regularly on the leading radio musical show, the Chesterfield Hour, along with such luminaries as Bing Crosby and Ruth Etting, and was twice voted top female singer on the air. Films, Broadway shows, recording contracts, nightclub and vaudeville engagements followed in profusion. In the parlance of show business, Jane became known as a classic interpreter of All-American standards.

Jane was a favorite of President Franklin D. Roosevelt, for whom she had performed five times. He particularly liked her rendition of Gershwin's "It Ain't Necessarily So." She was one of the first entertainers to volunteer for unpaid USO shows, appearing in the first camp show at Fort Belvoir, Virginia, in 1941. She had done many camp shows and war bond rallies throughout the country, and in the summer of 1942 she received a telegram from USO headquarters asking if she would be available for overseas assignments. She was then starring with Ed Wynn in the Broadway show, "Laugh, Town, Laugh." Within the hour she wired back that she would love to entertain the troops overseas, and thus became the first performer to accept this challenge. She was then placed on Saul Abraham's standby list, and was tapped by Saul for the February 1943 troupe. In the interim, she had to refuse lucrative stage and film offers to keep herself available for the USO tour. At 35, she was at the pinnacle of her career, and she still had the freshfaced girl-next-door look that often caused reviewers to call her "the All-American girl." She was one of the highest-paid nightclub performers but did not look like she belonged in nightclubs.

On February 19th, Saul Abraham went to Pan Am's ticket office and picked up the seven tickets as ordered. Then on February 21st he picked up the performers in Manhattan and drove them out to LaGuardia Field, still keeping their flight destination to himself. When they arrived at the LaGuardia Marine Terminal, Saul shepherded the seven volunteers through the paperwork that preceded their clearance to board the flight. He lined them up in front of the processing desks, and placed in front of each one his or her passport and ticket. Pan Am clerks tore off the first page of each ticket book and passed the tickets and passports down the line to the customs inspectors' desks as each performer was processed through. At the last desk, all the tickets and passports were handed back to Saul. He gave each performer the proper passport and a boarding pass. When the bell sounded signifying that the plane was ready for boarding, Saul handed all seven tickets to Roy Rognan, the only man in the troupe. It was only then that he told them they were boarding the *Yankee Clipper* for a two-day flight to Foynes, Ireland, by way of Lisbon. From Foynes the troupe would pick up another flight to England, and eventually would go on to North Africa to complete their three-month tour.

While the passengers were being processed, the crew was getting ready for what had become a routine crossing of the Atlantic. Although government regulations required physical examinations of pilots only twice a year, Pan Am's internal rules were much more stringent. Their ocean-crossing pilots were examined before every flight by Pan Am's doctors. Captain Rod Sullivan passed his pre-flight physical without any problems, as did the rest of the crew.

For this trip, the *Yankee Clipper* was manned by a crew of 12: two backup pilots, in addition to Sullivan and his co-pilot, First Officer Stanton Rush; two navigators; two engineering officers; two radio officers; and two stewards. This double complement enabled one crew to rest or sleep while the other shift was on duty.

It was nearly 9 a.m. when the entertainers boarded the plane, along with 20 other passengers—military officers, State Department officials, diplomatic couriers, war correspondents for newspapers and radio networks, business executives on wartime missions—all men. The performers were excited and pleased by their luxurious accommodations, for the B-314 was like no other other airplane they had ever seen. They settled into comfortable compartments—more like an ocean liner than an airplane—and chattered happily about their plans for entertaining the boys in England and North Africa.

The backup co-pilot, Fourth Officer John Burn, was making his first Atlantic crossing since joining Pan Am during the previous autumn. Earlier in the war he had been a ferry pilot, delivering military aircraft from factories to war zones. In the fall of 1942, when he left the ferry pilot job to start training with Pan Am in New York, he had seen Jane Froman perform at the Roxy Theatre in New York, and had become a fan of hers. One of his duties as the lowest ranking pilot aboard the *Yankee Clipper* was to walk through the passenger compartments with a sign showing the plane's altitude, speed, and estimated time of arrival at the next stop. As he did this, he recognized Jane Froman. She seemed so friendly that he wanted to speak to her, but he decided against it.

The *Yankee Clipper's* routing to Ireland was by way of Bermuda, Horta (in the Azores), and Lisbon. Although the B-314 was capable of flying non-stop from New York to the Azores, the stop at Bermuda gave them extra fuel insurance and enabled them to serve an important Allied wartime naval base. The flight to Bermuda was routine, landing at 2:10 p.m. After refueling and processing of mail, the flight departed Bermuda at 4:10 p.m., flying through the night to land at Horta at 10:14 a.m. the next day—Washington's Birthday, Monday, February 22, 1943. During the night the passengers had slept soundly in spacious berths that compared favorably with the most luxurious Pullman cars of the day.

The flight stopped at Horta for an hour and a half, departing just before noon for Lisbon, where they were scheduled to land at about 7 p.m. They proceeded routinely at 7,000 feet altititude from the Azores to the west coast of Portugal. For the approach up the River Tagus to Lisbon, wartime regulations required a flying altitude of 600 feet so that Portuguese authorities could clearly identify incoming aircraft. Rod Sullivan, at the controls for the landing at Lisbon, began his descent west of Lisbon and reached 600 feet as the flight headed eastward up the mouth of the River Tagus. Lisbon was to the north of their path, and came into view on the passengers' left. The USO entertainers gathered at the windows to catch their first glimpse of the fabled city. Lorraine and Roy Rognan held hands as they looked down on the docks of the Lisbon waterfront in the fading twilight. They noticed flashes of lightning in the distance behind the city.

Lisbon, set on seven terraced hills, is one of the great harbors of Europe. There are many ancient monuments to its maritime history. As the *Yankee Clipper* flew up the river, its passengers looking at the city to their left could see the magnificent monastery on the north bank of the Tagus, built by King Manuel I to commemorate the pioneering of the passage to India by Portugal's greatest mariner, Vasco da Gama. But on this February evening during the fourth year of World War II, Lisbon was as well known for its international intrigue as for its classic beauty.

Portugal remained neutral throughout the war, and was a hotbed of espionage for both sides. Everywhere there were spies, pretenders, and displaced persons seeking passage out of war-torn Europe to the New World. Many of the USO performers on the *Yankee Clipper* thought of *Casablanca*, the 1942 film starring Humphrey Bogart as Rick Blaine, proprietor of a nightclub in which half the patrons were trying to buy or steal the diplomatic clearances that would get them on the airplane to Lisbon.

Pan Am was an important part of the wartime Lisbon scene. Its radio station at Cabo Ruivo, the riverside airport from which the Clippers operated, was the only one in Europe that was not in Axis hands. Its westbound Clipper flights were the magic carpets to freedom sought by hundreds in Lisbon and thousands who were trying to get to Lisbon.

As the *Yankee Clipper* made its way up the river, Pan Am's ground personnel were busy preparing for the night landing that was the routine conclusion of the Horta/Lisbon leg of flight 9035. At 4 p.m., the *Yankee Clipper's* radio officer had sent the coded message "Enter" to Pan Am's Cabo Ruivo radio station. In their wartime code, this meant that they were expecting to land at Lisbon in three hours, which would put them down at 7 p.m. Pan Am's procedure called for its launch to leave the Cabo Ruivo dock 45 minutes before the flight was due to arrive, to allow sufficient time to lay out the lighted buoys that served as the runway for flying boat landings. Charles Bounds, Pan Am's assistant airport manager at Cabo Ruivo, was the control officer in charge of the principal launch, *Pan Air III-A*. He took the launch out onto the river with two Portuguese crewmen, Fernando Basto and Eduardo da Silva.

The runway formed by the lighted buoys was a product of Pan Am's long experience with flying boats. It is much more difficult for pilots to determine their altitude over water than over land, since the flat surface of water does not permit much depth perception. This is especially true at night, when the inky blackness of the water affords virtually no target for depth perception. While the Clippers were equipped with state-of-the-art barometric altimeters, there was considerable lag in their readings, and pilots could not safely depend upon these instruments to determine when to level off from descent, cut their throttles, and pull back on the stick to make a landing. These three final steps had to be completed very close to the surface, as determined visually by the pilot.

To overcome this difficulty, Pan Am had designed one of those simple solutions that made its operations work so well. The launch would lay out a string of five lighted buoys, about 1,200 feet apart, forming a lighted runway about a mile long. The first four lights were white, and the last light was red, indicating to the pilot that the landing would be made in the direction that the white lights pointed toward the red light. (See Figure 1.) The standard approach procedure called for the pilot to circle the runway to the right of the lights, flying from the white lights in the direction of the red light, and maintaining the prescribed approach altitude, which was usually 500 to 600 feet. When the pilot reached the red light, he would make a 90 degree left turn and fly across the red light, holding that course until he was to the left of the runway. He would then make another left turn and fly down the string of lights until he reached the first white light, at which point he would make another left turn and fly across to the right of the first white light. There he would make another left turn, line up with the runway of lights, and start a gradual descent from 500 feet down to the surface, using the string of lights to guide him down to the surface.

As the plane descended, the spaces between the lights would appear to get smaller and smaller, and when the pilot saw what looked more like a solid line than a string of separate lights, he would know that he was close to the surface. The launch would be anchored to the pilot's left of the red light, and when the pilot blinked the landing lights that were located in the airplane's wings, the launch officer would fire a bright flare that would illuminate the designated landing area near the red light, giving the pilot a good view of the water and helping him to accurately judge his height at the crucial time of leveling off, cutting power, and pulling the nose up into the stall that completed the landing.

All Pan Am pilots were trained to land parallel with the string of lights, from the white lights toward the red. This procedure provided two important safety factors. First, the area along the lights was patrolled by the launch, eliminating the dangers of floating logs and other debris that had sunk more than one flying boat. Second, paralleling the lights would give the pilot the depth perception without which he might either fly into the

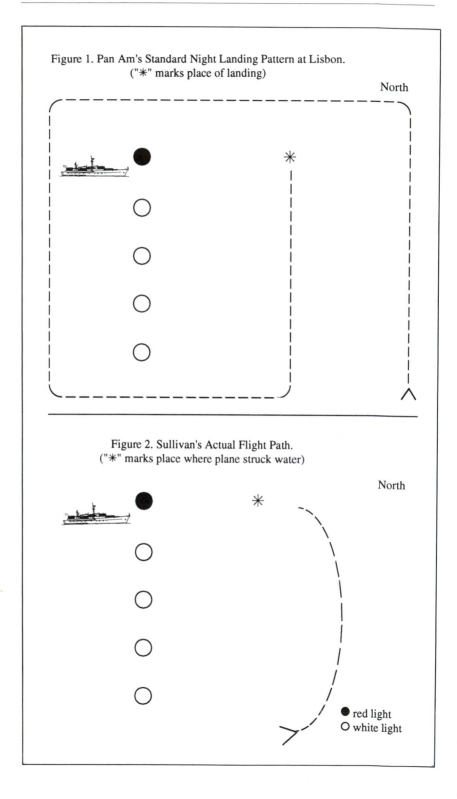

Figure 1. Pan Am's Standard Night Landing Pattern at Lisbon.
("✳" marks place of landing)

North

Figure 2. Sullivan's Actual Flight Path.
("✳" marks place where plane struck water)

North

● red light
○ white light

water or stall the plane at such a high altitude that a crash landing would result.

Landing at right angles to the lights would rob the pilot of both safety factors. He would not be landing in a patrolled area, and might strike a dangerous object on or just below the surface. And he would have no reference for depth perception, since the light he was approaching at right angles would look about the same to him at an altitude of 50 feet as it did at 500 feet. Only the narrowing of the gaps between the lights that became apparent when approaching parallel with the runway could provide the necessary depth perception. This was doubly important for night landings in the Boeing 314, the largest flying boat ever operated by any airline, with its wing span of 152 feet and its pilot sitting 27 feet above the hull bottom.

Charles Bounds and the crew of *Pan Air III-A* left the Cabo Ruivo dock at 6:20 p.m. and proceeded to lay out the five lights in a south-to-north direction, with the red light at the north end. The wind was coming out of the west, but since it was only blowing at 6 knots (6 nautical miles per hour) it was considered negligible. It was more convenient for Pan Am's flying boats to land north or south on the Tagus, rather than east or west, even in a slight crosswind. *Pan Air III-A* patrolled the area parallel with the lights and found it free from debris. Then the launch took up its regular position about 1,500 feet west of the red light, so that the pilot would see it to his left as he approached. Bounds checked and loaded his Very pistol so that he would be ready to fire the flare when Rod Sullivan signalled to him by blinking the Clipper's landing lights.

As Sullivan flew up the river toward the landing area, his co-pilot, First Officer Stanton Rush, spoke to Bounds on the launch by radiophone. At 6:44 p.m., Bounds advised that the lights were laid out south to north, and that the plane should land from the south to the north, with a crosswind from the west at 6 knots. At 6:45, Rush acknowledged the instructions, and asked Bounds to fire his flare when he saw both of the *Yankee Clipper's* landing lights blink. Rush reported that they were southeast of the light line and were going to circle it and come in for a landing. At that time, with darkness just settling in, Bounds could still see the *Yankee Clipper* flying a mile or two east of the light line, at about 500 feet, its position about abeam of the launch, which was just south of the red light. All this was according to established procedures, and Bounds expected that Sullivan would then make his first left turn, maintaining 500 feet altitude, to start circling the light line for a normal landing to the north. Bounds then turned away to make a final check of the designated landing area, since it was his responsibility to direct the plane into an area that was cleared of obstacles.

On the flight deck, Rod Sullivan was at the controls in the left seat, with his co-pilot, First Officer Rush, in the right seat. The spacious control cabin provided the opportunity for junior crew members to stand behind the pilots' seats to observe the landing. The relief pilot, Third Officer Andrew Freeland, stood behind Sullivan's seat; the head navigator, Second Officer Merwin Osterhaut, stood between the pilots' seats; and Fourth Officer John Burn stood behind the co-pilot's seat, happy at his first chance to watch a Master Ocean Pilot make a night landing. The other five cockpit crew members were seated at desks or jump seats in the rear of the control cabin.

At that point, when all the crew members and the launch personnel were expecting Sullivan to maintain his altitude and start circling the light line, the plane started to descend toward the water. Within less than a minute, the plane went into a descending left turn, changing its heading from north to west; it lost more than 400 feet of altitude; the left wing tip skimmed the surface of the river, then dug in deeper; and at 6:47 p.m. the great *Yankee Clipper* plunged into the river. It went down about a mile-and-a-half east of the red light, with its nose headed in a westerly direction, facing the red light.

If anyone on the flight deck had sensed any danger, they did not communicate it to the stewards who were back in the passenger compartments preparing the passengers for landing. The seat belt sign had flashed on and the stewards checked to see that all the passengers were strapped in. None of the passengers received any warning of a crash. Their first hint of trouble came when the left wing tip dipped into the water. When the crash followed in seconds, water rushed into the cabin and the plane began to sink rapidly.

As the wing dug into the river, the flying boat turned over on its back and hit the water with such a tremendous impact that it felt like an explosion. Roy Rognan was holding a briefcase full of music and other papers for the tour, including the tickets for the seven USO performers that Saul Abraham had given to him at LaGuardia Airport. When the water rushed in, his first thought was that he should get rid of his trousers and shoes so that he could swim freely and save his wife, Lorraine, who was not a strong swimmer. He yelled to Lorraine to take the briefcase so that he could strip. As she did so, the plane began to sink. Roy was knocked down, and as he grabbed desperately for Lorraine's hands, the water started to sweep him away. She screamed his name, and he cried her name back and waved frantically as the plane broke up and he disappeared into the black water. She was pushed out of the disintegrating hull and immersed in the water, quickly bobbing to the surface. In terrible pain from a broken ankle and in shock from having lost sight of her husband, she was picked up by Bounds in the *Pan Air III-A* launch.

Gypsy Markoff, Yvette Harris, and Grace Drysdale were all seated in a rear compartment, and were thrown clear of the *Yankee Clipper* as it broke up and sank. Gypsy's head, shoulders, hands, legs, and back were injured as she was dragged through the wreckage. When she came to the surface with a broken shoulder and her face cut open, she was doubly terrified because she could not swim. Barely able to lift her arms, she screamed for help. Out of nowhere, Yvette swam toward her and propped her up on a floating pillow from the wreckage. She clung to the pillow and it kept her head above water. She was close to panicking, but Yvette washed the blood from her face and tried to keep her spirits up. After 15 minutes that seemed like an eternity, the launch spotted Gypsy in its searchlight and she was hauled aboard. One of the crew members administered first aid to Gypsy's head wound as the launch moved on to search for other survivors. Yvette, a powerful swimmer and a junior lifeguard, continued to help others in the water, saving three injured men by pushing them toward floating debris that kept them above the surface until they were rescued. Unhurt herself, she finally swam all the way to safety on the shore, a distance of more than 2 miles, in the frigid water.

Jane Froman and Tamara Swann were in a rear compartment. In the prior landings at Bermuda and Horta, Tamara had taken the seat facing the rear of the plane, but as they prepared to land at Lisbon, she took the forward-facing seat. The sudden crash caught both singers by surprise. Jane was swept away by the surging water, and blacked out. She never saw what became of Tamara.

The icy waters of the Tagus revived Jane. She fought her way up to the surface, and knew immediately that she was badly hurt. She felt as though the impact of the crash and the collapse of the plane's structure had broken every bone in her body. As she came to the surface, she cried for help. She seemed to be alone in the darkness of the river. But then she heard the voice of a man who was cursing at the top of his lungs. Desperately she cried out, "Who's that? Would you help me, please?"

"Fourth Officer Burn at your service, Ma'am," came the reply from the darkness. "May I be of assistance?"

These were the first words spoken between Jane Froman and John Burn. Jane's right leg had suffered compound fractures and had nearly been severed below the knee. She also had several fractures in her right arm, two broken ribs, and cuts and bruises too numerous to count. John had fractures of the skull and two spinal verterbrae.

John quickly went to work to save them. He saw that they had both surfaced far from the main wreckage where the rescue boats were searching. They were going to be in those freezing waters for some time, and the odds were that both would die there within the hour unless he could keep them above the water until help came. Somehow John collected some floating life jackets and pieces of the wreckage, which he put together as a makeshift raft they could both cling to. Then he turned to conversation, hoping to keep Jane's mind—and his—off their terrible predicament.

"You know, Miss Froman, I've been a fan of yours for years. In fact, when I left the Ferry Command and came to New York for Pan Am training, I went to see you at the Roxy. I thought you were wonderful, but I never thought I'd meet you swimming in the Tagus River."

"How sweet," said Jane.

They both laughed, and then Jane said, "You know, I believe there are some some bones sticking out of my legs. I'm going to investigate."

John was gripped by the fear that if she felt bare bones, she would go into shock and hysterics. He would try to smooth-talk her out of it.

"Why, Miss Froman, your legs were beautiful the last time I looked at them. I wouldn't worry about it."

"Look," said Jane, "I asked you for assistance, not advice. I can't move my right arm, so you hold on to me."

She explored below the water with her left arm, and her worst fears were confirmed. "Yeah, just as I thought. Bones sticking out all over."

But instead of going into hysterics, she looked at John Burn, and became concerned at his wounds. "You've got blood all over your face!"

John laughed and said, "Don't be silly, it's oil."

"Look, lad, I know blood when I see it!" With that, she began to splash cold water into his face. The icy shock nearly drove John out of his mind, and he yelled, "Cut it out! Cut it out!"

She stopped splashing. Suddenly they started telling each other their life stories. Maybe they both felt the need to keep talking lest a deathly silence overtake them, or maybe it was the feeling that fate had thrown them together for a purpose. Whatever the reasons, they talked as if they had known each other intimately for years.

"You know, Jane, when I saw you, I thought you must have been a beautiful baby."

"I was born in University City, Missouri, and lived there till I was five. My mother and father separated and Mom and I moved to her home town, Clinton, Missouri. There were many debts and Mother began giving piano and vocal lessons to all comers for a dollar a lesson."

"Were you singing as a mere babe?" asked John.

"Well, I first remember singing arias at bedtime with Mom, and then when I was five I picked out 'Oh, You Beautiful Lady' after I heard a carnival carousel play it. I was all of eight when I started to sing at local churches and parties."

"Didn't you go to school?"

"Oh, yes," said Jane, "I went to a convent in Clinton and boarded there when Mom was teaching in other towns. I was terrible in math and very good in all the arts."

John told some of his childhood history, and Jane talked about the chilly atmosphere of the convent and how wonderful she had thought it would be to have a mother who didn't have to work so they could be home together all the time. Suddenly a launch swept into view, and they were spotted in its searchlight. Two excited boatmen, jabbering in Portuguese, reached out to pull them aboard. One leaned over too far to grab Jane, and fell into the water himself. The second boatmen lunged after the first, trying to keep him in the launch, and he too fell in. The helmsman screamed at the two clumsy boatmen and got so disturbed that he stalled the boat's engine, and the launch quickly floated away down the river. Jane and John laughed hysterically, as if to block out the thought that they had missed their rescue. But a small motorboat quickly came on the scene and they were hauled aboard. They had been in the water for 45 minutes.

Once ashore, John and Jane were taken by ambulance to San Jose Hospital, a tiny emergency facility where the survivors were crowded in, five to a room. The dismembered hull of the *Yankee Clipper* went to the bottom of the Tagus within ten minutes, taking with her 19 of the 27 passengers and 5 of the 12 crew members. Of the USO troupe, Jane Froman, Gypsy Markoff, and Lorraine Rognan were the most seriously injured survivors.

Grace Drysdale and Yvette Harris escaped relatively unscathed. But Tamara Swann and Roy Rognan were lost. Thus was broken the magic spell that had protected American performers who entertained troops throughout World War I (some of them right in the trenches of France) and World War II.

Captain Rod Sullivan survived with serious back injuries. The co-pilot, Stanton Rush, and the backup pilot, Andrew Freeland, who was standing behind Sullivan's seat when the plane crashed, were killed, as were navigator Ingles, engineering officer Vaughan, and steward Robinson.

At 8:10 p.m., Albert Anderson, Pan Am's manager at Cabo Ruivo, sent a radiogram to his superiors in New York:

SULLIVAN CRASH LANDED TWO MILES EAST OF CABO RUIVO STOP PLANE LOST DETAILS LATER ANDERSON

Such was the deference to the Master Ocean Pilots that when one went down, it was not reported as the crash of the *Yankee Clipper* or Flight 9035—just "Sullivan."

CHAPTER 5

Jane and John, 1943-1952

In Lisbon, Pan Am and the Civil Aeronautics Board (CAB), the government agency then responsible for investigating airline accidents, began to probe into the causes of the *Yankee Clipper* crash.

This was Pan Am's first accident in its transatlantic operations, which had previously covered 1,225 crossings, carrying more than 44,000 passengers without injury. It was known throughout the industry that Pan Am's safety standards were higher than the minimums required by the government. The CAB was a fairly new agency and did not have well-developed facilities for such investigations, particularly when accidents occurred outside the United States. Pan Am was the only American operator of the Boeing 314. This was the first crash of an American airliner in Europe, and with a war going on, one can understand why the CAB left much of the investigation to Pan Am.

The main wreckage of the *Yankee Clipper* was at the bottom of the Tagus, and the CAB had no facilities for recovering it. Two CAB investigators were dispatched to Lisbon, but could not get there before March 4th, ten days after the accident. While they were enroute, Pan Am itself was authorized to salvage the wreckage. They recovered most of the plane and deposited it in a warehouse at the Lisbon docks, where it was guarded by police until the CAB and Pan Am investigators had finished examining it.

Since the accident occurred in Portugal, the Portuguese government had the legal power to conduct its own investigation. Therefore, the questioning of Rod Sullivan and the other survivors and witnesses was conducted by a Portuguese Air Force officer, with the help of the two CAB investigators. In April 1943, when Sullivan and the other survivors had returned to the United States, a CAB Accident Investigation Hearing was held in New York. While such hearings were supposed to be open to the press and public, this one was a closed private hearing because of the secrecy of wartime overseas flight operations. The Clippers were officially owned by the Navy, and the armed forces continued to depend on Pan Am's transatlantic services for such precious cargo as President Roosevelt and General Eisenhower.

Unlike many aircraft accident investigations, this one was relatively simple. There was one basic question to be answered: Why did the *Yankee Clipper* descend to the water level when it was east of the light string, flying from east to west, instead of following the prescribed procedure that called for it to continue flying at 600 feet altitude until it had completely circled the light string so that it could then descend and land from south to north?

As it turned out, only one man knew the answer to that question: Rod Sullivan. His answer, as told to the investigators, was as follows:

He had intended to follow the prescribed pattern of circling the light string at an altitude of 600 feet and then land from south to north (see Figure 1). However, while he was still circling on a northerly heading and was abeam of (opposite) the first white light, the plane's nose started to drop. He was not alarmed until the plane descended to 400 feet, when he noticed that the angle of descent had increased to a dangerous 45 degrees. He was then abeam of the third (middle) white light. He pulled back on the elevator control to stop the descent, but there was no pressure whatsoever on the control wheel. It was absolutely dead, whereas normally in a descent there would be a lot of pressure on it. First Officer Rush also pulled back on his elevator control, which was a duplicate of the Captain's control wheel. When he and the co-pilot were unable to halt the descent by bringing the nose up, he knew that he was going to crash, and decided it would be best to reduce speed and have the wing absorb some of the impact. Therefore, just before the crash, he cut back the power on the engines in order to decrease the speed at which the plane would hit the water, and he threw the left wing down so that it would contact the water first.

Sullivan said that throughout this ordeal, there was no conversation between him and First Officer Rush or any other crew member. This was a sudden emergency that required him to make a snap judgement to avoid a total disaster. He was asked why he had not tried to increase engine power, which normally would cause the plane to climb. His reply was that he thought it too risky at low altitude with the nose down in such a dangerous descent and with no response on the elevator controls. He was asked whether he intended to land from east to west, perpendicular to the string of lights, instead of south-to-north, and he denied this flatly. He said that the only reason why he had made a descending left turn and put the plane into the water east of the red light (see Figure 2) was that it went into an uncontrollable dive at that point, and his only option was to try to cushion the shock of impact with the water by putting the wing down. It was natural for him to put the left wing down, since all turns in the traffic pattern were made to the left, and turning left rather than right would put the ship closer to the Pan Am launch and the rescue facilities on shore.

Sullivan's memory of the last few minutes of the flight was hazy, but the investigators ascribed this to the physical and mental shock he had suffered. Unfortunately, the one man who could corroborate his story, co-pilot Stanton Rush, did not survive. Two surviving crew members who had been standing behind the pilots' seats, 2nd Officer Osterhaut and 4th Office Burn, had been taken by surprise when the plane hit the water and did not have clear recollections of the descent.

When Sullivan returned to New York in April, Pan Am's investigating board, led by Master Ocean Pilot Harold Gray, took him up in another B-314 to simulate the descent at Lisbon, starting from 5,000 feet altitude so they would have plenty of time to recover. They also questioned Sullivan extensively and reached their own conclusions about the cause of the accident, but their report was considered an internal document covered by national security, and was not made public.

When the Pan Am and government investigations were completed, Sullivan was quietly retired from flight duty. He was then 51 years old, and the reason given for his retirement was the physical and mental aftermath of the Lisbon accident. While many of Pan Am's retired pilots stayed on in ground jobs, Rod Sullivan was not cut out for instructing or administrative work. His flying career ended, he went back to his home in Sanford, North Carolina, to devote full time to his electrical supply business.

At the tiny San Jose Hospital in Lisbon, Jane Froman was placed in the bed next to John Burn on the night of the crash. Both were given sedatives to ease their pain, but they could hear the team of doctors talking among themselves as they went from bed to bed. Some were speaking Portuguese and some English. The chief doctor examined Jane and read off a list of her injuries to the nurse who was taking notes. One of the doctors asked the chief doctor—in English—whether they were going to amputate Jane's right leg. Jane heard this clearly, and calmly said that if they intended to amputate, they should let her know first. The doctors promised to do so, and then moved on to John Burn's bed.

They looked at John's x-rays and conferred about his condition. "This man probably won't live through the night," said one of the doctors, "so there's no point in operating on him. Let's get on to the others."

Jane was taken to the operating room for emergency surgery in the wee hours of the morning, while John was left to sweat out the doctors' gloomy diagnosis. He lived through the night and went into surgery the next morning. Both came through the surgery without complications, John emerging in a full-body plaster cast for his spinal injuries and Jane with a heavy cast on her right leg. They were then moved to a convalescent hospital, Casa de Saude de Benfica, where there was much more room.

The first time John was allowed out of bed after his surgery, he went down the hall to visit Jane. They spent most of their waking hours together, and found that there was a powerful bond between them. It was more than the fateful 45 minutes in the River Tagus. There was a strong physical attraction and a sharing of many interests besides the immediate concerns about recovery. This was awkward, since Jane was Mrs. Donald Ross. Even though she was trapped in an unhappy marriage, Jane was the old-fashioned type who believed in loyalty. John played along, hoping that the problem would solve itself once they recovered from their crash injuries. As the weeks went by in the Lisbon hospital, they grew closer every day, but dodged open discussion of their romance as well as they could.

Jane had met Don Ross in Cincinnati in 1931, when he was half of the singing team of Brooks and Ross. Don was then an experienced vaudeville performer, ten years older than Jane. He helped Jane with stage presence, use of hands, walking, bowing—little touches that could polish her performances. Soon their friendship blossomed into romance, and they were married in 1933. Jane was then on the verge of stardom, while Don was wallowing in mediocrity. He had a fair singing voice but would not work hard to improve it. His worst fault was that he insisted on starting at the top, especially after he married a budding star. He got a few jobs from time to time but they all proved temporary. Gradually, he rationalized his own failures by devoting himself to management of Jane's career, even though she had the leading professional agents—the legendary William Morris Agency—representing her. He convinced himself that Jane needed his management, and that the demands of her booming career prevented him from developing his own.

This was a sure-fire formula for marital disaster, even with an easy-going wife like Jane. To justify his position, Don began to direct Jane not only in business affairs but in performance. After teaching her the rudimentary vaudeville moves in Cincinnati, there was really little Don could add from his limited theatrical know-how. He began to tell her to do things that she knew were wrong for her. She pretended to go along with his direction to preserve the marriage, but when she got on stage she did it the way she felt was right.

As the years went by, this time-bomb came closer to exploding the marriage. Don took to heavy drinking, and his egocentric complaints about Jane's career taking up all his time twice forced her to retire and act only as a housewife. This didn't work either as Don was beyond employment and they soon went broke. Jane went back to work and threw herself into her career, hoping that Don would mellow and the marriage would right itself in time. That's where they stood in the tenth year of the marriage when Jane boarded the ill-fated *Yankee Clipper*.

Jane's emergency surgery at Lisbon saved her leg, but the doctors told her that the damage was so extensive that bone grafts would be needed before she could think about walking again. The injuries to her right arm were also severe, but the prognosis for eventual recovery was much more hopeful than in the case of her leg. President Roosevelt himself arranged a special priority for Don Ross, and he flew over to Lisbon in March on another Pan Am Clipper. Jane was not able to fly back to the states, so they arranged passage on a small Portuguese freighter that would take two weeks to travel from Lisbon to Philadelphia. Jane was still in extensive pain and had many pieces of wood and metal from the plane embedded in her body.

John was still in his body cast, but he was 10 years younger than Jane, and was on the road to complete recovery. He planned to resume flying duties as soon as he got medical clearance. John and Jane did not spend as much time together after Don Ross's arrival in Lisbon, but the bond was still there. Both of them knew that they were deeply in love with each other. Neither knew what to do about it. They parted knowing that the first priority was to get Jane back to the states and into the hands of the best available surgeon so that she could walk and perform again.

Don and Jane weathered the rough crossing on the Portuguese freighter despite an attack by a Nazi submarine which fired a torpedo that narrowly missed. She was rushed to Doctors Hospital in New York, and Don engaged an orthopedic surgeon who had been recommended as the best. Unfortunately, he was along in years and had not kept current on the latest bone graft techniques. The older procedure was to take a large piece of bone from another part of the patient's body and use it as a splint. If infection set in (as it often did) the entire bone implant would fail to bond and the whole procedure would be useless. The newer technique was to use several smaller pieces of bone, so that if infection set in at some of the sites, the others would still have a chance to bond and all would not be lost. Jane's condition was precarious enough, as the Portuguese doctors had told her that if they had seen such devastating leg injuries on anyone but a stage performer, they would have amputated. Now her New York surgeon's obsolete methods robbed her of any chance for a speedy recovery. The first bone graft was unsuccessful. She still could not walk, and would need further surgery when she was strong enough. Meanwhile, President Roosevelt intervened again to provide her with penicillin, which was not then available to the general public. That saved her from the further spread of infection which would very likely have cost her the leg.

Discouraged by her slow recovery, which was complicated by the onset of osteomyelitis, Jane talked to Don about getting an opinion from another orthopedist. But Don saw this as a challenge to his judgment and authority. He was in charge, and he would not permit second-guessing. So Jane stayed with the first doctor, and was to face 25 more operations on the leg that was nearly severed in the River Tagus.

John Burn returned to New York a few weeks after Jane arrived. He visited her in the hospital and cheered her up immensely. But the romance was still problematical because Jane was loyal to her husband and would not consider imposing herself on another man as an invalid.

In August 1943, the doctors suggested to Jane that work would be her best therapy, even though her weight was down to 85 pounds (from her normal 128) and she carried a 35-pound cast on her leg. She agreed, and eagerly accepted an offer from producer Lou Walters (father of Barbara Walters) to star in a new Broadway show, "Artists and Models." Don Ross did the negotiating, and insisted that he be billed as the co-producer, a condition that Walters accepted in order to sign Jane.

"Artists and Models" proved to be a disaster for Jane. Her leg was not healing, and caused her constant pain and anguish. She had to be carried on and off the stage 22 times during each show. Jane herself wrote of this experience:

Men carried me on the stage, propped me up so my cast was hidden, and made me look as graceful as possible. Don Saxon and I sang a duet—accompanied by the appalling smell of putrefaction that went with osteomyelitis, the bone infection in my leg that simply would not heal. It is hard to describe the agony of my embarrassment when the heaviest perfume proved useless once the heat of the footlights began to get in its work. There was poor Don, singing me a love song; how could he pretend to ignore that poisonous reek?

The show itself was weak, lacking a comedy star to complement Jane's singing. The critics were kind to her but the show closed in six weeks. Jane immediately went back into hospital for more leg surgery.

By this time, Jane was drowning in the pain-killing drugs that had become part of her daily survival. In January 1944 she was hospitalized for an even tougher fight than the continuous battle to save her leg: she needed to withdraw from her dependence on the drugs. She was not helped by the self-righteous attitude of Don Ross and the orthopedic surgeon, both of whom lectured Jane on her moral duty to shake the drugs that had been thrust upon her as part of her medical treatment. Nevertheless, Jane fought and won this battle alone. Her reward for beating drug habituation was the news that she faced another bone graft. She went through that operation—again, done by Don's chosen surgeon with the outmoded splint technique, and again largely unsuccessful—and she recuperated without resorting to drugs.

Throughout this ordeal, Jane never lost faith that she would get well and walk again. But by the end of 1944 she was starting to lose faith in her marriage to Don. On top of all her pain and suffering, Jane had to pay her own medical bills. Neither Pan Am nor the USO paid for anything. Don would not work, claiming that Jane needed him full-time even though there would be no bookings until she got stronger. He became more dependent on alcohol. Jane had no choice but to put aside her pain and take on nightclub engagements, which were the highest-paying dates available to her.

To enable her to perform in nightclubs when she could not stand on her feet, an electrically-powered mobile piano was designed. Jane sat on the piano and sang from there while her accompanist worked the controls that moved Jane and the piano slowly around the stage. From November 1944 to April 1945, she dragged herself through successful engagements at Chicago's Chez Paree and New York's Copacabana, doing three shows a night. When the wartime brownout curtailed all nightclub shows, she took a vaudeville booking at New York's Capital Theatre, doing five shows a day.

When the Nazis surrendered in April 1945, the USO was called upon to supply more entertainers than ever for the wounded and homesick American service men deployed in the European theatre. Jane Froman had become a symbol of the courage to overcome the handicaps of wartime injuries. The USO begged her to go back to Europe and finish the job she had been forced to abandon at Lisbon. This time, she would give a tremendous lift to the wounded men who faced the daunting task of rehabilitation. If she could overcome her terrible injuries and perform as well as ever, there was hope for the G.I. who had lost an arm or a leg.

Still underweight, in constant pain and unable to walk on her own, she wanted desperately to go. Her orthopedic surgeon would not agree to release her. But Army doctors who examined her approved the trip, and that was enough for Jane. She sailed for France on May 10, 1945. She toured Europe for nearly four months, covering 30,000 miles and doing 95 shows. Her effect on the wounded men was charismatic, especially in those chauvinistic days when many of them said, "If a girl can overcome those injuries, I can do it." One group of soldiers, all in plaster casts, went AWOL in their pajamas and bathrobes to follow her show for nine days. Her triumphant tour ended only when she dislocated a bone in her spine.

Stranded in London, she put in a call to President Harry Truman. The White House arranged for her return passage on the Queen Mary. Coming into New York harbor on that huge ship with 15,000 returning servicemen, she was astounded when complete silence descended on the throng as they passed the Statue of Liberty.

By then it was the fall of 1945, and Jane faced new/old problems with her leg and her marriage.

X-rays revealed that the latest bone graft was not healing properly. It would have to be done again. Jane was warned, for perhaps the tenth time since that fateful night in Lisbon, that she might lose her leg. Again she wanted to change doctors, but Don would not hear of it, insisting that they had the best. She underwent the surgery, but was very sick in its aftermath. Coming out of the anesthetic, she called for John Burn. At the doctor's suggestion, John visited her at the hospital.

As 1945 ended, John was visiting Jane nearly every day. This time she made up her mind to end her marriage. She and John made plans to see each other in Florida in the spring of 1946, after she had time to recover from the latest operation and break the news to Don Ross. Jane told Don that there simply was nothing left of their marriage. He finally agreed and they parted as amicably as possible.

Early in 1946, Jane, under care of a private nurse, went to Miami Beach, Florida, to recuperate. John, who was back on flying duty with Pan Am, got himself transferred to Florida in February, and for the first time the lovers were together without the shadow of Don Ross hovering over them.

Her spirits lifted, Jane felt well enough to work. She took a booking at a popular Florida nightclub, the Colonial Inn, where she played to packed audiences through the winter season. John begged her to divorce Don and marry him. But she refused, saying that she was not out of the woods yet on her leg problem, and that she would not marry him if she lost the leg.

In the summer of 1946, Jane returned to New York, taking a cottage at Atlantic Beach on Long Island. With her private nurse at her side, Jane went back to work, doing a radio show for Shick and playing a long nightclub engagement at the Copacabana. In the fall, she, her mother, and her nurse moved to Coral Gables, Florida. She had left everything but her clothing with Don Ross. Her leg was acting up again. This time she was examined by new orthopedic surgeons, who told her that the present bone grafts were not taking properly. She would have to undergo that torture again, or the leg would atrophy and would have to be amputated.

Jane was practically broke, so she returned to the Colonial Inn, performing in great pain throughout December 1946 and January 1947 to raise enough money for the new surgery. She returned to New York in February, and selected as her new orthopedic surgeon Dr. Mather Cleveland, who had been the Army's chief orthopod in the European Theatre. Dr. Cleveland leveled with her: No less than five more bone graft operations would be needed, and even then the odds would be against success. And narcotics would again become a problem.

Without hesitation, Jane gave herself over to Dr. Cleveland. She checked into St. Luke's Hospital in New York and remained there eight solid months. The bone grafts were fairly successful, but she was threatened by recurrence of the dreaded osteomyelitis—infection of the bone marrow. Jane nearly died of shock following surgery.

John Burn spent his vacation with Jane and arranged a temporary transfer from Miami to New York to be with her between Pan Am trips. Jane left St. Luke's in October 1947, and returned to Miami with mother and nurse to recuperate and be near John. Then it was back to work on the Coca Cola radio show in January 1948, commuting from New York to Miami to be with John between shows.

She was divorced from Don Ross in February 1948. Jane and John were married at his house in High Pines near Miami on March 12, 1948. She walked down the aisle on crutches. Her long wedding gown concealed her crippled leg, but the horrible scarring of her right arm is plainly visible in the photos of the wedding, five years after the Lisbon accident.

They spent their honeymoon at Pirate's Cove in the Florida Keys, and then returned to the house in High Pines, which was to be their first home. John was flying out of Miami for Pan Am's Latin American Division. Jane was still on the air for Coca Cola, which required her to commute to New York. The bone grafts seemed to be holding up, but working caused her a great deal of pain, for which codeine was prescribed.

To eliminate Jane's commuting, John arranged a transfer to New York in August 1948. They took an apartment in Manhattan, and Jane played the Riviera nightclub in the New Jersey Palisades while still performing on the Coca Cola radio show. For the first time since her accident, she was able to walk on and off stage without crutches. But she still suffered great pain and needed her nurse in constant attendance. Her dependence on codeine was nearing the point of addiction.

Early in 1949, the Coca Cola program went off the air, and Jane decided to use her enforced break to eliminate the codeine problem. She was making good progress when suddenly Dr. Cleveland died. New doctors thought that nerve block surgery might improve the circulation in her leg and reduce the pain. She underwent this surgery at Presbyterian Hospital in New York in May 1949. It was not very successful. Meanwhile the codeine had been withdrawn abruptly and Jane had a ghastly time handling this. But she was determined to beat drug habituation again.

She returned from the hospital in June 1949, weak from her ordeal but proud of her victory over codeine. It was a very hot summer, so they decided to take a house on Fire Island. Jane's mother and nurse came along. As she regained her strength, she tried to exercise but overdid it, causing an abscess in her wounded leg. Again she was rushed to St. Luke's, terrified at the thought that the dreaded osteomyelitis had returned. The doctors brought the infection under control, but now Jane could fight no longer. She was on the verge of a complete mental breakdown from her long ordeal, and felt that she simply could not go on.

A committee of doctors met with Jane and John. Their spokesman said to Jane, "You are suffering from battle fatigue. You've had to go through ordeals that the human body wasn't meant to endure. You have had 25 operations, the total effect of which is the same as though you were being continually struck on the head with a hammer. We'd recommend that you check into the Menninger Clinic in Topeka, Kansas. There you could recover without risking further infection or physical injury, and you would receive the psychiatric guidance you now need to regain a healthy perspective."

Like many of her contemporaries, Jane regarded psychiatric clinics as funny farms. But in her condition she had no choice: it was Menninger or suicide. Jane and John went to Topeka in September 1949.

With typical Froman resilience, Jane threw herself into Menninger, determined to be a star there as she had been everywhere else. To her great joy, she thrived on the program. She busied herself in the arts and crafts shops, painting and working on leather, silver tooling, and ceramics. Gradually she began physical rehabilitation, and for the first time since Lisbon she discarded crutches and canes, playing golf, ping-pong, and dancing. Her appetite and sleeping improved, and her self-confidence returned. When John Burn visited her in Topeka at Christmas time, he could hardly believe the transformation.

Jane left Menninger in March 1950, traveling alone for the first time in seven years to rejoin John in New York. The seven months in Topeka had saved her life. She had achieved stardom at Menninger, and now she was determined to return to stardom as a performer.

In the early 1950's, Jane's improved mobility and her reborn spirit made her a greater star than ever. Once again she was in great demand for nightclub, radio, and recording dates. And now there was television. She made triumphant appearances on the leading shows of the day, Milton Berle's "Texaco Star Theatre" and Ed Sullivan's "Toast of the Town."

The crowning glory of her comeback was the Twentieth-Century Fox film of her life story, "With a Song in my Heart," released at Easter 1952. Jane recorded 26 songs for the soundtrack, and Susan Hayward, playing Jane, lip-synched the lyrics for the camera. David Wayne played Don Ross, and since Don's consent was required, it was a sympathetic portrayal, with the movie version of Don standing by Jane through much of her suffering and then stepping aside magnanimously when Jane no longer needed him. John Burn was played by Rory Calhoun, who was much younger and handsomer than Don Ross/David Wayne.

The film, corny 1950s sentimentality and all, was a hit. Alfred Newman won an Oscar for the score, and Susan Hayward was a runner-up for the best actress award. The film brought the Jane Froman story to millions, and proved to be a lasting inspiration to handicapped people all over the world. Ironically, Susan Hayward had suffered a crippling accident as a five-year-old living in Brooklyn. She was walking home from her first dancing lesson when she was run over by an auto. Both legs and both hips were fractured. She spent seven months in bed and six months more on crutches. This gave her special insight for the portrayal of Jane Froman.

In October of 1952, CBS gave Jane her own television program, "U.S.A. Canteen," a half-hour Saturday night show. It featured Jane and a weekly guest star. In keeping with the theme, members of the Armed Forces (particularly wounded veterans) were welcome in the studio audience. The show caught on immediately, attracting General Electric and Revlon as sponsors.

Since television shows were performed live at that time, lots of rehearsals were needed. Her rehearsals (and the shows themselves) were performed in a large Broadway theatre. Jane soon noticed that large groups of teenage fans—nearly all girls—were gathering at her stage door during rehearsals and performances. Rather than have her young fans standing out in the cold, Jane got permission from producer Irving Mansfield to invite them into the empty theatre during rehearsals. That band of rehearsal groupies was the start of the Fromanettes, a unique fan club.

Like any star, Jane was flattered by the attentions of her own fan club. But soon she saw a broader purpose for the Fromanettes. Many of these girls were inspired by the Susan Hayward movie and Jane's life story. They wanted to shower their adulation and celebrity worship on Jane, but they also wanted to emulate her in any way they could. Jane decided to harness this energy for her favorite cause: the Children's Division of the Menninger Institute. During Jane's life-saving stay there, she had been deeply impressed by the needs of disturbed children, and the pioneering work that Dr. William Menninger was doing through his Southard School, then one of the few residential centers for treatment of emotionally ill children who were too seriously disturbed to remain at home. So Jane turned the Fromanettes into a band of fundraisers and drumbeaters for Menninger's Southard School.

Jane and the Fromanettes (which quickly became a nation-wide and international network) promoted benefits and raised funds for Southard. Soon she incorporated the Jane Froman Foundation to carry on the work of helping the Southard School. The board of directors included Merv Griffin, Perry Como, Sophie Tucker, and other star performers. Of the many charities that Jane helped during her career, this was always closest to her heart.

As 1952 ended, Jane felt that she had it all together at last: a happy marriage, a newly nascent career, her fan clubs, her causes—all were flourishing as never before. She was energized as much by the inspiration she provided to others as by her own improved fortunes. Even her wounded leg had settled down to where she got around with only a light brace. Gone was the hell of surgery and pain-killing drugs. But now she had some bills to collect. Her medical expenses alone totaled more than $350,000, to say nothing of her lost earnings and the terrible pain and disfigurement she had suffered. Nobody had compensated her for any of this—not a penny from the USO, the United States government, or Pan American Airways. Like the other victims of the *Yankee Clipper* disaster, she had been forced to go to court for compensation.

The Lawsuit, 1943-1952

When Jane completed her perilous Atlantic crossing on the Portuguese freighter in Apil 1943, she went immediately to Doctors Hospital and began the long slow road to recovery. The last thing she thought of was starting a lawsuit against Pan Am. She assumed that some provision would be made to reimburse her for her medical expenses and other losses, but she put it out of her mind as she concentrated on the battle to save her leg and her career.

After her initial surgery in New York, she and Don Ross conferred with her lawyers. Jane was represented by one of the most prominent show-business law firms in New York. They specialized in negotiating contracts and protecting the business interests of performers like Jane. They were very competent in show-business litigation, but when one of their clients was injured, they turned to a negligence specialist since tort litigation was out of their field.

The New York negligence specialist that Jane's law firm brought in, Irving Lemov, was diligent, experienced in automobile accident cases, and competent by 1943 standards. Negligence claims usually arose out of auto accidents in those days, apart from the occasional case involving a railroad, maritime, or construction accident. Claims against airlines were almost unheard of, and their complexity was such that the negligence specialists simply were not equipped to handle them. Most resulted in complete losses for the plaintiffs, or cheap settlements for a fraction of the damage actually suffered.

Negligence specialists of the 1940s worked in small offices, typically as individual practitioners. The few that were organized as firms usually were headed by one lawyer who might have two or three supporting lawyers doing paper work. These specialists were able to handle auto accident claims because they did not call for much preparation or technical knowledge. There was a police report which could be obtained for a dollar or two, giving the names and addresses of the witnesses, who would be interviewed by the lawyer or by a staff investigator who was paid less than $50 per week. There would be one or two interviews with the injured client and the treating doctor. In serious injury cases, a medical specialist might be called in.

In other types of litigation, such as contract and business disputes, pre-trial "discovery" of evidence was permitted. This involved requests for the production of documents, and the taking of testimony of potential witnesses by depositions conducted in the lawyers' offices. The depositions were under oath and the testimony could be used at the trial just as if the witnesses were testifying in court. Pre-trial discovery increased the paperwork and preparation costs enormously, but it was not permitted in New York negligence cases, except for the depositions of the two adverse parties, usually the drivers of two cars that had collided, or a driver and a pedestrian.

As a result of these limitations, the file in a typical auto accident case was rarely more than an inch thick, even if depositions of the parties were taken. The cost of preparation normally did not exceed $200 to $250. And most important of all, the specialists representing plaintiffs did not develop the depth of litigation skills that was needed to equalize the scales of justice. Some made good livings, mostly by settling a large number of small cases before trial. But they all were considered small-time lawyers, outsiders, pushcart purveyors of legal services when compared to the Tiffany image of the Wall Street lawyers who represented business clients. The tort lawyers were Frank Capra's "little pushed-around guys." In routine auto accident cases, they could help clients collect more money for injury compensation than the clients could get on their own, but when it came to tough litigation they were usually no match for the clout that the firms representing insurance companies could muster in the courts.

Jane Froman's luck was bad all the way across the board. She volunteered for an unpaid USO tour that put her on the only transatlantic flying boat ever to crash. She suffered terrible injuries that became worse because she had the wrong husband and the wrong doctor. And when it came to recovering money for her expenses and injuries, she was confronted by another huge obstacle: the Warsaw Convention, an international treaty adopted in 1929 to deal with compensation of passengers injured on international flights.

In 1929, successful suits by airline passengers were almost unheard of. Most judges and jurors believed that airliners were expected to crash, and that passengers were adventurers who should assume the known risks of air travel. Any lawyer brave enough to take on such a claim would be outmanned by the large insurance firms defending the airlines, and by the vast amount of technical detail about aviation that the airline people knew and the plaintiff's lawyer did not. Furthermore, if all these obstacles were overcome and somehow the jurors found for the claimant, they were not likely to award more than $10,000 for even the most serious injuries—including death.

Therefore, the Warsaw Convention was considered a boon to air travelers when it was adopted in 1929, and when the United States adhered to it in 1934. In accidents arising out of international flights, it required the airlines to pay compensation to injured passengers and to the families of deceased passengers regardless of fault, thus eliminating the almost insurmountable burden of proving negligence. It limited compensation to 125,000 gold francs, worth about $8,300 in American money, which meant that cases involving deaths or serious injuries would automatically be settled for $8,300 without the need to file suit. The treaty helped the airlines to get liability insurance coverage in the early days of international air travel when the underwriters were wary of the potential risks.

The problem for Jane Froman was that by 1943, when she was injured, and especially by 1953, when her case came to trial, the passing decades had made the $8,300 Warsaw limitation far too low to provide real compensation. Her medical bills alone were more than 40 times the $8,300 limitation. But unlike federal or state legislation, the treaty could not be amended without consulting the 30 other signatory nations. So Jane was stuck with a total of $8,300 in compensation, unless she could somehow avoid the Warsaw limitation.

There were three possible escape routes. First, the Warsaw Convention required the airline to deliver a ticket that included a printed notice of the $8,300 limitation, and if this was not done, the airline could not claim benefit of the limitation. Second, if the transportation was performed by the U.S. government, the limitation would not apply. Third, if the ticket delivery requirement was met, the only other way to break the $8,300 barrier was by proving in court that the accident was caused by "wilful misconduct" of the airline or its employees. As of 1943, nobody had tried such a case in the United States, because it was considered next to impossible to prove that an airline would wilfully do anything that could cause a crash.

Jane Froman's show-business lawyers wrote to Pan Am soon after she returned from Lisbon, seeking a meeting to negotiate payment of her medical expenses and other losses. The reponse from Pan Am's insurers was that the Warsaw Convention applied, and that they would be happy to send a check for $8,300 in exchange for a full release of all claims. When Jane's lawyers rejected this, Pan Am's insurers refused to offer more than $8,300. At that point the show-business lawyers brought in Irving Lemov, the negligence specialist, who advised that they should file suit and seek a court ruling that the Warsaw Convention did not apply because of lack of ticket delivery, and because the transportation was performed by the U.S. government.

Irving Lemov and the lawyers representing the other USO victims thought they had a good chance of avoiding the limitation by showing that the airline had not delivered tickets as required by the convention. All seven of the USO performers' tickets had been given to Saul Abraham, who handed them all to Roy Rognan just before the troupe boarded the *Yankee Clipper*. Perhaps this was delivery to Roy Rognan, but how could it be delivery to Jane Froman and the other five performers? The delivery requirement was designed to give passengers notice of the limitation so that they could buy insurance, or even decide to cancel rather than take the financial risks involved. It could hardly be argued that the USO passengers had been given any reasonable opportunity to act on notice of the limitation. In fact, each of them found out about the limitation for the first time when their lawyers wrote to Pan Am about compensation after the crash.

Irving also thought he had a shot at avoiding Warsaw by showing that the transportation was "performed by the United

States government," since the tickets for the USO performers had been provided by the U.S. Army and the performers were to be conducted by Army personnel under Army orders throughout their tour.

Jane was preoccupied with the battle to overcome her injuries, and did not focus on the question of bringing suit until the summer of 1944. Finally she accepted the advice of her lawyers and authorized filing of suit in September 1944, in the New York State Supreme Court for Manhattan. (The Supreme Court in New York State is actually the lower or trial court. The state's highest court is the Court of Appeals in Albany.)

For the next three years, nothing much happened in the lawsuit. Jane was still concentrating on regaining her health, and Irving Lemov, the state-of-the art negligence specialist representing her, was not equipped to conduct such a complicated case. Pan Am's lawyers, a large Wall Street firm that specialized in defense of maritime, aviation, and insurance claims, were content to sit back and let the case gather dust. Finally, when Irving showed signs of trying to grapple with the case, Pan Am's lawyers made a motion to dismiss the part of Jane's complaint that sought damages of more than $8,300.

In support of this motion, Pan Am's lawyers attached copies of the Warsaw Convention and the ticket that they claimed had been delivered to Jane through her agent, Saul Abraham of USO Camp Shows, Inc. Their position was that Pan Am had complied with the Warsaw requirements, and therefore they were not liable for more than $8,300 unless Jane's lawyers could prove wilful misconduct. In opposition, Irving Lemov submitted affidavits from Jane Froman and Saul Abraham. Jane's affidavit recited the fact that she had never received a ticket, and indeed had never paid for a ticket, did not even learn her destination until after she boarded the plane, and had never authorized Saul Abraham or anyone else to accept a ticket for her or bind her to the Warsaw Convention limitation. Unfortunately, the affidavit which Irving Lemov drafted for her also said that Saul Abraham "was in charge of all arrangements up to the point of embarkation."

Saul Abraham's affidavit described the procedure he had followed in picking up the tickets from the Pan Am office and shepherding the performers through the embarkation procedure, during which he momentarily placed Jane's ticket on a desk in front of her, after which it was passed down the line to the customs inspectors without it ever being given to Jane. He confirmed that he had given all seven tickets to Roy Rognan just before the troupe boarded the airplane.

Based on these affidavits, Justice Bernard Botein granted Pan Am's motion in the trial court, holding that there was not even a question of fact to be submitted to the jury. He ruled that Saul Abraham had been Jane's agent, with at least implied authority to bind her to the Warsaw limitation by picking up the ticket. He quoted Jane's affidavit, prepared by Irving Lemov, that Saul "was in charge of all arrangements up to the point of embarkation." Irving, trying to wriggle out of his own admission, argued that this meant only that Saul was in charge of the formalities before they reached the airport, and that Saul could not be Jane's agent for a legal relationship that Jane knew nothing about.

The judge also brushed aside Irving's claim that the transportation had been performed by the U.S. government, quoting from the complaint that Irving had filed on behalf of Jane, which alleged that the *Yankee Clipper* had been "owned, operated, and controlled" by Pan Am. This was the boilerplate allegation about the car owner in the standard auto accident case, but should not have been used in a case where Irving was claiming that the U.S. government performed the transportation. Irving had never learned a key fact that might have won this point for his client: The U.S. Navy had taken over ownership of all the Pan Am B-314 flying boats shortly after the attack on Pearl Harbor. There were many regulations and documents detailing government control of Pan Am's wartime operations, but Irving was not aware of them.

Pan Am's motion was granted on February 20, 1948, nearly five years after the accident. This left Jane in the position of having to prove wilful misconduct in order to collect anything more than $8,300 unless the appellate courts overturned Justice Botein's ruling. New York procedure permits immediate appeal to the Appellate Division of the Supreme Court, and Irving took the case up there. That court affirmed Judge Botein's ruling without writing any opinion detailing the reasons, but one of the five Appellate Division justices dissented. He felt that the alleged ticket delivery was a question of fact that should be decided by a jury after hearing the witnesses' testimony during the trial rather than by a judge looking at affidavits. But since he was outvoted by four to one, Jane was still stuck with having to prove wilful misconduct.

Irving Lemov then appealed to the state's highest court, the Court of Appeals, which rendered its decision on April 14, 1949. By a vote of five to two, it upheld Justice Botein's ruling that the ticket was properly delivered and the transportation was not performed by the U.S. government. The Court of Appeals never clearly ruled that Abraham had been acting as agent for Jane. Apparently they were concerned about the long-standing principle, spelled out in many of their own prior decisions, that the existence of an implied agency (such as Saul Abraham being Jane's legal agent without any written contract) was a question of fact to be determined by the jury. They held that her passage through the boarding procedure at LaGuardia, with the ticket flashed in front of her momentarily, constituted "delivery" of a ticket to her under the Warsaw Convention. There was no finding of how long the ticket was on the desk in front of her, or whether she could possibly have read it. Indeed, there was no mention of the purpose for which the Warsaw Convention required ticket delivery: the opportunity for the passenger to buy insurance.

The Court of Appeals was really saying to Irving, "This international treaty, which protects important institutions like Pan American Airways, can't be attacked by the likes of Irving Lemov. We are ruling as a matter of law that this ticket was delivered to your client, and you can't raise the question of ticket delivery at the trial even though the facts are in dispute. You're way over your head in this case, so you'd better get your client to take the $8,300 that the treaty, signed by President Roosevelt and ratified by the U.S. Senate, has fixed as compensation for international passengers."

The New York Court of Appeals was considered one of the nation's most liberal courts in protecting the rights of plaintiffs to recover damages in accident cases. Yet they would not let Jane Froman present the facts about ticket delivery to a jury. And Irving Lemov had not even been able to get them to address the key question of how Jane Froman could possibly have bought flight insurance, given the manner in which the ticket was "delivered" to her. As we shall see, this debacle was caused largely by the lowly estate of plaintiff's tort lawyers at the time.

Historically, American courts have protected property rights in civil cases, and in the 1940s it would have taken a lot of lawyer power to overcome this basic posture, especially in a claim against a business icon like Pan Am. This was not true in criminal cases, where from the beginning the American courts have regarded it as their duty to protect the accused from the tyranny of the state. Although there have been some unjust criminal convictions, the presumption of innocence has generally been taken very seriously by our courts. The basic American distrust of monarchy and governmental authority protected most defendants from miscarriages of justice in criminal cases, but this did not help people like Jane Froman in civil cases.

There is a reason for this anomaly: Protection of people charged with crimes, at least to the extent of bending over backwards to assure a fair trial, costs the business establishment nothing. But the same degree of concern for the rights of people injured in accidents might well cost the business establishment a lot of money, either directly in large verdicts handed out by sympathetic juries or by increased insurance costs in the future. This helps to explain why a poor person accused of murder or other serious crime could be pretty certain of getting a fair trial even if his or her lawyer were only a run-of-the-mill single practitioner without the clout of a power law firm. Yet the supposedly liberal New York Court of Appeals denied Jane Froman any trial at all on the question of whether she had appointed Saul Abraham her agent or had received ticket delivery herself—questions that in a transaction between two business firms would surely have been treated as factual disputes requiring a trial.

Had Jane Froman been represented by an Equalizer like *L.A. Law's* Mickey Kuzak, Ann Kelsey, or Victor Cifuentes, she certainly would have gotten a jury trial on the issue of ticket delivery. Since the Warsaw Convention was written in French, they would have produced professors (probably professors of French law, American law, and international law) who would have testified as expert witnesses on the meaning of ticket delivery under Warsaw. And they would have done enough research to establish that Pan Am had the burden of proving ticket delivery in order to bring the $8,300 Warsaw limitation into the case. Irving Lemov did not mention the burden of proof, and he never dreamed of undertaking the extravagance of hiring law professors to give expert opinions in an accident case.

Pan Am's power law firm was ready to produce affidavits from such experts, but they didn't have to because Irving produced none and he failed to put the burden of proof on Pan Am. The courts simply accepted Pan Am's construction of the treaty because Irving submitted only his own uninformed, biased argument, without supplying any kind of authority to support his construction. Indeed, the affidavits of Jane Froman and Saul Abraham, the only evidence submitted by Irving, supplied Pan Am's lawyers with all the ammunition they needed to blow the ticket nondelivery argument out of the case. These affidavits enabled Pan Am to convince the courts that Saul had taken charge of all the pre-flight arrangements including ticket delivery, and that Jane's ticket had been laid out in front of her as she went through the processing line in Pan Am's departure terminal. Jane might have been better off without any lawyer at all, since the fatal admissions Irving had put into the two affidavits that he had drafted would not have been in the record, and the courts might have made Pan Am assume its rightful burden of proving ticket delivery.

Stunned by the Court of Appeals' final dismissal of his ticket nondelivery theory in April 1949, Irving found it difficult to cope with the task of preparing for trial on wilful misconduct. For a long time he did nothing. Then in 1951, he tried to discover some evidence of wilful misconduct by taking the deposition of Pan Am. For this purpose, Pan Am produced Master Ocean Pilot Harold Gray, then executive vice-president of the Atlantic Division. Gray was a clever witness who took advantage of Irving's ignorance of flight operations to thwart discovery at every turn. Nearly every meaningful question drew an answer couched in aeronautical jargon that no juror would be able to comprehend.

Irving knew from his experience with bus and railroad cases that common carriers usually had their own officials investigate major accidents. He got Gray to admit that there had been such an internal Pan Am investigation, called a "crash board," and that Gray had participated in it and submitted a written report relating to the cause of the accident. Irving then demanded that the crash board report be produced, but Pan Am's lawyers refused, claiming it was a private internal report. Irving asked a trial court judge to force Pan Am to produce the report. At that time, the scope of pre-trial discovery was gradually expanding in New York, but production of such internal reports fell into a gray area. Again Irving lacked the clout to make his case for production of the report. The trial court turned him down, and when he appealed to the Appellate Division, they too ruled that Pan Am did not have to produce the report.

Thus, Irving struck out at every level, first losing the ticket delivery battle that would have enabled Jane to win her case by proving ordinary negligence rather than wilful misconduct. Then Irving's weak discovery attempt produced no usable evidence of wilful misconduct, and succeeded in blocking Jane's access to the most crucial piece of evidence in the case: Pan Am's own investigation report which had led to the retirement of Rod Sullivan, written in 1943 when Pan Am could not have imagined that the report would ever be produced in litigation. Again, Jane probably would have been better off if she had not had a lawyer, for had she walked into the trial court and asked Pan Am to produce their investigation report, a sympathetic trial judge might have ordered Pan Am to do so. As it was, Irving's disastrous discovery campaign had shut the Pan Am crash board report out of the case for good.

Lest it appear that I am being too hard on Irving, I should make it clear that his misadventures were more the result of the general weakness of plaintiffs' tort lawyers than his own shortcomings. Indeed, while Irving was still knocking his head against the wall of Pan Am's impregnable legal position in 1951, the lawyers for the other *Yankee Clipper* victims had folded their tents and convinced their clients to accept the $8,300 Warsaw maximum. The only exception was Gypsy Markoff, who had joined forces with Jane Froman and was also being represented by Irving Lemov.

His case in shambles after he failed to get the Pan Am crash board report produced, Irving could think of nothing further to do. In April 1952, Pan Am actually got the case dismissed for failure to prosecute, meaning that the eight years that the case had spent in the courts was ample time to prepare for trial if Jane was serious about her claim. Fortunately, such a dismissal was a procedural matter rather than a final ruling on the merits. In order to clear the court calendars of cases that were not being prepared for trial, many negligence cases were dismissed for failure to prosecute. They could be restored to the trial calendar on a showing that the case was now ready for trial.

Jane met with her show-business lawyers, and they jointly decided that the case was beyond salvage if Irving remained in charge. They would have to get it into stronger hands, and for that purpose they selected the negligence lawyer who during the 1940s had developed into the first semblance of an Equalizer: Harry Gair.

Chapter 6

Can the Case be Won?

Based on the first 25 years of his life, it would be difficult to imagine anyone less likely than Harry Gair to lead the tort lawyers out of the pushcart age to the status of Equalizers.

Born in New York City in 1894, his family was so poor that they could not afford to let him attend high school. He worked in textile sweatshops of the type that actually supplied goods to pushcart peddlers. But he dreamed of greater things, and somehow he landed a job reading to a blind lawyer, Benjamin Berinstein. He absorbed most of what he was reading, including legal papers and court opinions, and became intrigued with the law. He wanted to become a lawyer, but had no way of getting a formal education, so he went to work for an insurance company as an investigator of accident cases. He continued to read law in the insurance company's library after working hours, devouring all the court opinions and textbooks he could lay his hands on.

In a few years, this unlikely investigator began writing legal briefs for Reed Jenkins Dimock & Finnegan, the in-house law firm that defended accident claims for his insurance employer. Then he began to go to court with the Reed Jenkins lawyers, helping them to defend negligence claims even though he was still on the payroll only as an investigator.

In those days, one did not have to be a graduate of law school (or even college) to take the bar exam. Many aspiring to become lawyers studied law on their own. In 1919, at the age of 25, Harry felt he had absorbed enough law to take the bar exam, which he passed on the first try, having never spent a day in any institution of learning higher than grammar school. He went to work for an older single practitioner, and in 1923 he opened his own one-room office at 130 West 42nd Street. The good addresses for lawyers were downtown on Wall Street, Broad Street, and Exchange Place, or uptown on Fifth Avenue, but Harry Gair started in the Tenderloin district of Times Square, which corrupt policemen considered a choice assignment because of the prevalence of brothels.

From this modest beginning, Harry built a reputation as a different kind of tort lawyer. He regarded each case as a challenge, to be studied, planned, and brought to trial scientifically. From his work with the insurance company and its law firm, he learned the inner workings of the system that would be his everyday adversary. Every move that he made in investigating, preparing, and trying negligence cases was designed to exploit the weaknesses of that system and force it to pay fair compensation to his clients despite the fact that it was designed for just the opposite purpose: to keep that compensation down to the bare minimum—indeed, to pay zero whenever possible.

The defendants in negligence cases are permitted to have their own doctors examine injured plaintiffs. In the days before the Equalizers, this work was usually assigned to undistinguished general practitioners who could be counted on to minimize trauma for a fee. Having worked with these doctors on the defense side, Harry Gair knew their shortcomings. He educated himself in medicine, and was among the first lawyers in the country to build a large medical library. He soon established a reputation for confronting defense doctors with medical literature that would embarrass them if they tried to minimize serious injuries.

Harry applied the same scientific approach to liability problems. He hired engineers and other experts to help explain complicated cases to jurors, at a time when such expenditures were rare. He disdained the florid oratory that many lawyers used to try to win cases by playing on the jurors' sympathies. Instead, he led the jurors in an exciting quest for the truth. He was the teacher, the guide, the illuminator, rather than the preacher. This was in keeping with his quiet, unassuming manner. He was about five foot six, of medium build, and there was nothing striking about him physically. His voice was raspy, with a nasal tone. It was the content of what he said that made judges, jurors, and even opposing lawyers hang on his every word.

From the start of his practice in 1923 through the end of World War II, Harry gradually built a supporting organization. While most negligence lawyers were happy if they could grasp the facts of a case, Harry insisted on careful legal research so that he mastered the law as well as the facts. By the 1950s, Harry Gair's "law man," Ben Siff, was recognized as an outstanding appellate lawyer whose grasp of New York negligence law has probably never been matched.

Gair was really the forerunner of the Equalizers, because he was way ahead of his time. He won most of the cases he tried, and usually recovered higher sums than the insurance companies were willing to pay in settlement. Usually his winning trial verdicts were sustained by the appellate courts. It was known throughout the insurance industry that he was always fully prepared on the facts and on the law. Often insurers would settle cases with him that they would have forced other lawyers to try. While he could balance the scales for most of the clients he took on, he still was a single practitioner with only a handful of assistants and a limited capacity. He was setting a shining example for the rest of the tort lawyers, but did not have the time or the facilities to lead a mass equalization movement.

When Jane Froman's show-business lawyers decided to make a change in 1952, Harry Gair was the natural choice. There were only a handful of negligence lawyers who had ever grappled with an airline case, and none who had tried a wilful misconduct case under the Warsaw Convention. By 1952, Harry had tried and won cases against domestic airlines, and in his prime at age 58 he was the acknowledged leader of the negligence bar. Jane's lawyers met with Harry to ask if he would take over the case. He was intrigued at the challenge, but told them that he would have to study the situation before making a decision. Part of that study involved him asking for my opinion of the prospects for winning the case.

Harry Gair called me late in 1952 and asked me to meet him for lunch to discuss the Jane Froman case. I was then 29, in my fourth year of practice, by which time I had originally hoped to be well along the track to partnership in a Wall Street law firm. Instead, I was operating a solo practice out of a one-room office at 25 Broad Street in lower Manhattan. Both the change of career path and the call from Harry Gair were results of my avocation: aviation.

After beginning studies at Columbia Law School in the summer of 1942, I had left to go into pilot training with the U.S. Army Air Force. Eventually I won my silver wings, became an airplane commander on four-engine B-24 Liberator bombers, and spent a leisurely war as a radar flight instructor and test pilot, much of it at Florida's luxurious Boca Raton Hotel and Club, which the air force had the good taste to commandeer as an officers' barracks. Before returning to Columbia in the fall of 1946, I flew as an aerial crop duster in Florida and Cuba, and I also worked as a broker in the sale of second-hand and surplus aircraft. I had not shaken off the flying bug, and when I graduated in June of 1948, I hoped to find a legal position that would enable me to use my aviation experience. I applied to several

New York law firms that represented airlines, but found no opening.

Like most of my fellow Columbia graduates, I thought only of landing with a firm that represented the business establishment. There seemed little future in representing individuals. Apart from Bill Kunstler, I can't remember anyone even mentioning this idea. I was happy to find a job with a smallish Wall Street law firm that represented, among others, a major league baseball team, a financial newspaper, a large department store, and several stockbrokers. I was assigned the job of assisting the senior lawyers in defending a firm of crooked "boiler room" stockbrokers who had fleeced widows, school teachers, and other vulnerable investors out of hundreds of thousands of dollars by selling them worthless stock. The boiler room operation was right in our building, and I witnessed their high-pressure telephone sales techniques when I visited their offices to work on defending them.

When I met with some of my Columbia classmates after working hours, we exchanged stories of our indoctrination into the great world of corporate law. I had thought that my boiler room defense assignment would be unique, but found that classmates who had landed jobs with bigger firms were also helping to defend stockbrokers and business executives accused of fleecing the public. They outshone me only in the respect that their clients were bigger fish who were accused of stealing much more money.

I wish I could tell you that moral indignation caused me to resign on the spot. I felt like doing so, but at that time moral indignation was a luxury that I simply could not afford. I did, however, start looking for a way out that would allow me to make a living at something that was a bit more palatable. I appreciated the importance of the presumption of innocence and believed in the right of every person to defend vigorously against criminal prosecution, but I did not believe I had any personal obligation to defend stockbrokers whom I knew to be crooked if other lawyers were available to them and if I could find a more rewarding role in life.

My deliverance from the boiler room came in the unlikely form of an Israeli crop duster. The new state of Israel, needing to increase agricultural production quickly, had commissioned Wim Van Leer, a Dutch pilot, to organize a crop dusting service. Wim came to New York hoping to find someone who could help him locate crop-dusting aircraft, pilots, pesticides, and other equipment. He also needed assistance with the then tricky job of exporting this sort of equipment to Israel. Since I was the only lawyer/crop duster in New York, Wim had no trouble finding me. We struck up a friendship as well as a business relationship. The Wall Street law firms could keep their airline clients. I now had my own aviation client: Chim Avir, owner of three dilapidated Piper Cubs.

At first I brought Chim Avir in as a client for the law firm that employed me, but as I began to bring in fees for locating and signing up pilots, equipping and exporting crop-dusting aircraft, and negotiating chemical distributorships, I realized that Chim Avir could be my escape route. Although the fees were very modest even by 1950 standards, they were enough to support me in a one-room aviation law practice. As soon as I could locate a room that was cheap enough, I resigned.

Soon after I opened New York's only crop-dusting law office, I discovered another field that few people had heard of: aviation negligence law. A lawyer friend of mine who worked for a negligence specialist told me his firm was representing a passenger whose arm had been seriously injured in the 1949 crash of an American Airlines DC-6 during an attempted landing at Love Field, in Dallas, Texas. The accident involved fuel management, piloting, and navigation of a four-engine airliner, and he remembered that I had been a four-engine pilot. He told me that their three-man law firm was having a lot of difficulty with the case, their first experience with an aviation accident. Finally he arranged for me to help his firm try to prove that the Love Field crash was caused by American's negligence. We needed only to prove negligence, since this was a domestic accident that did not involve the wilful misconduct requirement of the Warsaw Convention. Even though the DC-6's engines had been running on an empty gas tank while there was fuel in other tanks, proving negligence was difficult because the airlines won most of the trials in those days, and also because I knew practically nothing about accident litigation. Since the fee arrangement with the injured client called for a percentage of the amount collected, I agreed to work for a share of the contingent fee.

Through much trial and error, I managed to get the job done. Fortunately the case was pending in the federal court, where extensive discovery was available. I got hold of a book on federal discovery procedures, and used discovery for the first time in seeking production of American Airlines' records and then taking the depositions of key witnesses, including surviving crew members. Those rather primitive depositions spelled out a case of pilot error in failing to follow the prescribed procedures for fuel management, which required the pilots to shift from tank to tank while enroute but to make certain that the engines were hooked up to the fullest tank when coming in for landing. I even found a DC-6 pilot who was willing to testify at the trial that the American Airlines crew had not followed the fuel management safety regulations. The case was settled on the eve of trial for $30,000, a much larger sum than the plaintiff and his lawyers had expected. I earned the biggest fee I had ever seen, and apart from my work for Chim Avir, it was the first time I felt I had done something useful as a lawyer. I also had stumbled into a field of practice in which I could instantly become the leader, because there was nobody else in it.

In the Love Field case, American Airlines was defended by Haight Gardner Poor & Havens, a large admiralty law firm that often represented Lloyd's of London. Haight Gardner had a staff of pilot-lawyers, most of whom had finished law school after World War II. I also found that there were two other insurance defense firms—Bigham Englar Jones & Houston, and Mendes & Mount—that had established aviation departments to complement their maritime practices. Like Haight Gardner, they had pilot-lawyers on their staffs, but no pilot-lawyer had come along to represent the plaintiffs in cases arising out of aviation accidents.

After the Love Field arm injury case was settled, I learned that there were half a dozen other cases arising out of the same accident that were pending in New York courts. Again, the plaintiffs' lawyers had made little progress toward proving liability, because they were general practitioners or auto accident lawyers who had no aviation expertise and were therefore at a disadvantage against the experienced Haight Gardner admiralty-aviation defense lawyers. I was hired by the lawyers who represented the remaining Love Field plaintiffs to help them prove liability. I got to take the depositions over again, this time as an old hand at federal discovery procedures. Eventually, all the remaining Love Field cases were settled, as American Airlines' insurers did not want to take the risk of letting jurors fix damages after hearing proof of the egregious errors the flight crew had made.

I soon discovered that there were many cases still pending from accidents of the 1940s. Typically these cases sat for three to five years while the plaintiffs' lawyers tried to negotiate settlements from a position of weakness. When an airline accident occurred, often the family or business lawyer for the plaintiff would call in the negligence specialist to whom he customarily referred automobile cases, as happened in the Froman case. But even in domestic accidents, where the plaintiffs merely had to prove negligence rather than the wilful misconduct required under the Warsaw Convention in international accidents, the airline insurers did not offer settlements that approached the true financial losses. They were well aware of their tactical advantages in this type of litigation, with the mismatch of a Haight Gardner against negligence specialists whose usual fare was automobile accidents.

Even when a deceased passenger had an annual income of $15,000 to $25,000, a life expectancy of 20 years or more, and a wife and young children to be supported, settlement offers in domestic airline cases—even those with strong liability—rarely exceeded $40,000 in the 1940s and early 1950s. Each case had to be tried separately from others that arose out of the same accident, and each plaintiff had to prove the airline's liability before any damages would be assessed, even if other plaintiffs had won previous cases.

For most lawyers accustomed to automobile cases and other relatively simple suits (such as "premises liability" claims involving people injured in buildings), there was actually too much potential evidence available in aviation cases. They were not staffed either to digest or to use so much scientific information. The Civil Aeronautics Board (which investigated aircraft accidents until that function was taken over in 1967 by the National Transportation Safety Board) held public hearings and made transcripts of testimony and copies of exhibits available. These transcripts often ran to more than four hundred pages, and the exhibits added another thousand or so pages of technical information, such as diagrams of airline equipment, pictures of wreckage, complicated flight charts, and maintenance manuals. Lawyers who were used to spending only a day or two preparing for trial in auto or premises cases now faced the prospect of studying the government file for weeks, just to understand the significance of these strange documents. Then, after struggling to determine which evidence was helpful to the plaintiff, the lawyer had to spend more weeks trying to get that evidence into the case by taking the depositions of airline witnesses who were often hostile and could take refuge in the complicated terminology of aviation.

The Civil Aeronautics Board issued a public report giving the probable cause of each accident, but since the government did not want to take sides in civil litigation, a federal statute provided that this report could not be used in court. So even for the best plaintiff's lawyers it was a struggle to get ready for an aviation trial. The result in many aviation cases that went to trial in the early postwar years was that the plaintiffs either lost the case entirely or had to settle for much less than they would have recovered after an automobile accident.

Some plaintiff's lawyers tried to overcome these difficulties by relying on the doctrine of *res ipsa loquitur*—the thing speaks for itself. This may be used when the defendant has exclusive control of the instrument that caused the injury, and when the accident is one that would not ordinarily occur unless the defendant had been negligent. Since airplanes normally do not fall out of the sky unless someone is at fault, the law allows a plaintiff to submit such a case to a jury by simply showing the circumstances surrounding the accident. In relying on *res ipsa loquitur*, the plaintiff's lawyer hopes the jury will infer that the plane crashed because of the airline's negligence. But reliance on *res ipsa loquitur* did not prove fruitful for plantiff's attorneys. A study published in the 1951 *Virginia Law Review* showed that a total of 24 airline cases had been submitted to juries on the *res ipsa loquitur* basis. Of these, 22 had resulted in defendant's verdicts, meaning that injured passengers and families of deceased passengers got nothing.

The airlines usually came forward with positive evidence of the great care they took in training, maintenance, and flight operations. This evidence was presented by articulate, highly qualified pilots and engineers who often appeared in uniform, and who impressed jurors as more believable people than one would encounter on the railroads and bus lines. Since *res ipsa* cases did not pinpoint any act of negligence, jurors were reluctant to infer fault on the part of intrepid airmen or other clean-cut airline employees in the absence of specific proof. Take the case of Earl Carroll, the famous impresario of Earl Carroll's Vanities who was killed in the crash of a United Airlines DC-6 at Mt. Carmel, Pennsylvania, in 1948. His case was tried under *res ipsa loquitur*, but a Pennsylvania jury decided that the airline was not liable, so his heirs got nothing.

In countless other cases, plaintiffs' lawyers were forced to settle serious injury and death claims for fractions of their potential value because the risk of losing was considerable, and the defense attorneys sensed that the economic burden on the plaintiff's side was too great to bring the case on for trial. There were some early attempts at cooperation between attorneys for various plaintiffs involved in the same accident, but they did not meet with great success because there was always the problem of who would take on the heavy and unfamiliar work load. Even among groups of plaintiffs' attorneys, there were no pilot-lawyer specialists who could approach the case in the same depth as the admiralty-aviation defense firms hired by the airline insurers on an hourly fee basis.

That's where I fitted in. My work on the Love Field cases brought me to the attention of the small group of leading New York plaintiff's lawyers to whom most aviation cases (and other complicated tort suits) were referred in the late 1940s. Most of them were delighted to find this kid who had his own office and who would take on all the burdens of proving liability in aviation cases for a modest slice of the existing contingent fee. My fee was usually five percent of the amount recovered in airline cases, and in other aviation accidents (such as those involving light planes or company aircraft) it was ten percent of the recovery. Since the overall fee was usually thirty-three and a third percent, I was taking on the heaviest load of work for a reasonably small share of the fee. Bringing me into the case would not increase the fee to be paid by the plaintiffs, since it came out of the lawyers' share. If I did my work well, the negligence specialist could face up to the Haight Gardners and be ready to try aviation cases without turning his office upside down for months in the effort. And in large negligence cases, being ready for trial means that you will get the maximum settlement offer "on the courthouse steps," which usually translates to the time when the jury is being selected.

My exact role in those cases of the 1940s and early 1950s depended on the negligence specialist I was working with. The most capable tort specialists needed me only to investigate and prepare the liability phase of the case, taking the necessary depositions and discovery steps, engaging expert witnesses, and assisting the trial lawyer in court through whispered suggestions or scribbled notes. Others had me conduct parts of the liability trial, such as the questioning of each side's expert witnesses, who were usually pilots or aeronautical engineers. Some engaged me to conduct the entire liability case; others turned the client and the entire case (liability and damages, trials and appeals) over to me.

Early in my practice I met Harry Gair, and from that point on he hired me to assist him in all of his aviation cases. He had me investigate and prepare liability, conduct all the depositions and discovery, and sit next to him at the trial. He did all the talking in court, which was fine with me, since I had the world's greatest tort lawyer going for my stake in the case whenever he spoke. By the time of the Froman trial in 1953, we had worked together in half a dozen hotly contested domestic airline accident cases without a loss. He didn't really need me, but he was so thorough and painstaking in his preparations that he felt more confident going to trial against the aviation industry with the world's leading (and only) plaintiff's pilot-lawyer at his side. One day, after he had convinced a jury to hold an airline liable in a tough case, I got carried away with the excitement of working with him, and told him that I would gladly have paid for that seat at his trial table, just to get the experience and the radiated prestige. Despite this naive admission, he always paid my regular fees without quibbling.

I had heard that the Jane Froman case was still around, and sensed that Jane would have to call in Harry Gair if she was to have a chance to win. When Harry called and told me about his meeting with Jane's show-business lawyers, I literally ran the few blocks between my office on Broad Street and his at 84 William Street.

Harry was as excited as I was about the possibilies of the Jane Froman case. Having started his practice in the days when a $1,000 verdict was a big victory, he was now being offered the first case in history wherein the plaintiff's lawyer could reasonably ask the jurors to award a million dollars. Jane's inspirational life story, then playing movie theatres all over the country, made her case a once-in-a-lifetime spotlight opportunity for her lawyers. But that's where Harry's viewpoint diverged from mine. To me, struggling to build a reputation in my fourth year of practice, it was flattering just to be consulted by such a celebrity, even indirectly. To Harry, at the top of his field in his 30th year of practice, the spotlight was a special hazard. The media would cover every minute of the trial. If the verdict went to Pan Am, Harry would go down in history as the man who lost the Jane Froman case. He hadn't lost a jury verdict in ten years, but that one loss would get more publicity than had the hundreds of cases he had won in the past.

At lunch we discussed what little we knew about the liability phase of the case, and what proof we needed to muster in order to break the wilful misconduct barrier. A great deal would depend on how the trial judge treated "wilful misconduct" in his jury instructions. If he told the jurors that they had to find that Sullivan intended to crash the plane in order to hold Pan Am liable, obviously we didn't have a chance. We assumed that this would not happen, since the New York courts had defined wilful misconduct as "a conscious intent to do or to omit doing the act from which harm results to another, or an intentional omission of a manifest duty. There must be a realization of the probability of injury from the conduct, and a disregard of the probable consequences of such conduct."

We knew from the beginning that our wilful misconduct case would be based on charging that Sullivan deliberately tried to land across the lights from east to west, instead of completing the prescribed circle and landing with the lights from south to north. We would claim that he had a "conscious intent" to land across the lights, which was "the act from which the harm resulted." We would also claim that he intentionally omitted the "manifest duty" of circling and landing with the lights—a duty imposed by Pan Am's own regulations and practices. If the jurors accepted those claims, they could infer that Sullivan "realized the probability of injury" from a night landing without the depth perception provided by the light string, and that he went ahead with that dangerous landing "in disregard of the probable consequences." Thus, our theory would fit within the legal definition of wilful misconduct. If we could come up with convincing evidence that Sullivan was trying to land across the lights rather than struggling with an uncontrollable dive, it was worth taking a shot at the trial.

There was practically nothing in Irving Lemov's file that would help us to prove wilful misconduct. Harry Gair and I agreed that the first step was for me to get all the records of the Civil Aeronautics Board investigation and make a preliminary analysis of our liability proof problems before he decided whether he would take the case.

I went to Washington to get the CAB files, and found they were still technically classified as secret, but it was no problem to remove this classification and get copies. The two CAB investigators who had been sent to Lisbon had done a reasonably good job of questioning all the witnesses. They had taken depositions in question-and-answer form from the surviving crew members, passengers, and all the Pan Am ground personnel, including the airport managers and launch crews.

From these CAB depositions, I was able to put together a picture of what had happened at Lisbon. Everyone aboard the *Yankee Clipper* who had any recollection of the last minute of flight, passengers and crew members alike, testified that the plane appeared to be in a gentle descending left turn, with no hint of a dive or steep descent. (Everyone, that is, except Rod Sullivan, who insisted that the plane had been in an uncontrollable 45-degree dive.) The Pan Am employees in the airport manager's office and on the launch *Pan Air III-A* did not see very much detail, as they were preoccupied with their duties. The airport manager testified that he saw the plane at an altitude of about 400 feet "in a sharp descent, estimated at 20 degrees," which continued until the plane hit the water. Two other ground witnesses testified that the plane seemed to go down suddenly, but they were a long distance away and were not watching the flight steadily as they had functions of their own to perform at the time.

There was no clear corroboration of Sullivan's story, just pieces here and there which could be taken either way, depending on whether there was actually an uncontrollable dive or a gentle descending turn for an intended landing. The strongest evidence to me was the lack of any indication to other crew members that the ship was in a death dive. Sullivan testified that when the nose went down and he could not break the dive by pulling back on the elevator control wheel, First Officer Rush, the co-pilot who died in the crash, joined in this effort to pull the nose up, without a word passing between them. This didn't ring true to me, although it was possible to have an emergency come on so suddenly that there would not be time for talk. But it seemed to be too convenient an explanation for why the other surviving crew members who were standing behind the pilots, 2nd Officer Osterhaut and 4th Officer Burn, heard nothing and were taken by surprise when the plane crashed.

The 45 degree nose-down angle claimed by Sullivan was difficult for anyone with flying experience to believe. The normal angle for a landing descent was no more than five to ten degrees, and anything as steep as even 25 degrees would have made those aboard feel they were on a rollercoaster rather than an airliner. Osterhaut and Burn, the free-standing crew members, would have been propelled forward into the pilots' chairs, and even the passengers would have noticed the steepness of the dive. But of all those on board, only Sullivan noticed it, unless one believed his story that the co-pilot realized the predicament and joined the captain in pulling back the elevator control without saying a word.

Because of Sullivan's dive story, the CAB investigators combed the wreckage at Lisbon and closely examined the elevator cable control system. All parts of that system which could possibly have rendered the elevators inoperative were recovered from the River Tagus intact. The elevator control system parts were shipped back to Washington, where they were studied by metallurgists from the CAB and the National Bureau of Standards. Their conclusion was that there were no failures and that there was no physical evidence to corroborate Sullivan's claim of lack of elevator control. In other words, if his nose did go down, there was no reason why normal backward pressure on the elevator control wheel would not have raised the nose and kept the plane out of any unwanted descent.

Putting these pieces of the CAB investigation together, it was clear to me that Sullivan was either lying or had convinced himself that there had been an uncontrollable dive in order to assuage his guilt over having caused this terrible crash. A pilot of his experience would surely have increased engine power to lift the nose if it went down, whereas he testified that he cut the power when the nose dropped because he knew he was going to crash and wanted to soften the impact.

I checked these conclusions with several veteran pilots, some of whom knew Sullivan and were familiar with Pan Am's flying boat operations. Every one of them told me that Sullivan's dive story was incredible, and that nobody at Pan Am believed it. Most of them felt that Sullivan had been cutting corners, deciding on his own to land from east to west in the fading twilight even though the lights were laid out north to south. It would have taken him a few more minutes to complete his circling, by which time it would have been almost totally dark. There were some lightning flashes out to the west behind Lisbon, and the wind was coming from the west, which would have given him a slight crosswind for the south to north landing. Those who knew Sullivan said it was just like him to use his Master Ocean Pilot status and his extraordinary skills to make a spur-of-the-moment descending left turn and land to the west when he reached the red light. Had he completed the turn and lined up facing the red light, he could have signalled the launch to fire flares and set the plane down near the red light. (See Figure 2.) If he had completed the east-to-west landing safely, nobody would have dared to question the authority of the Master Ocean Pilot to come in that way.

Assuming that we could somehow prove all of this, it certainly would support a jury verdict of negligence; but negligence would only get us the $8,300 that had been offered ten years ago. Would it add up to wilful misconduct?

After a solid week of work on these questions, I met with Harry Gair again and told him my conclusions. The aviation pros felt that Sullivan's dive story was hogwash, but he was the only one who could tell a jury what his intent had been. Even if the jury didn't buy the dive story, how could we prove that he intended to land across the lights? Suppose he just became confused or miscalculated his position? That was mere negligence unless we could prove that he intended the act that caused the injury: the descending left turn that was part of an approach for landing from east to west.

The CAB investigators had pinned down Sullivan pretty well in their questioning. He testified that he was aware of exactly where he was, and that he was almost to the point where he would start a level left turn, maintaining his altitude at 600 feet as he started to circle the lights. That's when (according to his story) the nose went down into the uncontrollable dive, and he saved many lives by cutting back the power and throwing the left wing down to cushion the impact.

If he had been offered the case soon after the accident, Harry Gair would not have hestitated to take it on. Even with New York's limited discovery, we could have rounded up a lot of useful evidence to refute Sullivan's story. The opinions of the CAB and National Bureau of Standards metallurgists would not have been available to the jury, but by efficient discovery we probably could have pinned down Pan Am's own engineers and maintenance officials to the same conclusions: that the elevator control system was found intact after the crash, making Sullivan's dive story practically a physical impossiblity. But this weapon was not available to us, because Irving Lemov had exhausted discovery without producing any evidence on the post-accident condition of the elevator control system. Indeed, his losing efforts to force Pan Am to produce its crash board report had closed the door on that promising source of evidence.

It was clear to Harry and to me that the trial of Froman v. Pan American would come down to Gair v. Sullivan. We felt certain that Pan Am would bring Sullivan up from North Carolina to testify, as he was the only person who could say what his intent had been, and that intent was an indispensable ingredient of wilful misconduct. It was a pretty close call, but I thought that even with the little evidence available to us, Gair could convince the jury that Sullivan was lying. That was the whole case in a nutshell.

Gair himself was uncertain at that point. He said we would need a qualified flying boat pilot to testify as an expert, explaining to the jury the importance of landing parallel to the light string. Without such guidance, he thought the jury might not dare to brand Sullivan as the culprit. There was also the problem of establishing a *prima facie* case of wilful misconduct to the satisfaction of the trial judge. If we failed to produce evidence from which the jurors might reasonably find wilful misconduct, the judge would dismiss the case without submitting it to the jury. I pointed out that Sullivan himself, and other Pan Am witnesses, had testified before the CAB that it was Pan Am's standard procedure to land parallel to the lights, and that it was unsafe to attempt a night landing across the lights. But Harry insisted that we look for a qualified expert who was willing to testify against the Master Ocean Pilot, preferably someone who had been a Pan Am flying boat captain himself.

In 1952, that was a tall order. Juan Trippe had made it Pan Am policy to offer their veteran captains administrative or executive jobs when their flying days were over, and so most of the surviving boat captains who were retired from flying duties were working for Pan Am in ground jobs. Pan Am was the only American airline that had operated extensive transatlantic flying boat passenger service. Besides, in those days it was difficult to find a qualified airline captain willing to testify against any airline in an accident claim. This code of silence was not quite as tight as the one that kept physicians from testifying for plaintiffs in medical malpractice cases, but the same spirit of protective cameraderie prevailed. Pilots knew that there were only a handful of insurance companies that covered airline risks, and if they testified for plaintiffs, officials of those insurance companies would become aware of their names, as would the tight circle of chief pilots of airlines and aviation manufacturers. There was no formal blacklist, but many pilots whom I approached in the 1940s and 1950s refused to testify. They might help me behind the scenes, but there was not enough money available in expert witness fees to risk the consequences of publicly challenging the aviation establishment.

During my brief career as a used-aircraft broker, I had maintained a list of free-lance pilots who were available for delivery of planes to customers. This kept me in contact with many airline captains. Through this network I was able to come up with a qualified expert witness: Sherrill Shaw, retired Pan Am flying boat captain on the four-engine Sikorsky S-42, who had also been a flying boat instructor and check pilot for Pan Am. Serving with Pan Am from 1941 to 1948, he had logged over 3,000 hours in flying boats. He had made three transatlantic crossings on Boeing 314s as an observer, which included several night landings. As an S-42 captain, he had made at least 200 night landings, and had instructed other Pan Am pilots in the night landing procedures. Since the night landing procedures for the S-42 were the same as those for the B-314, he was as well qualified as anyone we could possibly find to testify. And as a little icing on the cake, before becoming a Pan Am captain he had served as the pilot of Pan Am board chairman Cornelius Vanderbilt Whitney's personal amphibious flying boat.

At my first meeting with Sherrill Shaw, we discussed the Lisbon accident and I briefed him on what we hoped to cover in his court testimony. He felt very strongly that Sullivan had been trying to land across the lights and that this had caused the crash. Part of this feeling was based on hangar talk with other Pan Am pilots at the time of the crash, but we could not use that hearsay evidence or any conclusions based on it. His testimony at the trial would have to based solely on the evidence in the trial record. I gave Shaw copies of the CAB depositions, and asked him to read them so that we could discuss his conclusions based on that evidence at our next meeting.

At the second meeting he felt even more strongly that Sullivan had intended to land across the lights. He was angered by Sullivan's "uncontrollable dive" story, which he thought was incredible and an insult to airline captains. He was eager to set the record straight, and he wanted to help Jane Froman. Of course, he would also be paid for his testimony. Since I was favorably impressed with his demeanor and his knowledge of flying boat operations, I decided that he could do the job. But the final decision was up to Harry Gair.

I had briefed Sherrill Shaw on the function of an expert witness. We did not want any emotional condemnation of Sullivan, or any histrionics. We needed him to describe Pan Am's night landing procedures to the jury in simple lay terms, and to explain why any captain who attempted to land across the lights would be consciously putting the plane into a dangerous maneuver that would rob him of his depth perception and create a strong risk of a crash. Harry Gair went over these points with him, asking questions in the same manner as he would in court in order to get a reading on Shaw's projection. Fortunately, Shaw was a clear thinker and speaker who did not try to embellish the facts. He and Harry got along well together. Captain Shaw was on board as our expert witness, and Harry Gair told Jane Froman's show-business lawyers that he would try the case.

We were now into November of 1952 and there were still some gaps in our case, thanks mainly to our inability to conduct discovery. Due to the 1952 dismissal of the case for failure to prosecute, we would have to make a motion to restore it to the trial calendar. That gave us the opportunity to include in the motion a request for further discovery, on the grounds that there were new lawyers in the case who had not had the opportunity to conduct any discovery. Since Jane Froman's previous lawyer, Irving Lemov, had exhausted her right to discovery, the odds were against such a request being granted. But it was discretionary with the judge hearing the motion, and Harry Gair might be able to persuade the judge. We decided to use this possible discovery as bargaining leverage with the attorneys defending Pan Am.

Haight Gardner was nominally representing Pan Am, but the real client was Pan Am's insurer, the United States Aviation Insurance Group. The lawyer in charge of the case was Bill Junkerman, Haight Gardner's senior aviation trial lawyer. Bill was a World War II Navy pilot, and had served as commanding officer of Johnston Island, a wartime Pacific naval air base. He had compiled an outstanding record in defense of airline accident claims, winning defendants' verdicts as often as he lost, and even when he lost, the amounts awarded were rarely much higher than his insurance clients had offered in settlement.

I met with Bill Junkerman in an effort to work out an agreement that would help to fill the gaps in our case. I explained that we were about to restore the case to the trial calendar, and would ask the judge to allow us to reopen discovery since neither Harry Gair nor I had been in the case when Irving Lemov's meager discovery took place. On the other hand, if Junkerman were willing to enter into a stipulation allowing both sides to use the 1943 CAB depositions as though they had been taken by discovery in the Froman case, we would forego the opportunity to reopen discovery. I knew there were a few gaps in his case too, since some of the witnesses who had been aboard the *Yankee Clipper* or on the ground at Lisbon in 1943 could not be located and brought into a New York court in 1953. Also, the CAB investigators had taken Rod Sullivan's deposition at Lisbon, but Irving Lemov had not done so. Junkerman's entire defense depended on Sullivan's alibi of the uncontrollable dive, which he had spelled out in the deposition he gave to the CAB investigators at Lisbon. If Sullivan died or was otherwise unable to testify at the trial, Junkerman's position would be difficult. He could buy insurance against that problem by agreeing to the use of all the CAB depositions by both sides.

Junkerman considered the proposal for a few days, and then agreed to it. Harry Gair and I were happy with this agreement, since we knew that even if we had been lucky enough to get a judge to reopen discovery, we could not have discovered very much in view of the standing order (affirmed by the appellate court) that Pan Am could not be forced to produce its crash board report.

Earlier in the case, when Irving Lemov was struggling with discovery, there were three Pan Am witnesses whose depositions were ordered, but Irving did not get around to questioning them before the case was dismissed for lack of prosecution. When Harry Gair took over, I was able to complete their depositions. They were the two surviving crew members who were still employed by Pan Am, Assistant Flight Engineer Manning and Steward Casprini; and Arthur LaPorte, a retired Master Ocean Pilot who had been operations manager of the Atlantic Division in 1943. I was able to pin Manning and Casprini down to their CAB statements that there was no dive and that they thought they were in a normal descent for landing. LaPorte's deposition was useless, since all of his knowledge was encapsulated in Pan Am's crash board report, which the courts had barred the plaintiffs from discovering.

The case was restored to the calendar and was scheduled for trial in March 1953. Gypsy Markoff had joined forces with Jane Froman, and their two cases were to be tried together, with Harry Gair representing both of them. Gypsy had made a better recovery than Jane since her back and arm injuries, though serious at the time, had healed without the agony that Jane had suffered. Even with that recovery, Gypsy had suffered much pain and shock, as well as loss of earnings due to cancellation of some engagements when she was recuperating. The damage she suffered was far beyond the $8,300 Warsaw limitation.

As we made final preparations for the trial, I got to meet Jane Froman, John Burn and Gypsy Markoff at Harry Gair's office. At 45, Jane was still beautiful, and had the brightest blue eyes I have ever seen. (An interviewer for a movie magazine had once written that "her eyes looked like there was a light bulb behind them".) She also had one of the worst stutters I had ever heard. She could hardly speak a sentence without tripping over a word, but she conversed cheerfully, as though the impediment did not exist. She told us that she had been stuttering since her father abandoned the family when she was five years old, but it had never affected her singing or performing on radio, television, or in movies. We learned that this peculiar ability of stutterers to perform in public without a hitch was shared by other singers, such as country music star Mel Tillis.

Gypsy Markoff was petite and exotically beautiful, with flashing black eyes and a streak of platinum blonde in her dark brown hair. Like Jane, she was utterly charming, and the way she told her story of the crash would have moved the most cynical listener. No tort lawyer could ever hope to have two clients who would make a more favorable impression on jurors than Jane Froman and Gypsy Markoff.

John Burn was trim and handsome, with a sensitive face and manner. He would be one of our trial witnesses, although we did not try to stretch his testimony too far because he was on record as having blacked out when the plane crashed and did not have much recollection of the final maneuvers. He was then a Pan Am captain, flying DC-6s in the Carribean division. If he testified at the trial as a Pan Am captain, his statements might be considered to be binding on Pan Am. Therefore, we expected Pan Am to lay him off temporarily when the trial came up.

As an offset to the good fortune of representing such story-book characters, there was a price to pay: Don Ross, the bad penny, turned up again. He had attached himself to Jane's lawsuit from its inception in 1944, claiming that he had sacrificed his own promising career to take care of her during her long disability. We knew that this claim, like Don's oily manner, would go over like a lead balloon with the jury. Originally Irving Lemov had represented both Jane and Don, but after their divorce in 1948 Don got his own lawyer to pursue his claims. Unfortunately the claims of Don and Jane had to be presented together as part of one case. Harry Gair met with Don's lawyer in an effort to work out an agreement for Don to stay out of court in exchange for a part of whatever compensation Jane received. Don's lawyer was a respected advocate who was receptive to Gair's proposal, but Don held out for such an unconscionably large part of Jane's prospective compensation that it proved impossible to reach an agreement. Don's stomach-turning claims would be presented to the jury by his own lawyer. I thought of suggesting to Harry that he send Don Ross on an extended trip and bring in David Wayne to reprise his movie portrayal in the courtroom. But we had enough problems in preparing for this monumental trial without my injecting gallows humor.

As we got down to final preparations, I rounded up all the documents I could find dealing with approach patterns, night landings, and angles of descent. The Pan Am System Operations Manual, an exhibit that we got from the CAB investigation records, covered the approach and landing procedures, including a description of the string of lights used for night water landings. It was important for Harry Gair to be armed with lots of ammunition to attack the credibility of Sullivan's 45-degree nose-down testimony, so I searched for documents that would force the Pan

Am witnesses to admit that such an extreme angle would have to have been noticed by all those aboard. There was nothing in the CAB depositions about this, but I found some reputable aviation and aero-medical textbooks that would serve the purpose. I gave all these documents to Harry, along with detailed written outlines for the questioning of all the potential witnesses. The outline for the expected cross-examination of Rod Sullivan alone was more than 30 pages long. But I knew that I could not possibly give Harry too much to read in preparation for a trial, no matter how technical the subject matter. He gobbled up all of it and discussed it with me in detail, making his own modifications and notes on my outlines. As usual, after the discussions with him, I understood the implications of all this potential evidence more thoroughly than before.

Finally, the trial was set to begin on Monday, March 9, 1953, and we learned that the judge would be Aron Steuer. I should explain that in 1953, New York still followed the archaic practice of assigning different judges to various phases of the case, depending on which judge was sitting in a particular part of the court when various questions arose. In the federal courts and in most other states, one judge would be assigned to each case from the beginning, so that he or she could become familiar with the details and make consistent rulings. New York later adopted that sensible practice, but during the life of the Froman case six different judges made important rulings, and Justice Steuer had nothing to do with the case until it was assigned to him for trial.

I had never appeared before Justice Aron Steuer, but like most New York lawyers, I knew him largely through the reputation of his father, Max D. Steuer, the most successful trial lawyer in New York—if not the entire nation—during the first half of the twentieth century.

Max Steuer arrived in the United States in 1877 at the age of 6, the son of a poor Jewish tailor. (Perhaps the word "poor" is redundant, since I have never heard of a rich Jewish tailor.) Max helped to support the family and paid for his education by toiling in the tailor shop. He graduated with honors from Columbia Law School in 1893, and sought employment with established New York law firms, but was turned away by all he approached. Having no other choice, he set up shop as an individual practitioner and took whatever clients he could pick up.

From this humble beginning he built one of the greatest trial practices ever enjoyed by an American lawyer. During his 47 years at the bar, he came to represent many prominent people and corporations, mostly in what today is called white collar criminal defense practice. He was often brought in by other lawyers (including some in prominent firms that had snubbed him for employment) to try difficult cases. His famous criminal cases included the successful defenses of Harry M. Daugherty, Warren Harding's Attorney General, on charges of defrauding the federal government in the administration of German property seized by the Alien Property Custodian during World War I; sports promoter Tex Rickard, on charges of statutory rape; and Charles E. Mitchell, president of what is now Citibank, on income tax evasion charges. Other prominent clients were singer Rudy Vallee, film magnate Alexander Pantages, actress Lillian Gish, chain store owner S.S. Kresge, and publisher William Randolph Hearst.

Once established, Steuer demanded and got a sizeable advance retainer in every case he agreed to take on. Even during the Depression years, he was charging the then astronomical fee of $1,500 per day for court appearances, over and above his initial retainer. Adjusted for inflation, this daily fee would be several times as high as the fees charged by the most expensive trial lawyers in the 1990s. Of special importance to our story, Max Steuer became very prominent in New York Democratic Party politics, serving as a member of the unofficial (backroom) board of strategy that made important decisions for Tammany Hall, the New York City Democratic organization. This was during the heyday of urban machine politics, and Tammany Hall ruled the rotten New York political scene with such an iron hand that it was able to elect its candidate, Asa Bird Gardner, district attorney of New York County in 1897 under the slogan, "To hell with reform!"

Max Steuer achieved part of the American Dream by doing very well financially and acquiring great power despite his lowly starting position, but he never demonstrated much interest in representing other underdogs, possibly because establishment clients were taking up all his time.

Max's son Aron, born in 1898, attended prestigious prep schools and went on to Harvard College. He interrupted his education to enlist in the Army in World War I, and on his return he played varsity baseball and graduated with honors. At Columbia Law School, he again received honors and was an editor of the law review. Unlike his father, he was able to land an associate's job at White & Case, one of the most prominent Wall Street law firms. After a few years there, he received the Democratic nomination for a seat on the City Court for New York County (Manhattan). Since that nomination was tantamount to election, he became a judge in 1929 at the age of 31. He served on the City Court until 1932, when he was elected to the Supreme Court for New York County, the seat he occupied at the Froman trial.

It would be easy to write off Aron Steuer as a product of his illustrious father's political and financial clout, but there was no denying that he was highly qualified and brilliant in his own right. He took special pains to demonstrate a high degree of scholarship in his judicial opinions.

In private life, Aron Steuer lived like a Brahmin. He married Virginia Clark, a Ziegfeld Follies beauty, and they toured Europe in the grand manner during summer recesses. He was a noted horseman and gained a coveted position on the Olympic Equestrian Committee.

I knew little of this in 1953, but I had the feeling that such an astute judge would quickly realize that Rod Sullivan's dive story was incredible, and that he would have the intellectual courage to break new ground if necessary to give us a fair shot at overcoming the $8,300 Warsaw Convention limitation. Harry Gair was more reserved, but he always took the position that his first hurdle was to educate the judge. For that reason, at the start of the trial he always submitted a detailed trial brief outlining the facts and the law — a common practice now, but rare in negligence cases before the 1960s.

As the trial date drew closer, I could barely contain my excitement. Yet, I knew that we faced a lot of tough obstacles. Pan Am was the world's leading airline and an icon of the business establishment, especially in New York. Juan Trippe was still presiding over his world-wide empire from his lair in the Chrysler Building. The flying boats had given way to long-range four-engine landplanes like the DC-6 and DC-7, and Pan Am, the pioneer of economy class service, was now leading the airlines into the jet age with the first Boeing 707s. We were attacking the Pan Am mystique head-on, accusing one of the Master Ocean Pilots of wilful misconduct in the only B-314 accident they had ever suffered. No Master Ocean Pilot had even been held to be *negligent*, let alone guilty of wilful misconduct. Nobody had ever taken Pan Am to trial on wilful misconduct, not even the families of the 19 dead *Yankee Clipper* passengers, some of whom were represented by leading law firms. Each of those families and all the other injured passengers had settled their claims for the Warsaw limit of $8,300, including Lorraine Rognan, who had suffered injuries serious enough to shorten her performing career, and had watched her beloved husband slip away forever beneath the waters of the Tagus.

This would be a particularly difficult wilful misconduct case because we were blaming the pilot, who usually has nothing to gain by breaking the rules. Airlines, on the other hand, can sometimes save lots of money by cutting corners. But Pan Am itself did not cut corners. Their rules clearly required circling and landing parallel with the lights at night. I wished that we could blame the Pan Am treasurer sitting in the Chrysler Building for directing a landing across the lights to save a few gallons of fuel, but that was not what had happened at Lisbon.

All these difficulties were apparent, but before the jurors ever got to the question of wilful misconduct they would see and hear Jane Froman, Gypsy Markoff, and Harry Gair. The jurors would be part of a fairy tale, and would have a chance to write a happy ending to a story that was much like the American Dream. In the end, they would be called upon to use the law to right a wrong, which is what tort cases are all about. I had no doubt that we were right, and that Harry Gair would make the jurors see that we were right.

I prayed that I would not do anything to spoil this dream scenario.

CHAPTER 7

The Trial Begins

The trial opened at 10 a.m. on Monday, March 9, 1953, in the Supreme Court for New York County, Trial Term Part IV. The courtroom's 200 seats were filled with media people, litigants, lawyers, witnesses, and interested onlookers. The guards were turning other would-be spectators away at the doors.

Justice Aron Steuer ascended to the bench and nodded almost imperceptibly to the lawyers and prospective jurors. He was a pallid, balding man of medium height and build who seemed older than his 55 years. His black robe looked shabby and disheveled; on close examination, I could see that it was held together in several torn places by safety pins. Harry Gair explained to me that years ago, one of Steuer's sons had committed suicide while attending prep school, and that he had made it a ritual to wear the same judicial robe from that time on.

The judge spoke deliberately, as though it required considerable effort. While not hostile or impolite, he seemed to have a condescending attitude toward the people in his courtroom. I got the impression that he considered himself intellectually superior to the lawyers, litigants, and jurors, and that he felt it was an imposition for him to be saddled with a negligence trial. This was disconcerting to me, but Harry Gair seemed unfazed, and since he was trying the case, I immersed myself in the work of supporting him.

The first task was one of the most important of the whole trial: selecting the jurors. Twelve prospective jurors were seated in the box, and the opposing lawyers were permitted to question them on their general attitude toward the case. The purpose of the questioning was to guide the lawyers in exercising their challenges. Each side had six peremptory challenges, meaning that each could exclude six prospective jurors without giving any reason. In addition, each side could challenge any number of jurors for cause, if there was any apparent reason why they could not judge the case impartially. For example, if any of the prospective jurors (or their relatives) worked for Pan Am or any other airline, or was related to Jane Froman, they could be challenged for cause, and such challenges would not be deducted from the available peremptory challenges.

In tort cases, challenges for cause are rare, especially in big cities where the odds are against the jurors being acquainted with or related to the parties. The lawyers for both sides try to use the peremptory challenges so that the final jury will be favorably predisposed toward their clients. This calls for a lot of guesswork. Over the years, trial lawyers have developed a mythology of juror selection. Supposedly, plaintiffs in tort cases should avoid employees of large institutions such as utilities and government agencies, and should shun persons of German and Scandinavian descent, on the alleged ground that such people are likely to be unsympathetic and parsimonious in their judgments. Defendants, on the other hand, are admonished to challenge the likes of housewives and bartenders because of their notorious sympathy for plaintiffs and their largesse in handing out other people's money.

Harry Gair did not have much faith in these stereotypes. From the outset of jury selection, he concentrated on telling the prospective jurors the story of his case so they would be conditioned for the evidence that would be presented. He began his role of teacher-guide-illuminator with the jury selection. He asked a few simple questions, such as, "If the proof that we present in this courtroom shows that Pan Am's pilot violated safety regulations by making an improper and dangerous night landing, and that this dangerous landing fits the definition of wilful misconduct, would you have any difficulty in finding for the plaintiffs?" He usually got a "no" answer, and would follow up with, "And would you still be comfortable finding for the plaintiffs if their injuries were so serious that large sums would have to be awarded for medical expenses, lost earnings, and the severe pain that they suffered?" Again, Harry knew that most jurors would deny any reluctance to render a fair verdict based on the evidence. He tried to gauge their real feelings by the way they reacted to his questions, rather than by their standard answers.

Bill Junkerman also took a low-key approach to jury selection. He tried to condition the prospective jurors to the very heavy burden the plaintiffs carried in seeking to prove wilful misconduct on the part of the pilot who was sitting up front and would be the first to hit the water in a crash landing. He asked the jurors whether they would be swayed by sympathy for two fine women who deserved their respect and admiration, if the judge instructed them to put sympathy out of their minds. None admitted that sympathy would play any part in their deliberations.

Harry used three of his six peremptory challenges, mainly to exclude men who looked like they might try to take control of the jury. In his long trial experience he had come across jurors who could dominate and even intimidate others on the panel because they were apparently more intelligent or more articulate. He felt that with a jury of 12 people selected at random, he had at least an even chance to win any case he took on. What he wanted to avoid was a jury of one domineering person whose ego and aggressiveness might keep the others from casting their votes based on the evidence. After nearly three hours of "voir dire," the jury selection process, both sides were satisfied that they had an impartial jury that was committed to deciding the case on the evidence in accordance with the instructions that Justice Steuer would give them at the end of the testimony. There were four women and eight men, mostly wage earners or their spouses, apparently people of average intelligence. There was nothing in their employment or personal histories to indicate any bias toward one side or the other.

Since the trial took place before airline travel became commonplace, most of the jurors had never been up in an airplane. That was a drawback in that such jurors were likely to consider flying to be an adventure in which the passengers took their own chances, especially on a wartime flying boat trip to Europe. On the other hand, we were wary about seating jurors who had a lot of flying experience, for they were likely to adopt the macho attitude that they were part of the airmens' brotherhood, which would tend to make them favor the airline. Besides, frequent fliers in those days were likely to fall into the dangerous category of domineering jurors who might take control of the deliberations and intimidate those who knew nothing about airplanes.

As the clerk swore in the final 12 jurors, Harry Gair got ready to give his opening statement. The counsel table faced the jury box at right angles, and Harry was seated at the end closest to the jurors. I was seated on his left. At my left was the lawyer for Don Ross, and next to him were Bill Junkerman and his partner John Osnato, one of Haight Gardner's most experienced personal injury defense lawyers. Among those in the spectator seats were Jane Froman; Gypsy Markoff; John Burn, who had been laid off temporarily by Pan Am as expected; Grace Drysdale, the puppeteer member of the *Yankee Clipper* USO troupe, who was on hand to lend moral support to Jane and Gypsy; and Donald Ross.

Harry began his opening in his customary way, telling the jurors that what he said (and indeed what any of the lawyers in the case said) was not evidence, and reminding them that they had sworn to decide the case solely on the evidence. That was all that he was entitled to ask of them on behalf of his clients, Jane Froman and Gypsy Markoff. Then he summarized the facts that he thought would not be contested by Pan Am: the history of the flight up to the last minute over the River Tagus. He took them through the events leading up to the crash landing, and then told them that Captain Sullivan wilfully disobeyed and disregarded the landing instructions he had received from Pan Am, as well as Pan Am's own regulations for night landings on water. This was not done because Captain Sullivan was inexperienced, but quite the reverse: "He had flown for so many years that he acted as though the safety rules which were binding on others did not apply to him."

Harry then used the railing of the jury box to orient the jurors to the landing scene. He asked them to visualize the railing as a line of five lights laid out at intervals of about 1,000 feet in the water, with a red light at the far end of the jury box—the end closest to the judge's bench—indicating north, where the landing was supposed to be made. He asked them to think of the five lights as a lighted runway that the pilot needed to guide him to a safe landing at night. He said that Pan Am's Assistant Airport Manager at Lisbon, Charles Bounds, in charge of the Pan Am launch that was anchored near the red light, had radioed instructions to Sullivan to circle the lights and land from south to north, toward the red light; that Sullivan had acknowledged and agreed to these instructions; but that in fact he did not circle the lights or land toward the north. When he pulled abeam of the red light, he made a descending turn to the left, trying to land from east to west, at right angles to the jury box railing instead of parallel to it.

Harry told the jurors that attempting to land at right angles to the lights was dangerous because it robbed the pilot of the depth perception needed to make a safe landing on water at night. And as Sullivan executed it, this improper landing across the jury box railing involved him in violation of another important safety regulation: All Pan Am pilots were required to maintain a "constant track" from an altitude of 500 feet to the surface of the water. They were prohibited from making the kind of descending turn that Sullivan attempted because turns below

500 feet in a large flying boat are dangerous, and can result in the wing striking the water, the very hazard that brought down the *Yankee Clipper*. He explained how the string of lights aided the pilot in maintaining the depth perception that was needed to avoid such dangerous descents, and how Sullivan ignored this vital safety provision by attempting to land across the lights. He simplified the case for the jurors, focusing their attention on the undeniable fact that Sullivan was supposed to land parallel to their railing, "on the lighted water runway that was created for him for the express purpose of safety," but that he landed instead way up at the back of the jury box where jurors 7 and 8 were seated. He told the jurors that the evidence would show that there was nothing wrong with the plane that might cause it to land at right angles if the pilot actually wished to land parallel to the light string.

Since we did not know at that point whether Sullivan would testify at the trial, or exactly what story he would tell, Harry left the explanation up to Bill Junkerman. Obviously, Pan Am knew more about the cause of the accident than Jane and Gypsy did, so Harry challenged Pan Am's lawyer to explain why Sullivan had not landed parallel to the light string. Harry said that the evidence required of the plaintiffs would depend on exactly what was conceded and what was contested by Pan Am during the trial.

That put the ball in Bill Junkerman's court, but he chose not to answer the challenge directly. He would not fall into the trap of assuming the burden of proof when that was the plaintiffs' job. He preferred to put the case in a setting of his own choice.

Bill was then 48 and in trim condition, but his bald crown and white sideburns made him seem older. Although not an Ivy Leaguer, he came across as the defender of the business establishment. He spoke in tones that would have been appropriate for the boardroom of a major corporation. Bill was a member of the Quiet Birdmen, a secretive society of aviation pioneers. When he defended airlines in court, he tried to maintain the mystique of aviation as a barrier against the possibility that mere lay jurors might dare to judge the intrepid aviators by the standards applicable to railroads, bus lines, and automobile drivers. He successfully projected the prestige of Pan Am, and tried to convince the jurors that they would have to hear a lot of very specific evidence of deliberate wrongdoing before they could dare to convict the world's leading airline of wilful misconduct. He told the jurors that at the end of the case, the judge would instruct them that the plaintiffs had the burden of proving wilful misconduct, and that while Pan Am did not have any such burden, he would do his best to demonstrate to them that the way the accident happened precluded any proof of wilful misconduct.

He reminded the jurors that the accident happened in 1943, and that it would be improper for them to apply the technical engineering and know-how of 1953 when judging the case. Then he told the jurors that the case had been dismissed for lack of prosecution a year earlier. This brought an immediate objection from Harry Gair. Justice Steuer did not rule on the objection, but he told Junkerman to go on without further mention of that subject or the length of time the case had been pending.

Now Junkerman launched into a short history of Pan Am's Atlantic Operations. The *Yankee Clipper* was christened in Washington by Mrs. Roosevelt in 1939, and it made the very first commercial crossing that year. Then the war intervened, and six days after Pearl Harbor all of Pan Am's Boeing 314s were taken over by the U.S. Navy. Thereafter Pan Am's transatlantic flights had to be conducted under wartime secrecy conditions, and were subject to Portuguese wartime regulations as well. So it was that Captain Sullivan had to descend from 7,000 to 600 feet in order to fly up the Tagus to Pan Am's landing area.

Junkerman described Pan Am's Cabo Ruivo seaport, and pointed out that it was actually owned by the Portuguese government, with Pan Am supplying the personnel. He adopted Harry Gair's prop of using the jury box rail to simulate the string of lights, and agreed that they were laid out to assist Captain Sullivan in making a south to north landing. His only departure from Harry's description of the facts leading up the crash was that he said that the plane arrived about 15 minutes ahead of schedule, and so it was not completely dark. The lights were laid out in the river in anticipation of a night landing. He intimated that if the plane had arrived when expected, Sullivan would have been required to execute a night landing in complete darkness; but since he was early and there was still some light—he left this question dangling, perhaps hoping to plant some doubt in the jurors' minds as to whether this was actually a night landing.

Having painted a picture of a U.S. Navy-owned flying boat approaching Lisbon in a manner required by Portuguese wartime regulations, and having questioned whether a night landing was required, Bill Junkerman stopped short of telling the jury what happened in the final minute. He said that the witnesses would tell the jurors what happened, and that he would not presume to testify in their place. He asked only that the jurors keep their minds open. Jane Froman and Gypsy Markoff are "charming ladies and talented actresses." Pan Am did not dispute that they were seriously injured. But the jurors should not let emotions influence their judgment. If they simply followed the evidence, at the end of the case they would realize that "there certainly was no intentional act causing this accident, and there certainly wasn't any wilful misconduct on the part of Pan American or any of its people."

The jury selection and opening statements had taken up most of the court day. There was just time for Harry Gair to start presenting his case by introducing into evidence some excerpts from Pan Am's records and operating manuals. These dealt with undisputed facts such as the procedures for laying out the string of lights for night landings; the positioning of the control launch near the red light; the clearances for landing to be given to the captain by the operations representative in the control launch; and the requirement that the captain land parallel to the string of lights, with the lights to his left. Harry read and showed these regulations to the jury, and then he showed them another important excerpt from Pan Am's System Operations Manual. Under the heading of "Flight Technique—Descent and Landing" it said:

> LANDING TRACK. Except when the nature of the terrain adjacent to the landing area renders a change in track necessary for safety, a constant track will be maintained from an altitude of five hundred feet to the surface.

In other words, no turns could be made below the altitude of 500 feet. The captain would have to complete all his turns and be lined up with the lights, pointed in the direction of the intended landing, before he could descend below 500 feet. This Constant Track regulation was designed to prevent pilots from making turns close to the water, where depth perception was often distorted.

To point up the dangers of attempting such low turns in the Boeing 314, Harry showed the jury a picture from the Pan Am manual indicating that its wing span was 152 feet. Thus he laid the groundwork for our claim that by making a descending left turn below 500 feet during his landing approach pattern, Sullivan had violated Pan Am's own Constant Track regulation and created a serious risk of having the left wing strike the water. After the jurors passed around the Pan Am manual page that contained the Constant Track regulation, Justice Steuer announced that court was recessed until 10 o'clock the next morning.

We thought that the first day had gone well. The jurors were paying close attention and seemed to realize what an important case they would be deciding. Harry Gair appeared to be in top form, and I could hardly wait for him to get on with the witness testimony that would be the heart of the case. That evening, I met Harry at his midtown apartment to go over the stenographers' minutes of the first trial day. In those days it was very expensive to get "daily copy"—the typewritten transcript of everything that took place in the courtroom on the same day. It required teams of shorthand reporters who would relieve each other every 25 or 30 minutes so that their notes could be typed up very soon after the words were spoken in court. Harry had arranged for daily copy to be delivered to his apartment each evening, so that we could study what had been said and use it to fashion the next day's strategy.

That first evening, all we had were the lawyers' opening statements. We studied Bill Junkerman's opening carefully, and found nothing that we did not expect. He was using everything at his command to magnify the difficulty of proving wilful misconduct. And he kept reminding the jurors of Pan Am's prestige and the wartime conditions of the flight. Gair made careful notes to remind himself to address these defenses when the questioning of witnesses started.

Our expert witness, Sherrill Shaw, came into New York that evening from his home in Florida. I met him at the airport and took him to the Hotel Astor in Times Square, where we reviewed the ground that would be covered in his testimony. At the end of that long first day, I bought every newspaper available. There were then half a dozen evening and morning papers published in New York, and every one had prominent stories on the opening of the trial, with photos of Jane and Gypsy entering the courthouse. It was a heady feeling. I could hardly wait for the witness testimony to begin.

Harry Gair began the second day by reading from the deposition of Charles Bounds, Pan Am's assistant airport manager at Lisbon. It was one of the CAB depositions that we had been able to get into the case through the agreement with Bill Junkerman that both sides could use this material.

Harry read Bounds's testimony to the jury. Bounds said that he was the control officer on the Pan Am launch, which was anchored at its customary place slightly southwest of the red light. He had supervised the laying out of the light string from the launch. He communicated with the *Yankee Clipper* crew by radiotelephone, advising them to land to the north. He assumed that he was talking to First Officer Rush, who acknowledged the instruction to land to the north and said they were then southeast of the light line, and would circle the light line before coming in to land. From these communications, Bounds concluded that the landing would be made in the customary way, landing to the north parallel to the light line. Rush told Bounds that he should fire flares to light up the landing area when he saw them blink the plane's landing lights (which were located in the wings). This too was routine procedure.

Bounds watched the plane in the air as it flew from south to north at an altitude of about 500 to 600 feet. It was flying level and was about two miles east of the launch and light line. He watched it intermittently because it was also his duty to keep checking the landing area visually to make certain it was clear of boats and other obstructions. When the plane was about abeam of the launch, Bounds looked away to make another check of the landing area. Before he looked back, one of the launch's boatmen, Eduardo da Silva, said that the plane was landing. Then, Bounds testified, "I immediately looked in the direction in which I had last seen the plane and saw a big splash of water. That is all I saw from the last time I had seen the plane in normal flight until then."

Bounds also testified that the weather was good, with a ceiling of 2,000 feet and unlimited visibility. He said that they were definitely using the night landing procedure, since it was dusk, "in the last stages of twilight."

Then Harry read from the deposition of the launch's coxswain, Eduardo da Silva, who, unlike Bounds, had watched the plane continuously untit it crashed. He testified that as the plane flew east of the lights and launch on its northerly heading, it maintained "the same altitude, the same speed, perfectly normal, the flight parallel to the landing lights" all the way from the first white light until it was opposite the launch and abeam of the red light. He was asked to describe the last moments of the flight from the time when the plane was abeam of the launch. He responded, "When the plane was at that point, it started a moderate left bank and a slight left turn. The first abnormal thing to me was the splash of the plane in the water." At another point, he said the plane "fell into the water." Thus, his testimony could be considered to be consistent with an attempt to turn and descend for a landing across the lights (our theory) or a sudden uncontrollable dive (Sullivan's story). I felt that if we could have questioned him in person, he would have supported our position that the plane crashed while in a gentle descending left turn rather than a dive. But we had to make do with the 1943 CAB testimony, and it was better for us to put it into the record than to let Bill Junkerman read it in a way which would indicate that it supported his defense.

Having set the scene with the depositions of the two launch witnesses, Harry then called our first live witness: George Spiegelberg, a prominent New York lawyer and law professor, a wartime army major who had been returning to his post in England aboard the *Yankee Clipper.* He had served as a dirigible pilot in World War I, and so was more familiar with aviation than most of the other passengers. He had been seated at a table in one of the lounges, with his back to the right side of the plane. He could see the outside through a window on the other side of the lounge, about 20 feet from his seat. In response to Harry Gair's question about the last minute of the flight, he said that they were flying up the river in a northerly direction. "It turned to the left, banked to the left as it turned. So that from my position on the right side of the plane, as I looked out the windows of the left side of the plane, I saw the water beneath me. I saw it dimly because it was dusk at that time. We proceeded on this left bank, losing altitude as we turned. The next thing I knew I saw the water rushing up at me as I looked down at the left wing and I was aware of the water rushing over the stub wing, which is a small wing under the large wing on the plane. The next thing I heard was one of the loudest crashes I have ever heard, and the last thing I remembered for some time was hitting something harder than I have ever hit anything."

Spiegelberg testified that the plane was heading toward the west when it struck the water, and that up to the time when the plane struck the water, he noticed nothing abnormal. Harry finished his questioning on that note, and now Donald Ross's lawyer took over. He brought out that Spiegelberg had been hospitalized for eight months, and that during his convalescence at Lisbon, he had met Don Ross, who was visiting his wife, Jane Froman.

Now it was Bill Junkerman's turn to cross-examine. Junkerman knew that Spiegelberg was a very impressive witness whose account of a descending left turn would have some impact on the jury. He took some time to place Spiegelberg's position in the plane as far from the window as possible. He also tried to minimize Spiegelberg's World War I dirigible service, distinguishing it from flying airplanes. At the end, he tried to support Sullivan's dive story by getting Spiegelberg to say that the time between the left turn and contact with the water was very short, but Spiegelberg could not estimate the time. He said only that there was "nothing untoward" about the descending left turn, and the first thing that riveted his attention was the water rushing up to the window of the plane.

The next witness was William Manning, the assistant flight engineer on the last flight of the *Yankee Clipper*. Ten years later, he was working for Pan Am as an assistant maintenance foreman at Idlewild Airport. Now we would see our first real combat, as Gair tackled a hostile witness whom he had subpoened to testify for the plaintiffs.

Manning was a bit evasive at first, but after Gair confronted him with the answers he had given in the deposition I had taken a few weeks earlier, his testimony became more straightforward. He testified that one of his duties was to inspect the plane's controls, including the elevator controls and cables before each departure; that he had done so at LaGuardia, at Bermuda, and at Horta, and had found everything in good condition. He was on duty during the approach to Lisbon, sitting at the flight engineer's station, about 15 feet behind the pilots. As they approached Lisbon, he became aware of a left turn and "apparently it did not level out." The pilots had controls for the throttles of each of the four engines, and these controls were duplicated at his station, so that either he or the pilots could work the throttles. He saw the throttle controls move to the "closed" position, shutting off the engine power, which to him was a normal incident of landing. Since he had definite duties in connection with the landing, he kept an eye on the throttles and also on the engine instruments at his station.

Now Harry Gair closed in for the crucial testimony from the only surviving crew member besides Sullivan who participated in the final descent.

[by Mr. Gair] Q. So far as all of the settings on all of the instruments are concerned, having to do with the landing, were they at the time you saw the throttles moving back, were they all settings which were normal for an immediate landing?
A. Yes, they were.

Q. In other words, there was nothing so far as engine controls, there was nothing left for you to do so far as actually landing the plane was concerned? A. No, sir.

Q. Everything had been done? A. That's right.

Q. And then the last thing to be done would be to pull the throttles back so that the plane could then land, is that right?
A. That's on the part of the captain.

Q. Pulling the throttles back happens just as the plane is ready to land on the water? A. Not necessarily.

Q. Soon before it hits the water? A. That's right.

Q. As a matter of fact, part of your duty as the throttles come back and the power is off, just at that time, isn't it your duty to get out of your seat in order to observe just where the water is with reference to the plane, so that you can work the throttles to give some power to continue the plane along on the water? A. It's not necessary to get out of the seat to do it.

Q. Well, did you on this occasion get up? A. I stood up on this occasion.

Q. Well, standing up—is that something that you did so that you could observe the situation as to what you have to do a little better? A. That's my own method of doing it.

Q. All right. And that's what you did on this landing? A. Yes.

Q. Is the term "normal glide" used with respect to normal landings? A. Yes, we have a normal glide.

Q. Well, as part of your job, do you know when a plane is making a normal glide for a landing? A. Well, if it is normal, it is not very much. You don't feel it.

Q. And that glide occurs just before the plane hits the water? A. That's right.

Q. Did it make a normal glide at that time, this plane? A. Yes, it was making a normal glide.

Q. Prior to that time, during all of these actions—the turn, the bank, the descent, the closing of throttles and so forth— prior to that, had you noticed anything abnormal anywhere and in any way about the plane? A. No, sir; we had a routine flight.

Q. Were there any emergency procedures laid out on this plane in the event that an emergency occurred? A. Yes, we had emergency procedures.

Q. Were you notified of any emergency by anybody? A. No, sir, no emergency procedure was given.

Q. And did you get any indication from anybody that the plane was out of control up to the point where you have just indicated that the plane was making a normal glide for land- ing? A. None whatsoever.

Mr. Gair: That's all.

Harry had done a masterful job of controlling this witness and making him tell the truth, painting a clear picture of an active crew member reacting to the many signs that Sullivan was attempting to land at the time of the crash. Bill Junkerman knew that Manning's testimony had taken Pan Am closer to the brink of wilful misconduct than they had ever been. He had to muddy up Manning's clear picture of a landing. He began by taking the flight engineer through all of the dozens of engine instruments that he had to monitor, describing the functions of each instrument. This had nothing to do with the accident, but it served to restore some of the mystique that Gair's questioning of Manning had swept away. Perhaps the jurors would believe that an engineer occupied with the reading of so many dials could not really tell when a landing was being made.

Then Junkerman led Manning into stating that the only indication of landing he received from the captain was the closing of the throttles, and that there was no way for him as the flight engineer to know whether the captain had any intention of landing at that point. Since he was 15 feet away from the captain's seat, he neither saw nor heard anything that could reveal the captain's intentions.

Manning's 1943 CAB testimony had been rather sketchy compared to the clear statements in Gair's direct examination. Therefore, Junkerman took the unusual step of confronting his own witness with the prior CAB testimony, in order to move him back to a less damaging version of the final seconds. Manning now adopted what he had said to the CAB investigators in 1943: "The last clear thing I can remember, we made a left hand turn and apparently we did not level out. The throttles were pulled back in a closed position, shutting off the power of the engines, and then I heard a sharp report, a distinct report, something new. From there on, I don't remember anything." Building on this earlier testimony, Junkerman got Manning to say that the closing of the throttles and putting the plane into a normal glide indicated to him that the captain "was preparing to land" rather than actually landing the plane. Then, despite an objection by Gair that Junkerman was leading the witness, the judge allowed the question, "When you said he was preparing to land, did you mean he was circling to land?" Manning hesitated a moment, and then said, "Yes." Harry Gair then confronted Manning with the answer he had given to me on his deposition a few weeks earlier: "Q. Was the cutting off of the power at that time an indication to you that the plane was landing? A. Yes." Instead of "Yes," Manning now answered, "That's right, he was preparing to go in, preparing to land."

This left Manning way out on a limb, since Junkerman next asked whether the plane could complete a circle of the landing area with the power cut off. Manning gulped and answered, "It is possible." I whispered to Gair that there was no way that this 40-ton flying boat could circle the landing area—a trip of at least 6 or 7 miles—with the power cut off. It would descend into the river long before completing a circle, and it would also immediately violate the Constant Track regulation by making turns below 500 feet altitude. Gair realized this, but he felt it was obvious that Junkerman was trying to lead Manning away from the damaging admissions he had made on direct examination. Manning's discomfort seemed to be projecting to the jury. Gair made a note to ask our expert, Captain Shaw, about circling with the power off. He preferred to avoid a technical confrontation with Manning, which might confuse the jurors and thus play into Junkerman's hands. Gair simply had Manning repeat that he had stood up when he saw the throttles shut off, so that he could be ready to open the throttles after a landing if necessary. Manning was then excused.

The next witness was another surviving crew member, Philip Casprini, the senior flight steward. His injuries had disabled him from flying, and he was now a reservations supervisor. His testimony was not as important as Manning's, since he was on the lower deck of the plane and was not part of the flight-deck team that actively participated in landings. He confirmed that the No Smoking and Seat Belt signs were on, and he had made sure that the passengers were prepared for landing. Then he went forward to take his assigned landing seat on the lower deck. He was about to sit down when he noticed that the plane was touching or skimming the water. He wasn't sure whether the hull or the wingtip was touching, but the skimming was similar to what he felt during normal landings. Immediately after that, he lost consciousness. He had not noticed anything abnormal, compared with other landings he had experienced. No emergency signal was given to him. When Gair asked him about the lighting conditions he had observed while in the river, he tried to give the impression that it was still light enough to see a short distance. But Gair confronted him with his recent deposition in which he had said that while he heard some voices in the water, he was not able to see anyone because it was too dark. He tried to wriggle out of this by saying that he was too seriously injured to determine whether it was dark.

Harry let Casprini go at that point, satisfied that we had one more crew-member witness who had felt no dive and who was going about his business as though the plane were about to land. Bill Junkerman's cross-examination was confined to showing that as a steward, Casprini had no flight training or duties related to the landing, which was solely the province of the captain.

As I saw it, the testimony of Manning and Casprini could not have gone better for us. The fact that they tried to fight off the truth and had to be confronted with their deposition testimony kept the jurors' interest at a high level. Harry seemed pleased and confident as he prepared to put Gypsy Markoff on the stand that afternoon. He would follow that with Jane Froman on Wednesday morning; then the medical experts; and would finish the plaintiffs' case with Captain Sherrill Shaw, our flying boat expert.

Gypsy Markoff was a magnificent witness. The jurors seemed to hang on her every word when she described her career as a professional accordionist in concert, stage, radio, and theatrical roles. When she spoke, she often tossed back her shoulder-length brown hair with its dramatic platinum blonde streak. She had toured the world for 15 years prior to the Lisbon crash. Her last engagement had been at New York's Waldorf Astoria hotel. It lasted six months and paid her $500 per week plus a hotel room. Like Jane Froman, she had done other USO shows and had been one of the first to volunteer for overseas assignments.

Under Gair's questioning, she described the last few minutes of the flight. She was sitting near the rear of the plane, with her back to the engines. She was near a window and could see outside. The flight seemed completely normal to her. The seat belt sign came on and she fastened her belt. She remembered seeing the wing "go down and down, and it seemed like moments and it kept going down. That's the last thing I remember." Nothing abnormal had happened up to that point.

Her next recollection was surfacing in the water. She had no idea how she got out of the plane's wreckage. She was panicky in the water since she knew she was seriously injured and she could not swim. She tore her hands trying to grasp some floating wreckage She described her injuries, including severe cerebral concussion, cuts that opened her face and forehead and bled profusely, her shoulder broken, her legs and back painfully bruised. She described how Yvette Silver had saved her life by keeping her afloat and helping her to hang on to a floating pillow until the rescue ship picked her up.

Her broken shoulder and the injuries to her hands had inhibited her ability to perform as before on the accordion. The instrument weighed over 30 pounds and required delicate finger manipulation. Gypsy spent 14 months in hospitals and medical treatment, including facial plastic surgery and operations on her broken right shoulder and the fingers of her left hand. As she testified, 10 years after the crash, she still could not bend three of those fingers. She had been forced to develop new accordion techniques to compensate for her disabilities, and took singing lessons to expand her routine. The overall effect of her injuries and the ensuing nervous shock was to drastically curtail her work schedule from the previous 48 weeks per year to less than half of that now.

Bill Junkerman was very careful in cross-examining Gypsy, for it was clear that she had captured both the admiration and sympathy of the jurors. He produced a *New York Times* clipping reporting a recital Gypsy had given at New York's Town Hall in 1945, and asked Gypsy if she recalled the occasion. She did remember, and said it was a sort of tryout to see how her new techniques would work. Junkerman read from the clipping, in which the reviewer said that Gypsy had given "a brilliant and exciting performance." "Well," replied Gypsy with a smile, "He certainly knew what he was talking about!" That was as far as Bill dared to go, and court adjourned for the day as Gypsy was excused from the stand.

That evening, I went to Harry Gair's apartment to read the daily copy, which often paid for itself handsomely by revealing gems that lawyers in the heat of battle did not fully record. Harry was already making notes for his final argument, and he marked up the Manning and Casprini testimony so that he could read the best parts to the jury at the end of the case.

On the third day, our star, Jane Froman, took the stand. She had never testified in court before, and despite her lifetime of public appearances, she was nervous. She managed to control her stuttering as Harry Gair took her through the story of her career, her volunteering for the USO overseas duty, and the early part of the flight to Lisbon. She remembered the plane going by the tomb of Vasco da Gama in Lisbon harbor, and then noticed a left turn and bank. When Harry asked her what happened next, she stuttered and could not speak for a minute. As she regained her composure, Harry brought out that the speech impediment had been with her since childhood, and was not related to the accident. To restore her confidence, he asked if it interferes with her singing. She smiled and said, "No, it doesn't."

Jane testified that after noticing the plane in a left turn, she blacked out, and could not remember anything else that happened before she came to in the icy waters of the Tagus. She described how John Burn had kept her alive in the water until they were finally rescued and brought to the dock. She lay on the dock in a stretcher for half an hour, until they took her to the tiny hospital:

> Q.[by Mr. Gair] When you came to the hosptial, were you admitted immediately? A. No, I was put in an anteroom for about 40 minutes.
>
> Q. Did you observe anything about yourself, your leg, or any other part of your body, at that time? A. Yes. I couldn't turn my arm at all, and the bones stuck out of my right leg.
>
> Q. You could see that yourself? A. Yes.
>
> Q. What's the next thing that happened? A. An intern came along and put a temporary splint on the leg and I was taken into a room with three or four other survivors.
>
> Q. What was done for you? A. As I recall, they gave me something to ease the pain, gave me an injection of anti-tetanus because of all the cuts, the open wounds. They finally got to me and took me to the operating room at twelve o'clock—midnight. They operated on me and at one point they thought I was gone—then they gave me a blood transfusion from a Portuguese sailor.

After Jane recounted her weeks of hospital confinement in Lisbon, Harry Gair read to the jury from the hospital records: "Patient very depressed...Patient feels life has nothing to offer...Pain very severe in right leg...Patient asks, 'give me a strong hypo; maybe I will be able to sleep and forget'...Patient very depressed, wants to die." As Harry read these passages, Jane fought to keep her composure on the stand. Then Harry took her through the years of surgery and the long struggle to resume her singing career.

In cross-examination, Bill Junkerman was brief and careful. Under the pretrial discovery rules, Bill had obtained all of Jane's tax returns and business records. This enabled him to bring out that Jane had a 44-week contract for her current television show at $4,000 per week, which would net her $176,000 for 1953, without considering additional income from nightclub appearances, movies, and recordings. She had been paid as much as $10,000 a week for doing three shows a day at New York's Roxy Theatre. Jane admitted that the television income alone was considerably more than she had earned in any year before the accident, despite having been a star of radio, stage, and films since the 1930s. Bill was laying the groundwork for a statement in his final argument that Jane had not actually lost money because of the accident.

When she completed her testimony, Jane had tears in her eyes as she stepped down to resume her seat next to John Burn. He squeezed her arm, and despite the ordeal, she seemed to be relieved at having told her story publicly for the first time. The press coverage was particularly heavy that day, especially in the tabloids.

The rest of the day was spent on testimony of three doctors, who described her injuries in medical terms and attested to the cost of her long treatment: over $300,000. An orthopedic specialist testified that there was considerable wasting of Jane's right leg, with heavy scarring and inability to place her foot flat on the ground. He said that her leg had withered more than an inch, and that if she tried to stand without the brace and boot that she was wearing in court, she would refracture the leg. Therefore, her leg injuries were permanent.

That evening at Harry's apartment, I did not read the daily copy, as the medical and damage part of the case was not my job. I went over the outline of Sherrill Shaw's testimony with Harry, and then we spent some time discussing the evidence with Ben Siff, Harry's law man. Harry would rest the plaintiffs' case the next day, at which time Bill Junkerman would move to dismiss for lack of evidence of wilful misconduct. He would ask the judge to take the case away from the jury right then and there, and so Harry had to be prepared to argue that we had made out a *prima facie case*—that we had produced evidence from which a jury could find wilful misconduct if they were so inclined.

The next morning, I took Sherrill Shaw to breakfast at the Astor Hotel. He was well prepared and calm—calmer than I was, knowing that my work on the case would face the supreme test as our expert took the stand.

This was the part of tort trials that Harry Gair disliked. He felt that he was in control of the case with ordinary witnesses, but expert witnesses had a lot of power to make or break a case. Harry prepared his expert witnesses meticulously lest they blurt out a damaging statement on direct examination or come unglued on cross. But despite his great care, he had suffered through some stomach-churning hours when a case hung on a expert witness who was trying to showcase his knowledge or who had overblown his qualifications. We hoped this would not happen to Captain Shaw, but in the meantime our stomachs were due for an even more severe test. Donald Ross was about to have his day in court.

As a plaintiff, Ross had the right to testify. All of Harry Gair's pleading could not prevent this ham actor from sharing the spotlight once more with the woman who had suffered him for so many years. Tall and still handsome, Don made a favorable first impression—until he opened his mouth. When his lawyer asked Don to give the jurors a brief sketch of his background, the answer went on for over ten minutes. Don's father had been a Methodist minister and a World War I army chaplain, so Don started with a long-winded speech about his father's career. Then his lawyer led him through the Don Ross saga: that he had given up his own promising singing and acting career to devote himself to Jane's great need for his coaching and managerial talents.

I fought to keep from squirming, and noticed that several of the jurors were shifting restlessly in their seats. As Don warmed up to his favorite subject—his aborted career—I noticed that one juror was shaking his head in disbelief. But Don did not reach his unctuous climax until he dramatized his role in the *Yankee Clipper* disaster and its aftermath. His story was that the accident had acccomplished the impossible by destroying the bond of love between himself and Jane. He read to the jury a letter that Jane had written to him on the day before the crash, when the *Yankee Clipper* stopped over at Bermuda. "Hello, darling," said the letter. "I'm sitting here in a deck chair. We are leaving in an hour. Darling, you'll never know how I hated to leave you this morning. Please remember I love you so much. I love you, I love you. Incidently, keep this letter. I want to save the stamp."

I will spare you the details of Don's testimony in support of his claim for huge damages. Basically, he told the jurors that because of the intense pain Jane suffered from her injuries and the ensuing surgery, she required "special pain-easing medica-tion" which so changed her that their "mad, idyllic love affair" was destroyed, leading to the 1948 divorce. His testimony seemed to go on forever. I could not bear to look back at the spectators' section to see how Jane and John Burn were holding up under Ross's allegation that Jane was not fit to live with him due to her medication. Finally he was finished. It seemed as though a blast of fresh air swept through the courtroom as Don Ross left the stand and Harry Gair called Captain Sherrill Shaw.

Harry took Shaw through his qualifications, including his government license as an airline captain and instructor; his Navy flight service, 1927-1931; his years as Pan Am Chairman C.V. Whitney's personal flying boat captain; and his 1941-1948 service with Pan Am. About two-thirds of his 7,000 flying hours (total-ling over a million miles) was on flying boats, mostly with Pan Am. He was a captain throughout his Pan Am career, and when stationed at Miami, he became both a check pilot and instructor on S-42s, the four-engine flying boats which, with 32 passenger seats and a crew of six, were in the same class as the B-314s. Indeed, Pan Am had used S-42s to survey the transatlantic routes that were later served by the B-314s. Shaw remained an S-42 captain and check pilot until Pan Am retired the flying boats in 1945. At the time he testified, he was in private business and also served as a captain on charter flights. Harry also covered Shaw's three transatlantic crossings as an observer on B-314s in 1941-1942.

Shaw had made over 200 night landings in Pan Am flying boats, and as an instructor he had taught other Pan Am pilots the night landing procedures. He explained to the jury that Pan Am's procedures for night landings on water were the same for all their flying boats, including the S-42 and the B-314. These procedures called for the string of lights to be laid out according to the wind direction, with the red light the last one in line. He explained how the lights provided the depth perception that would otherwise be lacking at night over water: "If the pilot was a mile back from the first light at an altitude of 1,000 feet, those lights would look fairly far apart, a wide space between them. If he was down to 500 feet, those lights would appear to be a little closer together. If they were in an exactly straight line, and he was at sea level, the lights would appear to be more or less one." But if the pilot tried to land at right angles to the lights, "The lights would be of little value as far as estimating his height off the water, because he has no means of observing the spacing between the lights."

We were getting down to the crucial point of his testimony, and Shaw was handling himself very well. There were many interruptions and objections from Bill Junkerman, but Shaw remained calm and unruffled. Now came the questions that would tie the night landing procedures to wilful misconduct:

Q.[by Mr. Gair] Was there a recognition among the pilots and the staff of Pan American that a landing at night at right angles to the lights was a dangerous procedure? A. Yes, there was.

Q. Will you explain that to us, please? A. Well, the light string was laid out to create a runway for the pilot.

Q. Captain Shaw, assuming that you were landing on water at night and you were going towards one light, that is, at right angles to it, as you gave us an example of earlier; what extent of depth perception would you have so far as the water beneath you where you were going down for that landing?

A. Well, approaching one light, there is actually no means of determining depth perception, if you can't see the water, and there is always the possibility of the pilot flying into the water due to that fact.

Q. And is that avoided by flying parallel to the lights?

A. That is correct; that is what the light string is for.

Q. Assuming that a series of landing lights is laid out from south to north, with the red light at the north, and that the plane makes its approach for the purposes of landing and travels parallel with the lights in a generally northerly direction until it reaches a point about two miles east of the red light, and then makes a left turn and bank and the throttles are cut; and assuming that the light string is of the ordinary length, with five lights—could you tell me, after the throttles are cut, whether that plane could complete the circle and make its landing south to north? A. Definitely not. The airplane could not continue the regular approach lane.

Q. What do you mean? A. The airplane could not continue around the regular approach lane due to the fact that he has no power after he has cut his throttles back.

Q. What happens after the throttles are cut back when you are making a descent to the water which you start from around 500 or 600 feet? A. Well, if the pilot had cut his throttles back, he had just better be ready to land.

Shaw's answers were given in his own natural conversational tone. They did not seem rehearsed, and yet he had given us exactly what we needed to get the case to the jury on wilful misconduct. He had branded the across-the-lights landing as dangerous and contrary to Pan Am's own safety procedures, and he had given the lie to Flight Engineer Manning's statement that the plane could continue to circle the landing area if the throttles had been cut way up near the red light. Now Harry would close out Shaw's direct testimony by covering the Constant Track regulation:

Q. Now, will you tell us just what those words "constant track" mean with respect to landing procedure over water at night? A. Well, that "constant track" means that the airplane, from his final turn on the approach pattern at 500 feet, will continue in a straight line to the landing area, the light string.

Q. Assuming, captain, that on this jury rail I set up five lights, and the red light is here to the north and the plane is seen to come up the river northerly some distance out from this light string, and then when it gets abeam of the red light, makes a left bank and descending turn until the wing of the plane enters the water; would such action be maintaining a constant track with respect to an approach and landing from south to north? A. Definitely it would not.

Q. What is the customary aviation practice, so far as maintaining a constant track is concerned, below 500 feet in a night landing? A. The pilot never makes a turn below 500 feet.

Q. And that would all the more apply to a descending turn below 500 feet? A. That is correct.

Q. What is the danger to be expected from such a turn?
A. The possibility of loss of altitude, the pilot highly absorbed in watching instruments in the turn, and the possibility, because of loss of altitude, of flying into the water.

Harry Gair ended on that high note. Bill Junkerman cross-examined for half an hour, but didn't get much. He took Shaw through all the different types of planes he had flown, to emphasize that he had never actually flown a B-314. He stressed the fact that Shaw was then flying for a nonscheduled airline. Finally, Junkerman brought out that Shaw's testimony about landing and Constant Track procedures assumed that everything about the airplane was normal.

Q. [by Mr. Junkerman] If there were something wrong, if the pilot were faced with a state of emergency, wouldn't he, with the company regulations, and every regulation that you have ever heard of, have discretion to take the emergency action that he deemed appropriate at that particular moment? A. The pilot always has the right to exercise his own judgment or use his own discretion in the case of an emergency.

We were happy with Captain Shaw's answer to the emergency question. We didn't want him to discredit himself by getting into an argument with Junkerman about whether Sullivan really had experienced an emergency, since there was no evidence as yet about the alleged nose dive. We knew now that Junkerman would be putting Sullivan on the stand to claim that he could not follow the prescribed landing procedure because he was overtaken by an emergency. As Captain Shaw left the stand, it was clear that unless there had been an emergency, Sullivan had violated the landing procedures and had put the plane into a position of danger by making a descending turn below 500 feet without any guide to depth perception because he was headed at right angles to the light string.

Harry Gair rested the plaintiffs' case, and then we faced the first moment of truth. It is customary for the defendant's lawyer to make a motion to dismiss the complaint at the close of plaintiffs' evidence. Usually such motions are routinely denied, but in a wilful misconduct case there was the question of whether we had produced evidence from which the jury might legally conclude that there had been wilful misconduct. As Bill Junkerman put it in his argument, "There has been no evidence to substantiate this charge. There is no evidence to indicate that Captain Sullivan intended to land in any way other than in a safe and standard manner. As a matter of fact, the only testimony bearing on Captain Sullivan's intention was that the flight crew had advised the launch that they intended to circle the light line in the usual manner. Plaintiffs' entire case rests solely upon speculation and conjecture which has no foundation in the evidence. There has been no proof that Captain Sullivan intended to land contrary to instructions, nor is there any proof that even if he had so intended, that he had knowledge that such a landing was likely to cause injury to the passengers aboard the *Yankee Clipper*."

I held my breath as Justice Steuer slowly opened his mouth and then said, almost inaudibly, "Motion denied." This meant that the case would go to the jury after Pan Am put on its evidence.

Now that Pan Am's insurers knew the case was going to the jury, would they offer to settle, as was often done at this point when the motion to dismiss had been denied? I hoped that they would not, for I wanted this case to go to the jury. Our evidence had gone in more smoothly than we could have hoped, and I felt that the jurors were with us all the way. Yet, if Pan Am had offered $250,000 for Jane's case and $100,000 for Gypsy's, I think Harry Gair would have recommended that they accept in view of the novelty and difficulty of proving wilful misconduct. Even if we won a jury verdict, the appellate courts might overrule the jury by finding that our evidence of wilful misconduct was insufficient as a matter of law.

There was no settlement offer, and Justice Steuer made no attempt to mediate or otherwise encourage settlement, although many trial judges did so at that point in the case. We left the court and met again that evening at Harry Gair's apartment to go over the daily copy of Captain Shaw's testimony and to prepare for Harry's cross-examination of the Master Ocean Pilots.

CHAPTER 8

Pan Am's Defense

It was Friday morning, March 13th, 1953, the fifth day of trial. Pan Am's first witness was Master Ocean Pilot Harold Gray.

Gray, then 47 years old, looked like a huskier version of Charles Lindbergh. He had a commanding presence that personified the aura of the world's leading airline. Although he was 14 years younger than Sullivan and 12 years younger than Musick, anyone listening to his authoritative testimony would not question why he had been jumped over the other Master Ocean Pilots to the executive suite in Pan Am's Chrysler Building headquarters. He then held the title of executive vice-president of the Atlantic Division. It was common knowledge that he was being groomed to succeed the then-54-year-old Juan Trippe as Pan Am's chief executive officer.

Bill Junkerman used Gray to dazzle the jury with the history of Pan Am. He did it in such a way that the Master Ocean Pilots appeared to be the main force in the airline's development and dominance, and every step of the way he wrapped Captain Rod Sullivan in the blue-and-white flag of Pan Am. As Gray went through the litany of the shrinking of the world by Pan Am's flying boats, Harry Gair objected several times to the relevance of this testimony, but the judge allowed it because Junkerman tied it into the qualifications and training of Captain Sullivan, which of course was a central issue in the case.

After half an hour of Pan Am's glorious history, Gray got down to describing the wartime operations into Lisbon, emphasizing the restrictions, such as yielding ownership of the B-314s to the Navy, having to communicate in code, having to preserve the secrecy of weather observations, and having to approach Lisbon at 600 feet altitude. None of these restrictions had anything to do with the accident, but they helped to shroud the flight in the mystique of wartime ocean flying so that the jurors would have another obstacle to push aside before branding Sullivan as the culprit.

Gray said that before Sullivan was transferred from the Pacific to the Atlantic, he had completed about 50 Pacific crossings.

That, coupled with his unparalleled record of more than 100 Atlantic crossings, had made him Pan Am's most experienced ocean pilot. Little wonder, then, that Rod Sullivan had been selected for the important ocean survey flights, and as captain of the first commercial flight across the Atlantic.

Junkerman then took Gray into a discussion of Pan Am's night landing procedures. Gray testified that the primary purpose of the light string was to mark the area that had been patrolled and found to be clear of obstacles such as boats and driftwood. He downplayed the usefulness of the lights in determining how far above the water the plane was at any particular moment, although he did say that "to some extent as the pilot approached those lights from a distance they were useful in determining generally how high the plane was." He said that the lights were too small to permit minute measurements, such as "I am six feet, or ten or fifteen feet" above the water. He said that Pan Am had cautioned their pilots not to rely on the lights to determine height above the water, but he did not produce any document that embodied such a warning.

Gray said that because the exact height could not be determined, Pan Am adopted the procedure of lining up with the light string and establishing a normal glide so that the plane could fly onto the water smoothly without the pilot knowing the exact moment at which the plane would land. This testimony was a smooth piece of sleight-of-hand work. Gray did not actually dispute anything that our expert, Captain Shaw, had said about the danger of approaching the lights at right angles, or the need to observe the diminishing spaces between the lights to monitor the descent. Gray had simply minimized the usefulness of the light string by truthfully stating that it could not be used for minute altitude measurements. Shaw had not testified that the lights were to be relied upon for determining exactly how many feet high the plane was. He had described use of the lights to give the pilot a general idea of altitude during descent, with the final seconds of landing to be illuminated by the plane's landing lights reflecting on the water, plus flares to be fired from the launch. But this was not the kind of nitpicking argument that Harry Gair wanted to get into, especially with a witness as articulate and impressive as Harold Gray. Besides, our position was that the crash occurred during a descending turn rather than during the final seconds of landing when the diminishing spaces between the lights would not help the pilot.

Gray closed his testimony by identifying a page from the Boeing 314 manual showing the dimensions of the windows in the passenger compartments. Each was 19 1/2 inches wide and 24 7/8 inches high. Junkerman put these dimensions before the jurors in order to impress them with the small size of the windows, which would tend to minimize the impact of the passengers' testimony about what they saw through those windows.

Harry Gair liked to begin cross-examination by turning the witness completely around to confirm the plaintiffs' position. He started this one by asking Gray whether the windows were put into the plane for ventilation or for the passengers to see out of. Gray replied that the windows were "to assist the passenger in avoiding claustropobia and seeing some of the things that went on outside of the plane." Finally he admitted that since the windows couldn't be opened, they were for observation rather than ventilation.

Gair then took Gray through the wartime restrictions, and established that they had nothing to do with the night landing procedures that Pan Am itself adopted and executed. Then he questioned Gray about the Constant Track regulation, at which point Justice Steuer, who had seemed bored with the proceedings up to then, suddenly took a hand:

> The Court: It doesn't say that you can't turn under 500 feet. It says you have got to come down on level. It doesn't say anything about what height you should turn in.
>
> The Witness [Harold Gray]: I think it does imply that the proper way to make a landing is to come down the last 500 feet with a constant track—I believe is what it says.

Thus, Pan Am's own witness, the greatest of its surviving Master Ocean Pilots, was telling the judge that the Constant Track regulation prohibited turns below 500 feet, but apparently the judge thought that the pilot could go below 500 feet and make all the turns he wanted, so long as he was not landing at the time. At one point the judge said, "There is nothing that says that a man can't come down to 200 feet and go up again." The problem with the judge's theory was that pilots were prohibited by the Civil Air Regulations from flying below 500 feet—with or without turns— except during landings and takeoffs. Harry Gair struggled with Justice Steuer's misunderstanding of this point throughout the cross-examination of Gray, but the judge stuck to his position that the Constant Track regulation did not prohibit turns below 500 feet unless we could prove that the plane was in the act of landing. After a while the colloquy between Gair and the judge began to sound like Abbott and Costello's "Who's on first" routine. It disrupted Gair's cross-examination of Gray, and finally he was forced to drop the subject.

Harry went on to ask Gray whether a landing at right angles near the red light would constitute a short cut. Gray fenced for a while, knowing that the short cut would provide a possible motive for Sullivan to pass up the circling in favor of a straight-in landing at the red light. Finally he minimized the time that the short cut might save, cutting it down to about two minutes by some very glib calculations.

Then Harry questioned Gray on the 45-degree angle of dive that we knew Sullivan would testify to. Harry had not brought it up in Sherrill Shaw's testimony because he thought it would have more impact if he could get Gray to admit that such a steep dive would have to be noticed by all aboard the airplane. We were very well prepared on this point, as I had found several textbooks on aerodynamics and on medical effects of flight maneuvers that supported our position. The leading textbook on medical effects of flight said that "any angle of descent greater than 25 degrees is considered practically intolerable from the point of view of the passengers." Harry took that textbook out of his briefcase and held it in his hands as he questioned Gray. I watched Gray's face as Harry leafed through the book to the page he was looking for. Gray was a scientist, an aviation inventor himself. I felt certain that he recognized the book and concluded that his leeway in answering these next questions would be limited if he wanted to maintain his credibility with the jury.

> Q.[by Mr. Gair] As a pilot, if a plane noses down, let's say at an angle of 45 degrees, is that a steep angle? A. That's quite a steep angle, I would say, for an airplane.
>
> Q. From the point of view of passengers, who are sitting, even strapped in, would they be noticeably affected by such a maneuver? A. I think that the average person would realize it.
>
> Q. Would it be something extremely uncommon? A. 45 degrees is a pretty steep angle and I think the passengers would realize that they were going down at that point.
>
> Q. How about anybody who would be standing on his feet in the plane, such as the steward? Would you say that a person standing on his feet, not strapped in, would be violently affected by such an angle of descent? A. It depends on how you went into it, whether it was a sudden thing or a gradual thing.
>
> Q. What if the plane descended suddenly at 45 degrees? A. If it went very suddenly, I think it would really be noticeable.

Q. You would fall over, wouldn't you? A. I think so—I don't know whether you would fall over.

Q. But you would be propelled forward, wouldn't you?
A. You are talking about something that's pretty hard to define, the suddenness of what you mean as compared to what I mean.

Q. In any event, as far as the angle is concerned, hasn't it been demonstrated to you in the course of your work, that any angle over 25 degrees is considered practically intolerable from the point of view of a passenger, intolerable for the purpose of standing up to the symptoms? A. With that particular kind of an airplane, the airplane seldom gets into an attitude of 20 degrees nose down.

Q. Would an attitude then of 40 or 45 degrees involve something extraordinary in relation to the comfort of those standing or sitting? A. I think so.

During the last two questions, Gair had been conspicuously consulting the textbook, and the message was not lost on Gray. Satisfied with the testimony on the angle of descent that would send the passengers and crew scrambling, Gair went on to his last point: a possible motivation for Sullivan's right-angle landing. He asked Gray if Pan Am had a procedure for the Captain to request a change in the direction of the light line if it is not pointing directly into the wind. Gray replied that the Captain can request the direction to be changed if he is concerned about the velocity of a cross-wind. Such a change would take about 40 minutes. Gair ended his questioning there, leaving it for his summation to argue that Sullivan might have been motivated to land east to west, into the westerly wind, rather than circle for 40 minutes while the lights were moved for a westerly landing.

Junkerman then opened a new line of questioning about the definition of a night landing. Gray said that there were "an infinite number of variations between daylight and darkness," and that you don't get complete darkness until about an hour and a half after "official sunset." He then launched into a technical discussion of terms like "nautical twilight" and "civil twilight." Finally, he said that often you can land a half hour after official sunset without it being a night landing, particularly if you land toward the west with a light sky that enables you to see obstructions on the water. Since the official sunset at Lisbon on February 22, 1943, was at 6:21 p.m., and Sullivan hit the water at 6:47 p.m., Gray's testimony, if accepted by the jury, would allow them to conclude that Sullivan was not obligated to land parallel to the lights as in a night landing, but could instead land to the west even though at right angles to the lights. But Harry Gair blunted that thrust by getting Gray to admit that if the captain decided that he was not going to make a night landing, after having told the control officer on the launch that he was going to circle and land parallel to the lights, the captain would tell the control officer of this change of plans.

That ended Gray's testimony, and I was happy to see him step down without hurting our case any more than he did. Undoubtedly he impressed the jury with his and Pan Am's accomplishments, and he confused them with aviation technicalities, but Gair's masterful cross-examination had added some important points to our case, especially the admission that a dive of even 25 degrees would have been "intolerable" to those aboard the plane.

Junkerman's next witness was Patrick Reynolds, a Pan Am navigation instructor who had been a merchant marine officer and surface navigator before joining the airline in 1941. He was a pedantic type who managed to confuse everyone in the courtroom with his explanations of various shadings of twilight, such as civil twilight and astronomical twilight. Junkerman brought out that at 6:47 p.m., when the plane crashed, Lisbon was still in the state of civil twilight, which did not end until 6:49 p.m. Civil twilight was succeeded by nautical twilight, which did not end until 7:19 p.m. He hoped to use this testimony to convince the jurors that Sullivan was free to approach the lights at right angles because he did not need to make a night landing during "twilight."

I had taken courses in celestial navigation, and had absorbed enough to recall that the various shadings of twilight related to the angle of the sun below the horizon. Trying to determine the lighting conditions at Lisbon at 6:47 p.m. on February 22, 1943, from these technical tabulations would be akin to a meteorologist giving the current weather conditions without looking out the window. I scribbled a note on this to Harry Gair, who then demolished the twilight/night ploy with a single question, which Reynolds answered honestly:

> Q. You are not saying to this jury that at 6:47 p.m., which is the precise moment of this accident, that it was light enough for the captain of that plane to really see objects below him on the water? A. Not in any sense.

The rest of Pan Am's first day of testimony was taken up by Albert Anderson, Pan Am's Cabo Ruivo airport manager at the time of the crash, who was now an engineer with General Electric in Schenectady, New York. In his 1943 CAB deposition, he had testified that he watched the Yankee Clipper intermittently from his office window, but was unable to determine its attitude (nose up or down) "because of the darkness." Now, in response to Bill Junkerman's questioning, he said that he saw the plane at the customary altitude—about 600 feet—abreast of Cabo Ruivo, then looked away briefly in his office, and then looked back and saw the plane in an abnormally sharp descent, with the nose down about 20 degrees until it crashed into the river. Gair and Junkerman went back and forth with this witness for a couple of hours, Gair trying to hold him to his 1943 statement and Junkerman trying to get him to explain how he had reconstructed the scene in his mind and was now certain that the plane was in an abnormal dive and that it was light enough for him to determine the plane's attitude. Anderson was a contentious witness whose testimony went on into the next morning, without producing anything more than a question of whether his recorded 1943 observations were more accurate than his 1953 reconstruction.

During this sparring match, I had little to do since Gair had the whole twilight/darkness picture in focus. I took this opportunity to study the jurors' faces, which is the only way of gauging their reactions since they are not permitted to talk to the lawyers or parties during trial. Some seemed impatient with the argument over which Anderson observation was correct. Others seemed restless or confused. Most were impassive, so I didn't really learn anything by looking at them.

We were into the fifth day of the trial, and with the weekend coming up, it became clear that Bill Junkerman wanted to save Rod Sullivan's testimony for the following Monday. He spent the Friday finishing up Albert Anderson's live testimony, and then read from the CAB depositions of two of Pan Am's Lisbon ground staff and three surviving crew members who were no longer with Pan Am.

The first deposition read by Junkerman was that of George Jordan, assistant airport manager, who had been in the airport office with Anderson. He first saw the plane flying normally at about 500 feet altitude, then looked away. He heard First Officer Rush say on the radiotelephone, "I will make a circle to the east of the lights," and then he glanced out of the window and saw the plane hit the water. There was a lapse of only about 30 seconds between the first officer's "circling" message and the plane hitting the water. After the crash, he saw what he thought were the plane's landing lights, which stayed on for about 10 minutes after the plane crashed. He had not observed the plane's landing lights at any time before the crash.

Junkerman then read from the CAB deposition of Fernando Basto, a Portuguese employee of Pan Am who was on the launch *Pan Air III-A*. He watched the plane as it flew up the river in the normal way, headed north on a straight line at 500 feet altitude, until it arrived abeam of their launch. "The plane then described a quick turn to the left, to the port side, and fell down. It was a very quick turn. I just saw the plane describe a sort of hook to the port side." He could not elaborate on this description because it was too dark to see details. He could not determine whether the nose was up or down when the plane hit. He did not notice anything abnormal about the plane's speed. Everything about the approach "seemed absolutely normal" until the crash. He too thought he saw the plane's landing lights shining for about 5 minutes after the crash. That was how those on the launch determined the location of the crash and went to the rescue.

The first flight crew member whose deposition Junkerman read was Charles Sanders, the radio operator who had been on duty on the flight deck when the plane crashed. He remembered nothing at all from about four minutes before the crash until the following morning when he awoke in the hospital. The last thing he remembered was talking to the navigator as they approached Lisbon, when everything was normal.

Next was the deposition of Robert Rowan, second radio operator who had been off duty at the time of the crash. As they proceeded up the river with the lights on their left, "We started to make the left bank, very slight bank, and I went back and sat down in the safety seat," which was directly in back of the navigator's table on the flight deck. That's the last thing he remembered before something hit him hard and he blacked out. At the time he sat down, he noticed that the altimeter at the navigator's table read 500 feet. He thinks they were descending slowly as the plane turned to the left, but he couldn't say for sure. He noticed nothing unusual at all, except that there were several flashes of lightning close to the plane about a minute before he sat down. The plane hit the water just as he was settling into the seat, before he had a chance to fasten the safety belt.

The last deposition was that of the navigator, Second Officer Merwin Osterhout, who had been standing directly behind Captain Sullivan, his usual place during landing. The last thing he remembered before regaining consciousness in the water was standing behind the captain's seat and looking at the lights of

Lisbon out to their left. The weather was generally good, although there was some distant lightning in the general direction of Lisbon, to the west of the plane.

As we packed our briefcases and left the courthouse for the weekend, we felt that the flight crew and Lisbon ground crew testimony had not hurt us. Most of it was inconclusive because the ground witnesses had not seen much in the darkness and the flight crew had not remembered much. While there were some hints of a rapid descent in what the ground people had seen, there was a complete absence of flight crew testimony to corroborate Sullivan's dive story. In fact, we had planned to read some of these depositions in our rebuttal case if Bill Junkerman had not read them.

Now we had the weekend to prepare for the showdown with Sullivan. I used the Saturday to catch up on other work in the office, and then on Sunday I met Harry Gair and Ben Siff at Harry's apartment to review our notes on Sullivan.

I had seen photographs of Rod Sullivan in aviation books that told the story of the *China Clipper* and Pan Am's conquest of the oceans. I finally saw him in the flesh as he took the stand on Monday March 16th, the sixth day of trial. He was just under six feet tall, and at age 61 he was stockier and his hair was whiter than in his earlier photos. But he still had the macho presence of a Master Ocean Pilot. I wondered whether his husky arms bore tatoos. He was wearing a gray business suit in which he seemed a little uncomfortable. He probably had worn it when he visited the White House a few weeks earlier to attend the inauguration of Dwight Eisenhower as a guest of the new president, his wartime passenger.

Bill Junkerman took Sullivan through his entire flying career, omitting none of the details of his Navy flight service (1919-1929) and his years at the helm of Pan Am flying boats (1929-1943). The jurors were treated to a first-person history of the pioneering survey flights in the Caribbean, the Pacific, and the Atlantic, in which Sullivan had played as important a role as any pilot. Although he did not have the polish of Harold Gray, Sullivan answered in a blunt, forceful manner that conveyed the impression of candor.

Finally Junkerman brought Sullivan to the flight of February 21-22, 1943, his 105th passenger flight across the Atlantic. Everything was normal as they came up the River Tagus at 600 feet altitude. He had decided "to make a circle, which was the usual rule, to make a circle before landing." He could see the landing lights laid out in a string to his left, and he intended to make a complete circle around the lights before landing.

> Q. [by Mr. Junkerman] And which way did you intend to land? A. Parallel with the landing lights.
>
> Q. You intended to land parallel with the landing lights? A. Yes, with the landing lights on my left.
>
> Q. That means you were intending to land which way? A. Well, approximately north.

I watched the jurors' faces as Junkerman asked Sullivan five consecutive questions about his intentions. They were all paying close attention, and seemed to be waiting for the explanation of why he did not in fact land parallel with the lights.

> Q. While you were in this left turn, preparing to circle this landing area, or this lighted area, what happened? A. Truthfully, I would like to know myself. I was making this circle and all of a sudden I felt the nose going down. Well, it didn't annoy me at first because I thought maybe it was somebody walking forward, a weight shift or something else, and I started pulling back on the control. But she was going down so far it was time to get annoyed. I started pulling clear back. Absolutely no feeling in the control. That's when I got annoyed.
>
> Q. You say as you pulled the control back— A. There was no feeling.
>
> Q. When you tell us that you got no feeling, what do you mean? You got no response? A. No response and no weight on it.

Junkerman then had Sullivan explain that normally he had to pull back hard on the control wheel to lift the nose, to use "a lot of muscle," because there is a lot of weight on the controls.

> Q. Did the plane respond? A. No response.
>
> Q. Well, now, at what altitude were you at that time? A. Well, I don't know for sure, but I have an idea around 400 feet.
>
> Q. Well, what did you do after that? A. I just pulled it completely back, and couldn't think of nothing to do—and, as far as that goes, I don't know what I did do. I might have done a lot of things. I don't remember at all. The next thing I knew, I realized that we was going, there was no chance, so I threw the wing down. The ailerons worked, I know.
>
> Q. You say that you threw the wing down? A. Yes, sir.

Q. Which wing? A. The left wing.

Q. You mean that you turned the wheel that controlled the ailerons, you say? A. Yes, sir.

Q. What did that do with respect to the bank of the plane? A. I just threw the wing down.

Q. In other words, did it make the bank steeper? A. Yes, sir.

Q. Why did you turn those ailerons up that way? A. Because I felt that the wing would take the bigger shock and it probably would save some of us.

Q. Did you know that the plane was going to crash? A. Absolutely.

Q. Why did you do that, so that the wing would hit first? A. Well, it would take the shock.

Q. Before or at about the time that you say that the nose started to drop and you pulled back on the control, and you got no response, did you get any warning from any source as to what was happening, or was there any indication to you? A. I had no indication of anything. Everything seemed to be normal up to the time when I had no control to bring the nose back up.

Q. What about the first officer who was sitting alongside of you? A. Well, the first officer, the last I know he grabbed the controls and was trying to help me pull them back, but there was no use pulling them, that's because they was clear back already.

Junkerman then established that Sullivan had not lowered his wing flaps or turned on the plane's landing lights. Normally these were among the last steps taken in the process of landing, and Sullivan testified that if it had been his intention to land instead of circling, then he would have lowered the wing flaps and turned on his landing lights. Sullivan also explained that the lights the Pan Am launch crews had seen shining on the plane after the crash were not the plane's landing lights. He had seen these lights himself when he surfaced after the crash. They were emergency flares that ignited automatically when the plane crashed into the water, and they did their job by guiding the rescue boats to the crash site.

Junkerman then brought out that Sullivan had flown some 14,700 hours as a captain, which added up to nearly 3 million miles. He had been seriously injured in the accident, with fractured neck vertebrae and back injuries. He was now retired from flying and was running his own electrical supplies business in his home town, Sanford, North Carolina. On that note, Junkerman finished his direct examination.

As Harry Gair got up to conduct the most important cross-examination of his career, I felt optimistic. Hearing Sullivan tell his story in his own words, I was more than ever convinced that he had to be lying. But he told the story without hestitation or embellishment. As the press was to report, Captain Sullivan was "solemn and regretful," but appeared genuinely mystified about how he had lost elevator control. At that moment all the jurors had before them as evidence of Sullivan's intention was his own statement that he intended to do the right thing, to make a normal approach and land parallel to the lights. We had the heavy burden of proving that this was not really his intention. Harry Gair had to demolish his story on cross, or our case would be in deep trouble. After all, Master Ocean Pilot Rod Sullivan had come up to New York to face the plaintiffs, the media, and the world, in order to clear his name. He swore that he had intended to land the proper way but the controls had failed him, whereupon his quick thinking had saved the lives of 15 of the 39 people aboard, including Jane Froman, Gypsy Markoff, and John Burn.

I had no idea where Gair would start. With typical ingenuity, he found a way of discrediting part of Pan Am's case without attacking Sullivan directly. He first brought out that Sullivan had been in the courtroom the previous week, when Junkerman tried to prove through Pan Am Navigation Instructor Patrick Reynolds that Sullivan's approach was made during "twilight" and that therefore it was not necessary to execute a night landing parallel to the light string. In response to Gair's questioning, Sullivan said that he had not suggested to Junkerman that Reynolds be called to testify about twilight calculations, and had not ever suggested to anyone that he had enough light to make a daytime-type landing instead of following night landing procedures. That gave Gair the ammunition to charge in his final argument that Junkerman had brought Reynolds in merely to confuse the jurors, when Captain Sullivan himself never suggested that it was light enough to make anything but a night landing.

With Sullivan thus committed to a night landing, Harry quickly moved to pin him down to the dangers of deviating from night landing procedures:

Q. [by Mr. Gair] Had you ever told anybody that you had decided not to follow night landing procedures? A. No, sir.

Q. Had you ever told anybody that you intended to follow daytime procedures? A. No, sir.

Q. Well, did you feel bound as a pilot to land in accordance with the lights? A. Yes, sir.

Q. As they were laid out? A. Yes, sir, I was bound to land in accordance with the lights.

Q. That was a company requirement, wasn't it, at that time? A. That's right.

Q. You couldn't just reject the lights as they were laid out and forget about them and land anywhere you wished, could you? A. I could do that, but that wouldn't be the proper thing to do.

Q. You could do it, but it would be the wrong thing to do? A. That's right.

Gair tried to move on from there to get Sullivan to admit that landing parallel with the light string was necessary for depth perception at night, but Sullivan resisted, saying that the lights marked the area that was clear of obstacles but "as far as depth perception, those landing lights mean very little." Gair reminded Sullivan that he had testified otherwise in his 1943 CAB deposition:

Q. In other words, your answer is that so far as landing parallel with the lights, you haven't found them of any great help to you in depth perception? A. No, sir.

Q. Have you ever said at any time that one of the reasons that you land parallel with the lights is because of the better depth perception that you get that way? A. (No reply.)

Q. Do you recall giving this testimony to the Civil Aeronautics Board in 1943— "Q. Do you regard the lights as a big help so far as your depth perception is concerned? A. Oh, yes. "Q. Is that one of the reasons you feel that it is necessary usually to land with lights? A. That is one and also that is the area you know is patrolled as well." You made those answers, did you not, Captain Sullivan? A. I reckon. You got them there.

Q. Is that answer, that you regard the lights as a big help as far as depth perception is concerned, true or not? A. The lights that we have there are really not any big help in depth perception.

Thus, even when confronted with his 1943 CAB testimony, Sullivan tried to discount the usefulness of the lights for depth perception. Gair again took him through the CAB testimony, and finally he admitted reluctantly, "Well, it is true that they would give you help in depth perception."

Harry then put the finishing touches on the twilight-darkness picture. His opening questions had established that Sullivan had not told anyone that it was light enough to land without the lights, but since this was such a crucial point, Harry tried to confirm that attempting a daytime landing would have been dangerous. At first, Sullivan resisted, saying that it wasn't actually dark, and that he could have landed without the lights.

> Q. In other words, you could have landed from east to west without lights? A. Yes, sir.
> Q. Is that what you did? A. I did not.

Gair then went back to Sullivan's 1943 CAB testimony and confronted him with his statements that it was dark at Lisbon, "because it was overcast and already dark," so dark that "you could not see anything on the water, only what had lights on." Then Gair asked:

> Q. You still say it was light enough to make a landing under daytime procedures? A. You could make a landing with daytime procedures. But it wouldn't have been the proper thing to do.
> Q. It would have been a dangerous thing to do, is that right? A. That's right.
> Q. It would, wouldn't it? A. Yes.

The more Sullivan resisted by contradicting his 1943 testimony, the more telling was Gair's nimble footwork in forcing him to admit the truth. Harry had to be careful about confronting Sullivan too often and too abruptly with the 1943 testimony, lest he create sympathy for the fallen pilot. On several occasions when he was confronted with the 1943 Lisbon testimony, Sullivan snapped that he couldn't be expected to remember such "details" after 10 years, and once he said, "I have tried to forget this thing, and 10 years later it doesn't help."

I felt that Gair had eliminated any chance that the jurors would believe that Sullivan could have landed at right angles to the lights intentionally without committing wilful misconduct. Now he moved on to the critical question of Sullivan's dive story. If the jurors believed that story, the rest of our case would go out the window, for our own expert had admitted that in an emergency the captain can use his judgment. Furthermore, if Sullivan lost elevator control and went into an irreversible dive when he was northeast of the light line, there was no way that he could have continued to circle and come in to land parallel to the lights.

Gair began with the 45-degree dive angle which Harold Gray had said would have been intolerable to the passengers and crew. Sullivan now said that he thought 45 degrees was too steep an estimate and that he had probably been mistaken in his 1943 testimony. He said that the 45 degrees had been a "guess," but Harry confronted him with the CAB record showing that Sullivan had carefully measured the 45-degree angle through a glass during a post-accident test flight in a Pan Am B-314 at New York.

Then Gair showed Sullivan a map of Lisbon harbor which he had used during his 1943 CAB testimony to indicate various positions of the plane during the final minutes of flight. Sullivan had marked the letters A,B,C, and D on that map, and had told the CAB that point B, to the east of the first white light, was where he first noticed the nose going down, and point C, about opposite the middle light, was where he first realized that the elevators were not working. Sullivan now claimed he could not remember what he had meant by those marks, nor could he remember his altitude at those points other than to say it was between 400 and 700 feet.

Now came the crucial testimony about the elevators. First Harry brought out that Sullivan had been part of the Pan Am acceptance team that visited the Boeing factory to make certain that the B-314 met the airline's specifications. Sullivan confirmed that he was familiar with the control systems, including those that worked the elevators. To orient the jury, Gair introduced a photo of the B-314 tail section, which he had Sullivan identify. The picture showed that the B-314 had a double tail section, with two sets of rudders and elevators. Harry wanted to establish that Sullivan was claiming he had lost all feeling in both elevators, which would have required the failure of two separate control cables:

Q. You have two elevators? A. Yes, sir.

Q. When you pull back on your yoke, does it operate both of them? A. Yes, sir.

Q. Suppose the control cables to one aren't working for one reason or another, if it has been broken or something happened to it, and the control cables to the other elevator are functioning, will you feel the controls on the one that is functioning? A. You would probably feel some control.

Q. In this particular instance, as you were coming along there, you pulled back your yoke, you said, and you felt no controls in either one of the elevators? A. That's right.

Harry brought out from Sullivan that he had used the elevators to descend from 7,000 feet down to 600 feet as he approached Lisbon about 10 minutes before the accident, and the elevators had worked normally at that time. Then Harry went on to the trim tabs, which are miniature elevators-within-the-elevators that can be set to keep the plane flying level without requiring any movement of the control wheel (yoke) by the pilot. Here the case was getting more technical than Gair was comfortable with, but he felt there were important points to be made about the trim tabs. He had Sullivan identify the trim tabs on the photograph of the B-314 tail section, and then asked:

Q. The trim tab which is on the elevator, this little trim tab, what is that used for? A. To trim the ship. It might be slightly nose-heavy or slightly tail-heavy. You could adjust those with a wheel on the side of the plane so the plane would fly level without any pressure whatsoever on the yoke.
Q. And if the plane is in descent, and you want to have the nose rise, you can do it by means of these trim tabs? A. That's right, sir.

Gair then established that Sullivan had set the elevator trim tab at 15 degrees nose down for the approach to Lisbon, meaning that the plane was a little tail-heavy and needed to have the nose held down in order to maintain level flight without the pilot having to hold the control wheel in a forward position. He asked Sullivan what would have happened if the elevators and the trim tabs had dropped completely off the plane, and Sullivan replied that this would make the plane dive. But he had given the CAB investigators the correct answer in 1943: that this would make the nose rise rather than fall. He resisted giving the correct answer, and Junkerman made several objections as Gair confronted him with his 1943 testimony. After more than 15 minutes of arguments and attempts to sidestep this issue, Gair finally was able to pin him down:

Q. So that we understand it: This ship was held in trim in a nose-down position by the trim tab setting, isn't that right?
A. Yes, sir.
Q. With the ship in trim that way, if your elevator control cables had gone, just parted, broke, anything—would the plane

have gone level, or would it have gone into a long dive, or would it have gone up? A. Up.

Gair followed up by asking whether Sullivan had tried to raise the nose by using the trim tabs. Sullivan had told the CAB investigators in 1943 that two or three turns of the trim tab wheel would normally bring the nose up even if there were no elevator control, and this would have stopped the dive "very quickly." In 1943, he could not remember whether he had tried to stop the dive by using the trim tabs: "If I did not, I should have. That really would have been the first thing I should have done. I don't know whether it was changed or whether it was not. I don't remember doing it." Again at the trial, he could not remember whether he had tried to use the trim tabs. Gair used this as a way of getting into the subject of how the other crew members reacted to the sudden dive that Sullivan had described:

> Q. Did you ask the first officer to work the trim tab? A. No, sir.
> Q. He has a wheel next to him, too, has he not? A. Yes, sir.
> Q. If you thought then that an emergency existed, wouldn't that be the first thing that you would do, use the trim tabs?
> A. It probably would.

Gair also tried to bring out that during the post-accident New York test flight conducted for the CAB investigators, Harold Gray had used the trim tabs to pull another B-314 out of a 45-degree dive very quickly, but Sullivan answered, "That was 10 years ago and I don't even hardly remember the flight." Gair let it rest there without again reminding Sullivan of his 1943 testimony, as he sensed that the jurors were tiring of these confrontations.

The last major gap in Sullivan's story—and to my mind the most compelling evidence that there was no dive—was the lack of any discussion or interaction with the other crew members on the flight deck. This was something that the jurors could understand more readily than the action of the trim tabs. Gair was more in his element as he put together the strands of Sullivan's story on the flight crew's reactions:

> Q. Under the Boeing manual as you remember it, wasn't it the first duty of the captain, where an emergency landing is being made, to notify the crew, "Stand by for an emergency landing"? A. I believe it was, sir.

Q. Well, after the ship had nosed down for a distance and you didn't worry about it, and then it started nosing down and you did worry about it, and you tried to stop it by various means you have told us about, did you mention this emergency to anybody? A. No, sir, I didn't have time to.

Q. Did you have time to grab for the automatic pilot? A. Well, that was one of the first things I checked when I felt the dive.

Q. And then you pulled back very hard on the elevator yoke, on the wheel, on the control wheel, you pulled very hard on that? A. I pulled it all the way back.

Q. While you were doing that, were you talking to anybody? A. No, sir.

Q. Was there anything to stop you from saying, "Emergency landing"? A. There probably wasn't.

Q. Well, did anybody say anything to you about the fact that the plane was going down in this steep descent? A. No, sir.

Q. You weren't alone there on the flight deck, were you? There were other officers there? A. I had the first officer in the seat alongside of me.

Q. But you knew there were other officers there behind you? A. They were behind, yes.

At that point, Gair introduced a photograph of the B-314 flight deck, and had Sullivan mark the positions of the five other crew members who were on the flight deck with him when the plane went down. He indicated that Burn and Osterhaut had been standing behind the pilots' seats, and that the other three were seated 10 to 15 feet behind the pilots' seats. Then Gair went back to the complete absence of any reaction from the other crew members:

Q. In whatever time is available, there are escape hatches to be pointed out and life preservers to get out and shoes to be taken off, things of that kind are involved in the emergency procedures, is that right? A. That's right.

Q. Is it your testimony then that you said nothing and nobody spoke to you about all this? A. It was a matter of a fraction of seconds and I had no time to say nothing to no one.

Q. In addition to the things you have mentioned before as to what you did, you remember that you turned the wing as well as cutting the throttles and pulling the elevator back and checking the automatic pilot, you also turned the wing in order to have it take the brunt of the shock. Do you remember that? A. Yes, sir.

Q. You say all this took a fraction of time. Was this a sudden dive? A. It was, the last part, yes.

Q. Did any of the officers who were standing behind you there on the deck, did anybody fall over on you by virtue of this steep descent? A. Not as I know of. I had my hands full without watching the rest of them.

Q. Nobody fell on you, nobody was pitched over your head, is that right? A. That's right.

Sullivan had been on the stand all day, and now it was drawing to a close. Gair had no more questions. Junkerman asked only one on re-direct:

Q. Were you rendered unconscious at the time of the accident? A. Yes, sir.

Sullivan was excused, and Bill Junkerman announced that Pan Am rested its case. Justice Steuer adjourned court until the next morning.

Ben Siff and I were jubilant. We congratulated Gair on a masterful cross-examination. He had gone just far enough to discredit Sullivan without taking the risk of trying to publicly destroy an aviation legend.

We had a short rebuttal case to put on the next day, and then would come the final arguments, called summations in New York. We also had to prepare to defend against another motion by Junkerman to take the case away from the jury and dismiss it, and we had to submit written statements that we wanted the judge to include in his instructions to the jury, known as "requests to charge". Ben Siff and I went back to the Gair office to complete work on the requests to charge, while Harry Gair worked alone at home on his summation.

CHAPTER 9

The Verdict

Tuesday, March 17th, the seventh day of the trial, was a beautiful spring day in New York. That morning I went to the East 93rd Street townhouse where Mr. and Mrs. John Burn lived, to review the questions that John would be asked in court. Jane looked beautiful as she hopped around the living room in pursuit of her pet dachsund.

John Burn took the stand as the last witness. Since he had blacked out at the time of the crash, there was little he could add, but Harry Gair felt we had to call him to make sure the jurors did not feel we were holding anything back. He was also the only surviving pilot of the four on board who could rebut Sullivan's dive story. He had been standing about two feet behind the co-pilot's seat. Gair had him describe the positions of the crew members on the flight deck, and then asked:

> Q. What did you observe about the course of the plane and the way it was flying up to the time you last observed it? A. I continued to observe the approach, looking at the surface below me, and the last thing I recall, sometime shortly before the accident occurred I had been looking around the cockpit making various observations, and for some reason I turned away, looking off to my right—I don't know whether someone else spoke to me or I was looking around to see what someone was doing, but I turned back and was looking around, and during this time I heard a crash, and that was the last thing I recalled until I came to in the water.
>
> Q. Up to the time that happened, up to the time that you turned around to talk to some person, had you observed anything abnormal about the movement of the plane in any way? A. No.
>
> Q. Had you felt any dive or forward motion of the plane? A. No, I didn't feel any dive. We were continuing along, of course, but I didn't feel a dive.

Q. Was your position as you were standing there in any wise changed forcibly by any movement that you observed of the plane? A. No.

Q. Or did you observe any such movement or change on the part of anybody standing near you? A. No.

On cross-examination, Bill Junkerman brought out that Burn had told the CAB that the crash occurred within "a very few seconds" after he had observed the altimeter reading of 450 feet, rather than "perhaps a minute" as he had testified during Gair's direct examination.

John Burn was excused, and Gair then read to the jury our last bit of evidence: admissions by Pan Am that the chief inspector of their Atlantic Division and two of his assistants had examined the wreckage of the *Yankee Clipper* at Lisbon after the crash. This was all the discovery we had been permitted to conduct on this subject, because of the previous court orders barring our access to Pan Am's internal crash board report. Little as they contained, Harry wanted these admissions before the jury so that he could point out in summation that Pan Am had access to the wreckage but did not call any witnesses who might have corroborated Sullivan's dive story by testifying to the condition of the elevator control systems after the crash.

That completed the short rebuttal case, and Gair rested again for the plaintiffs. Bill Junkerman also rested again, and then renewed his motion to dismiss the case without submitting it to the jury. Again he argued that the plaintiffs had failed to produce any evidence of a conscious intention to violate safe procedures, now buttressing his argument with Sullivan's own testimony that he intended to land properly. Justice Steuer did not permit extended argument of the motion. He ruled, almost inaudibly, "Decision is reserved." That meant that he was exercising his prerogative to rule on the motion after the jury rendered its verdict. This is often done by trial judges who want to encourage the parties to settle the case at that point without running the risks of a jury verdict. However, the judge said nothing about settlement, nor did Bill Junkerman, and so we knew the case was going all the way.

Reserving decision on the motion to dismiss is also favored by the appellate courts in cases where the judge has doubts about whether the plaintiff made out a *prima facie* case for jury decision. If the judge submits the case to the jury and they find for the plaintiff, the judge can then set aside the jury's verdict and dismiss, but the plaintiff can appeal the dismissal. If the appellate court finds there was an issue for decision by the jury, it will then reinstate the jury's verdict. If, on the other hand, the judge dismisses the case without submitting it to the jury, and the appellate court finds that he was wrong in doing so, the entire case must be sent back for trial before a new jury.

Harry Gair did not seemed disturbed by Justice Steuer's reserved decision. I would have preferred a denial, but it seemed a small point as we moved on to summations. In New York, the defendant's lawyer sums up first, and the plaintiff's lawyer has the last word. In many other states, the plaintiff's lawyer speaks first, followed by the defendant's lawyer, and then the plaintiff's lawyer may reply to anything said by the defendant's lawyer. Just to confuse you further, "summing up" in England refers to the judge's instructions to the jury rather than to final arguments of the lawyers. In our case, Bill Junkerman would sum up first for Pan Am; Harry Gair would sum up for Jane Froman and Gypsy Markoff; Don Ross's lawyer would follow with his summation; and then Justice Steuer would charge (instruct) the jurors just before they began their deliberations.

Junkerman summed up in his calm, authoritative style. He stressed the burden of proof that faced the plaintiffs: They had to provide evidence that the crash was caused by wilful misconduct, meaning an intentional act, and this evidence could not consist of speculation or conjecture. Bearing in mind that the accident had occurred 10 years ago under wartime conditions in a foreign country, and that even those who had witnessed the accident could not agree on what had happened, the jurors might well conclude that they did not have enough evidence before them to determine whether the crash was the result of an intentional act. In that case, they would have to decide in favor of Pan Am. Even if they found that Captain Sullivan had been negligent, they would have to find for Pan Am. Only if the crash was caused by a deliberate act could they find for the plaintiffs.

Junkerman reviewed all the evidence that tended to support Sullivan's dive story. Reiterating Harold Gray's detailed testimony on the glorious history of Pan Am, he emphasized Sullivan's outstanding record as a pioneer of ocean flying and the world's most experienced transatlantic captain. He said again that the only evidence of Sullivan's intentions was the captain's own testimony, under oath, that he intended to land parallel to the light string but was prevented from doing so by a sudden emergency that deprived him of elevator control. All of the Pan Am employees on the launch and at Cabo Ruivo airport who had spoken to the *Yankee Clipper* by radiotelephone verified that a landing parallel to the lights was intended. Junkerman stressed

Sullivan's testimony that he had not lowered his wing flaps or turned on the plane's landing lights, two steps that were required before he could attempt a landing. And he read excerpts from the trial testimony of those witnesses who had said that the plane "fell" or that they had seen the plane flying normally, when "suddenly" they saw it hit the water. Finally he paid gallant tribute to Jane and Gypsy, but said that the jurors were bound to decide the case according to the law, which required them to find for Pan Am because there was no evidence of wilful misconduct.

Harry Gair began in his straightforward manner—no fireworks, no flights of oratory, just the facts laid out clearly in a compellingly logical explanation that illuminated the dark scenario of the wartime crash into the black waters of the River Tagus. He reviewed the evidence that you have read in the preceding three chapters, explaining how each piece fit into the puzzle. He asked the jurors to think about why Junkerman had brought up false issues, such as the Portuguese wartime regulations, which Sullivan admitted had nothing to do with the accident; the almost comical attempt to prove through Pan Am's celestial navigation instructor from New York that it had been light enough to make a daytime landing in Lisbon that night, when Sullivan himself admitted that the darkness made this unacceptably dangerous; and Sullivan's own attempt to dismiss the value of the landing light string as an aid to depth perception, when he had told the CAB in 1943 that the lights were "a big help on depth perception." Why did Pan Am put up all these smokescreens, if not to keep the jurors from learning the truth for themselves?

Why did Sullivan try to change his story about the 45-degree dive, when he had carefully measured that angle through a glass on a test flight conducted at the request of the CAB after the accident? Because every witness who was asked about the 45-degree dive, including Captain Harold Gray, testified that such a steep dive would have been intolerable to the passengers and that the crew members who were standing on the flight deck would have been thrown off their feet. The jurors had heard the testimony of six crew members other than Sullivan, and three passengers, and not one had seen or felt the slightest indication of any abnormal descent or dive. And not a word about any dive or emergency was spoken on the flight deck, as Sullivan admitted, even though he had time to check the automatic pilot, pull his elevators all the way back, take readings of his altimeter and airspeed indicator, cut the throttles, and put the left wing down. Gair emphasized the live testimony of Flight Engineer Manning, still employed by Pan Am, the only surviving crew member whose job it had been to work hand-in-hand with Sullivan throughout the landing. Gair used the vaunted training and teamwork that had made Pan Am the world's leading airline to convince the jurors that Manning would not have stood up to perform his post-landing duties on the throttles unless he had observed that the plane was in a normal landing glide rather than a dive. Manning, Sullivan's teammate for the landing, testified that he had expected the plane to touch down normally on the water just before it crashed.

Harry reminded the jurors that even the Pan Am employees on the ground who had observed the plane's attitude (nose up or down) negated Sullivan's dive story. Bounds, da Silva, Jordan, and Basto all said they saw the plane flying north straight and level at 500 feet altitude all the way up the light string from the first white light to the last (red) light, whereas Sullivan claimed that the nose went down when he was opposite the first white light and that the plane was in a steep dive by the time he reached the middle (third) light. If the elevator controls had failed as Sullivan claimed, surely there would have been some indication of this in the wreckage that was recovered at Lisbon. Yet Pan Am did not bring in any of the three maintenance people who had examined that wreckage, so the jurors were entitled to infer that they found nothing to corroborate Sullivan's claimed loss of elevator control. And Sullivan admitted that even if the elevators and trim tabs fell off the airplane, the nose would go up rather than down.

Harry reviewed the testimony of our expert, Captain Sherrill Shaw, which stood uncontradicted even though Pan Am had many experts at its disposal. Shaw had described the well-known danger of miscalculating altitude during night water landings through loss of depth perception. Sullivan and Gray had agreed with Captain Shaw's testimony, even though they had tried to evade the question at first.

Harry argued that despite Pan Am's attempts to wrap the facts in a shroud of wartime secrecy and false defenses, it was clear from Sullivan's own reluctant admissions and from the testimony of everyone else who had been aboard the plane or had seen it come down, that he was making a left turn while in a normal gentle descent, trying to line up for an east-to-west landing toward the single red light, when he overestimated his altitude due to lack of depth perception, and the left wing tip caught the water, bringing the plane down into the river.

Bill Junkerman had stressed in his summation Sullivan's testimony that he had not turned on the plane's landing lights or lowered the wing flaps, two steps that remained to be taken before a landing could be executed. To counter this, Harry Gair reminded the jury that all five ground witnesses testified that they saw both landing lights on, shining from the wings at the wreckage site. They were trained to observe the plane's landing lights and to distinguish them from the flares that Sullivan says they mistook for the lights. As to the wing flaps, only Sullivan said that they had not been lowered. Normally the flaps would not be lowered until the plane was lined up for landing, and since Sullivan was still turning when the crash occurred, he probably felt that he had time to deal with the flaps after he rolled out of his left turn.

Harry said that the jurors need not speculate on the reasons why Sullivan decided to land to the west. Perhaps he wanted to land directly into the wind, even though the crosswind velocity of 6 knots was considered inconsequential. Perhaps he wanted to take advantage of a last sliver of twilight to land quickly without continuing the circle that would have taken a few more minutes. Perhaps he was a little concerned that the flashes of lightning behind Lisbon might be a sign of an impending thunderstorm that would delay his landing if he went all the way around the circle. Perhaps he just tired of following the regular routine on every landing, and felt an impulse to make a descending turn and land at the red light instead of circling. But none of these things mattered, because neither the plaintiffs nor the jurors were obligated to explain Sullivan's reasoning. The jurors only needed to conclude, from all the evidence, that he did in fact start to make a landing toward the west. This was an intentional act, and Sullivan himself had admitted that it would have been dangerous and improper to try such a landing. Thus, the plaintiffs had satisfied their burden of proving wilful misconduct by presenting the evidence from which the jurors could only conclude that Sullivan had been trying to land to the west.

Harry told the jurors that he did not expect Sullivan to come into court and admit that he had violated Pan Am's own landing procedures. Sullivan himself had said that he was trying to forget this tragic accident, and that process would probably include an effort to convince himself that he been forced into the landing by an emergency. Otherwise, with all the lives that had been smashed by this disaster, it would be very hard for Sullivan to live with himself. But the jurors should be guided by the evidence, especially the testimony of Pan Am's own officers and employees, which clearly demonstrated that Sullivan's dive story could not have happened. The jurors did not need a confession from Sullivan. They could infer, from his actions and from all the testimony of those on the plane and on the ground, that he was in the act of trying to land from east to west when the wing caught and the ship went down.

Harry was careful to point out that he was not accusing Sullivan of intentionally injuring the passengers. "That is not what wilful misconduct means," he said. "We have no such burden. We do say, and all the evidence says, that Captain Sullivan *intentionally* tried to make a daytime landing at night, in the course of which he misjudged his altitude and made a descending turn too close to the water—so close that his left wing tip hit the water and the plane fell from there."

Harry spent a lot of time on the ordeals that Jane and Gypsy had endured, and the difficult job of measuring their losses in dollars. No previous case had involved such large medical expenses and lost earnings. Tort lawyers got nervous when asking juries for as much as $100,000, and it was considered especially dangerous to try two serious damage cases together, because of the large overall sums the jurors would have to award. Harry handled the question of damages very carefully. He explained that the question of lost earnings focused on future earning *power*, not on a comparison of the absolute amounts earned in past years compared to what Jane and Gypsy were earning at the time of the trial. Their earnings in 1952 were much higher than they had been in 1942 because of inflation, but they still faced large future losses because the lingering effects of their injuries prevented them from filling all the dates available to them.

Harry told the jurors that the amounts involved in this case were so large that he would have to trust their judgment to calculate them. He pointed out that Jane Froman's medical expenses and loss of earning power added up to more than a million dollars at the time of the trial, without even considering her pain and future disability. That was probably the first time in history that a tort lawyer had mentioned a seven-figure damage award to a jury.

The summations took most of the day. Justice Steuer announced that he would instruct the jurors the next morning, and recessed court for the day. The newspapers reported the highlights of both summations, most of them devoting more space to what Harry Gair had said about Sullivan's intentions and the devastating financial impact of the crash on Jane and Gypsy.

The courtroom was packed the next morning, as it had been throughout the eight days of trial. Justice Steuer, quiet and seemingly detached from the courtroom conflict throughout most of the trial, now took over. The jurors, who had received practically no guidance up to this point, listened intently as he spoke to them.

> Members of the jury, it has come to my attention that some of you are sitting as jurors for the first time. Under those circumstances, for the benefit of those and to refresh the recollection of the others, it is fitting I should say a few words about the nature of your duties.
>
> There is an unfortunate popular misconception of the role that a jury plays in the determination of a litigation. Many people think that the duty of a jury is to decide the case fairly. If it were so all I would have to say would be, "You've heard the facts. Now do what you think is right." And no further instruction would be required.
>
> What your actual duty is, is to decide what the facts are, to decide what took place, and to apply to those facts the law which I will explain to you.

As the judge spoke, an icy feeling crept up my spine. What he had said was technically correct, but his one-sided approach and the way he spoke made it apparent to me that he wanted to prevent the jurors from finding for the plaintiffs. I looked at Harry Gair sitting next to me, and without a word passing between us, I sensed that he felt the same way.

The judge went on to discuss sympathy. He felt that the jurors understood they were not to decide the case on sympathy. In his experience, few juries knowingly base their findings on sympathy, but sometimes they use something that is similar to sympathy:

> What I have reference to is the desire which exists in all of us—and by "all of us" I mean all of us—to see that any situation has, as far as we can make it, a happy ending, and that has frequently prompted juries as well as others to decide not what they think happened but in order to bring about what they would like to see accomplished. And that is what I have already cautioned you against.

Having spent nearly ten minutes in this tortuous explication of the "no sympathy" admonition that most judges cover in a sentence or two, Justice Steuer moved on to explain the Warsaw Convention and how it impacted on this case. First he gave a long—and erroneous—history of how the convention came to be agreed upon by the 30 nations involved. He made it sound like a a great humanitarian breakthrough instead of the pragmatic step toward insurance coverage that it actually was. When he got down to the $8,300 limitation, he never mentioned the figure:

> The law provides that in the event of an accident of this charac-ter, the passenger can recover what his damages are up to a certain figure without any other consideration except the fact that the accident happened and that he was injured...So that the effect is that the prevailing law now is that if there is an acci-dent a passenger recovers his damage up to a certain point virtually automatically from the happening of the accident. Now, in this case the defendant has conceded that it is reponsi-ble to two of the plaintiffs [Jane Froman and Gypsy Markoff] up to the limit of the statute, and regardless of what the out-come of your deliberations will be, they will be responsible for and will pay to these plaintiffs the limited amount that is provided in the Convention. So that you are concerned solely with the claim which is for the excess of that amount.

He was telling the jurors that this wonderful convention would make Pan Am pay compensation no matter what they decided, and that they need only be concerned with the "excess" over a certain mysterious figure which he never mentioned to them. For all they knew, the convention amount might be enough to compensate Jane or Gypsy fairly without the jurors having to find wilful misconduct. It was clear to me that he witheld the $8,300 figure because he thought the jurors might find it so palpably inadequate as compensation that they would react by finding wilful misconduct.

Harry Gair shook his head in disbelief. But the worst was yet to come as Justice Steuer delivered his explanation of wilful misconduct.

> "Wilful" ordinarily means intentional; that the act that was done was what the person doing it meant to do. But the phrase "wilful misconduct" means something more than that. It means that in addition to doing the act in question, that the actor must have intended the result that came about or must have launched on such a line of conduct with knowledge of what the consequences probably would be and have gone ahead reck-lessly despite his knowledge of those conditions.

"That son of a bitch!" Harry Gair whispered to me. It was the first time I had heard him curse, other than when telling a joke.

"Son of a bitch" was mild compared to what I was thinking about
this judge.

As I listened to Justice Steuer's definition of wilful misconduct, I thought to myself that there never had been and never
would be any performance by an airline pilot that could possibly
fit that definition. As it turned out, I was mistaken. Nearly 30
years later, in 1982, Captain Seiji Katagiri, at the controls of a
Japan Air Lines DC-8 during a landing approach to Tokyo's
Haneda Airport, went berserk and deliberately crashed the plane
into Tokyo Bay in an apparent suicide attempt. Twenty-four people were killed and dozens were seriously injured, but the captain and co-pilot survived. Captain Katagiri had a history of
"psychosomatic illness." During the final minute of the flight, the
co-pilot sensed that Captain Katagiri had deliberately put the
nose down in a steep dive, and there was a struggle between the
two pilots for control of the aircraft. Nothing short of this Tokyo
Bay scenario would constitute "intending the result."

After delivering his "actor must have intended the result"
definition, Justice Steuer went on to give examples of wilful misconduct and ordinary negligence committed by automobile drivers, which only confused the issues because they were not
applicable to an airline pilot who owes his passengers the duty
of the utmost care.

Finally he applied his definition of wilful misconduct to this
case. He said, correctly, that the plaintiffs were claiming that the
act of wilful misconduct was "landing the plane in an east-west
direction when proper conduct would have been to land in a
south-north direction." He then gave the jurors a series of questions that they would have to answer affirmatively in order to
find wilful misconduct:

> Did this accident come about not only because of it, but, first of
> all, in the course of a voluntary descent in that direction?
>
> The plaintiff says it did. The defendant says it did not. The
> defendant says further that at no time during the course of the
> proceedings on the Tagus River on the occasion of this accident
> was the plane ever at a point or was the pilot actually engaged
> in bringing down the plane. It says that the plane fell.
>
> If that is the situation, if they are correct in that, then there
> was no act of wilful misconduct in this case and you cannot
> find it from anything other than the claim which has been
> made by the plaintiff and which I have just stated to you.

Thus, if the jurors believed that the plane "fell," as several of
the ground witnesses had testified, they could not find wilful

misconduct. He ignored the fact that it can be said of any plane crash that eventually the plane fell. The judge never mentioned Sullivan's story of losing elevator control and going into an uncontrollable dive, which was the real defense rather than merely that the plane fell.

The judge then told the jurors for a third time that if they found in favor of Pan Am, the plaintiffs "will still recover the amount provided for in the convention."

In case any of the jurors were not firmly straitjacketed by this time, the judge went on to tell them that even if they found there was "an intentional descent for the purpose of making an immediate landing," they could not find for the plaintiffs unless they found that landing at right angles to the light line was misconduct. Thus the judge put back into the case an issue that had been resolved by Sullivan's admission that landing at right angles would have been dangerous, and that he would thereby lose the aid to depth perception that was provided by landing parallel.

Finally, lest the jurors forget, he managed to work in a fourth reference to the unspecified compensation that the plaintiffs would receive regardless of the verdict:

> For convenience in this case, if you determine the questions that I have explained to you in favor of the defendant, your verdict will be for the defendant, although that does not mean, as I have explained to you, that the defendant will thereby be free of liability. They will still have the obligation of payment of the amount that the treaty provides, as I have explained to you, and that will be taken care of without any further act on your part.

Since I was one of the plaintiffs' lawyers, my feelings are naturally biased, and if I told you that these jury instructions could not have been more unfair to the plaintiffs if Pan Am's lawyer had written them, you might take such a statement with a grain of salt. But the fact is that these instructions went much further toward keeping the jurors from deciding for the plaintiffs than the instructions requested in writing by Bill Junkerman on behalf of Pan Am. His requests to charge did not contain any langugage instructing the jurors to disregard fairness or happy endings, nor did he request a charge that Sullivan must have intended the result, or that the jurors could not find wilful misconduct if the plane "fell." Those were the inventions of Justice Steuer.

When Justice Steuer finished charging the jury, our case was in shambles. Ordinarily, Harry Gair would have asked permission to approach the bench for a sidebar conference, so that he could argue for clarification of the instructions outside the hearing of the jurors. But this haughty judge, unlike the make-believe judges in *L.A. Law* and most real-life judges, did not permit conferences out of the hearing of the jurors. Most trial judges welcome oral and written arguments by the opposing attorneys, because this helps to frame the issues and avoid reversible legal errors. This applies particularly to the judge's jury instructions which are so vital to a fair trial and are so often the basis for reversals by the appellate courts. Many trial judges will hold conferences in their chambers before summations, allowing the opposing lawyers to argue for their requested charges, and informing them as to what the instructions will say. But a few judges consider themselves so intellectually superior to the lawyers appearing before them, particularly in accident cases, that they decide all legal questions imperiously without deigning to hear any argument. Justice Steuer fell into this category, and so none of the lawyers knew what he was going to charge before they delivered their summations.

Justice Steuer's aloofness also meant that if Harry Gair were to attempt to repair any of the damage done by these instructions, he would have to take the judge on directly, as the jurors watched and listened. There was a great risk that his attempts at repair would only emphasize the bad parts of the charge, or perhaps make them come out even worse than they had sounded the first time. But the charge was so one-sided and full of prejudicial errors that Gair felt he had no choice. As soon as the judge finished his charge, Harry stood up and addressed the bench:

> Mr. Gair: Since your Honor has adverted to the matter at one point in your charge, I ask your Honor to charge the jury that they are not to be guided in any way by what they may believe may be your opinion. As a matter of law, you have no opinion on the issues in this case.
>
> The Court: I believe I so stated. But if I didn't, that is my charge.
>
> Mr. Gair: I have some requests to charge that I handed up.
>
> The Court: As regards all of those, I have read them and except in so far as they were charged—it won't be necessary for you to read them. If there is anything that you feel I may have omitted you can call my attention to it.

Mr. Gair: Shall I do it now?

The Court: Now.

Mr. Gair: First, I would like the record to show an exception to so much of your Honor's charge as stated that the pilot in control of the "Yankee Clipper" must have intended the result. I don't know whether your honor intended to mean that. And I ask your Honor to charge that in order to prove wilful misconduct, plaintiffs do not have to prove that Sullivan intended to crash the plane or intended to injure or harm the passengers.

The Court: I didn't say that.

Mr. Gair: I know you didn't, but it may be misconstrued and that's why I am asking you for a clarification of "intended the result." I ask your Honor to charge that by "intended the result" you did not mean the result of crashing the plane or injuring the passengers.

The Court: I can't remember the exact words that I used, but I am confident that they accurately expressed my views. I am not going to restate them.

Justice Steuer had charged the jury without any written notes. He could have asked the court stenographer to read the charge back to him, but instead he simply refused to listen to any more argument or to consider clarifying the instructions which he had now further confused by declining to apply "intended the result" to the facts of the case before him.

Harry Gair asked that our other requested charges be given, but Justice Steuer insisted that he had covered the entire subject fully and fairly. Our requested charges included the New York definition of wilful misconduct as applied to this case: "If the jury find that Sullivan intentionally performed an act with the knowledge that the performance of that act created a peril of accident or injury, or that he intentionally performed an act which implied a reckless disregard of the probable consequences of the performance of that act, or that he intentionally omitted to perform a manifest duty, then the jury may find that Sullivan was guilty of wilful misconduct." We also requested that the judge apply the definition of wilful misconduct to the facts of this case, in order to supplement his inappropriate automobile examples: "If the jury find that the crash occurred during the course of a maneuver that was intended by Sullivan as a landing maneuver, and that the manner of performing the landing maneuver was in violation of ground control directions or standard landing techniques, and that Sullivan intended that manner of landing with the knowledge that a landing so performed created a danger of accident and injury, then the jury may find wilful misconduct on his part." Finally, we asked the judge to make it clear that Sullivan's intentions could be inferred from the regulations and from all the evidence before the jury, and that we did not have to produce an admission of wilful misconduct by Sullivan. All these requests were refused.

Despite all these setbacks, I still felt we had a good chance of winning. There were lots of cases in which judges were against the plaintiffs and attempted to "charge them out of court," only to have the jurors disregard the offensive instructions and find for the plaintiffs anyway.

Court stenographers are required to be precise in recording the times of jury deliberations, to preserve an accurate record in case one side or the other claims they were out for too short or too long a time to reach a reasoned verdict. Our jury retired from the courtroom to their private jury room at 11:05 a.m.

They returned to the courtroom in 15 minutes, at 11:20 a.m., and requested two exhibits. They were the radio log sheets of Pan Am's launch and airport stations, which summarized the radio contacts between the plane and those on the ground. They both showed that Sullivan had been instructed to land to the north parallel with the lights, and that he had acknowleged and agreed. The jurors also asked to have the testimony of George Spiegelberg read to them, which the court stenographer did. Spiegelberg, the Army major and former dirigible pilot, had testified to the lack of any dive or other abnormal descent. The jurors then returned to the jury room at 11:35 a.m. to continue their deliberations.

At that point, we couldn't decide whether the jurors' questions were a good or bad omen. Overall the log sheets and the Spiegelberg testimony were good for us, but there was no way of knowing how many jurors wanted to review this evidence. There could be a lone holdout who was trying to convince the other jurors to vote for the plaintiffs, or perhaps a large group favored the plaintiffs and was seeking to convince a few holdouts. A verdict in a New York civil case then required at least ten of the twelve jurors to agree, so the final vote could be 10-2, 11-1, or 12-0.

The next couple of hours seemed like an eternity, as they always do when a jury is out. The record of the trial concludes with these entries:

(The jury returned to the courtroom at 2:45 p.m.)
The Clerk: Members of the jury, have you agreed upon a verdict?
The Foreman: Yes.

The Clerk: How do you find?

The Foreman: Your Honor, the jury finds in favor of the defendant.

The Clerk: How do you stand on that verdict?

The Foreman: Eleven-to-one.

It was not difficult to determine who had held out for the plaintiffs. One of the women jurors in the back row dabbed at her eyes with a handkerchief as she returned to the courtroom, and after the verdict was rendered, she burst out sobbing. She was joined by Jane Froman and Gypsy Markoff. It was probably only shock and anger that held back my tears.

Justice Steuer had the last word. He thanked the jurors for their service, and went on to confirm what had been obvious to anyone who had heard his charge:

> The Court (to the jury): You had to do something which is essentially unpopular. I haven't the slightest doubt that your decision is absolutely correct upon the facts of this case and that if it had been a contrary one, that the duty would have devolved upon me to make a change. In that event I would confidently have expected to have been the recipient of countless letters from every neurotic who has followed the case and whose particular form of neurosis involves letter writing. It may be that if your names or addresses are discovered, you will be similarly honored. If so, don't take it to heart.

So the judge had been concerned that if he had dismissed the case without letting it go to the jury, the great unwashed who dared to follow the case would have written him some nasty letters. And if the jurors had defied his bizarre instructions and brought in a verdict for the plaintiffs, "duty" would have required him to set it aside and dismiss the case at that point, having reserved decision on the defendant's motion to dismiss at the close of evidence.

Formally, the verdicts were entered as $9,050 for Jane Froman ($8,300 plus $750 for lost baggage) and $9,580 ($8,300 plus $1,280 baggage) for Gypsy Markoff, whose accordions had been lost with her baggage. And for Donald Ross: zero.

Harry Gair and I tried to comfort Jane and Gypsy, but after the ten years of horror they had been through, what could we tell them? All I could say was that the appellate courts would never sustain Steuer's charge to the jury, and that they would give us a new trial before a different judge. Jane and Gypsy both said that they felt badly for us and all the work we had done on the case, for which we would get nothing. We didn't care a damn about the work. We only cared about losing the American Dream case.

As I walked back to my office from the courthouse, I tried to focus my thoughts on how unfair Justice Steuer's charge had been and how we could overturn it on appeal. I started working on the appellate brief that very afternoon, even though the main responsibility for the appeal would be in the hands of Ben Siff, Harry Gair's brilliant law man. Meanwhile I avoided reading the newspapers and listening to radio and television that night and the next morning because the crash of the Froman-Markoff case was headline news throughout the country.

We had the right to appeal to the Appellate Division of the Supreme Court for the First Department, which covers Manhattan and Bronx counties. There, a panel of five judges would hear the appeal. Their decision would be the final one, unless permission was given by the Court of Appeals, the state's highest court, to appeal to them.

Although our main hope for a new trial was the unfairness of Justice Steuer's jury charge, we decided to include an argument that the jury's verdict was against the overwhelming weight of the evidence. We did not expect to win on that ground, because legally the jurors could choose to believe Sullivan even if, as happened in this case, there were 14 other witnesses whose testimony was contrary to his. Strategically, we thought it was important to let the Appellate Division know that this was a very strong case of wilful misconduct, so that they would search the jury charge carefully for errors that might have caused the jurors to decide the case improperly.

In our appellate brief, we zeroed in on Justice Steuer's charge that wilful misconduct required proof that Sullivan must have intended the result. We cited the New York cases which defined wilful misconduct, none of which mentioned such a requirement of intending the result. All they required was that the actor must have intended the *act* (landing at right angles to the lights in violation of the night landing procedures) which brought about the result (the crash). We pointed out that proving wilful misconduct is difficult even with a fair charge, for the word "wilful" has criminal connotations that would make any juror hesitant to apply it to a civil case. This made it doubly important for the trial judge to clearly define wilful misconduct, without ambiguity or confusing appendages.

We argued that Justice Steuer's erroneous insertion of the intended-the-result requirement was compounded by his refusal to correct it when Harry Gair requested clarification. New York law requires that an erroneous instruction be clearly withdrawn and corrected, which Justice Steuer obviously did not do. If anything, his refusal to withdraw it in the face of Gair's objection, and his denial of our requested charge that the jurors could find wilful misconduct without proof that Sullivan intended to crash, intensified the prejudicial effects on the jurors.

We pointed out that Justice Steuer's charge had instructed the jury to decide an issue that was not contested: the improper and dangerous nature of landing at right angles to the lights at night. All the witnesses, including Harold Gray and Rod Sullivan, the Master Ocean Pilots themselves, had admitted the necessity of landing parallel with the lights to maintain depth perception. We cited New York appellate decisions that had granted new trials where the judge had erroneously required the jurors to decide an important issue that was not contested.

We also attacked Justice Steuer's misunderstanding of the Constant Track regulation, which caused him to erroneously remove this issue from the jury by stating that Sullivan was free to make as many turns as he desired below 500 feet, provided he went back up to 500 feet and then made no further turns below 500 feet before landing. We cited the Civil Air Regulations, which prohibited flight below 500 feet except during landing and take-off. We had requested a charge that any turn below 500 feet (other than turns made during an emergency) would violate the Constant Track regulation, but there was no mention of the Constant Track regulation in the charge, even though both Gray and Sullivan had admitted that it prohibited any turns below 500 feet.

We argued that Justice Steuer's four references to an unspecified amount of money the plaintiffs would be awarded under the Warsaw Convention were highly prejudicial, and were contrary to many New York decisions that prohibited mention of money (such as workers' compensation and insurance benefits) that litigants would receive beyond the sums to be awarded by the jurors.

Finally, we attacked Justice Steuer's long speech in which he charged that the jurors should not think about fairness or a happy ending. Harry Gair had never asked the jurors to decide the case on the basis of sympathy or a happy ending, but only on the evidence before them. Since the sympathy issue was never raised during the trial, we argued that it was improper for the judge to do anything more than give the standard admonition that the case was to be decided on the evidence rather than on the jurors' sympathies. As we argued in the brief, "The result of this comment was not to evenly balance the scales of justice between both litigants nor to call for a fair and just verdict based upon the evidence and the law, but rather to stamp happy endings as not justified in the realities of life, thus seeming to indicate that the Court was of the opinion that a happy ending in this case, meaning a verdict for the plaintiffs, would be unrealistic and contrary to law and justice."

When the day of the appellate hearing arrived, it became clear within a few minutes that the Appellate Division justices did not wish to hear argument. They had made up their minds that even if there were mistakes in Justice Steuer's jury charge, the plaintiffs could not possibly win a wilful misconduct verdict against Pan Am. Under the doctrine of "harmless error," they did not have to grant a new trial if they concluded that correcting the erroneous charges would not affect the eventual outcome of the case. Several of the judges indicated that they thought the treaty was designed to limit all claims to $8,300, and that they could not envision any scenario under which the limit could be broken. One of the more liberal judges took Bill Junkerman to task, stating that the Warsaw Convention had outlived its function of providing a basis for insurance coverage during the infancy of commercial aviation. The judge asked Bill to convince his clients that the $8,300 limitation was unfair and should be removed so that passengers on international flights would be able to seek compensation on the same basis as domestic passengers: by proving negligence, rather than shouldering the impossible task of proving wilful misconduct. Junkerman, aware that this meant he would win the appeal, graciously agreed that he would pass the message along to his clients.

During the trial, I felt that we were winning until Justice Steuer charged the jury on the eighth day. But our appeal never got off the ground, and it was no surprise that a few weeks later, the Appellate Division issued a terse order affirming the verdicts for the limited Warsaw damages. Although the Appellate Division panels usually write opinions explaining their reasons, they did not bother to do so in this case. Despite the fame of our highly admired clients, and the presence of the state's leading tort lawyer, Harry Gair, as well as the premier appellate lawyer, Ben Siff, our case was flicked aside without a word being written, as though it were a jailhouse appeal by a convicted criminal who did not have a lawyer. I realized then that even the biggest and best tort lawyers had no real clout against institutions like Pan Am. Despite our pretensions, we were nothing more than

Frank Capra's little pushed-around guys, and we didn't have Capra to write in a happy ending. We were certainly not Equalizers, since we could not prevent the scales of justice from crashing down on the side of Pan Am and the business establishment.

Since the Appellate Division unanimously affirmed the result in the trial court, there was no basis for taking the case to the state's highest court, the Court of Appeals in Albany. The case ended in 1954 with payment of the amounts awarded by the jury: $9,050 to Jane and $9,580 to Gypsy.

The Froman-Markoff case against Pan Am, in the hands of *L.A. Law's* Victor Sifuentes, Ann Kelsey, or Grace Van Owen, or any one of thousands of today's real-life Equalizers, would be settled out of court for $10 million or more. Pan Am would not dare to go to trial in such a case in the 1990s, even with the Warsaw Convention still in place. What happened to change this picture in the second half of the Twentieth Century? We'll discuss that in the following chapters.

Since you were patient enough to sit through the long story of the *Yankee Clipper* crash and its legal aftermath, you might want to know what became of the principal characters.

Starting from the front of the courtroom, *Justice Aron Steuer* remained in the trial court until 1961, when he was elevated to the Appellate Division. That post was better suited to his intellectual temperament, since he needed to spend no more than an hour hearing argument in each case, as one of five judges on an appellate panel. His written opinions were noted for their scholarship and acerbity. I was to encounter him again in the appellate court, most notably in the ultimate David-v-Goliath attack on the establishment, when I represented Ralph Nader against General Motors (a case we'll be discussing in the next chapter). When Justice Steuer reached the mandatory retirement age of 75 in 1974, his associates on the Appellate Division created for him the honorary non-salaried post of Judicial Administrative Officer, which he held until his death in 1985 at the age of 87.

Bill Junkerman put in another two decades of highly successful airline defense work before retiring in 1980. I was to lock horns with him again in several cases, including the litigation arising out of the 1976 Entebbe hijacking, highlights of which I will touch on in the coming chapters.

Harry Gair bounced back from the Froman loss and went on to his greatest triumphs during the next 20 years. He never lost another jury trial. I was privileged to work with him on all of his aviation cases until he died in 1975 at the age of 81. He became the true prototype of the Equalizer, and was the personification

of the American Dream, a self-educated and self-made Horatio
Alger success story in himself. He did well by doing good for
half a century, and by the shining example of his own conduct as
a scientific tort lawyer who always performed with integrity,
professionalism, and grace, he lighted the pathway for thousands of other Equalizers.

Captain Rod Sullivan returned to his electrical supply business
in Sanford, North Carolina. He suffered a heart attack and died
at his office desk in 1955, just two years after the trial, at age 63.
Obituaries in the local newspapers reported that his name had
been cleared by the 1953 jury verdict in favor of Pan Am.

Captain Harold Gray served as president of Pan Am from 1963
to 1968, succeeding Juan Trippe as chairman and chief executive
officer. His tenure was curtailed by cancer, which forced him to
retire in 1969. He died in 1971 at the age of 66.

Pan Am retained its world leadership throughout the tenures
of Juan Trippe and Harold Gray, pioneering wide-body jet service with the Boeing 747, but began a gradual descent soon after
Gray's departure. Its dominance had been built on a foundation
that could not be sustained indefinitely: Trippe's world-wide private diplomacy, and the unique ability of the airline, in the style
of its master surveyor, Charles Lindbergh, to span the oceans
safely and economically. Pan Am's success eventually created
competitors who could fly the same aircraft to the same places.
Lacking the domestic routes of their American competitors and
the government subsidies available to many of its foreign competitors, Pan Am's patented success formula finally ran out. Bad
management decisions, bad luck with its acquisition of National
Airlines, and fresh waves of competition brought on by deregulation, sealed the doom of Pan Am. The 1988 bombing of Flight
103 over Lockerbie, Scotland, cost Pan Am dearly in traffic. The
1990-1991 recession and the travel hiatus caused by the Gulf war
took a further toll, forcing Pan Am into bankruptcy in January
1991. Huge losses continued, and finally Pan Am closed its doors
on December 4, 1991. The scene in Stanley Kubrick's film, *2001*,
showing a space ship with the Pan Am logo operating regular
passenger service to the moon, would have to remain in the
realm of science fiction.

Donald Ross reached a new low in morality, even for him, by
attempting to collect a chunk of the $9,050 that Jane Froman
finally received from Pan Am for her injuries. The fact that all
her lawyers had waived their fees and expenses so that Jane
could get the benefit of that miniscule compensation did not
deter Ross from claiming most of it for himself. Nor was he

inhibited by his knowledge that the $9,050 represented less than three percent of her medical bills, which she would have to struggle for many more years to pay. In the only just result of the ten-year Froman litigation, Ross was denied any share of Jane's compensation. Jane was finally rid of him after the 1953 trial. He died in 1971 at the age of 72.

Gypsy Markoff, ever resilient, resumed her career as a concert accordionist. At this writing, nearly 50 years after the *Yankee Clipper* crash, she is still performing professionally.

John Burn, reinstated as a Pan Am captain soon after the trial, remained with the airline until his retirement in 1979. He closed out his career as a Boeing 747 captain, having flown most of Pan Am's major routes throughout the world. His storybook marriage to Jane Froman ended in a 1956 divorce, brought on by the demands of their separate careers and Jane's continuing health problems. They parted with great regret and undiminished mutual respect. John married again and raised four children.

Jane Froman continued performing on television and in nightclubs after the trial, determined to pay every cent of her medical bills, which eventually totalled more than $400,000. She never recovered from the devastating effects of the *Yankee Clipper* crash. By the time of the trial, she had spent 36 months in hospitals, but there was no relief in sight. As she drove herself to continue her career and pay her bills, she developed more ailments, the worst of which were spinal problems that began when she went back to Europe in 1945 to entertain wounded servicemen, and eventually required four major operations. When her marriage to John Burn broke up, she fell into depression again. But each time she fought back, determined to keep performing and to remain an inspiration to the thousands of handicapped people who had adopted her as their idol.

Finally, in 1960, at the age of 53, her medical bills paid and her strength depleted, she retired from show business, left New York, and moved back to her childhood home town of Columbia, Missouri. There she renewed an old college friendship with Rowland Smith, by then editor of the local Columbia newspaper. They were married in June of 1962, and for the first time Jane had a home life that was not encumbered by the demands of her career. Although she was in pain and misery most of the time, Jane enjoyed 18 years of happy marriage. By the time she died in 1980 at the age of 72, it was a release from a tortured existence. Throughout her later years, even though often bed-ridden, she continued her fund-raising and support of other pained people. She was honored by dozens of charitable and civic organizations, and kept in touch with the Fromanettes, the fan club members who had flocked to her when she lived in New York.

Probably her greatest legacy is the children's psychiatric hospital at the Menninger Clinic in Topeka, which her fund-raising and moral support helped to build and sustain.

When Jane sketched her life story at the request of the screenwriters who were working on the script of *With a Song in my Heart*, John Burn wrote this postscript:

> It would seem as though every possible obstacle were interposed between the girl and the thing she sought to attain, as though she were being submitted to a trial, infinite in its severity. She accepted such conditions; further, she imposed the strictest of ethics on herself. She must fight at all times honorably, ask little of others, and at the same time fulfill every obligation in a fuller measure than is asked of those not burdened as she.
>
> I think you may search back through the years, through history and legend, and never find an example of humanity at its best that will stir your heart more profoundly or give you greater pride in mankind.

I consider myself fortunate for having known Jane Froman, however briefly. I have never overcome the feeling of frustration and shame that came with the 1953 verdict which prevented me—and the legal system—from helping her. I can write no adequate words to end her story, and so I must fall back on one of her greatest song hits:

> Walk on through the wind, walk on through the rain
> Tho' your dreams be tossed and blown
> Walk on, walk on, with hope in your heart
> And you'll never walk alone
> You'll never walk alone.

Chapter 10

The Beginnings of Accountability

Jane Froman and Gypsy Markoff were devastated by the jury's verdict for two reasons. They were denied the compensation that they deserved and needed; and they were denied the satisfaction of holding Pan Am and the Master Ocean Pilots publicly responsible for their wrongdoing. Most people injured in accidents want more than mere compensation. They also want and need the final vindication that comes from finding out exactly why they were injured and holding the wrongdoers accountable. But few were able to obtain either compensation or accountability before the tort lawyers truly became Equalizers.

The image of the 1950s tort lawyer was formed by the likes of Irving Lemov (Jane Froman's original tort lawyer) rather than by Harry Gair, simply because there were thousands of Irving Lemovs and only a handful of Harry Gairs. Harry had to be very selective about what cases he took on, lest he expend his limited resources on losing causes, for there were few easy ones in those days. Gair turned down many cases pressed upon him by other lawyers who knew that his name on the file might produce a settlement for an otherwise hopeless cause.

Even Harry Gair suffered from the lowly image of the tort lawyer. He was successful in most of his own cases, but he could not carry all the Irving Lemovs on his back. Lawyers in the establishment firms admired and respected him, and when a relative, friend, or client was injured they would often refer such victims to Harry. But they still looked down their noses at the whole messy business of negligence practice, just as Douglas Brackman flinched when he visited the negligence office of his illegimate half-brother, Errol Farrell. Many establishment lawyers regarded Gair's efforts to build real litigation power into a tort practice as rather quaint.

This was brought home to me when Harry and I were invited to lunch by two partners of an old-line Wall Street law firm whose senior partner had been killed in an airline crash of the early 1950s. The deceased partner had been very prominent in politics, finance, and the law. His partners were pursuing his family's claims to recover damages for his death, and offered to cooperate with Harry Gair and myself, knowing that we represented most of the other families who had lost relatives in the crash. The two partners were gracious hosts at the Lawyers' Club, a posh private enclave atop a Wall Street skyscraper. As they questioned us about our plans for conducting our cases, a note of condescension crept in. It was obvious that they had an unlimited budget, especially when they described their elaborate plans for investigation and trial, for which they were considering Charles Lindbergh and General Jimmy Doolittle as expert witnesses. Harry and I had retained a couple of ex-airline mechanics as our experts, since the case involved an engine failure. As we left the Lawyers' Club after the luncheon, Gair and I agreed that it would be nice to have enough clout to hire the Lindberghs and the Doolittles. As it happened, with the help of our two undistinguished mechanics, we built up a strong case during discovery and were able to settle all of our cases. This helped the Wall Street lawyers, who also settled their case out of court without having to bother either Lindbergh or Doolittle.

Not only were we too weak to command an audience with the Lindberghs or the Doolittles, but in the 1950s we were still held in low esteem by the courts, the legislatures, the media, and the public. While jurors drawn mostly from working class families did not share this negative opinion of us, they did not think we were strong enough to overcome the establishment in the form of powerful defendants like Pan American Airways or aristocratic judges like Aron Steuer. Many jurors felt that we—and they—were far too insignificant to buck that kind of clout.

This weakness of plaintiff's lawyers had a long history. Consider some major twentieth-century disasters and the results achieved by tort lawyers for the victims. Major disasters are bound to attract the strongest plaintiff's lawyers, since the sheer number of victims guarantees that many lawyers will be involved, and the complexity as well as the potential rewards dictate that the leaders of the plaintiff's bar will take a hand. In most major disasters, even those of the early 1900s, public outrage and concern for future safety assured a more thorough public investigation than would accompany the average accident, thus making it easier for the claimants' lawyers to marshall the evidence needed to prove fault. Therefore, in selecting major disasters we are stacking the deck in favor of likely focus on the best results then attainable by plaintiff's lawyers.

The 1903 fire in Chicago's Iroquois Theater killed 602 people, mostly women and children. The theater had opened just a few weeks before, rushed to completion for the Christmas season through bribery of fire department and other public officials. Although advertised as "ABSOLUTELY FIREPROOF," there were no fire alarm boxes, fire extinguishers, or exit signs, nor was any water available to the firehoses. When the curtain brushed against a hot carbon lamp and started to burn, the fire quickly spread to the stage and throughout the theatre. Most of the orchestra patrons were able to escape through the exit doors. But the management, in order to prevent movement from the cheap seats to the better ones, had sealed off the balcony by locking two heavy iron gates—a violation of law, as was the locking of eleven of the theater's exits. The theater was gutted in 15 minutes. Public indignation ran high against the businessmen and public officials responsible for the carnage. But in the end all escaped criminal punishment, and after more than five years of inconclusive litigation, a few dozen of the civil suits were settled for payment of $750 per death. Most families received no compensation at all. So ended the worst theater fire in American history.

The 1904 burning and sinking of the New York excursion boat, the General Slocum, cost the lives of 1,021 passengers. Carrying 1,500 people on a church picnic outing, it caught fire in the East River. The crew members were untrained and had never held a fire drill. They tried to use the fire hose, but it had not been touched for 13 years, and it burst the moment that the water was turned on. The crew abandoned ship, leaving the passengers to fend for themselves. Many donned life preservers and jumped into the water, but most of the preservers were rotten and fell to pieces on impact. Many who jumped were drowned in the river, and hundreds more were trapped aboard and consumed by the flames. Captain William Van Schaick was prosecuted in the New York federal court. He was convicted and sentenced to ten years in prison. The prosecutors were Henry L. Stimson (later to become Secretary of War in the World War II Roosevelt cabinet) and Felix Frankfurter (later a Supreme Court justice). But no such legal clout was available to the bereaved families in their civil suits, and in the end they received no compensation. While a token measure of accountability was achieved by sending the captain to jail, the shipowners who were ultimately responsible for 1,021 deaths were left to go about their business, untouched by the legal system.

The 1911 fire at the Triangle Shirtwaist factory in New York City claimed the lives of 145 employees. Most of them were young women who were trapped in the sweatshop when a fire broke out near quitting time on Saturday afternoon. Since nearly $25 worth of piece goods had previously been stolen by employees, they were required to exit through a single door so they could be searched. Other exit doors were locked, and the building itself did not conform to fire laws in that it had only one staircase that went all the way from the street to the roof. Firefighters reached the building a few minutes after the fire broke out, but there was little they could do since their hoses and ladders could reach no higher than the sixth floor, and the fire had broken out on the eighth floor. Death scenes were viewed from the street by hundreds of horrified spectators, who stood by helplessly as more than 60 employees, trapped by the flames, jumped to certain death on the pavement below.

Issac Harris and Max Blanck, the owners of Triangle Shirtwaist, were indicted for locking the factory doors during working hours. Their lawyer was Max Steuer, father of Justice Aron Steuer. His brilliant defense won an acquittal despite the testimony of many witnesses, including firemen, that the locking of the doors had caused dozens of deaths. Many civil suits were filed, and Max Steuer defended those as well. Despite strong support from the International Ladies Garment Workers Union, newspapers, and civic organizations, and the availability of the evidence from the four-week criminal trial, the plaintiffs' lawyers presented their entire civil case in one day. The trial ended on the second day with the jury unable to agree on a verdict. That was the end of efforts to recover damages from the Triangle Shirtwaist owners. Within two weeks, the claims against the owner of the building were settled for $75 each, despite the clear violations of fire laws in its construction. The *New York World* tried to explain this travesty:

> The claimants have been tired out. Their money and their patience have been exhausted. So far as personal guilt is concerned the men whose methods made everything ready for the tragedy have gone free. So far as financial liability is concerned, the whole affair is in the hands of an insurance company and stricken families are not well equipped to carry on expensive litigations with corporations.

The 1912 mid-Atlantic sinking of the British White Star liner Titanic cost the lives of 1,517 of the 2,207 people aboard. Under maritime law, the liability of the shipowners was limited to the value of the ship *after the accident*, plus the amount paid on that voyage for freight and passenger transportation, which in the case of the *Titanic* came to a total of $97,772 for all of the 1,517 claimant families, an average of $64.45 each. In order to circumvent the limitation and recover full compensation, the claimants would have to prove that the ship was unseaworthy or that negligence of the crew was within the knowledge or "privity" (participation) of the owners. As history buffs and moviegoers know, the iceberg that cut a 300-foot gash in the *Titanic*'s hull did not injure a single passenger. Had there been enough lifeboats, all on board could easily have been saved. The 1,517 people who remained on board as the band played "Nearer My God to Thee" died only because there were not enough lifeboats. This shortage was known to the owners, whose chief executive, J. Bruce Ismay, was aboard for the maiden voyage. He acted as a super-captain, giving the chief engineer orders concerning the speed of the ship without consulting the captain, and ignoring ice warnings in order to stay on schedule for the festivities and press coverage awaiting in New York. He managed to slip into one of the last lifeboats. Despite this hands-on control by Ismay, the courts ruled that whatever negligence caused the deaths was not within the knowledge or privity of the owners, and the $64.45 limitation was upheld.

The 1915 sinking of the SS Eastland in the Chicago River cost between 815 and 1,100 lives. The exact number was never determined because the ship had been grossly overloaded and the owners were able to prevent disclosure of the full extent of the disaster. Again this was a picnic outing. The crammed ship capsized and sank just as it pulled away from the dock. A federal grand jury indicted the owners, the captain and chief engineer, and two government ship inspectors. But with Clarence Darrow defending, the indictments were dismissed when the judge ruled that the government had failed to make out a criminal case. The civil suits brought by the bereaved families were filed in Chicago as early as 1915, but the plaintiffs' lawyers were so weak that they were unable to bring the case to trial until 1933, some 18 years later. The claimants were turned out without a penny of compensation.

You have seen in the preceding chapters that as late as the 1950s, the two plaintiffs (out of 27 passengers killed or injured in the *Yankee Clipper* accident) who took Pan American Airways to trial were unsuccessful despite their representation by the leading plaintiff's tort lawyer of the day.

In addition to these examples of complete lack of accountability in major disaster cases, there were thousands of cases in which the plaintiffs won jury verdicts approaching their actual losses, only to have judges reduce those verdicts arbitrarily because they broke through the judicial barriers erected to block full compensation. An apt example is the case of Ken Strong, a famous athlete of the 1930s.

Strong was a unanimous all-American football selection as a halfback in 1928, his senior year at New York University, in which he set a collegiate record of 2,100 yards gained. Since he was equally talented in baseball and it offered more money than professional football, Strong signed a contract to play for the Detroit Tigers after setting a minor league record of 41 home runs in 1930. But a minor wrist operation in Detroit went awry when the surgeon removed the wrong bone, ending Strong's baseball career because he could no longer grip or throw the ball properly. The negligence was admitted by the surgeon in a letter to Strong. When no settlement was forthcoming, Strong decided to sue the surgeon in Detroit. Despite the admission of culpability, Strong could not find a suitable lawyer from the plaintiff's bar, so he retained Stevens T. Mason, one of Detroit's leading insurance defense lawyers, who always wore a swallowtail coat and striped black trousers in court.

In 1933, after a two-week trial, the Detroit jury awarded Strong $75,000, an unprecedented amount at the time. Mason then faced the task of keeping the judge's scalpel from cutting the award, despite the fact that the jury's verdict was almost exactly the amount that an unchallenged expert witness had calculated as Strong's loss of earnings: average annual future salary of $7,780 for a 15-year major league career, which came to $77,022 even after discounting to present value at 5 percent per year. Mason knew that he faced an uphill battle, so he tried to convince the judge to apply the principles of business contract cases, in which courts rarely disturbed jury verdicts if the amount awarded was supported by evidence. "This case resembles a breach of contract case more than a personal injury case," he argued, "because all the plaintiff is claiming is loss of his ability to perform his contract with the Detroit baseball team." But Mason was unsuccessful, and in the end Ken Strong had to settle for $15,000—two years' pay for a smashed 15-year baseball career. Strong then turned to professional football, where he was able to work around his stiff wrist and eventually became a member of the Pro Football Hall of Fame. But thousands of other plaintiffs who did not have such career alternatives fell into poverty because they were unable to overcome the short-changing of their compensation claims.

American tort practice began in the second half of the nineteenth century, which coincided with the high point of laissez-faire, a philosophy little concerned with social justice. "Survival of the fittest" was the ruling creed, in society as in nature. Those injured in accidents were widely regarded as victims of bad luck who would have to look to their families and to charities for assistance. This general attitude persisted well into the twentieth century, as evidenced by the USO calling on Jane Froman and other prominent entertainers to fly overseas during wartime without giving a thought to providing accident insurance. Nor was any health care insurance available to her privately in 1943.

The negative image of the tort lawyers, which the courts consistently transferred to their clients, arose from rough-and-tumble skirmishes between outlaws on both sides of accident cases. An America preoccupied with industrial expansion was not going to spend much time worrying about accident victims whose claims might delay or inconvenience the march of true progress. In the name of free enterprise, railroads and industry were permitted to deal brutally with injury claims. They had notorious claims departments whose moral standards were below those of Butch Cassidy and the Sundance Kid. Given this background and the weakness of the struggling lawyers who came to represent accident victims, early tort litigation could not help but turn into a perjury contest.

When a serious accident occurred, the defendant's "investigators" would sweep into action, often buying up witnesses, creating their own eyewitnesses where there were none, falsifying records, and sometimes inducing severely injured victims to sign away their rights for a few dollars in cash laid on a hospital bed. It was not necessary for defendants to hire lawyers for this work, since they could get "investigators" and "claims adjusters" at lower rates. For the few cases that came to court, the railroads and other frequently-sued companies could afford to hire the best lawyers (such as Clarence Darrow) to represent them.

This practice bred its own antidote. The early plaintiff's lawyers were faced with the problem of overcoming the handiwork of the claims department if they were to have any chance to settle or win the case. The plaintiffs had no claims department, so the dirty work had to be done by their lawyers. Some plaintiff's lawyers became adept at the game of buying up witnesses and creating evidence.

As tort practice began to develop in urban centers, many of the early cases involved claims of pedestrians injured by streetcars that were operated by street railway companies, most of which had claims departments modeled on those of the intercity and transcontinental railroads. Their investigators would usually get to the witnesses first, finding an ample number who, for a few dollars, would testify to whatever version of the accident would help the company to avoid liability. The most enterprising of the plaintiff's lawyers also knew how to buy the desired testimony, either directly or through their own "investigators." Thus, it was not uncommon for the trial of a street railway accident case to start with the testimony of witnesses who lived on the first, second, third, and fourth floors of an apartment house overlooking the accident scene. The witnesses for the plaintiff (whose case was presented first) would testify that they were looking through their windows at the time of the accident and observed that the motorman was going very fast and was looking off to the side when the streetcar ran over the plaintiff. When the street railway put on its defense, it would produce witnesses who lived on the first, second, third, and fourth floors of the same building, or one across the street with an equally good view of the accident. The defense witnesses would swear that, as they looked through their windows, the motorman was proceeding slowly and was looking straight ahead, but was unable to stop in time because the plaintiff carelessly darted in front of the streetcar at the last moment. An observer of tort trials might well have concluded that most of the residents of apartment houses in New York and other big cities spent their time looking out of their windows waiting for accidents to happen.

That was tort law as practiced by the strongest plaintiff's lawyers—those who had the money and the determination to take on the street railways at their own game. At least they were trying to provide effective legal services for their clients by bringing their cases to trial, and they did it in the one way that offered them any chance to win: by fighting fire with fire. There was, however, an even lower rung to this ladder: the plaintiff's lawyers who took on such cases with no capability of ever bringing them to trial, but in hopes of promoting a small nuisance settlement (often no more than twenty-five or fifty dollars). They would start the lawsuit by typing up a very short standardized form of complaint, and would then attempt to settle the case, often as part of a wholesale batch of claims. If no settlement was forthcoming, they would drop the case, even if it had merit. They settled many serious cases for small amounts and made their profit on volume, quick turnover, and the low overhead that went with their lack of any truly professional services. Many a badly injured plaintiff was sold out by his lawyer in that way.

Aron Steuer, in his 1950 biography of his father, noted that these early tort lawyers were not vicious people, but:

> Put into a profession by the sweat and sacrifice of their families, they lacked both the skill to make a living at the law and the character to abandon it for a livelihood more suitable to their talents.

This type of practice also lent itself to ambulance chasing—the solicitation of clients by lawyers or their paid intermediaries. This happened predominantly in the ghettos and ethnic neighborhoods of big cities, where few residents read and spoke English and even fewer had their own attorneys. It was easy for enterprising bilingual intermediaries to contact accident victims, sign them up to contingent-fee agreements, and feed them to hungry lawyers. Often the more advanced plaintiff's lawyers who hired their own investigators would also use these sleuths to procure cases. This was both illegal and unethical, so that lawyers caught at this game could be suspended or disbarred. Today it is still illegal for lawyers to pay intermediaries to sign up cases, but direct solicitation by lawyers is allowed in some states and advertising for clients is permitted in some form everywhere.

If these vulgarities were not enough to discourage the better lawyers from entering tort practice, there was a final hurdle: the contingent fee. This was at the very heart of the system, since the plaintiffs could hardly ever afford to hire a lawyer on any other basis. Apart from the economic drawbacks of contingent fees to the plaintiff's lawyers in those days when the court system was rigged in favor of defendants, many lawyers shrank from them because they saw themselves as successors to the tradition of the English barrister, which had evolved from the feudal concept of advocates as champions who were acting out of kinship or nobility rather than commercial considerations.

The earliest English and European advocates were not paid at all, and in later years when advocacy became a lifetime vocation, it was considered unprofessional for the payment to be contingent upon the outcome of the case. The Roman emperor Justinian disallowed contingent fees, and in his *Digest* he likened them to the "morals of a pirate." Justinian's condemnation was mild compared to that of the leading nineteenth-century American authority on torts, Thomas M. Cooley, who wrote in 1881 that contingent-fee lawyers were a contemptible lot, debasing the legal profession and creating "a feeling of antagonism between aggregated capital on the one side, and the community in general on the other." Apparently it did not occur to Mr. Cooley, who also served as a law professor and a justice of the Michigan Supreme Court, that the "community in general" would have to suffer almost unlimited injuries at the hands of "aggregated capital" unless contingent fees were permitted.

Even as recently as 1948, when I began practice, most attorneys felt that the lawyers who got paid for their time, win or lose, were the only real pros. Contingent fees have been legally and ethically permissible throughout the United States since the nineteenth century. But those of us who had to rely on a cut of our client's take were looked upon as crapshooters, not good enough to command real lawyers' fees. The tugboat operators who engaged in marine salvage work had a quaint term for their fee arrangements: "No cure, no pay." But professionals like physicians and dentists certainly didn't follow the practice of the tugboat market. And the level of professionalism among tort lawyers in the 1950s *was* quite low, apart from the few Harry Gairs. Most plaintiff's lawyers depended on the natural sympathy of jurors for the plight of an injured person. They did as little investigation, discovery, preparation, paperwork, and legal research as they could get away with.

The small-town lawyers were truly general practitioners in the early tort days, and many took on all types of cases that came their way, including representation of accident victims on contingent fees. Many did a good job for their clients, considering the difficulties of overcoming the investigation tactics of the railroads and insurance companies. Often the small-town general practitioner would have a good rapport with jurors, and sometimes that would help to win an accident case for a plaintiff. At that point, the superior clout of the defendants came into play at a different level. Defense lawyers were often able to get trial or appellate judges to reduce the amount awarded, or to set the verdict aside entirely, on grounds that it violated some provision of law or was contrary to the weight of the evidence. The judges were selected by the establishment, and the great majority of them followed the establishment's laissez-faire philosophy. While this philosophy was usually left unspoken in the courts because it did not square with equal protection of the law and other democratic ideals, as late as 1922 a federal judge wrote in an appellate court decision:

> It should be remembered that of the three fundamental principles which underlie government, and for which government exists—protection of life, liberty, and property—the chief of these is property.

Francis Hutcheson Hare, a leading Alabama plaintiff's tort lawyer who began practice in 1927, wrote of that era in his memoirs:

> When the young lawyer graduated he was met with the proposition that defense counsel had almost a monopoly on prestige. The smartest law graduates went with the big corporate law firms and the plaintiffs were represented by lawyers who relied largely upon the sympathy or prejudice of the jury. The defense lawyer mousetrapped the plaintiff in the pleadings or reversed him on refused written charges, and, if he got a good-sized verdict without other error, the Supreme Court would reduce it as excessive. "The simple truth," [said Supreme Court Justice Felix Frankfurter] "was that the leading lawyers of the United States had been engaged mainly in supporting the claims of corporations, while the people and their interests had been represented generally by men of very meager legal ability."

What, then, happened in the last half of the twentieth century to make it realistic for *L.A. Law* to show McKenzie Brackman doing battle on equal terms with the leading lawyers of the United States? The basic law, that everyone must use reasonable care for the safety of persons who might otherwise be injured, has not changed. While there have been some statutory changes by the legislatures, most of the progress in tort law has been accomplished by the courts, which began to *enforce* the same law that was supposed to be applied to the Triangle Shirtwaist Company in 1911. There were also contingent fees and jury trials in 1911, so that system has not changed. What has changed is the lawyers, who are now enforcers and Equalizers.

We shall go on to learn just how and why the lawyers changed. But now let's examine my statement in the preceding chapter that if the Jane Froman-Gypsy Markoff case arose in the 1990s, it would be settled for $10 million or more without a trial.

First let's dispose of two evolutionary changes outside of the law that would help such plaintiffs today. Airliners are now equipped with flight recorders ("black boxes") and cockpit voice recorders, which are usually recovered from the wreckage of accidents. A flight recorder recovered from the *Yankee Clipper* would have shown the airspeed, angle of descent, power setting, and degree of turning for the entire flight, including the final minutes that led up to the crash. If these readings indicated a descending turn preparing for landing instead of an uncontrolled dive, Rod Sullivan's dive story would have been put in greater doubt. And the cockpit voice recorder probably would have told a different story than the complete silence of the crew that Sullivan testified to.

Also, most jurors today have some experience as airline passengers, since flying is now the major method of public transportation, especially for overseas trips. During the 1940s and 1950s, many people still considered flying to be a risky adventure for passengers, who should expect the possibility of a crash. Although airline pilots are still highly respected, they no longer command the status of demigods, certainly not to the extent of the Master Ocean Pilots. On the day following the *Yankee Clipper* crash, Lorraine Rognan, interviewed at the Lisbon hospital after losing her husband and having her own career smashed by crippling injuries, told the press that she would gladly fly with Rod Sullivan again. We wanted to believe in heroes then.

But I don't believe that these factors, important as they are, would have been sufficient to change the result in the *Yankee Clipper* case, without a much more significant advance: the development of tort lawyers as Equalizers, able to overcome the clout of the business establishment represented by our leading airline and the mystique of the Master Ocean Pilots, Harold Gray and Rod Sullivan.

Today, if Victor Sifuentes were representing Jane Froman and Gypsy Markoff, he would have broad discovery at his command. He could force Pan Am to produce its crash board report and any other documents relating to the crash. He would be able to question all the Pan Am officials, including those who served on the crash board, at pretrial depositions. Indeed, he could force Pan Am to produce the wreckage of the *Yankee Clipper* itself, and he would have the working capital to hire aeronautical engineers to examine the elevator system and testify that it must have been operating normally at the time of the crash. If Pan Am persisted in blaming failure of the elevators, Victor would sue Boeing, the airplane manufacturer. Then he would have Boeing's vast resources working for him, and their engineers would demonstrate to the jury that there could not have been any malfunction of the elevators.

Victor Sifuentes would have all those things going for him, which Harry Gair did not have in 1953. And to top it off, the ticketing charade at LaGuardia Marine Terminal—during which the tickets were flashed in front of Jane and Gypsy for seconds and they were never told of the Warsaw Convention limitation—would not be considered a valid or binding delivery. My firm took care of that in a return bout with Pan Am, again represented by Bill Junkerman. Our 16-year-old client had been a passenger on a Pan Am plane that was attacked by terrorists at Fiumicino Airport in Rome in 1973. She was part of a charter group, and her individual ticket had not been delivered to her before departure from Kennedy airport. After the trial judge held that Pan Am had the burden of proving ticket delivery and had failed to meet that burden, the case went up to New York's highest court, the Court of Appeals, which upheld the trial judge by a vote of seven to zero. Since there had been no proper delivery of a ticket warning the passenger of the Warsaw Convention liability limitation, the limitation would not apply, and Pan Am would be liable for ordinary negligence to the full extent of the damages proven. No showing of wilful misconduct would be required of us. Pan Am then agreed to a settlement that compensated our client (as well as money could do) for the serious burns she suffered during the firebomb attack.

Even if Victor Sifuentes had to prove wilful miscondct, he would have a much easier task than Harry Gair shouldered in 1953. As plaintiff's lawyers became stronger in the 1960s, they were able to convince the courts to follow the established definition of wilful misconduct in Warsaw Convention cases. No other judge gave Aron Steuer's jury charge that the pilot had to intend the result (i.e., the crash) as well as the act. As we shall see, the definition of wilful misconduct became flexible enough to support a jury verdict against Korean Air Lines in the trial arising out of the shooting down of its Flight 007 by a Soviet fighter plane which occurred over the Sea of Japan in 1983.

Whether he tried the case under the wilful misconduct requirement of the Warsaw Convention, or (because of improper ticket delivery) he could get full compensation merely by proving ordinary negligence, Sifuentes would be the odds-on favorite to win a jury verdict in favor of Jane and Gypsy. Based on today's levels of medical costs and ·lost earnings, their damages would be way up in the millions. Probably Jane's damages from lost bookings and the shortening of her career would total over $5 million today. And thanks to decades of uphill fighting by the Equalizers, the trial and appellate courts are much more sensitive to the human tragedies involved in such disasters. The physical and mental pain inflicted on both women, whose lives were never the same after the *Yankee Clipper* went down, would cry out for multi-million dollar compensation today. I'm sure that Bill Junkerman would consider it a job well done if he could settle with Victor Sifuentes for $10 million the two cases in which Pan Am paid a total of less than $20,000 in 1953.

The underlying reason for this dramatic change was not the mere passage of time. It was brought about by the development of the Equalizers into a force that can hold the establishment accountable for its mistakes and transgressions.

We next look at a case that brought the concept of the establishment's accountability to a new level: the executive floor at the Detroit headquarters of General Motors. The case is the classic David/Goliath litigation: *Ralph Nader v. General Motors*, in which I was privileged to represent David in the form of a Lebanese-American consumer advocate who lived in and worked out of a boarding house in Washington, D.C.

Unsafe at Any Speed

In 1964, Ralph Nader, then 30 years old, worked in Washington as a free-lance writer on auto safety. Later in the year, he became an unpaid voluntary adviser to the staff of the Senate Subcommittee on Executive Reorganization which was headed by Abraham Ribicoff, the Democratic Senator from Connecticut. Ribicoff was holding hearings on auto-safety problems, and Nader worked with the subcommittee staff to prepare for those hearings. He supplied the staff with many embarrassing questions that were put to General Motors' executives during 1965.

In 1964-1965, Ralph completed work on his first book, *Unsafe at Any Speed*, which revealed General Motors' Chevrolet Corvair as an example of irresponsible and dangerous auto design. The book blamed auto manfacturers rather than drivers for much of America's annual highway carnage of 50,000 deaths and 5 million injuries. After the book was published in November 1965, Ralph continued his work with the Ribicoff subcommittee. Early in 1966, he began to notice some strange happenings. When he attended auto safety hearings in Iowa, he noticed a man who seemed to be keeping an eye on him. Then he began to get harassing phone calls, more than two dozen over a two-week period. Some were merely designed to annoy him, but others were more threatening, culminating in "*Why don't you go back to*

Connecticut, buddy-boy!" at three-thirty in the morning of the day he was scheduled to testify before the Ribicoff subcommittee about the allegations made in his book.

On the day after that testimony, February 11, 1966, there ensued an historic comedy of errors. At 1:30 p.m., Ralph went to the Dirksen Senate Office Building to record a television interview. He stayed in the ground-floor television studio for about half an hour. As he left the studio, he took the elevator, intending to go down to the basement to eat in the cafeteria, but he pushed the wrong button and the elevator took him upstairs instead. Realizing his mistake, he quickly pressed the down button and took the elevator to the basement. Unknown to Ralph, he was being followed at the time by two private detectives from New York. But his rapid reversal of direction shook off the bloodhounds. Having lost their quarry, they asked a building guard where Nader had gone. The guard became suspicious and called in a Capitol Police lieutenant, who promptly told the private eyes that they were not allowed to follow people in the Senate Office Building and that they had better leave at once. Then the guard saw Ralph leaving the building, and told him that he had been followed by two private detectives.

His suspicions now confirmed, Ralph then learned that investigators had interviewed some of his friends and past associates, under the pretext of checking his qualifications for an important job. He again noticed men following him, and he was accosted in a drug store and a supermarket by attractive young women who asked him to accompany them back to their apartments. Ralph related these facts to journalist friends, some of whom wrote articles seeking to smoke out the people behind this intimidation campaign. On March 6th, the *New York Times* published Ralph's charges that the auto industry was attempting to harass and discredit his book and his testimony before the Ribicoff subcommittee.

Now Senator Ribicoff took a hand, announcing that he was asking the Department of Justice to investigate a possible criminal attempt to intimidate a witness before a Congressional committee. This brought statements from Ford, Chrysler, and American Motors denying any involvement. From General Motors came a "no comment," followed by a late-night press release which admitted they had launched an investigation of Nader. But they claimed it was only "a routine investigation through a reputable law firm to determine whether Ralph Nader was acting on behalf of litigants or their attorneys in Corvair design cases pending against General Motors." They denied involvement in "any of the alleged harassment recently reported in the press."

The next day, Senator Ribicoff announced that he was requesting Nader, the president of General Motors, and the "detective agencies" to appear before his subcommittee on March 22, 1966, for a public explanation of the alleged harassment of a Senate witness. Senators Robert Kennedy and Gaylord Nelson joined in the request. Senator Nelson said:

> If great corporations can engage in this kind of intimidation, it is an assault upon freedom in America. No average citizen can face up to a corporation the size of General Motors which sets out to destroy him.

But the Senate and millions of people around the world watching on television were soon to learn that General Motors had not selected an average citizen to intimidate.

On the appointed day, GM President James Roche appeared before the Ribicoff subcommittee, flanked by his lawyer, Theodore Sorensen, who had been John F. Kennedy's speechwriter and was a long-time associate of Ribicoff. Roche read a prepared statement that seemed to accept responsibility for the Nader fiasco, but if you read it carefully it was an apology for doing nothing wrong. Mr. Roche wanted to apologize there and then to the senators and Mr. Nader—"to the extent that General Motors bears responsibility." Then he proceeded to deny that the GM investigation—which he said was for legitimate Corvair litigation purposes—had employed detectives using false names, or had Nader under surveillance on the day he testified before the subcommittee, or made threatening phone calls. Roche portrayed it as a routine litigation check that had gone awry because of the overzealousness of the main private eye, ex-FBI agent Vincent Gillen of New York. He assured the senators that if he had been told that the detectives were going to prowl around Nader's home town in Connecticut and interview more than 60 people who had known him from childhood through the other phases of his life, asking searching personal questions that had nothing to do with the Corvair litigation, he would have stopped the investigation immediately.

Roche, who came across like a kindly small-town high school principal, was permitted to get away with this whitewash. The senators were satisfied that they had summoned the president of GM before the nation and that he had humbly apologized. It was a fine bit of lawyering by Sorenson.

The star witness was Vincent Gillen, the great detective himself. He was a Runyonesque character who sensed that he was being set up as the fall guy, and he wasn't about to accept that role graciously. He insisted that everything he had done, including the interviewing of 60 people under the pretext of a pre-employment check, had been approved by GM. But he had been cast as the villain of this TV show, and Senators Ribicoff and Robert Kennedy denounced him heatedly. Finally, Roche was allowed to repeat his statement that the nefarious Gillen tactics were not within GM's instructions.

Satisfied that bringing GM's president to heel had given a strong impetus to passage of the first federal auto safety legislation, Senator Ribicoff adjourned the six-hour hearing. At the close, he waved the voluminous Gillen investigation report toward the camera, and said to Ralph:

> And I may say to you, Mr. Nader, that I have read these reports very carefully, and you and your family can be proud, because they put you through the mill and they haven't found out a damn thing against you.

Ralph was now a national hero, thanks to the magic of television—and to Vincent Gillen's gumshoes who lost his trail in the Senate Office Building. But when Ralph tried to get a copy of the Gillen investigation report, he was informed by the subcommittee staff that it had been sent to the National Archives for safekeeping and would not be available to the public or even to him.

Ralph was ambivalent about suing GM at first. He consulted me, since we had known each other earlier when I helped him in a small way with his efforts to pioneer auto safety regulations. Some of his journalist friends convinced him that his crusader image might be tarnished by suing, and that his future auto safety activities would be branded as support tactics for his lawsuit. I tried to convince him that he could protect his image by announcing at the start of the lawsuit that the proceeds would be dedicated to his publc interest work, since he told me that was what he planned to do. In the end, Ralph came up with his own convincing reason to sue. He wanted all the facts brought out, so the whole world would be able to see the extent of GM's involvement; and he wanted to broaden the law's protection against corporate harassment so that future consumer advocates would not have to rely upon acts of personal courage for survival.

Just before the one-year statute of limitations ran out, Ralph gave me the green light to sue. A few weeks earlier, he and

Senator Ribicoff were honored guests at the White House, look-ing on as President Lyndon Johnson signed into law the National Traffic and Motor Vehicle Safety Act, the first statute to impose safety standards on auto manufacturers.

This was an exciting case to be in, even if it did not promise large financial rewards. Since GM had not published any of its investigation data, Ralph could not sue for libel or slander. His main claim against GM would have to be brought under the heading of "invasion of privacy." Although it appeared in the textbooks as a well-established form of tort, it had proven to be more of a plaything for law professors than a means of collecting damages. In all the state and federal courts there had been only twelve reported cases in which damages had been awarded for invasion of privacy. The awards ranged from $250 to a high of only $12,500, and in some states (including New York) the pro-tection of privacy was very narrow. Ralph himself pointed out that while GM had the worst of motives, they had unwittingly increased the sales of his book (his major source of income at the time) and had helped him to become a national hero, much in demand as a lecturer and television show guest.

Ralph was properly concerned that if he sued GM, they might file counterclaims against him in the same suit, such as claims that his book or other statements libeled or slandered GM's products. I agreed that we would defend him against any such claims without any fees other than the contingent fee of 30 percent of the amount we collected for him from GM.

Ever since the last losing appeal in the Jane Froman case a dozen years before, I had been hoping for another shot at the dream tort case. Whatever Ralph Nader had become to idol-hun-gry admirers—knight in shining armor, the consumer's cham-pion, the last honest man, even a sex symbol—in my narrow sights he was one thing above all else: the perfect plaintiff. And General Motors was a perfect target defendant: hated by millions of disgruntled car owners and unlikely to get sympathy from a jury when it came to fixing damages. To be handed the repre-sentation of the perfect plaintiff against the ultimate big-business icon in a classic David-Goliath confrontation that had climaxed in a nationally televised apology was the second chance I had been praying for. And this time Aron Steuer would not charge us out of court, because he was safely ensconced on the Appellate Division bench, where he would have only one out of five votes if the case came before him on appeal.

In the twelve years since the bitter ending of the Froman case, a lot of things had changed. The plaintiff's lawyers were becoming better educated, better organized, and more of a match for corporate litigation power. I felt that in this case, I might be able to play GM's bigness against them. But when I filed the suit in the fall of 1966, I did not kid myself that it was going to be easy, for there never had been a case like this one involving the attempt of a giant corporation to silence a lone critic.

The main legal problem, apart from the fuzziness of the right to privacy and the low damage awards, was that GM had taken the precaution of erecting a Maginot Line of attorney-client privilege to protect all records of the Nader investigation. GM's legal department in Detroit had initiated the inquiry, supposedly as part of their defense of the Corvair product liability suits. Attorney-client privilege protected communications of the client (GM) with its own house counsel, even though they were employees rather than independent lawyers. Not content with that protection, the GM legal department had not hired Gillen directly, but instead went to the trouble of paying a fee to a Washington lawyer, Richard Danner, for the sole purpose of having *him* hire Gillen, who was himself a lawyer as well as a private investigator. I had to figure out a way to get around those privilege barriers or I would never get my hands on the evidence needed to establish the reponsibility of GM for the actions of Gillen. If I failed, all we could get would be a judgment against Gillen and his agency, which was not what Ralph wanted even if it could be collected. He was determined to hold GM itself accountable.

The law gives strong protection to the attorney-client relationship in order to encourage clients to confide completely in their attorneys without fear that such confidences will ever be used as evidence in court. The attorney-client privilege belongs to the client, so that GM could prevent Danner, Gillen, and the lawyers in GM's legal department from testifying, if the claim of privilege was upheld. The privilege might be waived by public disclosure, which explains why the Gillen investigation report, which was seen from a distance by millions of viewers as Senator Ribicoff waved it to the TV cameras, quickly found its way into the National Archives. If that report had become a public document, the attorney-client privilege protection might have been lost.

Once again, fate took a hand, as it had when Ralph unknowingly shook off Gillen's operatives by pushing the wrong button in the Senate Office Building elevator. On the day that Gillen was served with the suit papers, he gave an interview to the *Detroit Free Press* in which he said of Ralph, among other things, that "I would refer him to a psychiatrist." Gillen was enjoying the media interest in his role, appearing on TV talk shows and giving expansive interviews all over the country. Ralph was in the early stages of establishing his reputation and did not want to suffer any further smears. We decided to start a separate lawsuit against Gillen, seeking damages for libel in the *Detroit Free Press* interview. We hoped that this would deter him from further media attacks.

From the beginning, Gillen's legal position in the GM investigation had fascinated me. I felt that GM's lawyers were facing a delicate balancing act in their dealings with him. Using him as the fall guy at the Ribicoff hearings had served GM well, but the lawsuit would raise tougher questions. Normally GM would provide defense counsel for Gillen and agree to pick up the tab for any damages assessed against him. But if we were able to tell the jurors that GM was backing Gillen in the lawsuit, they might decide that GM must have authorized his activities, or at least that they were ratifying his "frolic" and thereby made themselves responsible for what he had done. On the other hand, if they cut him adrift and let him defend himself, they would be giving him a strong incentive to come forward with whatever evidence he might have that GM had instructed him to go as far as he did. Otherwise, he might have to pay a jury's award all by himself.

Since Gillen was an adverse party in two lawsuits, I could not discuss these problems with him. But now that I had started the separate libel suit against him, I decided to take his deposition immediately. I could do this without GM's lawyers being present since GM was not a party to the libel suit. Indeed, they didn't even know it existed because New York practice did not require it to be filed in court until a later stage.

Vincent Gillen arrived at my office for his deposition with his lawyer/brother-in-law, Francis Maguire, who had been a member of Thomas E. Dewey's crack young prosecuting team in the New York of the 1930s. Gillen's appearance and his gravelly voice reminded me of Paul Douglas, the New York radio sportscaster who had become a popular comic film star in the 1950s. I began by asking questions that enabled him to talk about his favorite subjects: himself, and the importance of his detective agency. Then, since his statement about referring Nader to a psychiatrist was based upon what happened during the Gillen-GM investigation, I started asking him about that investigation. I was delighted to find that Gillen was willing to respond at length on that subject, as on most any other. What was even more important was that his knowedgable lawyer was letting him answer detailed questions about the investigation. That told me that GM had probably refused to indemnify him, and so he was being forced into the position of disgorging the truth to protect himself from a ruinous judgment.

The deposition stretched out over five days. Each day I encouraged him to produce more documents, which were pure gold for our side since we probably would never have gotten GM to produce them because of the attorney-client privilege. From the five days of testimony and the hundreds of pages of documents Gillen produced, this picture emerged:

From its inception, the GM investigation of Ralph Nader was designed to "get something on Nader" that GM could use to shut him up, to discredit his auto safety work and "get him out of GM's hair." In all the communications and instructions to Gillen, there was never any mention of the Corvair litigation. At GM's request, Gillen conducted wide-ranging interviews with more than 60 people who knew Nader, from his grade school teachers to his legal associates. Gillen's operatives questioned these people about drug use, sexual practices, and financial manipulations, making it appear that others had given such information about Nader to them. Gillen reported these interviews immediately to Danner for transmittal to GM's legal department, whose response was that Gillen was not digging deeply enough and was not coming up with the dirt that they wanted. Gillen and all the GM people involved knew that Nader was scheduled to be a witness before the Ribicoff Committee, but they put him under surveillance anyway, and GM paid an extra fee for this surveillance. Gillen had done 26 previous jobs for GM, and each time he had dealt directly with GM instead of going through a lawyer-intermediary such as Danner. And after Senator Ribicoff summoned GM to explain the Nader investigation, Gillen was flown to Detroit to participate in a session with GM's legal department that was designed to cover up the true purpose of the investigation, and he was ordered to alter or destroy some key documents.

But Vincent Gillen, who was rapidly emerging as the smartest person involved on the GM side of the investigation, kept copies of all the documents he was ordered to destroy, since they proved that he was acting within GM's instructions at all times. He produced those documents at the deposition—69 exhibits in all, some of them running into dozens of pages of notes, instructions, and records of intimidating interviews, including the detailed Gillen report that had found its way into the National Archives after the Ribicoff hearings. The most revealing document was a letter from one Eileen Murphy of GM's legal department in Detroit. While this letter was sent by Murphy to Richard Danner, it did not show any addressee. It was typed on plain white paper rather than on GM's letterhead, and since it began with "Dear Dick," it became known as the Dear Dick letter. Written about midway through the investigation, it complained about the lack of dirt in Gillen's reports. GM's frustration came through in this sentence: "It also strikes me that everyone is going overboard to impress us with what a great, charming intellectual this human being is—Eagle-Scout type." Eileen went on to complain that numerous personal questions she had ordered the investigators to ask about Nader had not produced any useful information. She gave further detailed instructions, listing questions about Ralph's private life to be checked out by the detectives. And of course, she did not mention the Corvair litigation. She signed off with, "Well friend, have fun. Sincerely, Eileen." Writing about the Dear Dick letter in his *New York Post* column, Murray Kempton titled his article, "Have Fun, Friend."

Danner himself was an interesting character. An ex-FBI agent who had headed the Miami FBI office during World War II, he later left the FBI and became campaign mananger for George Smathers in his famous 1950 senate race against the incumbent, Claude Pepper. According to Pepper, Dick Danner played an important role in producing faked and composite photographs that purported to link Pepper with prominent communists, which helped Smathers to defeat Pepper. Later, Danner went to work for the Howard Hughes organization in Las Vegas, during which tenure he delivered $100,000 in cash taken from the Silver Slipper gambling casino to President Nixon's close friend, Bebe Rebozo. Danner told the press that this was a contribution to President Nixon's reelection campaign.

When the contents of the Gillen deposition were made public, GM was put on the defensive. Since the deposition was evidence only in the libel suit against Gillen, GM's lawyers quickly moved to prevent its use in the invasion of privacy suit against GM and Gillen. They asked the court to suppress the Gillen deposition, charging that the libel case against Gillen was a "sweetheart suit" which must have involved collusion between Nader and Gillen or their lawyers. The court found that there were serious questions of fact about the nature of the Gillen deposition, and ordered a trial on the issue of collusion. But GM was not able to produce any evidence of collusion, even after subpoening the lawyers' diaries, because there was none. I had never spoken to Gillen or his lawyer before we started the libel action and took his deposition. The judge decided the collusion issue in our favor.

GM took that decision up on appeal to the Appellate Division, where Aron Steuer was one of the seven judges. But only five sat on any given case, and when I arrived at court to argue for our side, I was delighted to see that he was not on the panel. He would not have taken kindly to the spectacle of a boarding-house-based consumer advocate embarrassing the ultimate corporate power symbol, General Motors.

A few weeks after the argument, the Appellate Division affirmed the lower court's finding that there had been no collusion in obtaining the Gillen evidence. The vote was five to zero in our favor. GM then sought leave to appeal to the Court of Appeals in Albany, but that was turned down. All this legal maneuvering, including the trial on the collusion issue, took nearly two years. But now we knew that we had hurdled the attorney-client privilege barrier and were armed with overwhelming evidence that GM's investigation of Nader had been designed to intimidate him and stop his crusade for auto safety. Prudence dictated that GM's lawyers would then try to negotiate an out-of-court settlement rather than giving Gillen the chance to display GM's dirty linen in front of a jury. But GM did not roll over so easily. Their lawyers still had some legal games left to play.

As noted, we could not sue GM for libel or slander because they had not published anything about Ralph. We could only sue for the tort of invasion of privacy. There are two types of privacy invasion: *appropriation*, which usually involves unauthorized publication or other use of the plaintiff's name or picture; and *intrusion*, which covers the harassment, surveillance, and other indignities involved in the Nader case. New York law permitted invasion of privacy claims only for appropriation. Fortunately for us, most of the harassment took place in Washington, and District of Columbia law had no such restrictions. While it did not clearly grant the right to sue for intrusion, it did not rule out such claims. GM tried to get out of the case by asking the court to rule that Ralph had no right to sue for intrusion.

To oppose GM's motion to dismiss Ralph's case on those legal grounds, I turned to our firm's ultimate intellectual weapon: our law man, our version of Harry Gair's Ben Siff, Al Gans. For many years prior to joining our firm, Al was managing editor of *American Law Reports*, the most exhaustively annotated set of legal reference books, known to lawyers as *ALR*. As part of his regular editorial duties, he read every court decision published in the United States—state and federal courts at the trial and appellate level—plus many English decisions and at least fifty law reviews. He maintains that schedule even now, when he is in his eighties. He also gobbles up novels and periodicals at the same pace, and is a fountain of knowledge in history, chemistry, philately, Russian literature, and baseball.

Al looks the part of a judge right out of Hollywood central casting—tall, white-haired, distinguished—and he actually played the judge in an educational film produced by the American Arbitration Association. But his kindly demeanor does not inhibit his fighting instincts. An incident in Al's career as an Air Force legal officer during World War II is illustrative. Early in the war, Al was posted to the Judge Advocate (legal) department of the Air Transport Command in Alaska, which was not formally designated as a combat zone. This meant that service men were allowed to have their wives and other dependents living with them. The commanding general decided to order all dependents back to the continental United States. There were rumors that this move was inspired by high-ranking officers who had managed to create some Arctic warmth though liaisons with eskimo girl-friends.

This order required endorsement of all the Alaskan command's legal officers in order to become effective. All duly signed off in approval—except for one: a mere captain, Al Gans. Al not only refused to sign, but he wrote and sent to the general a memorandum on constitutional law, demonstrating that nobody had the power to "deport" American citizens from Alaska. Captain Al was put under extreme pressure by generals and colonels, but he stuck to his position, shooting back another memo that quoted from the Civil War era Supreme Court decision in *Ex parte Milligan*: "The Constitution of the United States is a law for rulers and people equally in war and in peace, and covers with the shield of its protection all classes of men, at all times, and under all circumstances." The case finally wound up in the Alaskan federal court, which upheld Al Gans's position and kept the dependents in Alaska throughout the war.

GM's legal team filed a 52-page brief in support of their motion to dismiss the case "for failure to state a cause of action," meaning that even if everything Ralph alleged in his complaint was true, he could not recover any damages because he had no right to sue for intrusion and there had been no appropriation or publication. Al Gans countered with an equally weighty brief, and then he went in to argue against the dismissal motion before Justice Joseph A. Brust in the Supreme (trial) Court for New York County. This was a smashing success. Not only did Justice Brust uphold our position that District of Columbia law allowed Ralph to sue for intrusion, but he went further and agreed with Al's

contention that even under New York law Ralph should be allowed to sue for privacy invasion, since the federal constitution
established a *constitutional* right of privacy that overrides New
York's narrow limitation of that right to appropriation cases. As
Justice Brust wrote:

> However, there is presented a constitutional right of plaintiff to
> privacy—a right to be left alone. The right of privacy stands on
> high ground, cognate to the values and concerns protected by
> constitutional guarantees (see 4th, 5th, and 14th Amendments,
> Federal Constitution).

GM's lawyers weren't about to accept that defeat lying
down. They quickly appealed to the Appellate Division, and this
time we weren't so lucky. Aron Steuer was one of the five judges
before whom Al Gans argued the appeal on January 8, 1969. We
knew which way Steuer would go. We could only pray that he
did not drag more than one other justice with him.

Two months later we learned that we had won by the narrowest of margins. Three justices decided in our favor. Aron
Steuer voted for GM, and one other justice joined him. The majority decision noted that while the District of Columbia had
never expressly allowed a privacy action based on intrusion,
neither had it ever barred such an action. Citing the leading torts
textbook, *Prosser on Torts*, which said that the law in most jurisdictions was moving toward allowing suits for intrusion, the
majority, led by Justice Owen McGivern, concluded that the District of Columbia would allow it in the Nader case. As Justice
McGivern wrote:

> And since we are not dealing with the laws of the Medes and
> the Persians, the lack of an exact precedent is no reason for
> turning the plaintiff out of court when receiving his action will
> further the bringing of the law into harmony with the known
> practices of our modern society.

Justice Steuer, still garbed in his worn and patched robe, saw
a potential for "great mischief" in permitting such suits. His dissenting opinion stressed the fact that the only District of Columbia cases in which money had been recovered for privacy
invasion involved publication. He felt that any extension of privacy to include intrusion should be left to the legislature. Apparently he was unfazed by the fact that there was no District of
Columbia statute on invasion of privacy, so that it was up to the
courts to fashion this remedy. Nor was he bothered by the prospect that dismissing Ralph's case would permit GM to get away

with a blatant attempt to intimidate a critic whose sole objective was to save thousands of lives.

Al Gans, a former left-handed catcher on the Ohio State baseball team, was still batting one thousand. The last hurdle was the Court of Appeals in Albany, which heard GM's appeal on October 28, 1969. This time Al won by a more comfortable margin. All seven judges voted in our favor. They held that District of Columbia law should apply, and that it permitted actions for invasion of privacy by intrusion. Their decision came on January 8, 1970, a little more than three years after we had filed suit. We had been through the entire three-layer court system twice and had won every contested issue. Now it was time for GM to pay.

In addition to all the Gillen evidence which was now officially in the case, GM had other incentives to settle. The public relations battle, which was as important to Ralph as collecting money in the lawsuit, had been going against GM since the day suit was filed. Every major development in the case was covered nationally by the media. The Dear Dick letter and other Gillen disclosures kept turning up like bad pennies for GM. The Gillen evidence wiped out the portrait of GM as the victim of the detective's overzealousness that President Roche had painted at the Ribicoff hearings. Now the media stories about the lawsuit were saying that Roche had apologized for hiring detectives to smear Nader's reputation. By 1970, there was a new GM president, and the people in the GM legal department who had masterminded the Nader campaign were gone. The new officials had no incentive to prolong the agonized defense of GM's detective misadventure.

After prolonged negotiations, I was able to get a final settlement offer of $425,000, which was more than 30 times the size of the highest previous award for invasion of privacy, even in cases where there had been loss of income or destruction of a business. While Ralph would have preferred to bring GM to trial and play out the sordid harassment scenario again for the public, he realized that most of the facts we would ever learn were divulged in the Gillen deposition. He also knew that it would be years more before we could ever get to trial if we forced GM to use all their delaying power. His small staff of Nader's Raiders were working almost on a volunteer basis, and he could do a lot more good if he had the money to hire more consumer advocates. With this in mind, on August 13, 1970, Ralph agreed to settle for $425,000.

The settlement was a front-page media story throughout the country. The *New York Times* carried an editorial which concluded:

The settlement is significant in ways that go beyond Mr. Nader's own case. It gives added legal standing to the developing notion that an individual's private life must be safeguarded from intrusion and snooping by various institutions. And it provides further recognition to the problems of automobile-caused hazards without making these vital matters appear to be merely the concern of one bold consumer gadfly.

But it remained for Ralph himself to supply the final punch line, as quoted in *Newsweek* for August 24, 1970:

The $425,000 settlement will be General Motors' contribution to the consumer movement. They are going to be financing their own ombudsman.

Al Gans and I were delighted to have been able to help Ralph Nader become GM's ombudsman. But as lawyers we took even greater pride in what Professor William Prosser wrote about the Nader-GM case in the 4th Edition of his widely-quoted *Handbook on Torts*: The most significant American decision on invasion of privacy was the trial court's finding in the Nader case that there was a constitutional right of privacy.

Few corporate executives or legal advisors would dare to launch a Gillen-type investigation against a critic today. But the most important effect of the case was one that Ralph Nader's lawyers had nothing to do with: Ralph used the settlement proceeds to build the world's first effective consumer movement, saving thousands of lives and changing American government, business, and society as no private individual had ever done before. And now his influence has spread around the world, as his successful consumer crusades are copied in many countries, often with Ralph's assistance.

Nader v. General Motors helped to speed up diffusion of litigation power, so that many individuals and small companies can wield power in the courts—power that once was reserved for corporate giants like General Motors and Pan American Airways. It furnished a winning model for David-Goliath confrontations, giving other individuals the inspiration to criticize, to challenge, to sue if necessary, to hold the establishment accountable. Its ultimate results can be seen on *L.A. Law*, in the readiness of McKenzie Brackman lawyers to represent the underdogs in suits against the establishment and to do well by doing good—all in the tradition of the American Dream.

In 1971, Frank Capra addressed a seminar of the American Film Institute that was discussing his movies. He said, "Ralph Nader would make a perfect Capra hero."

CHAPTER 11

Onassis, Gucci, and the End of Impunity

We have seen how wealth and power were used to forestall accountability. As the concept of accountability gained impetus during the 1970s through cases like *Nader v. General Motors*, there remained a hard core of holdouts who refused to consider themselves accountable to anyone because they believed their lofty financial status entitled them to impunity. Most of these holdouts were egocentric tycoons who were not receptive to sound advice because they believed themselves to be above the law.

In his 1911 book, *The Devil's Dictionary*, Ambrose Bierce defined wealth as "impunity." We now consider two cases that might have caused Ambrose to revise this sweeping definition.

First, a personal reminiscence. Early in my practice I attended a Florida meeting of plaintiff's tort lawyers who were trying to help each other become Equalizers. The group was addressed by Fuller Warren, a distinguished-looking, silver-haired, southern gentleman who had served as governor of Florida and was now in private law practice. To our consternation, he excoriated us for sitting around in a hotel discussing legal principles and courtroom strategy. "I'm ashamed of you fellows," he said. "Instead of pontificating on the law, you ought to be bringing tort suits against the likes of J. Paul Getty and Howard Hughes. It doesn't matter what torts you charge them with, and you don't need any proof. As rich as they are, they have plenty of skeletons in their closets—so go out there and sue the hell out of them for torts!"

Fuller Warren was a great jokester. Any plaintiff's tort lawyer following Fuller's tongue-in-cheek advice would find himself surrounded by dozens of unsympathetic lawyers from the powerful firms that handle the legal business of tycoons like Getty and Hughes. The super-rich are accustomed to receiving many requests for handouts and frequent threats of extortion and blackmail. Given the spotlight of publicity that is focused on the super-rich, the first hint of their susceptibility to these financial demands would bring forth thousands more. Therefore, the tort lawyer representing a client with a claim against such a tycoon has to think at least twice before launching a suit that is likely to be contested to the hilt even if the claim is meritorious.

Nevertheless, I must admit that I thought back to Fuller Warren's speech when I was asked to sue Aristotle Onassis and Aldo Gucci.

Onassis

Like the Jane Froman case, this one arose out of a flying boat crash that occurred in Europe. But the script was much different this time, although the owner of the flying boat, Aristotle Onassis, was even more powerful in his own domain than Juan Trippe or Pan American Airways.

Befitting his enormous ego, Aristotle Onassis owned a private yacht, the Christina, that was large enough to accommodate a twin-engine Piaggio amphibian airplane. (An amphibian can operate from land airports, and with its wheels retracted it becomes a flying boat which can take off and land on water.) Aristotle used the Piaggio for personal transportation to and from his island of Scorpios, and he also carried it aboard his yacht so that when he was in a hurry to get to shore, the yacht crew would lower the plane into the water and the pilot would fly him to his destination. Aristotle's only son, Alexander, a pilot himself, was the head of Olympic Aviation, a subsidiary of Aristotle's Olympic Airways that operated a fleet of small aircraft like the Piaggio in air taxi and charter service to the smaller Greek islands. Donald McGregor, a veteran BOAC flying boat captain, was the regular pilot for Artistotle's Piaggio. In January 1973, McGregor developed eye trouble and was temporarily grounded. This was most inconvenient for Artistotle since he was planning a cruise aboard the *Christina* from Greece to the Caribbean. He ordered Alexander to sign up another Piaggio pilot in time for the cruise.

Alexander, then 25 and still dominated by his iron-handed father, had been trying for years to replace the outmoded Piaggio with a helicopter. Finally Aristotle agreed, but the Piaggio would be used one last time for the January 1973 Caribbean cruise. Finding no suitable Piaggio pilot in Greece, Alexander advertised for one in America. His ad was answered by Donald McCusker, a decorated World War II Navy pilot and former test pilot for major American aircraft manufacturers. Besides having excellent credentials, McCusker had considerable flying time in amphibians. Alexander arranged his passage on Olympic Airways to Athens, where he would be checked out on the Piaggio and if satisfactory, would be hired as Aristotle's pilot.

After sitting up all night on the Olympic flight from New York, Donald McCusker arrived at Athens International Airport on Monday morning, January 22, 1973. He did not realize that his checkout flight would take place that same day. But Alexander Onassis was in a hurry because he was under pressure from his father to hire the replacement pilot. He was also eager to get away to London that afternoon to be with his 41-year-old girlfriend, the Baroness Thyssen-Bornemisza, daughter of a British admiral and formerly a famous fashion model under the name of Fiona Campbell. Married and then divorced from Baron Thyssen, she had an ongoing five-year affair with Alexander, and was helping him to assert his independence from Aristotle.

The Piaggio had been down for overhaul, which was performed by the maintenance department of Aristotle's airline, Olympic Airways. The plane was supposed to get a maintenance test flight before returning to passenger service. Alexander decided to combine the maintenance test flight with the orientation of McCusker. Alexander took the right seat, where the instructor/check pilot usually sat. McCusker was in the left seat, normal for the pilot being checked out. Donald McGregor, Aristotle's former pilot, sat in a rear seat. The plan was for Alexander to talk McCusker through a few takeoffs and landings at the Athens airport, and then do some water landings and takeoffs at the nearby islands of Aegina and Poros. Then, when they all thought McCusker was ready, Alexander would take the afternoon airline flight to London, leaving the rest of McCusker's orientation to Captain McGregor.

Under instruction from Alexander, McCusker taxied the Piaggio up to the takeoff runway. When they received takeoff clearance, McCusker opened the throttles, and as the plane reached the takeoff speed of 100 miles per hour, he eased the stick back and the plane left the ground normally. But almost immediately after takeoff, the plane banked sharply to the right. Its right wing tip struck the ground to the right of the runway. Then the plane cartwheeled in a circle for more than 400 feet, smashing its nose, its tail, and both its wings as it crashed to the right of the runway.

The airport emergency rescue trucks sped to the crash scene. The three pilots were pulled from the wreckage, unconscious and bleeding badly. They were rushed to a hospital, where it was determined that McGregor and McCusker had been lucky and would survive without permanent injuries. But Alexander was not so fortunate. Sitting on the right side at the point of the most severe ground impact, he had suffered crushing head injuries. He underwent a three-hour operation to remove blood clots and relieve the pressure on his brain.

At the time of the accident, Aristotle Onassis and his wife Jacqueline were in the United States. They flew to Athens immediately, bringing along a Boston neurosurgeon and a Texas heart specialist. But by the early afteroon of the day following the crash, all the doctors agreed that there was no hope. They kept Alexander alive until his sister Christina arrived from Brazil. He died that evening.

Aristotle Onassis was at once inconsolable in his grief and irrational with rage. He was convinced that the Piaggio had crashed because of sabotage, and he thought the saboteurs had meant to kill him rather than his son because he was the plane's most frequent user. It was the time of the dictatorship of the colonels in Greece, and Aristotle, as the sole owner of Olympic Airways and the nation's most visible business icon, could have his way with the Greek government. The official investigation was conducted by a court-appointed team, most of whom were Greek Air Force officers. Their report was suppressed, because it reached conclusions that did not please Aristotle.

The cause of the fatal accident quickly became apparent to the investigators. During its overhaul by Olympic mechanics (who worked for Aristotle) the Piaggio had its aileron controls rerigged. This meant that the controls that made the wings bank during turns were removed and then reinstalled. Unfortunately they were put in backwards, so that when the pilot turned his wheel to the right to put the right wing down in a bank for a right turn, the plane would actually turn to the left. And when the wind caused the Piaggio to drift to the right on its final takeoff with McCusker at the controls, his normal corrective action—turning the wheel slightly to the left to counteract the wind and stop the drift to the right—would cause the plane to turn even further to the right, because of the reversed aileron controls. At that point, any experienced pilot would turn the control wheel even more sharply to the left. Given the slow airspeed and low altitude at the time of takeoff, the right wing would dig into the ground and the crash sequence would follow exactly as it did.

Since the maintenance test flight that was supposed to be conducted after overhaul was combined with Alexander's checkout of McCusker, the opportunity to discover the reversal of the aileron controls was lost. So the primary cause of the accident was the negligence of Aristotle's mechanics in rigging the ailerons backwards, and a contributing cause was Alexander's failure to follow the checklist that required a walk-around inspection of the controls and then a maintenance test flight, both of which would have revealed the misrigging. McCusker did not know that the Piaggio had just come out of overhaul, and in any event he was being instructed by Alexander rather than the other way around.

But none of these sobering facts broke through the blind rage of Aristotle Onassis. He contrived to have Donald McCusker and three Olympic mechanics indicted for manslaughter. McCusker was then flat on his back in a Greek hospital, leveled by hepatitis that had set in during his post-accident treatment. His passport was confiscated, and during the six months of his slow recuperation from hepatitis he was too weak to do anything about defending against the criminal charges. There was little he could do anyway, for although he was certain that he had not been at fault in the accident, he could not remember anything about it, nor was he told about the misrigged aileron controls found by the Greek Air Force investigators. Finally, through the intercession of the American ambassador to Greece, McCusker regained his passport and was allowed to return to America in July of 1973. But he was still under indictment for manslaughter, as were the three mechanics.

On his return to his wife and seven children in Ohio, Don McCusker found that his distinguished flying career, which had included the testing of the Gemini space capsule, was now in ruins. He was known throughout the world as the pilot who had been at the controls of the plane that killed the son of Aristotle Onassis, and he was still under indictment for manslaughter. He used up much of his savings before he finally found a job in South Dakota, flying a 40-year-old World War II surplus Beechcraft in aerial mapping work, at a salary lower than that of a truck driver.

Don McCusker and his wife Helena were to endure their nightmare for another five years. They kept corresponding with a Greek lawyer whom they had hired to get the manslaughter indictment lifted and to seek compensation for Donald's injuries and expenses. But the lawyer was not able to make any progress during Aritstotle Onassis's lifetime. Aristotle went to his grave in March of 1975 without ever having relented in his quest for revenge and expiation of his own guilt. It was not until November of 1977 that the indictment was finally dismissed. Even then McCusker's name was not cleared because the indictment was merely dropped for lack of proof. He remained at his low-paying job in South Dakota, and renewed his request for compensation through his Greek lawyer.

Finally, Olympic Airways authorized an American lawyer to negotiate a settlement with McCusker in 1978. All that McCusker asked was reimbursement of his out-of-pocket expenses and financial losses, which then totalled a modest $65,000. When the American lawyer for Olympic was about to approve a $65,000 settlement, Don McCusker phoned to ask my advice about settling for that amount.

After meeting with Don and Helena McCusker and studying the documents they left with me, I thought it was worth trying to collect more than $65,000. While Don had recovered his health to the point where he could pass the stringent commercial pilot physical examination, he had been robbed of his good name and the ability to earn his living as a pilot at the accustomed level. Clearly, he should get more than $65,000 if he could prove that someone other than the Greek government was resonsible for the harsh treatment he received as an innocent victim of the Piaggio crash. While it was common gossip that Aristotle Onassis was the responsible party, proving this in court would be extremely difficult since he was now dead and it was unlikely that we would find either witnesses or documents attesting to his complicity. There were other serious problems with the case, most notably the passage of more than five years since the accident. The New York statute of limitations for McCusker's physical injury claim was three years, and there were even shorter time limits for some of the other torts involved, such as defamation. There was also the hazard that if McCusker brought suit, the $65,000 offer that emanated from Greece might well be withdrawn, leaving him even worse off than before. Despite all these obstacles, I had a strong feeling that if we could sue the estate of Aristotle Onassis, the technicial problems of our case would quickly be solved.

I had another reason for wanting to take a crack at Aristotle's estate. Years before, during the era before the tort lawyers became Equalizers, I had been retained by Aristotle's cousin, who had been driven out of the shipping business by him because he did not want anyone else using the Onassis name in that industry. Since Aristotle's shipping empire was legally domiciled in Monaco and his repressive actions against my client originated there, I tried to find a Monaco lawyer who would file an action there. But I discovered that Aristotle had every lawyer in Monaco under retainer, so that it was impossible to sue him there. I then took steps to try to sue Aristotle in New York, at which point he turned up the financial pressure on his cousin to the extent that the cousin suffered a heart attack. The client's wife tearfully informed me that their doctors had ordered that the suit be dropped. Thus Aristotle proved that Ambrose Bierce had been correct in equating wealth with impunity in the pre-Equalizer days. But now I would have another chance as an Equalizer—provided that I could find a way to sue his estate in New York.

I checked the court records and found that no estate of Aristotle Onassis existed in New York or anyplace else in the United States. This was not surprising since Aristotle was averse to paying taxes of any kind, and had arranged his affairs so that his property would be passed on to his heirs without using the courts. Although he owned the Olympic Tower on Fifth Avenue and other property in New York, officially he was a citizen of Argentina. But as things then stood, three years after his death, neither the Internal Revenue Service nor the state tax authorities had tried to collect anything from his estate.

There is a procedure under New York law through which you can have an administrator appointed for the estate of a deceased person whom you wish to sue, even if that person's heirs have taken no steps to administer the estate. Upon a showing that the deceased left property in New York, the Surrogate's Court may appoint an administrator. Usually this is done in cases where the deceased did not leave enough property to warrant expenditures by the surviving relatives for administration through the regular court procedures. There is a county official called the Public Administrator who usually is appointed to administer such estates. Therefore, at the time I filed suit for the McCuskers in June of 1978, I also filed a petition in the Surrogate's Court for the County of New York, asking that the Public Administrator be appointed as administrator of the estate of Aristotle Onassis.

When the Public Administrator received a copy of the petition, he thought at first that it was a practical joke. Most of the estates he administered were of paupers, and now he was a candidate to handle the property of one of the world's richest men. The petition was also served on the two people who would have the right to act as administrators themselves: Jacqueline Kennedy Onassis, the widow, and Christina Onassis, the only surviving child. A hearing was set for August 16, 1978, in the New York County Surrogate's Court to determine who should be the administrator of the estate of Aristotle Onassis. I thought that I might get a phone call from a lawyer prior to the hearing, and I was not disappointed.

A hastily-arranged conference took place at my office, attended by three Wall Street lawyers representing Olympic Airways (and possibly other interests). Each was equipped with the standard legal-size yellow pad. As I spelled out the details of Don McCusker's injuries and financial losses, I noticed that the lawyers were not writing anything on their pads. The same thing happened when I summarized the proof I had assembled on the cause of the accident, including photographs showing the faulty rigging of the aileron controls. It was only when they broached the subject of settling the case out of court prior to the appointment of an administrator for Aristotle's estate, that they wrote down the figure I demanded: one million dollars. They said that they were authorized to offer $500,000, but would recommend to their clients that they pay $600,000. I told them that I would report the offer to the McCuskers but would recommend that they reject it.

After the meeting broke up, I called Don McCusker. He could hardly believe his ears when I told him that there was now an offer of $600,000 for the claim that he had been willing to settle for $65,000 just a few weeks before. I told him that I thought we could get a little more, and he authorized me to settle for anything over $600,000.

I called the Olympic lawyers and within a few minutes the case was settled for $800,000. That same day a cashier's check for $800,000 was hand-delivered to me, even before the McCuskers had signed a release or settlement agreement. Apparently the Olympic lawyers wanted to be certain that the case was officially settled before the date of the hearing scheduled in the Surrogate's Court. Thus did the Public Administrator of New York County miss out on the opportunity to become the administrator of the estate of Aristotle Onassis.

I mention the amount of the settlement (with the permission of Don McCusker) because it stands as a clearance of his name and vindication of his performance during the fatal Piaggio flight. It confirms that he was the victim of Aristotle Onassis's overbearing ego which precluded Aristotle from accepting any of the blame for his son's death.

I was proud to represent Don and Helena McCusker. Their five-year Greek nightmare had an American Dream happy ending because the American legal system gave them the firepower they needed to overcome the arrogance of a tyrant who was able to manipulate the legal system of his own nation to the point of impunity.

Gucci

Our next underdog is unusual in that he is a multimillionaire with the name of Gucci. Our case is actually a maze of litigation involving many civil and criminal actions that unfolded during the 1980s from New York to Europe and back. The story of this litigation was told in some detail by the English author Gerald McKnight in his 1987 book, *Gucci: A House Divided*.

The House of Gucci was founded by Guccio Gucci in Florence, Italy. Guccio, whose initials are the basis of the famous "G.G." trademark, had worked as a waiter and dishwasher at the Savoy Hotel in London. He took careful note of the expensive leather luggage that accompanied the Savoy's patrons, and thought that he could improve upon it. When he returned to Florence he set up his own leathergoods company in 1923. It provided an adequate living for the family, but did not really blossom until Mussolini's invasion of Ethiopia caused the League of Nations to impose sanctions on Italy in 1935. Up to that time, Italian leathergoods manufacturers had obtained their supplies of tanned leather mostly from Britain. Those supplies were cut off by the League's sanctions, and this forced Guccio to improvise. He developed his own leathers, and also designed the leather-and-canvas combination bags that minimized his need for leather and at the same time created a fashion sensation.

Guccio had three sons: Aldo, Vasco, and Rodolfo. It was the charismatic eldest son Aldo who made Gucci a worldwide symbol of high fashion, opening the first Gucci boutique in New York in 1953, the year that Guccio died at age 72. Through Aldo, a master of hype, the loyal wearers of Gucci fasions came to include the likes of Grace Kelly, Sophia Loren, Katharine Hepburn, Jacqueline Onassis, Audrey Hepburn, and the Duchess of Windsor. By 1980, the middle son, Vasco, had died, and Aldo and younger brother Rodolfo each controlled half of the worldwide Gucci fashion empire. Aldo himself had three sons (Giorgio, Paolo, and Roberto) all of whom worked in the family business. Aldo's brother Rodolfo was something of a playboy, and even had a fling as an actor in Italian films. He was content to draw down millions from the business, leaving the management to Aldo, until his later years when he became concerned about future control and the position of his only child, son Maurizio.

When Paolo Gucci came to see me in 1980, I was probably the only lawyer in New York who did not own a pair of Gucci loafers. (This might be explained by the fact that Gucci did not carry my size: 14 AAA.) His reason for selecting such an unfashionable attorney was that he had read about the Nader-GM case and had heard from others that I was willing to fight the establishment on behalf of the underdog. As Paolo sat there in about $5,000 worth of clothing (not counting the jewelry), I found it difficult to believe that he was disadvantaged. But when he told me the story of what his family had done to him, I realized that even a Gucci could be an underdog.

Besides being handsome and debonair and thus looking the part of a Gucci, Paolo was the most talented designer in the Gucci empire. He thumbed through the 1980 Gucci catalogue and showed me that he had designed most of the Gucci line himself. He had worked at the main Gucci office and factory in Florence, but his innovative ideas and the questions he raised about distribution of the profits incurred the wrath of his Uncle Rodolfo, who had assumed control of the Italian company when Aldo moved to New York. By 1978, the rift between Paolo and Uncle Rodolfo became so wide that Paolo was forced to move to New York to work under his father. Aldo appointed Paolo vice-president and a director of the American Gucci company, known as Gucci Shops, Inc. There he was supposed to be in charge of design and development of new products.

Paolo found that working for his father in New York was not much better than the old Florence days under Uncle Rodolfo. If anything, his father was more devious, promising Paolo free reign but rarely performing. Although Paolo was a shareholder in both the American and Italian companies, he was never able to find out much about the ultimate resting places of Gucci's huge worldwide profits. He received a good salary and liberal expense account, but there were no dividends. Whenever he asked questions about where the money was going, Aldo would scream at him as though he were a child.

By the time he retained me as his lawyer in 1980, he had been cut off from any meaningful activity in the Gucci business. His salary had been stopped; his business and travel expenses remained unpaid; and the entire Gucci staff had been told to pay no attention to anything that he said or asked for. This was his punishment for continuing to ask where the money was going. Paolo decided that he would set up his own business as "Paolo Gucci, Designer," using a "P.G." label instead of the familiar "G.G." Quickly, his father and uncle instructed their lawyers to prevent him from using his own name in his own business, even though they would not permit him to function in the established Gucci business.

Paolo wanted me to accomplish two things for him. First, he wanted an American court to rule that he had the right to use his own name as a designer without interference from the old Gucci companies. (This may sound like a simple task, but if your name happens to be Gucci or Berlitz or any other household word, the courts will be looking out to protect the public from the confusion of dealing with a similarly-named entity.) Second, he wanted an accounting of the past profits and payment of the dividends which he was certain were due to him out of those profits.

I set out to do this, and quickly found that I would have to modify my customary stance as a champion of the downtrodden. During the first of many court hearings, the judge asked the lawyers to come into his chambers to argue a motion. "It's going to be a pleasure for me to hear this argument," said the judge. I took this as a great compliment, but was quickly deflated when the judge explained: "Nearly every case that comes into my court involves some kind of human tragedy, and often I'm torn between two heartbreaking choices. But in this case, who gives a damn which Gucci wins?" I resisted the temptation to tell the judge that I represented an unemployed shoemaker. Fortunately, the judge really did care that the party who was in the right should win in his court.

As the marathon litigation got under way, I discovered that Paolo was a pretty good investigator himself. He was able to furnish me with documentary proof of how the profits had been siphoned away by his father Aldo and his Uncle Rodolfo. When I read the documents, I found it mind-boggling that Aldo Gucci, the tycoon of high fashion, would even consider becoming a party to such a blatant fraud. It was even more difficult to believe that he had created this Mickey Mouse scheme himself. The scam was designed to divert millions of dollars in Gucci profits to a Hong Kong corporation known as Fashion Design Consultants, Ltd. (FDC). Ostensibly, FDC was supposed to be designing much of the Gucci line, and for this they were paid 20 percent of the value of the items that the American Gucci company purchased from Italian suppliers, which amounted to most of Gucci's inventory. However, FDC did not employ any designers or actually do any designing. Its only employee was a Chinese accountant in Hong Kong, whose sole function was to deposit the checks that the Gucci companies sent to FDC each month,

and then distribute these funds equally to two Panamanian corporations—one owned by Aldo, and the other owned by Uncle
Rodolfo. Thus the two old smoothies diverted millions each year
from the other Gucci shareholders, including Paolo. It was of
more than passing interest that they were also depriving the
treasuries of the United States of America and the State of New
York of millions of dollars in taxes on what would have been
taxable income but for the remarkable Hong Kong contract with
FDC.

Paolo presented me with a copy of a three-page letter addressed to Aldo, written in 1975 by Edward Stern, the New York
Gucci accountant.The letter proudly announced that Stern had
followed Aldo's instructions by going to Hong Kong and setting
up FDC to do exactly what I have described above. Armed with
that letter, even the greenest of prosecutors would have had no
difficulty in sending the schemers to jail for income tax evasion
even if they were defended by the team of Clarence Darrow,
Edward Bennett Williams, and Abraham Lincoln. Paolo also had
copies of the annual financial statements of FDC, showing that
FDC had received millions of dollars for doing nothing and had
no payroll or other overhead expenses apart from its accountant.

The Gucci litigation turned into an eight-year marathon, during which it became apparent to Aldo that Paolo would have to
present proof of the FDC Hong Kong scam to support his claims.
One of the actions I filed for him was a "whistleblower" suit,
claiming that he had been wrongfully discharged as vice-president of the American Gucci company because he insisted on
finding out what happened to the money that was sent to Hong
Kong. Aldo had many opportunities to settle this litigation without forcing Paolo to reveal the Hong Kong scam, but he would
not do so. Several times over the eight years he actually reached
oral agreements with Paolo to settle, but he always reneged
when it came to putting these settlement agreements in writing.
Finally his arrogance forced Paolo to instruct me to file in court
the accountant's letter and other evidence of the Hong Kong
swindle. Paolo, a considerate person and a dutiful son, was reluctant to do this, for he knew that these revelations posed a
criminal threat to his father and would also hurt the Gucci companies in which Paolo owned shares. But Aldo's deviousness
stripped Paolo of his dignity and his means of earning a livelihood, and in the end there was no basis for Paolo to believe
anything that his father said.

Once in the public court record, the damning documents
were quoted by the media. Soon the Internal Revenue Service

picked up the scent and pursued a tax fraud case all the way to Hong Kong, where it won a monumental court struggle to force the Hong Kong branches of American banks to hand over their records showing the diversion of taxable Gucci income. Thus did Aldo Gucci follow in the footsteps of Oscar Wilde and Alger Hiss, both of whom were convicted of crimes and imprisoned because of evidence that originally came to light in civil litigation.

In the end, Aldo Gucci pleaded guilty to federal income tax evasion, and was sentenced to a year in jail. He also had to pay $7 million to the IRS for evasion of his personal federal income taxes. Further huge sums were paid by the American Gucci company for corporate taxes and penalties on the income that had been diverted to Hong Kong. In all, after the many civil and criminal cases had run their course, Paolo Gucci was granted the right to use his name as a designer, with appropriate safeguards against confusion with the products of the old Gucci companies; his father served his jail sentence, and then died a broken man in 1990; and the old Guccis and their companies probably paid out more than $100 million in their fruitless efforts to fight the underdog Paolo in the courts. As federal judge William C. Conner wrote in his decision granting Paolo the use of his name as designer:

> Since the time of Cain and Abel, family disputes have been marked by the irrational and impulsive decisions of those involved, the fierce battles which ensue, and the senseless destruction they cause. This case is but a skirmish in one of the must publicized family disputes of our times, among the heirs of Guccio Gucci, who founded the business empire which bears his name.

The entire war could have been avoided by settlement in 1980 for a fraction of the ultimate $100 million cost, but the imperious Aldo Gucci would not hear of it. Like Aristotle Onassis, he thought he was a law unto himself.

At one point during the war of the Guccis, I attended a shareholders' meeting of the American Gucci company at its New York headaquarters. The luxurious board room, on the penthouse floor of the main Gucci shop on Fifth Avenue, was decorated with expensive modern art. Behind the seat where Aldo presided as chairman there hung an oil painting of Guccio Gucci, looking to me like the great tenor Enrico Caruso. I was representing Paolo, who had warned me that his father had a penchant for throwing heavy ashtrays at people (including his sons) who tried to ask embarrassing questions at such meetings. With this in mind I had carried to the meeting my hard-sided attache case in lieu of the canvas one that would give me less protection against such missiles.

The meeting was the last one held in America which both Aldo and Rodolfo attended. Both brothers were handsome septuagenarians. Rodolfo's resemblance to Maurice Chevalier, which probably prompted his fling at movie acting in the 1930s, was still discernible. Both men were affable to a fault; I thought they were going to kiss me when Paolo introduced me as his lawyer. But their smiles turned to frowns when I introduced the third member of our entourage: a legal stenographer who would be taking down the minutes of the meeting. This was unprecedented in Gucci company practice; not only were no official notes taken, but no coherent reports were ever disseminated. Aldo conferred with his own lawyer, and when he called the meeting to order, he asked that our stenographer leave the room. When I refused to allow this, he exploded. Turning purple with rage, he started screaming at Paolo: "I took you from nothing and made you a great man! Is this the thanks I get?" As his trembling hands moved toward a large marble ashtray on the conference table, instinctively I gripped the handle of my attache case. Fortunately, his lawyer calmed him down, and before I could ask any questions about the diversion of funds to Hong Kong, Aldo shouted that the meeting was over.

Thereafter the old Guccis held the directors' and shareholders' meetings in Italy, even those for the American company. The next shareholders' meeting after the one I had attended was scheduled for Florence in July 1982. Since Paolo was going to the meeting, I suggested that he take along a tape recorder so that we would finally have a record of what was said at a Gucci meeting. This sage advice nearly proved the undoing of my client. When he produced the tape recorder and announced that he was turning it on, Aldo went into his screaming act, at the same time ordering Paolo's brothers to relieve him of the tape recorder. In the ensuing scuffle, Paolo was cut over the left eye, and bled rather heavily. While he recovered without lasting injury, he felt the affront so deeply that he instructed me to file suit in New York for battery. Of course, the press picked up the story, and when Aldo was questioned by a reporter about the alleged assault, he replied, to the consternation of his lawyers, "Who is the father who has not given a slap to a reckless son?" That slap cost Aldo a six-figure settlement.

Aldo Gucci went to jail and lost his empire because he was living in the past. Had Paolo's legal challenge been launched a few years earlier, back in the pre-Equalizer days, Aldo probably would have succeeded in squelching his upstart son and keeping his Hong Kong tax-cheating scheme a secret. Paolo himself pronounced the epilogue during a 1988 *60 Minutes* segment on the Guccis. Diane Sawyer began it by saying, "If you were writing a television soap opera, you'd have to invent a family like the Guccis, the family behind one of the world's most famous designer labels." She finished by asking Paolo, "If you could say one thing to the other members of the family now about all this, what would it be?" Without hesitation, Paolo replied, "Do you see? I was right. From the beginning."

Thus in real life, the balance of litigation power shifted away from the likes of Aristotle Onassis, Aldo Gucci, the Master Ocean Pilots of Pan American Airways, and the faceless General Motors legal department, just as in the land of television it tilted toward the underdog clients of McKenzie Brackman. The Equalizers took away the impunity of Ambrose Bierce's *The Devil's Dictionary*, and in its place sought to impose financial accountability.

Was this a revolution? And if so, how was it pulled off?

CHAPTER 12

Kicking in Rotten Doors

The economist John Kenneth Galbraith observed that most revolutions resulting in human progress have come about through the kicking in of rotten doors. So it has gone in the saga of the underdog's progress in American tort cases, which some observers have described as a litigation revolution. Those of us who happened to be in the practice when the empowerment of the Equalizers took place in the last half of the twentieth century would like to think of ourselves as the architects or master builders of a brand new legal system. But in truth we were more like a band of hikers wearing hobnail boots. Rather than erecting glittering new edifices, the real contribution of the Equalizers has been to use our hobnail boots to kick in the doors that were kept locked over the centuries to protect the powerful against enforcement of the existing laws by the underdogs.

One Equalizer, Melvin M. Belli, kicked in more of the rotten doors that blocked the enforcement of tort law than did any other lawyer, judge, scholar, or public official. One day in 1958 I sat in his Los Angeles hotel room, getting ready to work with him in court for the first time. I was dazzled by his costume, which included bright red trousers that I hoped he would not be wearing in the courtroom. I glanced down at his feet and noticed that he was wearing high black shoes that looked to me like traditional western cowboy boots. When I complimented him on his boots, he informed me that they were not cowboy boots at all, but "Congress gaitors" that had been made to order for him by Peal's of London. So much for my romantic notion of hobnail boots. But even handmade Congress gaitors can be used to kick in rotten doors if they're on the feet of a Melvin Belli.

Belli's office was in San Francisco, but the rotten doors he aimed at were barring the way to justice in every state. To extend his reach, he needed a vehicle, which he found in the form of a unique nationwide bar association, at first called NACCA (National Association of Compensation Claimants Attorneys) and later renamed ATLA (Association of Trial Lawyers of America).

ATLA and Melvin Belli

ATLA was founded in 1946 by a group led by Samuel B. Horovitz, a prominent Boston worker's compensation lawyer. Until the 1950s, it concentrated on worker's compensation issues, and its membership was limited to "lawyers helping injured workers." This was not as broad a mandate as tort law, since worker's comp statutes provided benefits that were supposed to be paid automatically by the employer, without having to go to court. In exchange for this, the benefits were very limited, falling far short of providing real compensation to people injured on the job.

In the early 1950s, Sam Horovitz decided to expand ATLA's horizons to encompass the tort lawyers who had to go to court for compensation. For this expansion, Sam wisely chose to hook ATLA's tail to a comet: Melvin M. Belli, of San Francisco, Hollywood, Rome, and points east and west. This was an unlikely combination of personalities, for Belli was the flamboyant traveling mate of Errol Flynn, while Sam was so conservative that he paid his law firm's entire annual office rent on January 1st so that he wouldn't have to worry about paying the rent for the rest of the year. Belli had won some landmark victories on points of law in the California trial and appellate courts, but his forte was breaking through the artificial barriers to achieve true compensation—what he called the Adequate Award. This he did by a unique combination of forensic skills, scholarship, and showmanship. Belli barnstormed around the country, preaching the gospel of the Adequate Award and attracting hundreds of embryo Equalizers to the ATLA banner.

Learning the dramatic qualities of the fingerprint and the smoking gun by trying criminal cases, he was the first to feature this "demonstrative evidence" in civil cases, which until then turned mainly on spoken evidence. He once brought his bedridden 500-pound client to the trial by having a crane hoist him through the courtroom window. And he delighted in wrapping props (such as artificial limbs) in butcher paper, leaving the menacing package on his table throughout the trial to build the jurors' curiosity to a climax when he unwrapped the package during final argument. Not every judge took kindly to his cowboy tactics, but he backed them up with scholarship and solid trial skills that usually won the day.

If there was a Rosetta stone of the Equalizer movement, it was Mel Belli's 1951 article, "The Adequate Award," published in the prestigious California Law Review. Its main point was that tort awards had not risen proportionally to the increased cost of living, even though the early awards themselves never had represented real compensation. Trial and appellate judges reviewing jury verdicts had taken an extremely narrow viewpoint, usually looking backwards to older decisions that had been erected as barriers to adequate compensation. Thus, if the highest award for the loss of a leg was $15,000 in a particular state, even if it had been granted in 1910, the courts of the 1940s and 1950s would raise that old award to the lofty status of a legal precedent, without bothering to make any adjustments for the decreased value of the dollar. Belli's article cited many shortchanging decisions, such as an 1896 Indiana case holding that a verdict of $1,100 was adequate for the loss of a leg by a seven-year-old girl, and a 1911 Arkansas case in which a verdict of $10,000 was ordered reduced to $5,000 even though the plaintiff had lost both his legs.

Then Belli's article documented the decreased value of the 1951 dollar, using common items such as the cost of a four-room house, the hourly wages of carpenters, and the quarterly tuition fees at Stanford University. Many of these costs had multiplied by five to ten times in the first half of the twentieth century, but the ceilings imposed by courts on jury verdicts for personal injuries and death had been allowed to rise by only a small fraction.

Belli demonstrated through analysis of hundreds of decisions that there was a sound barrier in the vicinity of $50,000, beyond which most state and federal judges got their knives ready to perform surgery on jury verdicts. But he went on to cite dozens of isolated cases in which plaintiffs had collected amounts exceeding $50,000. These data, which had not been collected or published anywhere, he had obtained from plaintiff's lawyers in various states, and they included many cases that were settled before trial. In order to avoid raising the general level of verdicts, insurance companies and railroads had long made a practice of settling their severest cases before trial when they involved strong liability and heartbreaking injuries. Settling a handful of such cases for comparatively generous amounts was much cheaper for them than allowing juries to pass on them and thereby running the risk that judges would start to back away from outmoded precedents in ruling on the excessiveness of awards. Belli's unique scholarship on settlements was more significant than the old shortchanging decisions that one could find in the lawbooks. Here was a register of the true value of serious injury cases in the current marketplace, which trial and appellate judges should take into account when deciding on excessiveness.

Belli's eye-opening 1951 article was quoted by many formerly backward courts to justify the affirmance of much higher awards than had been allowed to stand before Mel wrote "The Adequate Award." Included among them were the supreme courts of Mississippi, Arizona, and Oregon, which in the 1950s had been classified as "low- verdict areas" that used nineteenth-century yardsticks of compensation.

As he wrote, lectured, and traveled around the country trying cases, Mel put the blame on plaintiff's lawyers for failing to pick up the gauntlet he had thrown down to them: the challenge of using "The Adequate Award" and demonstrative evidence to lift their local courts out of the gaslight era. As he wrote in his 1954 textbook, *Modern Trials*:

> That too low a standard had been put upon man's life, his mind, his members, his family, has been almost entirely the fault of the plaintiff's trial lawyer himself in failing, in the so-called low-verdict centers, properly to educate juries, trial judges, and appellate judges. Adequate preparation and adequate use of demonstrative evidence has produced adequate awards.

It was this challenge, plus Mel's charisma and his own record of success in trial and appellate courts, that convinced many plaintiff's lawyers to try his methods of education, first teaching themselves and then educating judges and jurors. Mel himself used a courtroom blackboard like a high-school or college instructor, printing key words and figures in chalk to make a more lasting impression than his spoken word. He also had a skeleton named Elmer, whose component parts he used in courtroom anatomy lectures that helped jurors to understand and evaluate serious injuries.

Belli had the drive to package his courtroom victories, his books and law review articles, his blackboards and blown-up photos, and Elmer the skeleton into a traveling circus of legal seminars which were unlike anything that had ever been seen in law practice. From 1951 through 1956 he conducted a five-year cross-country crusade, lecturing in 44 states under ATLA auspices. He became president of ATLA in 1951, and attracted hundreds of tort lawyers throughout the country into membership. As he barnstormed the country, he often made side trips to try cases, especially in low-verdict areas. In 1954, for example, he interrupted a lecture tour to spend four weeks trying a case in Montana. In a county where the highest previous award had been $30,000, he achieved a jury verdict of $183,000 for a man who had lost his leg and suffered other serious injuries in a gas explosion.

At the height of Belli's five-year crusade to build ATLA's influence, there occurred what was then the world's worst air disaster. On June 30, 1956, two airliners departed from Los Angeles International Airport within a few minutes of each other on cross-country flights. TWA Flight 2, a Lockheed Constellation, departed at 9:01 a.m., bound for Kansas City, Missouri. United Air Lines Flight 718, a Douglas DC-7, took off at 9:04 a.m., scheduled to fly to Chicago. According to their flight plans, both planes were scheduled to fly over the Painted Desert and the Grand Canyon in Arizona, an area that was not then on the civil airways and was therefore considered "uncontrolled airspace." At 10:31 a.m., the two airliners collided near Painted Desert and fell into the Grand Canyon, killing a total of 128 persons. The time was fixed by the chilling radio message received from the United crew at 10:31 a.m.: "Salt Lake, United 718—ahhh!—we're going in!"

The passengers had come from cities across the country, and so their families consulted law firms in different states. Both airlines blamed the accident on the FAA (then called the CAA) air traffic control personnel, but legally there was no basis for suing the U.S. government since the crash occurred outside its traffic control jurisdiction. The insurers refused to pay compensation, and all of the families were forced to file suit. Because they were dispersed around the country, lawsuits were filed in a dozen different states. I had been retained by the families of the New York and New England passengers, and tried to figure out how I could help to coordinate the efforts of those representing the other 120 families in Los Angeles, Kansas City, Chicago, Pittsburgh, and other places.

The airlines' insurers, of course, had no problem coordinating their defenses. They appointed two major New York admiralty/aviation defense firms, who were defending the suits I had filed in New York, to handle the discovery and trial preparation for all the suits, and to assist the local defense lawyers in trials held outside of New York. I felt that the claimants needed this kind of coordination even more than the airlines' insurers did. But how could we accomplish this? As of 1956, there had never been an airline crash that involved such widely dispersed litigation. Usually there were no more than a dozen suits filed, mostly in one state. And there had never been a major midair collision involving the arcane question of whether the government air traffic controllers, who had been told that both planes would be

over the Painted Desert at the same time and altitude, had a duty
to warn the pilots (which they did not do.)

ATLA provided the answer to this problem. In 1955, I had
been designated to organize an ATLA Aviation Law section, the
first such section in any bar association. (As it turned out, I was
to serve as its chairman for the first 10 years of its existence.)
That section helped to establish communications among plaintiff's lawyers throughout the country in aviation accident cases,
through educational seminars and the pooling of information
about specific cases. Through the Aviation Law section of ATLA,
we assembled a group of Grand Canyon plaintiff's lawyers who
knew each other and were eager to cooperate—leading tort lawyers such as Craig Spangenberg of Cleveland, Jim McArdle and
Dennis Harrington of Pittsburgh, Jim Dooley of Chicago (later to
become Justice Dooley of the Illinois Supreme Court), Everett
Hullverson and Orville Richardson of St. Louis, Bill de Parcq of
Minneapolis, John McGeehan of Newark, and Mel Belli of California.

After several organizational meetings, it was decided that I
would be designated to investigate and prepare the liability
phase for all cases in the group. My contingent fee for these
services would be paid by each plaintiff's lawyer out of his own
contingent fee. In addition, each plaintiff's lawyer was to pay
$250 per case into a joint expense fund. This group was the first
effective network of plaintiff's lawyers involved in nationwide
tort litigation. In the end, the group included most of Grand
Canyon claims that were filed in court.

Our first task was to prove that a collision had occurred, and
who had hit whom. Even though the accident was known
throughout the world as the Grand Canyon Midair Collision,
there were no eye-witnesses, and in the court cases, the airlines'
lawyers denied that the planes had collided. Their strategy was
to make us prove even the most obvious facts, hoping that this
burden would overwhelm our jerry-built group. The Civil Aeronautics Board had issued a report concluding that there had been
a collision, but a federal statute prohibited use of the CAB report
in litigation.

My first discovery thrust was a motion for production of the
aircraft wreckage. I was not about to let the airlines get the only
look at their own wreckage, as had happened in the Jane Froman
case. Most of the wreckage was still at the bottom of the Grand
Canyon, but the government investigators had recovered portions of the left wing of the United airplane and the tail section
of the TWA plane, which they brought out of the Canyon with

the help of helicopters and a team of professional mountain climbers flown over from Switzerland. These key pieces enabled the government investigators to determine the angle and other details of the collision. They had assembled these pieces of wreckage on the floor of a hangar at Washington National Airport, and had then taken photos and made laboratory tests from which they concluded that the left wing of the United DC-7 had hit the tail of the TWA Constellation from behind. After the government investigation was completed, the wreckage was returned to the respective airlines that owned it. Our discovery motion was granted, and the airlines were ordered to produce the wreckage for our inspection at Washington National Airport.

The wreckage was produced on the appointed day. But instead of neatly tagged pieces that we could assemble on the hangar floor as the CAB had done, the airlines produced assorted jagged metal parts that gave no clue to their identity or position. Fortunately we had the CAB committee report, which included photos of all the recovered wreckage. From these we were able to puzzle out the reconstruction, but it was slow work. Two and a half days later, we had completed the reassembly on the hangar floor, and Sam Tour, a metallurgist we had brought down from New York, was ready to go to work with his cameras and spectrographic analysis equipment. We hoped that he would be able to determine the fact and angle of collision from the paint of the United Airlines wingtip that had lodged on the TWA tail and from other markings on the wreckage, as the CAB had done. But at that point, before Sam could do anything, the airline lawyers announced that we had had enough time for discovery, and that they were shutting down the operation.

After the hangar door was shut in our faces, we went back to the federal court in Manhattan and requested an order requiring the airlines to let us complete the discovery. The judge was impressed by our plight, and he granted our motion. We took Sam Tour back to the Washington hangar, where he completed his photos and tests. Then we took his deposition for all the cases in the group, so that each plaintiff's lawyer could prove the fact and angle of collision. The defense lawyers tried to discredit his testimony because he was not an aeronautical engineer. At that time, it was almost impossible to find qualified aeronautical engineers who would testify against any branch of the aviation industry. But Sam was an experienced expert witness on metallurgy and was not about to be downgraded. When a defense lawyer asked him on his deposition whether he had ever made an analysis of a midair collision before, he gave one of those classic answers that trial lawyers pray for: "No, but a piece of metal is a piece of metal, whether it is on an airplane or on a stove!"

It took me the better part of two years to prepare the liability phase of the Grand Canyon case, with dozens of depositions taken in Washington, D.C., where the principal CAA Air Traffic Control officials were located; Salt Lake City, where the controllers working these flights were stationed; Kansas City, Missouri, the headquarters of TWA; and Los Angeles, where United's regional supervisors had their offices. I had to reconstruct the whole history of CAA Air Traffic Control, to prove that the airlines had not expected to receive traffic information or separation when off airways, and that they were legally responsible to avoid such a collision by the "see and be seen" method. Even after this exhaustive discovery, the airlines' insurers were confident that we could not win the case. The first trial was scheduled to begin in Los Angeles in October of 1958. The plaintiff's lawyer was Mel Belli. I was delighted and flattered when he asked me to come out to work with him at the trial.

Mel was then 51 years old, and could easily have been cast as one of McKenzie Brackman's leading trial lawyers. He was handsome, brilliant, sure of himself, and equipped with a great stage voice. I had never worked with him before, and in common with most other lawyers, I had mixed feelings about him. He had received enormous publicity, notably in a 1954 *Life Magazine* article that crowned him "The King of Torts." Though his boyish pranks and blatant egotism rubbed a lot of people the wrong way, he was creating great public interest in tort cases and was forcing tort lawyers all over the country to push themselves beyond their limitations to emulate his pathfinding courtroom victories.

Mel's clients were the three orphaned children of a California lawyer who, along with his wife, had been killed in the Grand Canyon disaster. The deceased lawyer, whom we'll call Bill Harkness, was 42 years old when he died, and his wife Mildred was 40. Their son was 14, and the two daughters were aged 11 and 8. Bill Harkness was a small-town general practice lawyer who handled some tort cases and was a member of ATLA. The family had moved from Oklahoma to California in 1955. Bill had been making about $10,000 a year as a single practitioner in Oklahoma, and was just getting started in California when the crash cut him down.

The trial went on for more than six weeks, most of it devoted to fighting over liability. Mel did most of the talking in court, and did a brilliant job. I was delegated the task of combatting the main defense of both airlines: that the CAA controllers at Salt Lake City had been told that both planes would be over the Painted Desert at the same time and altitude, but did not warn either plane. The airline lawyers relied on some ambiguous CAA publications which mentioned that the CAA would warn of "potentially hazardous conditions" even off the airways. After much testimony and argument, I finally succeeded in convincing the judge that this applied only to weather conditions, not air traffic, which could not be safely monitored off the airways. After the airline lawyers had committed themselves to reliance on the CAA for traffic separation, the judge granted our motion to strike out this defense, ruling that as a matter of law, there was no air traffic control or information provided off the airways.

On damages, Mel presented two star witnesses to the ability and earning power of Bill Harkness. Both of them were distinguished appellate judges before whom Harkness had practiced when they were trial court judges—one in Oklahoma and one in California. Justice Ben T. Williams of the Oklahoma Supreme Court went through a list of cases that Bill Harkness had tried, recounting the details to the jury in a folksy Will Rogers style. He rated Bill among the top ten percent of Oklahoma trial lawyers. And Justice Walter J. Fourt of the California District Court of Appeal testified that if Bill had been alive then (in 1958), he would have been earning about $25,000 per year, based on the amounts then being earned by lawyers of similar skill. Mildred Harkness had worked as a school teacher, earning about $5,000 a year, and was scheduled to work her way up to $7,000 over a ten-year period. The school principal testified to her earnings and told the jurors that he rated Mildred a superior and dedicated teacher. The three children also testified, rounding out the picture of an All-American family in the Norman Rockwell image.

Mel made a magnificent final argument, raking the airline lawyers over the coals for taking up weeks with untenable arguments that there had not been a collision and that the CAA was supposed to exercise traffic control off airways. On damages, he filled the blackboard with figures that were based on the evidence. He took the $25,000 earning potential of the lawyer-husband, added $3,000 per year for the teacher-wife, and multiplied the $28,000 total by 30 years, their joint life expectancies, to reach a total of $840,000. The law required adjustments for personal living expenses and taxes that would reduce the $840,000 figure, but there were other calculations that would offset the reductions, and so Belli argued in round figures that the financial loss to the three orphaned children was close to $1 million. He told the jurors that if a $500,000 racehorse had been destroyed, they would have to award the full $500,000. He urged them to treat these orphaned children as fairly as they would the owner of a racehorse, by awarding them the full damages prescribed by law, dollar for dollar.

The jurors deliberated for the better part of two days. Finally, on the 43rd day of the trial, they announced their verdicts. They found in favor of the plaintiffs against both airlines, and awarded $200,000 for the death of Bill Harkness and $20,000 for the death of Mildred. The Clerk then polled the jury. There were nine "yes" answers and three "no" answers, meaning that we had won the case by the narrowest margin allowed by California law.

The total of $220,000 probably seems pitifully low to you, even in terms of 1958 dollars. But we were still in the dark ages of artificial barriers to fair compensation, and in fact there had only been a handful of wrongful-death jury verdicts above $75,000 at that time. The airline lawyers were shocked at the award, which was more than twice what they had been willing to offer in settlement at any time. They immediately asked the judge to set aside the verdicts as excessive and order a new trial. A few weeks after the jury verdict, the trial judge lopped $50,000 off the Bill Harkness verdict, reducing it to $150,000. Mercifully, he let stand the $20,000 verdict for the death of Mildred, the mother.

Trial judges do not actually have the power to rewrite the jury's verdict, but they do so indirectly through *remittitur*: they order a new trial unless the plaintiff agrees voluntarily to "remit" part of the jury's verdict. This is an important power which I feel is needed to correct the occasional jury verdict that exceeds reasonable compensation. However, it has been used traditionally in accident cases to keep jury verdicts within predetermined limits *regardless of the evidence of real loss*. Thus, in the Harkness case, the only evidence of future earning power was that the 42-year-old lawyer was capable of earning $25,000 per year in 1958—and that evidence came from a respected California appellate judge who had observed Harkness at work in the trial courts. Although the jury could consider his past earnings ($11,000) as some indication of his probable future income, they were not restricted to a verdict based on maximum earnings of $11,000 for the last 30 years of his life. They could have selected any figure between $11,000 and $25,000 and multiplied it by the 30-year life expectancy.

The jurors were instructed that this gross earnings figure would have to be adjusted for various factors, but the adjustments largely cancelled each other out, so that any verdict between $330,000 and $750,000 would have been supported by uncontroverted evidence in this case. The jury had been conservative enough in awarding $200,000. Yet the trial judge, an eminently fair and scholarly jurist, felt compelled to reduce it by a quarter, to keep it within the tradional limits of accident awards. He cited no precedents and gave no reasons. He simply held the line because the California courts were not ready to allow any family to collect $200,000 for the death of the breadwinner, regardless of the real financial loss.

Despite the reduction, the Harkness family eagerly accepted the $150,000 for Bill's death and $20,000 for Mildred's. Otherwise they would have to endure the delay and expense of a second trial, and even if they won the case again, it was doubtful that the trial judge would allow any larger verdict to stand.

I was angry at the reduction because we were still Frank Capra's little pushed-around guys. If we had represented the owner of the $500,000 racehorse that Mel mentioned in his final argument, or a museum that had lost a $2 million painting in a fire, we would have been awarded those amounts, and because property rather than a human being was involved, the trial judge would not have reduced the verdicts. This was what Mel Belli's Adequate Award crusade was all about. We had to content ourselves with the knowledge that collecting $150,000 for the death of one man was an important step toward adequate awards, for the airline insurers had rarely paid more than $50,000 for such a life until the Equalizers began to develop some clout.

The Harkness trial did not end the Grand Canyon litigation. In those days each case stood on its own, and we had to endure another half dozen trials on liability and damages before the insurers finally agreed to decent settlements in the remaining cases. Today, with modern consolidation procedures, there would probably be only one trial on liability for all the families involved.

The experience of working in court with Mel Belli at the height of his powers was exhilarating. I learned a lot of fine points that I have often used since then, although I never did summon the courage to wear fire-chief red trousers to court. There was also a lot of fun to working with Mel—if one was not too faint-hearted to enjoy it. During the trial Mel was frequently visited at his hotel by Mickey Cohen, the notorious Los Angeles hoodlum, who was trying to convince Mel to defend him in a pending criminal case. During this wooing process, the two went out to fashionable restaurants and night spots several times during the trial. Mel invited me along several times, but I always told him I was too busy preparing for the next day's courtroom work. I also tried to discourage Mel from being seen in public with Mickey Cohen. I was not being snobbish. I simply thought it might hurt our case if Mel's picture appeared in the paper with Mickey. On our jury of twelve people, we had eight middle-aged women, most of whom looked conservative enough to be Daughters of the American Revolution. Also, there was a lot of gang warfare buzzing around Cohen, and I did not want to wind up with a bomb in my shrimp cocktail, even if Mickey was picking up the tab. (Sure enough, thirty years later, *L.A. Law's* Grace Van Owen was to experience the fatal shooting of her racketeer client as he sat talking to her in a fashionable Los Angeles restaurant.)

Despite my evasive maneuvers, Mel trapped me one night during the trial. I was climbing into an automobile to join Mel for dinner before I realized that he had Mickey and Mickey's current girlfriend in the car with him. It was too late for excuses, and so I decided to make the best of the evening. Mel had not forgotten my reluctance to join the Cohen party. As a special treat, he arranged for me to sit in the back of the car, next to Mickey Cohen's English bulldog, who was addressed as "Mickey Junior." I don't mind English bulldogs as a breed, but this one was something special. Mickey had trained the dog to go into a growling, drooling tantrum at the mere mention of the names of law enforcement officials. As we drove along the Sunset Strip, Mickey was showing off his dog-training prowess. He said to the dog, "Junior: J. Edgar Hoover!" At that point, the four-legged Mickey started growling, drooling, and foaming at the mouth, mostly in my direction. It occurred to me that he might have Junior trained to tear apart Hoover and any other lawman who came within his range. Mickey and Mel were convulsed with laughter as I cringed in the corner, completely intimidated by the English bulldog. Mickey and Mel ran through the names of most of the top echelon of the Los Angeles Police Department before they finally broke up the act when we arrived at Dino's Lodge for dinner.

This was my first (and last) dinner with a famous racketeer. I was not prepared for the bowing and scraping that would precede our entry into the restaurant, then one of the most popular in Hollywood. We had the best table in the house and were swarmed over by captains and waiters. On the way back to our hotel I managed to slip into the front seat so that Mel Belli could have exclusive jurisdiction over Mickey Cohen's bulldog.

Mel was so devoted to clowning, and so adept at it, that it was difficult to perceive him as the great legal statesman he became. In 1959 he bought an old building on Montgomery Street, which had been a saloon during the San Francisco Gold Rush, next door to the house in which Bret Harte had written "The Luck of Roaring Camp." Mel had his building restored to the decor of the nineteenth-century Barbary Coast. His personal ground-floor office became a tourist attraction, as he could be seen through the large glass windows working at his desk with his faithful skeleton Elmer sitting nearby. On display in the front window was a photo of seven Mexican bandits, complete with rifles and cartridge belts, right out of the annals of Pancho Villa. The inscription under this photo, which Belli had printed in old-English lettering, reads: "Adjusters of the Holy Grail Insurance Company." He also installed a roof flagpole on which he ran up the Jolly Roger whenever he won a case.

Over the years I had the privilege of working on other cases with Mel Belli. When he called on the phone, I cringed instinctively, wondering what new challenge he might drop in my lap. Once it was the case of Ferdinand Waldo (Fred) DeMara, the self-styled "world's greatest imposter," who wanted to halt the filming of his life story (starring Tony Curtis) because he claimed he had been bilked into signing his rights away. The only problem with the case was that it turned on a question of credibility, and DeMara himself, our only witness, had made a career of lying, sailing under false colors as a Trappist monk, an assistant warden of a Texas prison, a surgeon in the Canadian Navy, and a lecturer to brain surgeons, despite his complete lack of traditional qualifications for any of those jobs. With some trepidation I filed suit for DeMara. With Mel's help, I was able to work out a financial settlement for Fred, who later became an investigator in Mel's San Francisco office. Then came the case in which Mel himself had been sued, along with his client, Phyllis McGuire of the McGuire sisters. Phyllis had sent a necklace to the renowned jeweler, Harry Winston, for cleaning, and she claimed that he had substituted and returned to her a worthless paste necklace. Mel had been a little overzealous in pursuing her claim, placing newspaper ads that asked others who had been similarly cheated by Harry Winston to get in touch with him. The first to get in touch with Mel were Winston's lawyers, who filed suit in New York against him and Phyllis McGuire for defamation. Cooler heads finally prevailed, and the whole matter was settled out of court.

Mel Belli was and is important to nearly every person who has suffered a serious injury since the 1950s. Without the life work of this one man, millions of injured persons would have much smaller chances of recovering adequate compensation. And many lawyers would still be struggling to eke out a living from unrewarding law practices, shackled by nineteenth-century concepts designed to protect property rights.

The Grand Canyon litigation broke the pattern of isolation and dispersion of the victims that had been maintained so carefully by the airline insurers in the past. The insurers did not welcome this development. They made every step of the case expensive and time-consuming, knowing that lawyers working on contingent fees would find it difficult to keep pace with the powerful hourly-fee defense firms that were brought in against us all over the country. But by proving our staying power and establishing our ability to take the necessary thousands of pages of depositions and fashion them into a successful trial presentation, we made some important progress. At a cost of only $250 per case for expenses, we centralized a nationwide effort that was successful in meeting the heavy demands of the Grand Canyon litigation. I took some pride in this bit of pioneering, but my satisfaction was blunted when I faced up to the fact that our clients had been shortchanged. I feel quite certain that all of the money paid to the families of the Grand Canyon passengers ran out long before the expiration of the life expectancies on which the right to compensation was based. We had a long way to go before we could call ourselves Equalizers.

The Grand Canyon experience furnished a working model for cooperation (later called "networking") among plaintiff's lawyers who had similar cases arising out of a mass disaster or injuries inflicted on many people by defective products. Our firm was to build on the Grand Canyon model when we were called upon to organize a group of lawyers representing victims of the anti-cholesterol drug MER/29, which had side effects that included cataracts. Led by Paul Rheingold, who joined our firm after working at ATLA headquarters, we were able to coordinate the efforts of MER/29 plaintiff's lawyers throughout the country. The group's efforts produced many favorable verdicts and settlements, including the first punitive damage awards in pharmaceutical cases.

ATLA seized the opportunity to institutionalize this networking. Today, through its Product Liability Exchange, its affiliated state chapters, and its litigation groups, ATLA supplies its 60,000 lawyer-members with computerized backup services that would cost of tens of millions of dollars to duplicate. It has more than 75 litigation groups, each one dedicated to a particular field of litigation, such as Asbestos in Schools, Breast Implants, Dalkon Shield IUD devices, Formaldehyde, Nursing Homes, Tire/Rim Mismatches, and Yugo Automobiles. These action groups supply members with copies of technical literature, expert opinions, trial transcripts, settlement data, and other materials that are priceless to the plaintiff's lawyer, putting him or her on a level playing field with corporate giants: the insurers and manufacturers who are their opponents in litigation. In addition to helping injured victims recover compensation, these efforts have also led to improved product warnings and instructions, more thorough investigations by regulatory agencies, and more responsible business practices. ATLA itself has become a great Equalizer, and it serves as the command post in the continuing battle to achieve justice for the underdog.

In 1982, leaders of ATLA formed Trial Lawyers for Public Justice, a separate organization that serves as a national public interest trial law firm, taking on groundbreaking cases that private lawyers and other public interest organizations would not pursue because of the financial risks. This unique task force has compiled an enviable record in difficult environmental, civil rights, and consumer rights cases.

ATLA and its state affiliates produce educational seminars somewhere in the country every week. Thousands of ATLA members contribute their time and talents to these seminars, often traveling at their own expense to divulge techniques that have won cases for them. This gesture is not entirely philanthropic, for in addition to the ego gratification that goes with being recognized as a teacher by one's professional peers, it can also produce referrals of cases from lawyers in the audience.

Equally important has been ATLA's development as a legal authority. Again the organizational genius of Sam Horovitz was decisive. After he got Mel Belli started on his nationwide barnstorming crusade, Sam pulled his greatest coup by signing up Roscoe Pound, dean emeritus of the Harvard Law School, to become editor of the *ATLA Law Journal*. Pound was renowned as the chief American advocate of sociological jurisprudence, which required old legal precedents to be adjusted to contemporary social conditions. He and his colleagues, including Felix Frankfurter, were credited with inspiring and providing the legal underpinning for much of Franklin D. Roosevelt's New Deal legislation in the 1930s. Pound's enormous prestige and scholarship established ATLA's journal as a serious professional publication which judges throughout the country read and cited.

Dean Pound was in his early eighties when Sam Horovitz recruited him for ATLA. He stayed on for two years until his eyesight began to give out. Then Sam came up with a replacement for Pound who was to prove as important to ATLA as the great dean himself. His choice, recommended by Dean Pound as his successor, was Professor Thomas F. Lambert Jr. Tom was a Rhodes scholar who served as trial counsel on the staff of the chief American prosecutor at the Nuremberg trials, Justice Robert H. Jackson. Tom prepared the American trial brief against the Nazi party leaders and delivered the final trial argument against party chief Martin Bormann. His extraordinary writing and speaking gifts were a godsend to ATLA as he took Dean Pound's place in 1955. He soon became known as the Poet Laureate of Torts. (Commenting on a statute that would have limited damages for pain and suffering, he quoted Shakespeare: "They jest at scars who never felt a wound.") He has inspired many an ordinary lawyer to reach out for excellence and become an Equalizer.

ATLA and Mel Belli were largely responsible for turning the rag-tag band of plaintiff's tort lawyers into a nationwide force of Equalizers. This helps to explain one of the swiftest and most significant sea changes in all of legal history: the development of "strict liability" for injuries caused by defective products.

Strict Liability for Defective Products

Lobbyists for business interests who seek to limit the responsibility of manufacturers for the damage done by defective products describe strict product liability as the revolutionary invention of greedy tort lawyers. But legal responsibility for dangerous and defective products, with or without proof of specific negligence, was part of the earliest Anglo-American tort law. Indeed, the tort law on both sides of the Atlantic originally provided for strict liability—regardless of fault—for any personal injury, whether caused by a manufacturer or anyone else. The early law was preoccupied with breaches of the peace. Damages were offered primarily to induce injured persons to refrain from resorting to private vengeance. This overall strict tort liability lasted well into the nineteenth century. It was a cheap giveaway for the establishment since there were no Equalizers to enforce these rights.

Consequently there were few tort claims brought to court, and those who sued rarely recovered more than a fraction of their actual losses.

When the Industrial Revolution changed society in the nineteenth century, the requirement of proving fault came into Anglo-American law; but there remained underpinnings of strict liability that the courts could have leaned on if there had been Equalizers capable of presenting the right cases to them in the right way. There was the long-standing concept that a manufacturer or seller of goods impliedly warranted that the goods were "fit for the use intended"—that the seller stood behind his product, at least to the extent that it was suitable for the purpose for which it was marketed. This implied warranty of fitness originated in tort law and then became part of the law of sales, protecting purchasers who were sold unmerchantable goods. As we shall see, it was this implied warranty that the courts used as a foundation for strict product liability when the time of the Equalizers came.

Meanwhile, in the 1842 case of *Winterbottom v. Wright*, an English court erected a door that barred those injured by defective products from suing manufacturers unless they had bought the defective product directly from the manufacturer. This became known as the "privity" rule, since it prohibited suit by all those who were not in "privity of contract" with the manufacturer. Note that privity was required before anyone injured by a product could sue the manufacturer, not only for strict liability but also for negligence. The nineteenth-century American courts quickly adopted the privity rule. There was nobody around to speak effectively against it. Indeed, given the weakness of plaintiff's lawyers at that time, it is doubtful whether any of them could have undertaken so complicated and expensive a project as a suit against a manufacturer even if privity were not required.

A century later, the injustice of the *Winterbottom v. Wright* privity rule had become apparent. It was shielding manufacturers from responsibility for poisoning and maiming unsuspecting victims of dangerous and defective products simply because the products had been bought from a dealer. First the privity rule was abandoned in negligence claims, led by a famous 1916 decision by New York Court of Appeals Judge Benjamin Cardozo. In *MacPherson v. Buick Motor Co.*, he ruled that Donald MacPherson, a Saratoga gravestone contractor, could bring a negligence action against Buick for injuries he suffered when a defective wheel came off his 1911 Buick runabout and dumped him into a ditch, even though he had bought the car from a dealer rather than directly from Buick. Cardozo's reasoning was based upon long-standing legal protection against inherently dangerous articles; he simply extended this principle to the automobile as an article that may reasonably be expected to inflict harm if defectively made. This was one of the most important American tort decisions, but it still left the claimants with the burden of proving *negligence* in the design or manufacturing process, a task that was beyond the skills of most tort lawyers during the first half of the twentieth century.

After Cardozo's 1916 *MacPherson* decision, the courts began to move away from the negligence requirement toward strict liability for a few product groups. They broadened the protection of the implied warranty of fitness by creating exceptions to the privity rule, most notably that the implied warranty applied even without privity to food products and others that were dangerous to life or limb if negligently made. Even though there were no strong plaintiff's lawyers capable of mounting a sustained assault on privity, there was grave public concern about adulterated food products, dramatized by Upton Sinclair in *The Jungle*, his muckracking attack on the putrescent Chicago stockyards. As Al Gans wrote in 1946, when he was editor of *American Law Reports*, "the exceptions have swallowed up the rule," since virtually any product that was the subject of a personal injury suit could be dangerous if defective.

Finally in the 1960s, privity faced its last stand. The Supreme Court of New Jersey struck a telling blow in 1960, allowing an automobile owner whose wife was injured by a defective steering gear to sue the manufacturer, Plymouth, for breach of implied warranty as well as negligence, even though the car had been bought by her husband from a dealer. In 1963, the California Supreme Court went New Jersey one better by allowing William Greenman to sue Yuba Power Products, Inc., the manufacturer of a "Shopsmith" power tool that Greenman's wife had bought as a Christmas present for him from a dealer. Like many a Christmas gift, the Shopsmith failed to perform according to the owner's manual. When Mr. Greenman deployed it as a wood lathe, it hurled a large piece of wood at him like a projectile, inflicting serious head injuries. Mr. Greenman was permitted to sue the manufacturer directly for "strict liability in tort," thus extricating product liability actions from the intricacies of sales and contract law.

Strict liability, like breach of implied warranty, meant that manufacturers and sellers could be held liable for injuries caused by defective products even if negligence could not be proved. The plaintiff would have to prove just two things: that there was a defect, and that the defect caused the injury.

This was an important advance for victims of defective products, for it relieved them of the burden of delving into the manufacturing process, which might involve thousands of laboratory experiments and blueprints, as well as complicated theories of how to design and make the product. It was difficult enough to prove a defect and causation, without undertaking to reinvent the wheel by showing just how and why the product came to be defective. Another advantage of eliminating the privity requirement was that the plaintiffs now had a direct suit against the manufacturer, which was often needed to overcome lack of insurance and limited assets on the part of dealers, who might just fold up their corporations if hit with a large judgment in a defective product case.

The 1963 California Shopsmith power tool decision was written by Justice Roger Traynor, one of America's most respected judges, who authored over 140 opinions on tort law during his 30 years on the California Supreme Court. It was based on views that he had expressed nearly 20 years earlier, in the 1944 case of *Escola v. Coca Cola*, which was argued for the plaintiff by Mel Belli. Gladys Escola was a waitress in a California restaurant who was seriously injured when a Coca Cola bottle exploded in her hand. The bottle had been supplied to her employer by a distributor, but she sued Coca Cola directly for negligence. Belli managed to win the case on negligence, using circumstantial evidence and the principle of *res ipsa loquitur* (the thing speaks for itself), which allowed him to argue to the jury that Coca Cola bottles do not explode by themselves unless someone has been negligent in the bottling process. The California Supreme Court affirmed Belli's negligence verdict, but Justice Traynor went further. He wrote a concurring opinion that called for the courts to apply strict liability to Coca Cola and any other manufacturer of a defective product that caused injury. The other California Supreme Court justices were content to stay with the negligence standard in 1944. But in the 1963 Shopsmith case, the entire court joined with Traynor, now the chief justice, in finding strict product liability. They adopted the core of his 1944 *Coca Cola* decision:

> Public policy demands that responsibility be fixed wherever it will most effectively reduce the hazards to life and health inherent in defective products that reach the market. It is evident that the manufacturer can anticipate some hazards and guard against others, as the public cannot. Those who suffer injury

from defective products are unprepared to meet its consequences. The cost of an injury and the loss of time or health
may be an overwhelming misfortune to the person injured, and
a needless one, for the risk of injury can be insured by the
manufacturer and distributed among the public as a cost of
doing business.

That simple statement opened the way for California victims
of defective products to be compensated without having to
prove negligence. Other states followed, some continuing to
cling to the "breach of implied warranty" language that furnished the historical basis for the breakthrough, and others following California by calling it "strict product liability." Justice
Traynor, in both his visionary 1944 Coca Cola opinion and the
unanimous 1963 Shopsmith decision, relied heavily on the writings of William Prosser, author of the leading textbook on torts,
first published in 1941 when Prosser was teaching at the University of Minnesota Law School. (In 1948, Prosser moved to the
University of California, where he taught torts until his death in
1972.) In a *tour de force* of legal scholarship, Prosser demonstrated
that the implied warranty of fitness had its historical roots in tort
law rather than in contract, and that there was no historical or
logical basis for the decadent privity rule. Prosser's writings in
law reviews and in his own textbook opened the way for the
courts to bring tort law into harmony with property law in its
treatment of those who sold defective products. If the buyer of a
defective product could get the purchase price refunded without
proving any more than a defect that caused the product to be
unfit for the use intended, why shouldn't those who suffered
physical injuries from the defective product be able to bring their
claims to court on the same proof?

The 1960 Plymouth case in New Jersey and the 1963 California Shopsmith case dealt with products that someone in the
plaintiff's family had purchased for direct use within the family.
But what about the carnage caused by defective products that
were bought by service companies for use in their business,
which inflicted injuries on those who bought the services rather
than the product—e.g., the airline passenger injured or killed by
a defective airplane? Because I was representing victims of most
of the major air disasters at the time of the assault on privity, it
fell to me to do the door-kicking in that field.

On February 3, 1959, a Lockheed Electra operated by American Airlines crashed into New York's East River as it was approaching LaGuardia Airport for a night instrument landing
after a flight from Chicago. Sixty-five of the 73 persons on board

were killed. Among the eight survivors were the co-pilot and the
flight engineer, both of whom testified that just before the crash
the plane's two altimeters indicated that the plane was 500 feet
high instead of at the level of the airport. The Electra then was a
fairly new aircraft, in which Lockheed had installed a new
"drum" type altimeter in place of the older "three-pointer" type
that its crews were accustomed to. The government accident investigation report concluded that one of the causes of the accident might have been the crew's misreading of the new
drum-type altimeters. A few days after the accident, the FAA
raised the minimum ceiling and visibility requirements for Electra landings. In response, American replaced the drum-type altimeters with the conventional three-pointer types, whereupon
the FAA restored the lower minimums. Thus, the confusing design of the new (and short-lived) drum-type altimeter was found
to be a possible cause of the East River disaster. It was clear that
the crew had become confused during the final approach, and
there were no other failures to account for an experienced airline
captain flying his plane into the river.

This was a domestic accident that did not come under the
Warsaw Convention, so we only had to prove negligence (rather
than wilful misconduct) in order to recover against American
Airlines. But the altimeter problem raised the specter of the
"empty chair" that we had faced in the Jane Froman case. American Airlines could blame the accident on the defectively designed drum-type altimeter, and unless we sued Lockheed (and
thus forced them to either blame American Airlines or take the
blame themselves) there was a chance that the jury would blame
Lockheed completely and let American off, turning our clients
out with nothing. I didn't want a repeat of Rod Sullivan's defective elevator story, so I decided early on to sue Lockheed. I could
sue them for negligence even though my clients had not bought
the airplane, thanks to Judge Cardozo's 1916 ruling in *MacPherson v. Buick*. But winning on negligence would require us to go
beyond proving that a defective altimeter had caused or contributed to the crash. We would have to go through the entire design and manufacturing process and pinpoint just where
Lockheed (and Kollsman Instrument Company, who actually
supplied the altimeter) went wrong. That was a staggering burden for my four-man law firm which in 1959 was struggling to
become an Equalizer on a small scale.

I decided that in addition to suing American Airlines for
negligence, we would sue Lockheed for both negligence and
strict liability, based on the implied warranty that the Electra was

fit for use in passenger service and free of defects that endangered the passengers. This was in 1959, before the New Jersey Plymouth case (1960) and the California Shopsmith power tool case (1963) established the right to sue for strict liability in those states. Since the only things my clients had purchased were tickets on American Airlines, and therefore they had no privity with Lockheed, they had no established legal right to sue the manufacturer for anything other than negligence. But I felt the wind of change in the air, and decided that I would try to get the New York courts to lead the parade toward strict product liability.

I knew that Lockheed's lawyers would quickly make a motion to dismiss our claims of warranty and strict liability, since they didn't want that issue to arise at the trial. I didn't expect to win the argument in the lower court, since that judge would be bound by past appellate court decisions holding that privity was required. I hoped that the lower court judge would take note of the developing trend toward narrowing the privity requirement through the many recognized exceptions, thus opening the door a crack so that the appellate courts might focus on the need for change. In the event, we drew Justice Aron Steuer, then in his last year on the trial bench before being elevated to the Appellate Division.

By this time you must think that Aron Steuer was the only judge in the Supreme Court of New York County. Actually, he was one of more than 30 judges before whom this case might have come, but it was our luck that he fixed his cold gaze on our bold request to allow airline passengers to sue a manufacturer for defects in an airplane which they had not purchased. It would be unsporting of me to keep you in suspense, so I will tell you quickly that he was unreceptive to this new idea, and found it necessary to rule against us. He dismissed the portions of the complaint which alleged breach of implied warranty and strict liability of the manufacturers, Lockheed and Kollsman. He based this conclusion solely on the ground that the passengers had not bought the airplane and therefore had no right to claim warranty or strict liability. As if to smother the movement toward strict liability in its incubator, he decided that the entire subject was unworthy of serious legal discussion:

> It must be conceded that the efforts to extend the doctrine of liability for breach of warranty, proceeding, as they do, on emotional rather than logical grounds, produce situations which are not easily resolved by reason. Basic principles are lost sight of or ignored.

Thus Justice Steuer, steadfast in his support of the eighteenth-century principle that form is more important than substance, disposed of decades of scholarly research by Roger Traynor, the highly regarded chief justice of the California Supreme Court, and Professor William Prosser, universally recognized as America's leading authority on tort law.

Our next stop was the Appellate Division. We struck out again, by a vote of five to zero, without even meriting a written opinion. The Appellate Division also refused us permission to go on to the Court of Appeals, the state's highest court. Our last hope was to get permission from that court to take the final appeal there. Finally in July 1962, the Court of Appeals granted us leave to appeal the case to them. And on May 9, 1963, came a collect telegram from Raymond Cannon, Clerk of the Court of Appeals in Albany, informing us that by a vote of 4-to-3, Justice Steuer's decision was reversed. Our clients would become the first victims of an airline crash to proceed against the airplane manufacturer without having to prove negligence.

The majority opinion by Chief Judge Charles Desmond was short but sweet. He noted the then very recent California Shopsmith case (decided in January 1963, five months before the Lockheed Electra case) and adopted the reasoning of Chief Justice Traynor, even to the extent of saying that California's strict product liability was "surely a more accurate phrase" than New York's "breach of implied warranty." Since strict product liability was so new, Judge Desmond's slim majority applied it only to Lockheed and not to Kollsman, the altimeter manufacturer, because "adequate protection is provided for the passengers by casting in liability the airplane manufacturer which put into the market the completed aircraft." (After Judge Desmond's decision, all of our clients' claims were settled at what were then considered excellent levels of compensation.)

Thus by the spring of 1963, the highest courts of New Jersey, California, and New York had permitted people injured by defective products to sue the manufacturers directly without having to prove negligence. From there, in a little over a decade, the other states fell into line, by allowing suits for either breach of implied warranty or for strict tort liability. In the slow-moving game of kicking in rotten doors, this was wildfire speed. It took years to get test cases up to the highest court in each state, and there was plenty of resistance along the way. Much of the credit for the speed of this change must go to William Prosser, whose writings had inspired California Supreme Court Justice Traynor to pioneer strict liability in the 1944 Coca Cola case.

Yale Law School Professor George Priest, writing the history of the movement toward strict liability, described Prosser as a legal magician who was able to fashion a landslide out of a handful of scattered decisions. Prosser was the main architect of the 1964 revision of the Restatement of Torts, a collection of legal principles drafted by leading scholars. Nearing the end of his career, Prosser was determined to write into the Second Restatement the principle of strict liability for injuries caused by defective products. Professor Priest noted that in support of this thrust, Prosser had only "three genuine strict liability cases" and six "possibles." The three genuine cases, all decisions of states' highest appellate courts, were the 1960 New Jersey Plymouth auto case; the 1963 California Shopsmith case; and my 1963 New York drum altimeter case. The six possibles did not carry as much weight as those three because they were decisions of lower courts that had not yet reached the appellate level. Of the six possibles, three were 1960 decisions in other aviation cases in which I had convinced the trial judge to apply strict liability against airplane manufacturers whose products had crashed in Texas, Michigan, and the Gulf of Mexico. Thus, four of the nine arrows in Prosser's quiver were airplane cases.

Armed with this mixed bag of authorities that surely appeared skimpy to some of his colleagues, Prosser announced that the dam of privity had been busted, "and those in the path of the avalanche would do well to make for the hills." Prosser's genius for achieving consensus on the need for equalizing the rights of tort victims with those of property owners won the day, and Section 402A of the Restatement of Torts Second, adopted without opposition, proclaimed that manufacturers of defective products should be held strictly liable for injuries caused by those products.

Prosser's Restatement victory gave plaintiff's lawyers strong scholarly authority for spreading strict product liability to the states that still clung to the privity rule. Despite Prosser's vision of an avalanche, the privity states still constituted a vast majority. The change to strict liability without privity spread with unusual speed because it developed during the time that Ralph Nader was building nationwide support for consumerism. But even more important was the fact that for the first time, there was a budding group of Equalizer lawyers who had the resources, drive, and creativity to carry on this expensive and demanding litigation all the way through the trial courts and intermediate appellate courts, to the highest court in each state. This was the first great nationwide victory of the Equalizers. In that sense, strict product liability was the creation of the tort lawyers, but as we have seen, the act of creation was the kicking in of 50 rotten doors marked "DO NOT ENTER UNLESS YOU HAVE PRIVITY."

Without the hobnailed boots (and Congress gaiters) of the Equalizers, the privity doors would still bar the way to any real consumer protection. Your childrens' children would be forced to inhale asbestos in their school rooms, because there would never have been enough pressure from business-oriented government agencies to force removal of asbestos or withdrawal of thousands of other dangerous products.

This victory cost tort lawyers many millions of dollars in expenses and lawyers' time. It had to be won state by state, and sometimes product by product, until the last rotten timber was kicked away. This huge outlay was a highly speculative undertaking by the Equalizers. It was an investment in the future of their own practices, but at the same time it proved to be the only real protection of the public against greedy manufacturers who could not be forced to withdraw defective products except through tort lawsuits.

Those who would like to turn the clock back to the old privity days sometimes say that strict product liability makes the manufacturer an insurer, since plaintiffs can win money without proving that the manufacturer did anything wrong. But as we saw in the Lockheed Electra case, plaintiffs still have to prove that there was a defect, and that the defect caused the injury. That is still a formidable task. The Civil Aeronautics Board, which investigated the Electra East River crash, did not delve deeply into the manufacturing or design process that produced the drum-type altimeter. The CAB was satisfied to rest on the existence of the design defect—the confusing altitude presentation that caused both surviving crew members (and probably the dead captain) to misread their altitude.

The bottom line of strict product liability is that the *defect* injures the consumer. Who but the manufacturer should have the duty of avoiding or curing defects? If a product cannot be made without a defect, do we want that product on the market? If a manufacturer insists upon marketing defective products, do we want to subsidize his business by making his victims—or government welfare agencies—absorb the costs of injury and death?

Even after strict product liability was accepted by the courts, it was nothing more than an empty legal theory. It required the further work of thousands of Equalizers to breathe life into it, using the hard-won appellate victories of the early 1960s as the incubator. After all, as we have observed, there was strict liability for all kinds of torts in the time of Thomas Jefferson, but this afforded no protection to the public because there was no way that individuals could win lawsuits against manufacturers or other large organizations whose products or services caused widespread suffering. The Equalizers sustained the second incarnation of strict liability by using key elements of the American Dream: achieving excellence at their own risk and expense, through education and hard work, without government subsidies or access to bank or equity financing.

So it was that the fledgling Equalizers, usually in law firms even smaller than *L.A. Law's* McKenzie Brackman, took on the world's most powerful manufacturers, making them compensate victims of their defective products and, as we shall see, sometimes forcing them to take dangerous products off the market even though the manufacturers were able to forestall government regulatory agencies from issuing recall orders.

Becoming a Legal Authority

By the mid-1950s, it was clear that Mel Belli was leading tort lawyers toward achievement of the Adequate Award. He inspired me to try to make a contribution toward increasing our clout, our ability to influence the judges—our *authority*. After Grand Canyon I reduced my participation in trials, and decided to try to become an authority by writing legal textbooks that would be recognized and cited by the courts. First I needed to bring some more lawyers into the firm to carry the courtroom load. Since my practice consisted almost entirely of aviation accident cases in the 1950s, all the lawyers who entered the firm then were also fliers. At one time, we were a firm of eight lawyers, all of whom had flying experience either in military service or with the airlines or government aviation agencies. In 1959, Charles F. ("Chuck") Krause, who was then attending Rutgers Law School, became the first in a succession of jet pilots who would work in our office as clerks and then join our firm after graduation. Chuck is an ex-football star whose service as a Marine Corps fighter pilot during the Korean War included aircraft carrier duty. At Rutgers, he served on the law review. He kept up his flying proficiency by joining a Marine reserve squadron. He was to develop into our leading trial lawyer, and took over as senior partner and chief executive officer when I formally retired in 1988.

To make time for me to write authoritative textbooks, I delegated as much litigation work as possible to Chuck Krause and
others. While New York had been the traditional center of aviation accident litigation up to the 1960s, this was beginning to
change. To meet the need for specialized services in other areas,
we opened offices in Washington, D.C., California, and Texas.

I decided that the first area of tort law in need of an authoritative text was that of fatal accident claims, known in American
law as wrongful death actions. I chose wrongful death because it
was the rottenest door of all those blocking the path to the Adequate Award. I encountered this barrier more than most lawyers
because my specialization in aviation meant that most of my
work would arise out of fatal accidents that occurred all over the
USA and in foreign countries, thus bringing into play the wrongful death laws of many jurisdictions—including, as we shall see,
New York, Massachusetts, Oregon, Texas, England, Scotland,
France, and Turkey.

CHAPTER 13

How to Shortchange Widows and Orphans

In the infamous 1808 English case of *Baker v. Bolton*, a husband sued for the injuries he suffered in a stagecoach accident, and he also sued for the loss of his wife, who was killed when the coach overturned. Lord Ellenborough, the reactionary lord chief justice of England, presided at the trial. He allowed the husband to recover damages for his own bruises but ruled out the claim based on the wife's death, holding that "in a civil court, the death of a human being could not be complained of as an injury." Lord Ellenborough cited no precedent for this ruling, nor did he explain the reasoning behind it. But such was the temper of the times that the holding of *Baker v. Bolton* became an immutable rule, eagerly adopted by English and American judges who were concerned with protection of stagecoach (and later railroad) operators against sympathetic awards by outraged jurors.

Thus began the institutionalized shortchanging of widows, orphans, and other relatives aggrieved by fatal accidents, which continues today to an unconscionable degree. Under Lord Ellenborough's view of the law, it became cheaper to kill a victim than to scratch him. Compensation was allowed for personal injuries, but not for the ultimate personal injury: that which destroyed life. This gave rise to the grisly fable that axes were carried aboard railroad coaches so that conductors could finish off passengers who were merely injured in accidents.

Until 1808, wrongful death cases were treated like any other accident claims. Under the English common law, which was used in the American colonies and then adopted by the states of our new nation, those damaged by the accidental death of a relative could sue for damages. I should explain here that the English common law consisted mostly of the decisions of judges, rather than statutes enacted by Parliament. It was more flexible than the legal systems that depended on statutory codes, such as those of France and other European nations, because the judges were free to adapt the law to the living values of the day without waiting for corrective legislation that might be long delayed and distorted by political forces. But Lord Ellenborough's 1808 decision in *Baker v. Bolton* detached wrongful death cases from the common law and set them on their own back road to becoming the stepchildren of tort litigation.

Lord Ellenborough was described by his biographer as one who "attached excessive importance to penal methods of defending property and privilege." But his perversion of justice in *Baker v. Bolton* was too extreme to be swallowed whole even in the nineteenth century. The reaction was Lord Campbell's Act, an English statute passed in 1846, which gave surviving relatives the right to sue for damages in fatal accident cases. This was an improvement, but the construction of the statute by the English courts limited the damages to *pecuniary loss*, a standard guaranteed to shortchange widows and deprive children of real compensation. In addition to keeping damages for lost support to a minimum, it completely excluded the human losses such as the grief caused by death and the deprivation of companionship and parental care.

In America, the states followed the English lead, with New York enacting a statute similar to Lord Campbell's Act in 1847. Eventually every state adopted a wrongful death statute. While this alleviated the complete absence of legal remedy for wrongful death, it put the method and amount of compensation in the hands of the nineteenth-century state legislatures, which were dominated by the best statesmen that money could buy. Railroads were the main targets of wrongful death cases, and their lobbyists found it easy to write into the state statutes the protections that their clients desired. (Accident victims had no lobbyists until a century later, when the Equalizers would take on that role.) Not content with the strictures of the pecuniary loss standard, the railroad-dominated legislatures went even further than England by placing arbitrary monetary limits (usually $5,000) on compensation in many states.

Since there were no Equalizers around, there was little outcry against the cheapening of human life by railroad lobbyists. The most influential nineteenth-century American torts authority was Thomas M. Cooley's *Treatise on the Law of Torts*. Cooley was a justice of the Michigan Supreme Court, a law professor at the University of Michigan, and a prolific writer, mostly in defense of laissez faire and social Darwinism. His biographers say that he was closely connected to railroads and was very successful in private investments. In the first edition of his torts textbook, published in 1880, Cooley commented on an English wrongful death case in which the court had set aside an award of 75 English pounds as *excessive*. The plaintiff was the father of a 21-year-old working man who had been killed on the job. The father himself was old and infirm, and therefore suffered a devastating financial blow when he was deprived of the support of his son. This case seems to have touched Cooley. Perhaps he thought it was a bit unfair to rule that 75 pounds was an excessive amount to pay for the taking of a human life. As he put it, "This seems a very strict application of the law. An American court would probably not disturb a verdict, unless the excess appeared more manifest." But Cooley went on to set his own value on human life:

> Thus, if the deceased is a common laboring man, and it is not shown that he could bring to the assistance of the family other resources than his daily earnings, an award of five thousand dollars is clearly excessive. Many of the statutes fix a maximum of recovery, five thousand dollars being a common limitation.

Perhaps such comments were to be expected in an 1880 textbook which reflected the primitive first century of American law, especially when the author was the same Mr. Cooley who denounced all contingent-fee lawyers as a contemptible lot who were debasing the legal profession and creating "a feeling of antagonism between aggregated capital on the one side, and the community in general on the other." But the same statements about $5,000 being excessive for the death of a "common laboring man" were repeated verbatim in Cooley's second edition (1888), the third edition (1906), and the fourth edition—mercifully his last—in 1932. So it was that in the formative period of American tort law, when the courts were struggling with the difficult problem of appropriate compensation for wrongful death, all they had before them were the many state statutes that arbitrarily limited damages, and Cooley's equally barbaric evaluation. Judges who were sympathetic to the need for reform were hesitant to blaze new trails without some authority to lean on. Not even Professor William Prosser's monumental textbook on torts, first published in 1941, provided such authority, for it was a one-volume work covering the whole field of torts, which required him to declare the complicated subject of damages for wrongful death to be beyond its scope. There being no other volunteers, I laced up my hobnail boots and took aim at the rotten door erected by Lord Ellenborough, Justice/Professor Cooley, the crooked railroad lobbyists, and their even more corrupt friends in the state legislatures who sold out widows and orphans without losing any sleep.

The result was *Recovery for Wrongful Death*, first published in one volume in 1965. The second edition (1975) went to two volumes, and the third edition, co-authored by Chuck Krause and Juanita Madole, was published in three volumes in 1992. When I started work on the first edition, fully a third of the states still had statutory limits on the amounts that could be recovered for the deaths of human beings. This included some large states like Illinois, Massachusetts, and Missouri. These arbitrary pricetags on human life were to be my first target.

I should explain that one seeking to change the legal system through the writing of textbooks does not have the privilege of making polemical statements of what the law should be. To command respect as a legal authority—indeed, to get the book into print under the label of an established legal publisher—unbiased legal scholarship is required. As former federal judge Robert H. Bork put it in his book, *The Tempting of America*: "A judge who announces a decision must be able to demonstrate that he began from recognized legal principles and reasoned in an intellectually coherent and politically neutral way to his result. Those who would politicize the law offer the public, and the judiciary, the temptation of results without regard to democratic legitimacy."

My job would have been easier if I had been a law professor rather than a plaintiff's tort lawyer, since the impartiality (if not the wisdom) of professors is assumed. I had to try to emulate Professor Prosser, who built consensus among judges and his academic colleagues by making the need for change appear to be self-evident. I found that the most effective way to accomplish this was to put the spotlight on inconsistencies between the treatment of property rights and personal rights which were not justified by accepted legal or moral principles. Although the overall legal protection of property rights remains stronger than that accorded to personal rights, no constitutional, legal, or moral principle supports such discrimination. It remains in place only because of historical inertia—rotten doors. The rottenest of all the doors were the statutory ceilings—the pricetags on human life—that persisted in many states.

In *Recovery for Wrongful Death*, I suggested, as several respected legal scholars had previously asserted, that the entire movement of wrongful death cases away from the common law that began in 1808 with *Baker v. Bolton* had been an historical mistake. I began by pointing out that although Lord Campbell was a Scotsman, no Lord Campbell's Act was needed in Scot-

land, for Scottish law never accepted Lord Ellenborough's unprecedented, unreasoned holding that the courts could not compensate the relatives of those killed in accidents. Indeed, the last
paragraph of Lord Campbell's Act specifies that it does not apply to Scotland. My book pointed out many legal anomalies
caused by the statutory pricetags, even though they were updated every 15 or 20 years by raising the maximum slightly. As I
wrote in the preface to the first edition:

> Families of Massachusetts residents who were killed in their
> home state cannot recover more than $30,000 in death cases,
> but if the same person was killed in New York, or if his survi-
> vors can bring suit in New York for a death in a third state, they
> may be able to recover damages limited only by the proof of
> actual losses. If a Harvard professor is killed in a train accident
> in Massachusetts, his survivors can recover only $30,000, but
> the survivors of a railroad conductor killed in the same acci-
> dent would have an unlimited claim under the Federal Em-
> ployers' Liability Act [a federal statute covering railroad
> workers.] North Dakota has no limitation on death damages,
> but South Dakota has a $30,000 limitation. When you scramble
> these elements together in knotty conflict of laws "omelets," the
> public begins to realize that these archaic death statutes have
> created a considerable body of second-class citizens in this
> country.

Conflicts of law occur when the laws of two or more states
may be involved and the courts must choose to apply the law of
one of these states. We shall now examine some of the conflict-of-
law (also called "choice-of-law") situations that brought this second-class citizenship into the public eye and hastened the
demise of the statutory pricetags.

Three Tickets to Nantucket

On August 15, 1958, a Northeast Airlines Convair 240, groping
through the late night fog while trying to land at Nantucket Island, Massachusetts, crashed and burned 1,500 feet short of the
landing runway, killing 24 of the 34 aboard. The airport had practically no state-of-the-art landing aids, and had been condemned
by the Air Line Pilots Association as unsafe for low-visibility approaches.

At that time, Massachusetts limited damages in wrongful
death cases to even less than the $30,000 mentioned above. Fami-

lies of fatal accident victims would receive between $2,000 and $15,000, depending on the "degree of culpability" of the defendant, i.e., how negligent the defendant had been in causing the accident. The claims of the ten surviving passengers were not limited, since they were governed by the common law that left the fixing of compensation to the jury—the law whose protection Lord Ellenborough had snatched away from the families of fatal accident victims in 1808. Therefore, even those passengers who survived with relatively minor injuries stood to collect more compensation under Massachusetts law than the families of deceased passengers.

At the time of the Nantucket crash, the law of the place of the accident was always applied in tort cases, regardless of where the parties resided and where the suit was brought. Thus, it appeared that the families of the deceased Nantucket passengers were stuck with the $15,000 Massachusetts limitation, regardless of where they brought suit. Several New York families refused to settle for $15,000, and brought suit in New York, hoping to circumvent the $15,000 Massacusetts limitation and proceed under New York law, which had no arbitrary limit on damages for wrongful death.

The cases brought in New York by three deceased passengers' families made legal history. The three passengers, all New York residents, were Edward Kilberg, 33, an unmarried economist who was survived by his parents; John Pearson, 35, an executive of an insurance company, who was survived by his wife; and Gordon Dean, 52, a former government official and later a vice-president of General Dynamics, who left his widow and two young children, aged 2 and 4. Our firm represented the families of John Pearson and Gordon Dean, while the Kilberg family was represented by Kreindler & Kreindler, another New York Equalizer firm.

In the Kilberg case, the Kreindler firm devised an ingenious method of getting around the $15,000 limitation. They sued for breach of contract, claiming that Northeast Airlines had contracted to provide safe passage for Edward Kilberg from New York to Nantucket, and that it had breached the contract by failing to carry him safely. If the contract theory was upheld, the estate of Edward Kilberg would be able to collect as damages the amount of money he would have accumulated over his normal life span. It was necessary to go this route because Edward had left no dependents, and under the pecuniary loss standard of damages, as we shall see, the awards to parents of unmarried children were very small. Indeed, in the 1950s, the Kilberg parents could not have collected as much as $15,000 for pecuniary loss under either Massachusetts or New York law, even if there had been no limit.

The Kreindler firm was successful in the lower court. The trial judge held that there was a right to sue for breach of contract, and that the estate could recover lost accumulations even though there was no dependency or loss of support. But Northeast Airlines, represented by Bill Junkerman, took that decision up to the Appellate Division and got a reversal, based on the long-standing principle that accident claims fall into the tort law classification even if there is a contract of carriage. The contract, according to that principle, is merely an undertaking to use due care, and the absence of due care is negligence, so that the existence of the contract does not really change anything. But the Kreindler firm persisted, and got the Court of Appeals in Albany to review the decision of the Appellate Division.

Looking back on his long string of successes in defending claims against airlines, Bill Junkerman is still bugged by the Court of Appeals decision in the Kilberg case—for he won the battle but lost the war. The Court of Appeals agreed with the Appellate Division that the contract theory did not apply, and so the Kilbergs were left with a tort claim that was worth less than $15,000 because of the lack of dependency. But by a 4-to-3 majority, the Court of Appeals went a step further and constructed its own theory, one that was not argued by the Kreindler firm because it would not have benefitted their clients. In the majority opinion, Chief Judge Desmond said that dismissal of the breach of contract claim did not mean that the Kilberg family was limited to a maximum recovery of $15,000, because modern conditions made it "unjust and anomalous" to subject New York citizens to arbitrary limitations in the laws of other states through and over which they travel. Judge Desmond went on to say:

> His plane may meet with disaster in a State he never intended to cross but into which the plane has flown because of bad weather or other unexpected developments. The place of injury becomes entirely fortuitous. Our courts should if possible provide protection for our own State's people against unfair and anachronistic treatment of the lawsuits which result from these disasters. There is available, we find, a way of accomplishing this conformably to our State's public policy and without doing violence to the accepted pattern of conflict of law rules.

Judge Desmond then proceeded to find that New York's strong public policy against such arbitrary limitations, first expressed in the state constitution of 1894, prohibited the New York legislature from imposing any such limits because they were "absurd and unjust," and that this public policy cried out for the New York courts to refuse to enforce the Massachusetts limit against a citizen of New York state. He and three of his colleagues held that while the Kilbergs could not sue for breach of contract, they could amend their complaint to sue for more than $15,000 under the Massachusetts wrongful death statute, which the New York courts would apply *without* the limitation.

The concurring opinion agreed that the breach of contract action should be dismissed, but said that this was as far as the court could go, especially since the public policy question on the $15,000 limitation was not raised, argued, or briefed by any of the parties. The three concurring judges also said that the action of the four-judge majority probably violated Article IV, Section 1 of the federal constitution, which requires that "full faith and credit" be accorded to the acts of every state legislature. All of this only made Bill Junkerman more furious, for he felt he had been sandbagged by the court without getting a chance to argue this constitutional issue.

In the end, the Kilberg case was settled for a little less than $15,000, since that was all that could be recovered in the absence of dependency. Great credit is due to the Kreindler firm for taking a case that did not involve a large fee all the way to the Court of Appeals. As Equalizers, they had learned that progress often came at unexpected times, and that the important thing was to fight every case to the finish in the hope that the appellate courts would eventually discard the remnants of nineteenth-century tort law.

The Kilberg decision was a godsend to the Pearson and Dean families, since both had lost breadwinners and were in a position to collect much more than $15,000 if the jury found that the crash was caused by the airline's negligence. First up for trial was the Pearson case, which was pending in the New York federal court before District Judge John F.X. McGohey. It was an especially poignant case because John Pearson had survived internment in a Japanese prison camp during World War II, and had been married just a few months before the Nantucket crash. Bill Geoghan, then our leading trial lawyer (and now head of his own firm), tried the Pearson case. After Judge McGohey ruled that the Kilberg decision removed the $15,000 Massachusetts limitation, the jury awarded Mrs. Pearson $160,000. Today that

seems a paltry sum for the death of a promising 35-year-old
junior insurance executive who left a young widow, but I remind
you that this case was tried in the era of the knee-jerk reduction
of verdicts that approached $200,000, as we saw in Mel Belli's
Grand Canyon case. In fact, Bill Junkerman, who defended for
Northeast Airlines, made a motion to reduce the verdict as excessive. Only after long deliberation did Judge McGohey let the
$160,000 verdict stand. At that point, Junkerman appealed the
case to the U.S. Court of Appeals for the Second Circuit, and
looked forward to his first opportunity to challenge the constitu-
tionality of the Kilberg decision which had enabled Mrs. Pearson
to win a jury verdict more than ten times the size of the $15,000
Massachusetts limitation.

I took over at the appellate stage, and at first it looked like I
had managed to undo Bill Geoghan's brilliant work in the trial
court. The three-judge appellate panel consisted of Chief Judge
Edward Lumbard and Circuit Judges Thomas Swan and Irving
Kaufman. Judges Lumbard and Swan held that the Kilberg decision (and therefore Judge McGohey's application of it in the
Pearson trial) violated the Full Faith and Credit Clause of the
federal constitution, which required New York to enforce the
Massachusetts statute, including the $15,000 limitation. Judge
Kaufman dissented, in a scholarly 20-page opinion which
pointed out that the majority holding was based on the "vested
rights" doctrine of territorial sovereignty proclaimed by U.S. Supreme Court Justice Oliver Wendell Holmes in 1904. Judge Kaufman then cited some more recent decisions, starting in 1923, that
had discredited the Holmes doctrine by demonstrating that it
had outlived its usefulness and was now too inflexible to govern
our more sensitive legal system. The only real question, he said,
was whether New York had sufficient interest in or contact with
this multi-state transaction (the flight from LaGuardia Field to
Nantucket) to apply its own law and policy.

Judge Kaufman then analyzed the contacts and the state interests involved in the case, including these events that occurred
in New York: sale of the ticket; boarding of the flight by John
Pearson; his widow's residence in New York; and New York's
interest in protecting its citizens from negligent operation of airlines which sell a lot of tickets in the state. He pointed out that in
contract cases, the courts were moving away from automatic
application of the law of the state where the contract was made,
in favor of the more flexible "significant contacts" test. Why not
apply the same protection to those killed in accidents, as New
York's highest court had done in the Kilberg case?

Judge Kaufman's opinion was a blueprint for an enlightened approach to the choice of which state's law should apply in such situations. But it was a minority opinion, and we stood as the losers by a 2-to-1 vote. At that point, I tried a longshot: a petition for rehearing *en banc*—a request that the entire bench of the Second Circuit, consisting of nine active judges, review the 2-to-1 panel decision and reverse it so that Mrs. Pearson's $160,000 verdict would be reinstated. The great majority of such *en banc* petitions are denied. Only those involving compelling issues such as constitutional questions are seriously considered. Rarely does this occur in accident cases. In fact, this was the first such petition I had ever filed, and my inexperience is on the record for posterity, as I called it "in banc" rather than "en banc."

Despite the misnomer, my petition for rehearing *en banc* was granted. The case was reconsidered by the entire nine-judge bench. By a vote of six to three, the Second Circuit adopted Judge Kaufman's position that the Kilberg/Pearson applications of New York law and policy did not violate the Full Faith and Credit Clause or any other part of the constitution. One of the six who voted in our favor was Judge Thurgood Marshall, then sitting on the Second Circuit before his elevation to the Supreme Court.

Bill Junkerman tried to take the Pearson decision to the Supreme Court, but they refused to hear the case. Mrs. Pearson collected her $160,000, with interest. Now we were down to the last Nantucket case: the death of Gordon Dean.

Gordon Dean began his American Dream career as a law professor at Duke University, where one of his students during the 1930s was Richard Nixon. Dean found that his real dream was to be elected president or at the very least to become a member of the cabinet or the U.S. Supreme Court. He moved to Washington in 1935, and became chief of the appellate section of the Justice Department's criminal division, in which job he argued many criminal cases before the Supreme Court. He then hitched his wagon to the rising star of Robert Jackson, who became U.S. Attorney General in 1940. Dean became Jackson's chief executive assistant, but left in 1942 to serve as a Naval intelligence officer. With the end of the war in Europe, Dean again became Robert Jackson's assistant when the latter, now a justice of the U.S. Supreme Court, was assigned to Nuremburg as the chief American prosecutor for the Nazi war crime trials. After returning from Germany, Dean came to the attention of President Harry Truman, who appointed him to the newly organized

U.S. Atomic Energy Commission, and in 1950 moved him up to chairman.

That prestigious appointment was intended as a launching pad for even higher posts, but when Dwight Eisenhower ousted the Democrats from power in 1952, Gordon Dean's government career had to be put on hold until the Republican regime ended. He decided to try his hand at high level jobs in the private sector, but as a favorite protege of ex-President Truman he kept his hand in the Washington power structure. Truman arranged for Gordon to receive top-secret briefings from government officials, as a member of the unofficial "shadow cabinet," a small group of Democrats considered potential future candidates for cabinet posts. Gordon moved to New York City in 1953, where he became Senior Vice-President for Atomic Energy of General Dynamics Corporation and a consultant to the investment banking firm of Lehman Brothers.

For the summer of 1958, Gordon Dean rented a getaway cottage on Nantucket Island. His lovely wife, Mary, and their two young children spent most of the summer there, while Gordon commuted to his General Dynamics office in New York. August 15th, 1958, although a Friday in summer, was a typically busy New York work day for Gordon, what with his duties at General Dynamics and Lehman Brothers, as well as numerous chores that his charitable, public service, and political activities imposed on him. He had to settle for Northeast's last flight of the day to Nantucket, leaving LaGuardia Airport at 8:20 p.m., and scheduled to arrive at 9:28 p.m. Delays pushed the actual departure back to 10:30 p.m., putting the plane in the Nantucket area at 11:30 p.m., just as heavy fog swept in—fog that the crew could not cope with, given the lack of adequate runway lighting and electronic landing aids.

On August 16th, the day after the Nantucket crash, an unusual Saturday session of the U.S. Senate was held to honor Gordon Dean. President Eisenhower sent a message that eulogized Dean as an able administrator and a great patriot. "The nation has lost a distinguished citizen whose contributions to our welfare and progress were many," said the president's message. Seven senators added their eulogies.

Devastated by the crash that killed her husband, Mary Dean gave up their Fifth Avenue apartment a month later, and moved to her family's large farm in Maryland. There she sought the solace of her mother and other relatives who would help her to raise the children, both of whom were less than five years old. That move was to have a profound effect on her claim against

Northeast Airlines, for when the case came up for trial, Judge McGohey ruled that the Kilberg/Pearson principle applied only to those widows and surviving children who remained residents of New York. I argued that this was too narrow a construction, but Judge McGohey stood by his ruling and granted Bill Junkerman's motion for a $15,000 judgment.

Back up to the Second Circuit Court of Appeals I went, and this time drew Chief Judge Lumbard and Circuit Judges Waterman and Anderson as the panel. I argued that under both New York and Massachusetts law, the residence of the widow and children at the time of death was the crucial date. Otherwise widows could move back and forth at later dates, and some who had never been New York residents could claim the benefit of its law if they simply moved to New York before filing suit. It was clear that the Dean family had been residents and citizens of New York for more than five years before the accident, and it was unconscionable to shortchange Mary Dean because she had taken refuge with her family in Maryland to rebuild the damage that Northeast Airlines had inflicted on her and the children. I also argued that the Pearson *en banc* decision was not based merely on New York's public policy of protecting its own citizens, but established a broader rule: that the courts must analyze and weigh the interests and contacts of each state to determine which law should be applied.

This time the appellate court voted unanimously to reverse Judge McGohey's decision. Analyzing the interests of New York, Massachusetts, and Maryland, and weighing the contacts of each state with the issues involved, they found that New York had the strongest interest and the most significant contacts. Therefore, New York law would apply regardless of the residence of the Dean family after the accident, for New York had sufficient interest in the regulation of major carriers that sold tickets and conducted flights in the state to apply its own rules of compensation.

I was especially gratified that Chief Judge Edward Lumbard, who had voted against us twice in the Pearson case, joined in the Gordon Dean decision that spelled out an even more sweeping change in choice-of-law rules. From then on, as a result of the Three Tickets to Nantucket—Kilberg/Pearson/Dean—and other cases that Equalizers were taking to appellate courts all over the country, there would be no automatic deference to the law of the place of the accident. The law of the state having the greatest governmental interest, or having the most signficant contacts, would be applied. Once again it was California's Chief Justice

Roger Traynor who kicked in this rotten door for the people of his state. As he said in the California decision that refused to apply Missouri's arbitrary pricetag for wrongful death cases:

> Interest analysis, like other methods of approaching choice-of-law, is not perfect. But it has the virtue of recognizing that laws are adopted in order to accomplish social goals and that they should be applied so as to carry out their purpose.

The new flexible approach to choosing the applicable law spread throughout the country, so that by 1992 only a handful of states still clung to the old *lex loci* rule that the law of the place of accident must be applied. This change is a great tribute to the care taken by American judges to see that justice is done, for it would have been much easier on the judges to retain the automatic *lex loci* rule. Interest analysis adds a complicated chore to the judges' burdens, but many seem to enjoy the intellectual challenge and the opportunity to apply the law that is most appropriate under all the circumstances of the case.

Kilberg/Pearson/Dean also hastened the demise of the statutory pricetags, for they threw a nationwide spotlight on the second-class status of citizens of Massachusetts and the other states whose legislatures had refused to undo the nineteenth-century shortchanging of widows and dependent children. Soon those legislatures were forced to remove the monetary limitations. It was the ATLA state chapters that fought these final battles in the judiciary committees of the state legislatures. I am proud to say that my book, *Recovery for Wrongful Death*, was used to advantage by many of these ATLA groups.

In the Second Circuit's decision that removed the $15,000 limitation on the compensation of Gordon Dean's family, the three judges also agreed with another of my contentions. Since Northeast Airlines had moved for a judgment of $15,000 against itself in an effort to end the case, it had admitted liability for the accident. Now it was left bare with that admission, without the protection of the $15,000 limitation. This meant that we could try the Gordon Dean case on damages only, without any risk of losing on liability. We moved ahead with preparations for the damage trial, and our star witness would be none other than Harry S. Truman. He had agreed to have his deposition taken at his office in Independence, Missouri. He had not committed himself to come to the trial as a witness, but he had not turned us down, either. I had the feeling that if Northeast Airlines' insurers continued the effort to shortchange the widow and children of Gordon Dean, perky old Harry Truman just might decide to testify at the trial, even though we could read his deposition to the jury if he did not come to the trial.

In the event, his attendance was unnecessary, for the notice of the taking of his deposition was enough to galvanize the insurers into action. They did not want to deal with the Truman factor in a jury trial, especially since Gordon Dean had been an exemplary citizen with a long record of earning more than $100,000 a year, which put him well up in the top one percent of the working population at that time. I was invited to a meeting with the insurers' claims director to try to work out a settlement before the trial began.

At that time, the highest amount actually collected in any accident case, whether involving personal injuries or death, was less than $400,000, and there had been only a handful of jury verdicts exceeding $300,000. As I prepared for the settlement meeting, I guessed that they might offer between $400,000 and $500,000. Even though that would have been the largest amount ever paid in an accident case, I felt that I should advise the Dean family to reject it and take their chances with the jury. In addition to Harry Truman's testimony, we had lined up witnesses from the top ranks of General Dynamics and Lehman Brothers, who would attest to Gordon Dean's extraordinary earning power and future career prospects. These were establishment leaders whose testimony would carry great weight with the federal court jurors, many of whom were drawn from the ranks of business.

At the meeting, the claims director did not beat around the bush. Before I was settled in my chair, he announced that he was offering $750,000. I told him that I would pass it along to my clients and let him know. A few days later the case was settled for $760,000, more than double the amount collected in any previous accident case.

On reflection, I think the insurers were wise to pay $760,000. Facing Harry Truman, General Dynamics, Lehman Brothers, the widow, the two infant children, and the life story of Gordon Dean, they could well have suffered the first million-dollar jury verdict in an accident case. Judge John McGohey was a laid-back man who called them honestly as he saw them. He was not known for interfering with the functions of the jury or ruling verdicts to be excessive when the evidence supported the jurors' findings. Nor was he an elitist. He had come up the hard way as a federal prosecutor, and had earned his seat on the bench by sending the leaders of the Communist Party USA to jail in one of the most difficult and exasperating criminal trials on record. Given the solid business record of Gordon Dean and the evidence that would document his future earning power, Judge McGohey might well have let a million-dollar verdict stand.

The Gordon Dean settlement helped all the Equalizers to appreciate that we were making some progress toward eliminating the short-changing of accident victims. There weren't many Gordon Deans around, but the sound barrier that had held death claims (and most injury claims) below $200,000 regardless of the evidence was now a thing of the past. And soon came the first million-dollar jury verdict, achieved by Bill Geoghan of our firm for the family of California financier Arnold Kirkeby, who had been killed in the first major American jetliner disaster, the crash of an American Airlines Boeing 707 in Jamaica Bay, New York, on March 1, 1962. It was ironic that we, the Equalizers, who saw ourselves as champions of the underdog, scored this victory for the family of a multi-millionaire whose Bel-Air mansion was so much a symbol of opulence that it was used as the setting for the *Beverly Hillbillies* television series. But that was the only way we could make the breakthrough, because Lord Ellenborough, Professor Cooley, and their cohorts had made wrongful death litigation a game of pecuniary loss that could be won only by people who were already comparatively wealthy.

The next task was to rewrite the nineteenth-century Ellenborough/Cooley script to conform to the egalitarian American Dream—to move from *Beverly Hillbillies* to *L.A. Law*.

Two Nuns from Oregon: Humanizing Pecuniary Loss

When Lord Campbell's Act was adopted by Parliament in 1846, it said nothing about creating a method of fixing damages that would be different from the methods used in personal injury cases. Indeed, the reverse was true, for the act provides for the preservation of legal rights as they would have existed "if death had not ensued." The only specific provision for damages was this:

> And in every such action the jury may give such damages as they think proportioned to the injury resulting from such death to the parties respectively for whom and for whose benefit such action shall be brought.

Yet, soon after its enactment, Lord Campbell's Act was rewritten by the English courts. In *Blake v. Midland Railway Co.*, the jury's power to award damages was limited to pecuniary loss, which the court construed as the actual loss of financial support suffered by surviving relatives. This eliminated compensation for all the humanitarian impacts resulting from the death of a loved one, including grief, loss of companionship, and loss of parental guidance.

In Scotland, the human factors were always considered in fixing damages for wrongful death. An excerpt from an 1813 Scottish case, *Brown v. MacGregor*, captures the moral force of the Scottish award for "solatium"—damages for injured feelings:

> Lords Meadowbank and Pitmilly were of opinion that the loss of a husband or father was not to be estimated merely by the pecuniary advantages which the family derived from his exertions; he was not to be considered merely as if he had been a part of the goods in his shop. A man may be a burden instead of an advantage to his family, and yet if his life be improperly taken away, the Court must give damages in solatium of the wounded feelings and affliction of his relatives, which were surely of more deep importance than the tangible injury that could be instructed from the loss of emoluments derived from his exertions.

But the English court held that Mr. Blake *was* to be considered merely as if he had been a part of the goods in his shop. Although the Blake family's lawyers argued that Lord Campbell's Act assimilated English law to the existing law of Scotland, the court was more concerned with protection of the Midland Railway. Pecuniary loss remains the standard in England even today. In practice, this measure yields far less than actual loss of support, since the award is determined by a rigid mathematical formula that is designed to minimize the amounts collected by widows and dependent children.

The American wrongful death statutes written by the state legislatures followed the wording of Lord Campbell's Act, giving the surviving relatives the same legal rights as the deceased would have had if death had not ensued from his injuries. Some legislatures (e.g., California and Arizona) went further and provided that the jury should award "such damages as are fair and just under all the circumstances of the case." But the American courts proceeded to negate these statutory rights by limiting awards to pecuniary loss, as the English courts did in following *Blake v. Midland Railway Co.* About a quarter of the state legislatures (e.g., New York and New Jersey) wrote the pecuniary loss limitation into their wrongful death statutes, while the others reached the same result through court decisions that followed the English model.

The most dehumanizing effects of the pecuniary loss restriction came in cases involving the deaths of young children. The law in its majesty held that parents did not suffer any pecuniary loss on the death of a child, since the child was not contributing to the support of the parents. Only by the greatest restraint did the courts decline to give the defendant credit for relieving the parents of the financial burden of raising the child. Even in a "liberal" state like New York, appellate judges still place an arbitrary cap of about $100,000 on such claims, regardless of the devastation wrought on the parents by the loss of a child. As we saw in the Nantucket cases, the parents of Edward Kilberg could not even collect the $15,000 Massachusetts maximum back in the 1950s. Inflation has pushed the New York awards up to the very low six-figure range, but they are still based upon pecuniary loss and therefore can never achieve justice.

American juries do not take kindly to the pecuniary loss limitation, especially in cases involving the deaths of children. During the nearly 150 years since the wrongful death statutes separated fatal accidents from the common law, thousands of substantial awards have been made to parents of children killed in accidents. It is doubtful that many of these awards were actually based on jurors' attempts to calculate pecuniary loss. Judges called upon to reduce these awards as excessive have often winked at the law, allowing the jurors some leeway to speculate that the child might have contributed to the support of the parents in their old age. This is the contrived basis on which New York courts permit jurors to award anything. Clearly the jurors are awarding damages based on the emotional impact of the loss of a beloved child, rather than the "goods in the shop" approach of pecuniary loss.

Meanwhile, in millions of personal injury cases, jurors have evaluated the emotional and non-pecuniary effects of injuries sustained in accidents, without resorting to pious fictions such as the probability of children supporting their parents. The common law of personal injury cases has scientifically developed a body of jurisprudence by which juries, trial judges, and appellate judges fix the damages for such non-pecuniary injuries. But because of Lord Ellenborough's miscarriage of justice in 1808, the families of fatal accident victims have been deprived of such access to the common law.

In my 1965 book *Recovery for Wrongful Death* I took aim at the rotten door of pecuniary loss. There were two ways to kick the door in. Appellate courts could rule that pecuniary loss includes anything that can be reduced to money, and so the common law damage rules governing personal injury cases could be applied to wrongful death cases as well. Or, the wrongful death statutes could be amended by the state legislatures to bring them in line with the damages available in personal injury cases, including solatium for grief. I hoped that the book would provide a useful authority to both the courts and the legislatures.

In 1972, a case came before the Supreme Court of Oregon that threw the inhumanity of the pecuniary loss stricture into bold relief. Margaret Mary O'Donnell and Mafalda Maria Zucca, two nuns who were members of the Sisters of the Holy Names of Jesus and Mary, were killed in an automobile accident that was apparently caused by a defect in the Chevrolet in which they were riding. Both nuns had taken vows of poverty. Neither had ever received any pay for her work, and neither left any dependents. Oregon's wrongful death statute had swallowed the English rule whole, since it provided for such damages as "will reasonably and fairly compensate the spouse, dependents, or estate for *the actual pecuniary loss, if any*." Suit was brought by the executrix of the estates of the two nuns and also by the religious order. Interpreting the wording of the Oregon wrongful death statute literally, the trial court threw out the case with no damage award on the ground that no pecuniary loss could be shown. The plaintiffs appealed this dismissal to the Oregon Supreme Court, which had to face the question of whether Oregon law must brand as worthless two human lives that were dedicated to doing good rather than collecting money.

I am proud to report that the Oregon Supreme Court unanimously held that "all human life has pecuniary value in terms of either actual or potential earning capacity," and that it was basically unfair to permit a defendant who has negligently killed two human beings to escape liability merely because the victims had volunteered to contribute their services to a nonprofit organization. The court found that Sister O'Donnell had a Master of Education degree and would have earned at least $13,000 a year if she had been employed in the Oregon public school system, and that Sister Zucca was a trained school librarian who would have earned at least $10,000 in the public schools. The court said that the plaintiffs were entitled to have these figures submitted to a jury as evidence of potential pecuniary loss, and that it would be up to the jury to determine the question of fair and reasonable compensation to the order which had lost their services.

The Oregon Supreme Court went on to say that in adopting the wrongful death statute, the Oregon legislature intended to leave to the courts the question of defining pecuniary loss in each case. This holding means that pecuniary loss includes anything that can be reduced to a monetary award. As the court concluded:

> We believe that this result is in accord with the present trend to liberalize the rule of "pecuniary loss" in wrongful death cases and to respond to "new emergencies" in this often perplexed and tortured field of the law.

To overcome this perplexity and tortured reasoning, the Oregon Supreme Court needed some legal authority. In their 18-page opinion, they cited my book *Recovery for Wrongful Death* 12 times. Something I had written helped to win a case for someone I had never met. I found this fully as satisfying as winning a case for my own client, especially when the result was to kick in a rotten door so that future victims could walk through without impediment.

The case of the two Oregon nuns spotlighted the injustice of the pecuniary loss rule because it forced the lower court to place a zero valuation on human life. But in a quiet way, virtually the same thing was happening to thousands of families that had lost mothers and housewives. If the mother/housewife was not employed (as most were not in the 1950s) there was virtually no pecuniary loss allowed for her household services. As we saw in Mel Belli's Grand Canyon case, the award for the death of the mother was only $20,000, and this was based almost entirely on the fact that she had been employed as a school teacher, earning about $5,000 a year, with raises scheduled to about $7,000 over a ten-year period. Since she was only 40 years old when killed, the $20,000 verdict figures out to an award of only $800 per year for the remaining 25 years of her working-life expectancy.

Some of us would-be Equalizers tried to plug this hole in wrongful death law by calculating for the jury the actual dollar cost of replacing a deceased mother/housewife. We drew up lists of the chores that women performed regularly in the home, such as nursemaid, housekeeper, cook, dishwasher, laundress, chauffeur, and half a dozen others. We estimated the number of hours per week devoted to each function, and multiplied those by the hourly rates charged by people who earn their livelihoods by performing such services. We came up with average figures of close to 100 hours a week, which, when multiplied by the then minimum wage of $2.65 per hour, added up to $265 per week, or over $12,000 per year. To present these figures in court in a way that would be most useful to jurors, we called as expert witnesses people who dealt with these costs regularly: managers of employment agencies that supplied domestic servants. Despite the fact that we were playing by the strict rules of the pecuniary loss game, reducing the deceased homemaker's value to the actual marketplace figures, the courts were slow to accept this innovation.

We used such an employment expert in a case tried by Bill Geoghan, arising out of the same 1962 American Airlines crash in which the California financier Arnold Kirkeby was killed. A week before the Kirkeby verdict, Bill presented to another jury the case of a father and mother who died together in the crash, orphaning their four young children, one of whom was mongoloid. While the mother was not employed outside the home, she had her hands full with the four youngsters and the special care required for the mongoloid child. The costs of a substitute mother-nurse-homemaker were toted up by our expert, and they must have impressed the jurors, for they returned a verdict of $200,000 for the death of the mother, in addition to $550,000 for the death of the father, based on the loss of his support of the household. The trial judge allowed the expert testimony and refused to reduce the verdicts, but the Appellate Division disagreed. They reduced the verdicts to $350,000 for the death of the father and $125,000 for the mother's death. Even at that level of $125,000, this was important progress beyond the $20,000 allowed in the case of the Grand Canyon working mother, since it was based entirely on the mother's services in the home. But the Appellate Division disapproved of our use of an employment expert to calculate the cost of a substitute wife, holding that expert testimony is only permitted on matters that are unfamiliar to the average juror.

Going back to the drawing board in an attempt to convince the courts to allow expert testimony, I realized that the substitute homemaker valuation was part of a larger problem. For more than a hundred years, jurors had been called upon to appraise the value of human life by guesswork. They were given actuarial tables that helped to determine life expectancy, but all the other variables, such as the amount of money that an accountant or a bricklayer or a schoolteacher would probably earn over the next 40 years, were left to guesswork. At that time, there were a few scattered cases in which innovative plaintiff's lawyers had used professional economists to appraise the present value of lost future earnings in wrongful death cases. I decided to try to institutionalize this movement, by using economists in our death cases, and by writing a book that would establish legal authority for their use. The result was the *Economic Handbook*, first published in 1970 as a companion volume to *Recovery for Wrongful Death*.

The theme of the handbook was that use of economic data and the testimony of economists as expert witnesses were commonplace in commercial litigation. Antitrust cases, for example, were mostly about market shares and projections of future business prospects. Even though it involved some guesswork, the courts did not hesitate to allow such evidence, since it had some scientific underpinning and was the best estimate available for guidance of the jury. Indeed, such data were considered reliable enough to guide momentous business and governmental decisions about spending huge sums of money. Given this acceptance in matters of property, why not provide the jurors with this type of scientific evidence to guide them in determining the pecuniary value of future earnings? As I wrote in the handbook's preface:

> As shown in the text, there are striking similarities between the factors underlying valuation of the assets of a business, and those involved in determination of pecuniary loss arising from the death of a human being. Indeed, many business decisions (such as those involving purchase of automated equipment) require immediate parallel determinations of the value of a man's work as against the value of a machine. Therefore, there is no reason why economic data and economists' forecasts should be used for determining the value of a business or a machine over the next 40 years, and then be ignored when trying to determine the value of a man's earning power over the same period in the same economy.

Eventually these arguments, aided by many Equalizers throughout the country who began to use economists as expert witnesses, convinced the courts. Today it is common for plaintiff's lawyers to use economists as appraisers in death cases, and also in personal injury cases involving loss of future earning power. Economists are especially useful in appraising the probable impact of future inflation, as well as the pattern of future interest rates that must be considered in determining the present value of a lump sum award. The *Economic Handbook*, the third edition of which was published in 1988, is an unusual lawbook. It is replete with the tables, statistics, and economic studies that economists use in courtroom appraisals of human earning power. It helped to create a new source of income for many economics professors, who are used by both plaintiffs and defendants as expert witnesses in wrongful death cases.

We found that the courts were more receptive to the substitute homemaker cost appraisal if presented by an economics professor rather than someone from an employment agency. By the 1990s, it became commonplace for economists to appraise the cost of replacing the deceased homemaker. Awards for the loss of these ordinary services frequently range between $250,000 and $500,000, depending on the amount of time involved in the household chores. That award would be added to the value of lost earnings in cases where the homemaker was also employed outside of the home.

Thus the alliance between law and economics helped to make awards for pecuniary loss a little fairer. But there was still a vast area in which the pecuniary loss standard itself perverted justice. Despite the admonition of the Scottish court in 1813, many American courts were still treating deceased accident victims like the goods in a shop. There was a lot of work to be done in the courts and in the legislatures to restore the dignity of human life.

In the 1974 case of *Sea-Land Services v. Gaudet*, the U. S. Supreme Court was called upon to decide whether Helen Gaudet, the widow of Awtrey Gaudet, a seaman who was killed aboard his ship, could recover damages for loss of society, in addition to loss of support. This case was governed by federal law since the death occurred outside the reach of state wrongful death statutes. In a 5-to-4 decision, the Supreme Court held that the widow could recover for loss of society, which the majority defined as follows:

> The term "society" embraces a broad range of mutual benefits each family member receives from the others' continued existence, including love, affection, care, attention, companionship, comfort, and protection. Unquestionably, the deprivation of these benefits by wrongful death is a grave loss to the decedent's dependents.

The court reviewed the history of wrongful death statutes dating back to Lord Campbell's Act, noting the effort to restrict the definition of pecuniary loss so as to exclude loss of society. In rejecting that restriction and broadening the defintion of pecuniary loss to include loss of society, the Supreme Court's principal authority was my book *Recovery for Wrongful Death*, which they cited eight times. They also adopted my definition of loss of society, including the distinction I drew between loss of society and the mental anguish of surviving relatives.

The Supreme Court's *Sea-Land* decision was a turning point. Its holding has been adopted by many state appellate courts, and has influenced state legislatures to amend wrongful death statutes that would otherwise deprive grieving relatives of damages for loss of society and mental anguish of surviving relatives. The experience of Texas is an apt illustration.

The Texas wrongful death statute was copied verbatim from Lord Campbell's Act, and so it did not contain the words "pecuniary loss." But in 1877, the Supreme Court of Texas held that since the statute was based on Lord Campbell's Act, the measure of damages would be the English standard of pecuniary loss laid down in *Blake v. Midland Railway Co.* Texas remained one of the strict pecuniary loss states until Eugene and Angelica Sanchez brought a wrongful death suit against Charles Schindler, whom they accused of negligently killing their 14-year-old son Johnny in a 1979 collision between Johnny's motorcycle and Schindler's pickup truck.

The jury found that Schindler's negligence caused the fatal accident, but they decided that the Sanchez parents had not suffered any pecuniary loss through the death of their son. Nevertheless, they awarded the mother, Angelica Sanchez, $102,500 for the mental anguish she had suffered because of her son's death, based on evidence that she was suffering from traumatic depressive neurosis. The trial judge ignored that award since he considered it outside the realm of pecuniary loss. So did the intermediate appellate court in Corpus Christi. Facing a zero award for the taking of a human life, the Sanchez's lawyer appealed the case to the Supreme Court of Texas in 1983.

By a 4-to-3 vote, the Supreme Court of Texas threw out its century-old pecuniary loss restriction, and restored the $102,500 mental anguish award to Johnny Sanchez's mother. As Justice Spears wrote in the majority opinion:

> The jurisdictions that do not limit recovery to pecuniary loss realize that damages for loss of companionship and society of a child are not too uncertain to be measured in pecuniary terms in an attempt to redress the actual loss which a parent suffers. These elements of damage are not too speculative to be given a monetary value. Recovery is allowed in other tort areas for injuries which are equally intangible: e.g., pain and suffering. The fear of excessive verdicts is not a sufficient justification for denying recovery for loss of companionship. The judicial system has adequate safeguards to prevent recovery of damages

based on sympathy or prejudice rather than fair and just compensation for the plaintiff's injuries.

In a concurring opinion, Justice Ray stated that recovery should be allowed for the emotional impact of the loss of any close relative, whether a spouse, a parent, or a child; and that proof of physical manifestations such as that provided by Mrs. Sanchez should not be required.

Among the authorities cited by the Supreme Court of Texas was my book *Recovery for Wrongful Death*, as well as a 1976 article I had written for the *Tulane Law Review*. In the *Tulane* article, I had called attention to the ultimate absurdity in wrongful death law: New York, which would not permit a daughter to sue for the mental anguish caused by her mother's death, in a 1975 case allowed a daughter to sue for mental anguish caused by a telegram erroneously informing her that her mother had died in a state hospital. In other words, mental anguish damages could be awarded in New York because of a false report of death, but not for the actual killing of a human being! The sole reason for this mindless distinction was that the action for the false death report came under the common law, whereas the action for a real death had to be brought under the wrongful death statute that carried its own nineteenth-century pecuniary loss stricture.

Soon after the Supreme Court of Texas allowed Johnny Sanchez's mother to recover for mental anguish, it adopted the suggestion of Justice Ray and extended the humanization of wrongful death compensation to include awards for mental anguish and loss of society for all those allowed to sue under the wrongful death statute: parents, children, and spouses of those killed in accidents. In doing so, the court again quoted the statement in my Tulane article that "the emotional impact of the loss of a beloved person is the most significant damage suffered by surviving relatives." The court also allowed a separate award for loss of society, adopting the position I took in *Recovery for Wrongful Death* that loss of society and mental anguish were separate injuries that should not be lumped together. My reasoning was that mental anguish dealt with the negative question of what harmful effects the death had upon the relatives, while loss of society dealt with loss of the positive benefits which flowed to the family from the dead person having been a part of it. This reasoning was first adopted by the U.S. Supreme Court in the 1974 decision, *Sea-Land Services v. Gaudet,*, which we discussed above. In turn, the Supreme Court of Texas adopted the Sea-Land decision in 1987.

As a result of this turnabout by the Supreme Court of Texas in the 1980s, the killing of human beings is now a very expensive activity in Texas. The separate awards for loss of society and mental anguish often run between $250,000 and $500,000 for each parent, child, and spouse left surviving. Thus, each parent of a young child killed in a school bus accident will probably receive $250,000 to $500,000, making a total award of $500,000 to $1 million for the human effects of the death of a young child. It makes no difference whether the child was from a family of Mexican migrant workers or was the scion of an oil baron. If a father or mother is killed in an accident, the surviving spouse will likely receive separate awards of $250,000 to $500,000 for mental anguish and loss of society, making a total of $500,000 to $1 million, in addition to the spouse's award for loss of support. In addition, each child will probably receive separate six-figure awards for mental anguish and loss of society, as will each parent of the deceased person (the grandparents of the surviving children). Accordingly, it is not uncommon for those who cause fatal accidents in Texas to face damage payments of $3 million or more for each death, in addition to whatever loss of support has been suffered. This furnishes a stronger incentive to inspect the brakes of school buses than any administrative regulation.

Since the advent of the Equalizers, many state appellate courts have humanized wrongful death compensation in the way that Texas has done. In addition, some of the state legislatures have rewritten their wrongful death statutes to eliminate the injustices caused by the nineteenth-century pecuniary loss restriction. In most of the latter states, the Equalizers led the way by demonstrating to the legislative committees that the differences between the common law of personal injuries and the statutory law of wrongful death were historical anomalies, based on nothing more substantial than the nineteenth-century distrust of jurors' ability to assess emotional injuries fairly. Since jurors are called upon to assess emotional injuries every day in personal injury cases, there is no longer even a shred of justification for adding to the devastation of fatal accidents by denying just compensation to the victimized families.

When the Maryland legislature amended its wrongful death statute in 1969, the preamble stated that the pecuniary loss restriction previously applied in the state had caused many injustices, and needed to be replaced by a valid legal test of damages. The 1969 amendment provided that damages would no longer be restricted to pecuniary loss, "but may include damages for mental anguish, emotional pain and suffering, loss of society, companionship, comfort, protection, marital care, parental care, filial care, attention, advice, counsel, training, guidance, or education where applicable." That amendment and similar measures in other states have followed guidelines in the Model Wrongful Death Statute that I drafted and published in *Recovery for Wrongful Death*.

As of the time of writing (1992) the states are far from uniform on pecuniary loss. New York, the leader in development of many other branches of law, is still mired in nineteenth-century wrongful death restrictions. It adheres strictly to the outmoded pecuniary loss rule, a position that lessens respect for the law in the eyes of jurors as well as claimants. How would you like to tell the parents of a teenager killed in an accident that according to New York law, their child's life is worthless, except to the extent that the jurors are allowed to guess at what the child might have contributed to the parents' support in later life?

Because Lord Ellenborough severed wrongful death cases from the common law in 1808, Anglo-American wrongful death law is an outcast among civilized nations. Most other countries have adopted the *Code Napoleon* (derived from Roman law) as the cornerstone of civil law. Under the French construction of that code, followed in most other code nations, both "material" and "moral" damages must be paid in all tort cases that are won by the claimants. No distinction is made between personal injury cases and fatal accidents. Moral damages include grief and loss of society. While the amounts paid for moral damages in wrongful death cases are low by American standards, they are consistent with the foreign awards in personal injury cases. Even at nominal levels, they reaffirm the dignity of human life and create a sense of justice being done. This is missing from the American courts that are reduced to invoking fictional notions of young children supporting their parents.

In New York and other states that shortchange the families of fatal accident victims, the Equalizers continue to fight the battle to undo the handiwork of Lord Ellenborough and Professor Cooley. Time and history are on our side, for every amendment of wrongful death statutes in the second half of the twentieth century has kicked in part of the rotten doors of statutory pricetags on pecuniary loss. But patience is required, since it took more than 100 years to rip off the last of the statutory limits (pricetags), and vestiges of the pecuniary loss stricture are still with us even though *Blake v. Midland Railway Co.* was decided in 1852. Perhaps by the year 2000 the legislators or judges of New York and the other holdout states will cease to impose second-class citizenship on victims of the ultimate tort: the wrongful taking of human life. As we have seen, this can be done by the courts, as in Texas, or by the legislatures, as in Maryland. It can be accomplished either by discarding pecuniary loss as the standard, or by broadening the definition of pecuniary loss to include all the common law elements that are now considered in personal injury cases.

Some well-meaning people balk at the notion that there should be substantial damage awards for wrongful death. Some feel that it is difficult and degrading to try to put a pricetag on human life. It is not an easy job, but isn't it highly preferable to compounding the trauma of the victimized family by making them shoulder the financial as well as the emotional costs? And isn't it important to furnish strong incentives for all of us to do everything possible to avoid killing innocent people through carelessness, selfishness, and callous disregard for human life?

I was gratified by the authoritative status accorded to *Recovery for Wrongful Death*, not least by Prosser's appraisal of it as "an excellent text." Encouraged by that reception, I have tried fill some of the historical sinkholes in other areas of tort law. When I started practice, New York had no organized source of jury instructions, despite the fact that many other states had printed formbooks for the guidance of lawyers and judges. New York judges kept their own loose-leaf notebooks full of jury instructions, and no two were completely alike. I published a book of jury instructions for tort cases, which was used for a few years until the New York judges themselves published an authoritative set of Pattern Jury Instructions. The law of *res ipsa loquitur* was also in disarray, a problem that I tried to solve in 1972 by publishing the first—and hopefully the last—text on this arcane subject. (Some unkind critics felt that it was the height of pettifogging to write two volumes on a subject that is supposed to speak for itself.) In collaboration with Al Gans and Chuck Krause, I wrote a three-volume set on *Aviation Tort Law*. This was a warmup for our most ambitious undertaking: a ten-volume work titled (perhaps immodestly) *The American Law of Torts*.

In the last two chapters, I have tried to explain how the kicking in of rotten doors opened the way for the Equalizers to enforce the long-standing — but largely theoretical— rights of the underdog in tort litigation. As we have seen, this was accomplished by following the examples of a few giants like Gair and Belli; by self-education and networking, largely through ATLA; and by scholarship that led to the recognition of intellectual authority, which in turn gave us some clout in the courts and the legislatures. All of this adds up to the pursuit of *excellence*. To the extent that we have achieved excellence, we, like the legal stalwarts of McKenzie Brackman, are able to win for the underdogs. And since this excellence is self-made, springs from self-interest, requires hard work and personal risk, produces lucrative income, results in happy endings for the underdog, and therefore enables the Equalizers to do well by doing good, it conforms to the American Dream.

Now let's consider two questions about this pursuit of excellence.

First, what will the tort lawyers of the twenty-first century be like?

And second, is the Equalizers' quest for excellence significant only within the legal profession, or does it have any broader implications?

CHAPTER 14

The Equalizers' Continuing Quest for Excellence

The plot was bizarre enough for a James Bond movie. It even had a 007, but in this case it was the flight number rather than the secret agent's designation. Korean Air Lines Flight 007, a Boeing 747 jumbo jet flying from New York to Seoul, South Korea, on August 31, 1983, made its regular refueling stop at Anchorage, Alaska. From there it was scheduled to fly nonstop to Seoul along Route R-20, the one-way east-to-west airway over the Northern Pacific. It was due to land at Seoul's Kimpo International Airport about 6 o'clock the next morning after an eight-hour flight, mostly over water. When 007 failed to arrive at Seoul, a massive international search and rescue mission was launched. After several false reports, including one that the plane had landed safely on Sakhalin Island in the Soviet Union, the world finally learned the chilling truth: KAL Flight 007 had flown over Soviet territory and had been shot down in the Sea of Japan by missiles fired from a Soviet fighter plane. All 269 people aboard were lost, and only a few fragments of aircraft wreckage, personal possessions, and human remains were found.

1983 was the year in which President Ronald Reagan branded the Soviet Union "the evil empire." He denounced the shooting down of a defenseless civilian airliner as an "unspeakable act" and urged the world's leaders to defy "the system that excuses it and tries to cover it up." Soviet President Yuri Andropov, former head of the KGB and one of the last of the hardline cold warriors, responded in kind, claiming that the plane had been on an American-controlled spy mission. Although Flight 007 was operated by the privately-owned Korean Air Lines, the U.S. government was involved politically because most of the passengers were Americans or orientals with ties to the United States. The day after the shootdown, the Soviet-American ideological confrontation was played out on worldwide television at an emergency session of the United Nations Security Council.

The Soviets insisted that they never knew KAL 007 was a civilian airliner, since the shootdown occurred at night and they claimed that an American spy plane—an RC-135 military version of the Boeing 707—was flying so close to the airliner that the two images merged on Soviet air defense radar.

Although many official and unofficial investigations have been made and more than a dozen books have been written about the shooting down of KAL 007, there has been no conclusive determination of what actually happened. But one thing is clear: the plane did penetrate Soviet air space—indeed, it flew all the way across the southern tip of the heavily fortified Sakhalin Island, gateway to the strategic port of Vladivostok—and thus became a candidate for interception by armed fighters. Flight 007 was commanded by Captain Chung Byung-in, one of KAL's leading international pilots, who was on the short list of captains selected to transport South Korea's president on official flights. Like all KAL pilots, Chun was highly sensitive to the need to stay out of Soviet airspace because another KAL plane—this one enroute from Paris to Seoul over the polar route—had been shot down by the Soviets in 1978. The pilot of that Paris flight had managed to avoid total disaster by landing safely on a frozen lake, but two of his passengers were killed by shrapnel and 13 were injured.

Knowing that Route R-20 from Alaska to Korea would take his plane within a few hundred miles of Soviet territory, how and why did the highly rated Captain Chun allow his Boeing 747 to stray more than 300 miles off course and become a sitting target for a missile attack?

The history of Flight 007 only deepened the mystery. Captain Chun's Boeing 747 was equipped with all the current navigation and communication aids. For ocean flying, the key component was the Inertial Navigation System (INS), a combination of gyroscopes and computers derived from the American space program that made navigation almost foolproof. To operate the INS, the crew had to program it on the ground by punching in the longitude and latitude of the takeoff airport, the destination airport, and the "waypoints" in between that would serve as checks on the progress of the flight. Once this programming was done properly on the ground, the crew could sit back and let the INS send the signals to the automatic pilot that would keep the plane precisely on course regardless of wind conditions. So reliable was the INS that many flight crews took to playing cards during long ocean flights, since there was little for them to do other than to check the plane's progress at the waypoints that came up about every 300 miles. For that purpose, the plane was equipped with DME (Distance Measuring Equipment), VOR (very-high-frequency omnidirectional radio range receivers), airborne radar, and other devices that would enable the crew to verify its position.

For 007's flight to Seoul, there were 17 waypoints at which the crew was required to report to air traffic controllers, by calling Anchorage radio in the first half of the flight and Tokyo radio in the second half. Route R-20 from Anchorage to Seoul ran in a southwesterly direction over the Pacific Ocean, slightly south of the land masses of the Soviet Union, China, Japan, and Korea. To visualize the scenario, imagine that the plane was to fly nonstop from New York west to Seattle, remaining south of the Canadian border because Canada was a hostile nation with a known penchant for shooting down any aircraft that intruded over its territory. The INS on our imaginary flight would be programmed to fly over waypoints Cleveland, Chicago, Minneapolis, Bismarck, and Helena, before arriving at Seattle. But instead of following this route, somehow our pilot flew north of the prescribed track, entering Canadian airspace and flying over strategic military installations at Calgary, Alberta, where it was shot down more than 300 miles north of the prescribed course.

After KAL 007 was shot down, ICAO (the International Civil Aviation Organization, an affiliate of the United Nations) launched an investigation. ICAO obtained some degree of cooperation from the USA, the USSR, Japan, and Korea, and enlisted experts who attempted to recreate the flight. The position of 007 throughout much of the flight was determined by collecting radar sightings from stations in Alaska, the USSR, and Japan. The radar sightings showed that the plane had actually flown considerably to the north of each waypoint along R-20, even though the crew had reported flying directly over these waypoints as planned. All the radar plottings and the other technical information about the flight were assembled by the ICAO team, which then used a Boeing 747 simulator to test several theories as to how the plane could have flown so far off course. The most likely 007 scenario postulated by the ICAO investigators was one that had happened before and that arose out of a hazard of INS navigation: the tricky task of programming the system.

In order to program the INS properly, a crew member had to insert in proper sequence the geographical coordinates (longitude and latitude) of each location: the takeoff airport, all the waypoints, and the destination airport. This was done by punching numbered buttons that would spell out the longitude and latitude of each location. Each coordinate consists of a long figure, in degrees, hours, and minutes of longitude or latitude. For example, the coordinates for Bethel, Alaska, the first waypoint to be programmed into the INS, are latitude North 61 degrees 25 minutes 3 seconds, longitude West 161 degrees 58 minutes 9 seconds. For a long ocean flight, there were dozens of such figures to be punched in. Fortunately the INS has built-in safeguards which enable pilots to detect programming errors and correct them in flight, with one exception: If the wrong coordinates for the takeoff airport are punched in, this error cannot be corrected in flight, and the whole navigation program will be incorrect. Therefore, if the pilot of an ocean flight discovers that his INS has the wrong coordinates for the takeoff airport, he is required to return to the takeoff airport and reprogram the INS on the ground before departing to resume the flight.

This embarrassing error has occurred more frequently than one might expect from professional flight crews. In KAL operations, there were three documented instances of misprogramming the takeoff airport coordinates. In each instance, the pilot picked up the error fairly early in the flight and returned to the takeoff airport for reprogramming.

The ICAO investigators simulated 007's flight by programming longitude of West 139 degrees instead of the correct coordinate of West 149 degrees for Anchorage airport. This single-digit error of 10 degrees longitude—punching in 139 instead of 149—produced a simulated track that came very close to the actual route that 007 had flown. The simulated flight missed the first waypoint at Bethel by flying about 12 miles north of it, and wound up over Soviet territory at Sakhalin Island, more than 300 miles north of Route R-20. The single-digit programming error theory emerged as the most likely 007 scenario, although it could not be conclusively verified without the plane's flight recorder, which was never recovered.

The programming error may explain how 007 flew north of its course toward Soviet territory, but it does not explain how or why Captain Chun, a latter-day equivalent of Pan Am's Master Ocean Pilots, did not detect the error and then return to Anchorage to reprogram the INS. It seems inconceivable that he would not have noticed the error, since he had little to do enroute other than to use his sophisticated electronics to verify his position at each waypoint. His Distance Measuring Equipment, VOR, and radar would have told him that he was not flying anywhere near the R-20 track once the 10-degree programming error took the plane farther and farther north of the proper course. He should have been alerted to the error at the very first waypoint, Bethel, which he missed by at least 12 miles. The INS itself and several other instruments would have shown that he was well north of his R-20 course. As soon as he noticed the error, it was clearly his duty to turn around and fly back to Anchorage.

Returning to Anchorage within the first few hours of the flight would have required him to dump some fuel to lighten his load sufficiently to maintain control during landing. You will recall that Pan Am Master Ocean Pilot Ed Musick's flying boat exploded during fuel dumping at Pago Pago in 1938. But by 1983, fuel dumping was a safe and routine operation in the Boeing 747. Indeed, KAL had designated a specific area for dumping fuel in the Pacific Ocean near Anchorage, and the pilots of the three previous KAL flights in which the INS was improperly programmed dumped fuel before returning to the takeoff airport. Therefore, Captain Chun's failure to return to Anchorage cannot be explained by any hazard associated with fuel dumping.

Without the black boxes (the plane's flight recorder and cockpit voice recorder) we can never be certain why Captain Chun flew off course, or why he failed to return to Anchorage if he had misprogrammed the INS. This made an intriguing scenario for books and television programs about unsolved mysteries, but it was not an appetizing prospect for our law firm as we took on the job of representing the largest group of plaintiffs in the suits to collect compensation from KAL. This was, of course, an international flight, and our old nemesis, the Warsaw Convention, was again blocking the way to adequate compensation unless we could prove that the loss of KAL 007 was caused by wilful misconduct. As in the crash of the *Yankee Clipper*, the negligence of Captain Chun in flying off course was clear enough. But even if the jury bought the somewhat speculative single-digit INS misprogramming theory, how could we prove that Captain Chun intentionally refused to return to Anchorage?

Suits were filed on behalf of families of the KAL-007 passengers in federal courts throughout the country, since the plaintiffs could sue KAL wherever it maintained an office. Under *Multidistrict Litigation* procedures adopted by the federal courts in 1968, all the cases would be sent to one federal judge for determination of liability in a single trial. We chose to file our cases in the federal court for the District of Columbia, since many of the potential witnesses were government employees living in the Washington area. Also, we wanted to avoid New York because the prior Warsaw Convention cases tried in the District of Columbia had produced jury instructions on wilful misconduct that were much fairer to the plaintiffs than Judge Steuer's "intending the result" charge in the Jane Froman case. Since ours was the largest group of cases, the Judicial Panel on Multidistrict Litigation transferred all the cases to the District of Columbia, where they were assigned to Chief Judge Aubrey E. Robinson, Jr.

Under the Multidistrict Litigation (MDL) procedures, the trial judge appoints a Plaintiffs' Steering Committee consisting of several lawyers who are entrusted with handling the liability phase of the case on behalf of all the plaintiffs. If the plaintiffs win on liability, the MDL judge (Chief Judge Robinson in this case) usually will send each case back to the district where it was filed originally for trial on damages. The Plaintiffs' Steering Committee for the KAL-007 case included two lawyers from our firm's Washington office: Donald W. Madole and George E. Farrell. In addition, Juanita Madole of our Washington office was appointed Liaison Counsel, which involved coordination of the logistics and paperwork of more than 100 separate actions, and the financial management of the Plaintiffs' Steering Committee.

The Plaintiffs' Steering Committee (PSC) included prominent tort lawyers from New York, New Jersey, Illinois, and Michigan, all of whom made valuable contributions. Initially the PSC hoped to get the cooperation of the U.S. government, whose intelligence agencies knew far more about the shootdown than the PSC lawyers could ever hope to learn. But in the end the U.S. government refused to disclose anything but the facts that had already been made public, even though our firm represented the families of a congressman and a State Department official who had been killed in the shootdown. Government officials claimed it would endanger national security if they disclosed the sources and extent of their knowledge of Soviet military operations in the Pacific. (To this day, there are investigators and journalists who believe that U.S. military forces used KAL 007 to spy on Soviet air defenses.) The Soviets, of course, were even less cooperative, and our attempt to sue the USSR government was unsuccessful since they claimed immunity from such civil suits. To round out the governments opposed to us, the Republic of Korea was not interested in cooperating either. KAL originally was owned by the Korean government, and even after it was sold, the private owners maintained strong clout with the government, in keeping with the overall coziness of that government with the Korean business establishment. (Governmental cover-ups are the main theme of Seymour Hersh's book on the 007 shootdown, *The Target is Destroyed*.)

Given this phalanx of governments arrayed against us, and the paucity of evidence available from a plane that had disappeared almost without a trace, it was not surprising that KAL's insurers refused to offer anything more in settlement than the maximum provided in the Warsaw Convention. The limit was now $75,000 per passenger, up from the $8,300 of Jane Froman's day but still only a minor fraction of the real damage done to these families. The PSC fought valiantly to put together a wilful misconduct case, but in the first two years of the litigation there was little evidence to be discovered. KAL's insurers were confident that we couldn't prove Captain Chun did anything intentionally that caused his plane to be shot down. After all, Captain Chun and KAL itself were victims of trigger-happy Soviet pilots, along with the passengers.

Then late in 1985 came a ray of hope. When KAL 007 departed from Anchorage on August 31, 1983, another KAL Boeing 747 took off 14 minutes later, heading from Anchorage to Seoul on Route R-20, the same route being flown by 007. It was KAL Flight 015, commanded by Captain Park Yong Man, a long-time close friend of 007's Captain Chun. The two captains had served together in the South Korean (ROK) Air Force. Captain Park, nine years older than Chun, was a colonel at the time that Chun was a second lieutenant. After their combat flying in the Korean war, both men had joined KAL in 1972. Captain Park was like an older brother to Captain Chun, and he was to play a key role in Chun's last flight.

Captain Chun was required to report his position over all his waypoints to Anchorage Air Traffic Control (and later to Tokyo Radio when he got closer to Japan). But from the second waypoint, which came up only 90 minutes into the eight-hour flight, 007's crew had difficulty reaching Anchorage by radio. When Chun's copilot was unable to get through to Anchorage radio, he called Flight 015 by radio and requested its crew to relay 007's position report to Anchorage, which 015 did. (Chun's inability to contact Anchorage should have warned him that he might be off course, but this was not conclusive because atmospheric conditions at different altitudes can cause variations in the clarity of transmissions, and it is fairly common for one airliner to relay the position report of another airliner.) In all, 015 relayed two position reports to Anchorage for 007.

Later in the flight, Captain Chun wanted to change his altitude but could not reach Anchorage radio for the necessary clearance. Again he asked Flight 015 to relay this request, and Captain Park's copilot obliged. But something about Chun's reported position worried Captain Park. He got on the radio himself and called Captain Chun to discuss his concern. When Park told Chun that 007's weather and position reports did not seem to jibe with his own progress over the same route, Captain Chun explained that he was experiencing strong headwinds. This did not quite make sense to Captain Park. He was flying the same route and indeed was at a higher altitude where the headwinds should have been even stronger, but he seemed to be making better progress than Captain Chun. In his polite oriental manner, he did not question Captain Chun's explanation. Instead he turned off his cockpit lights so he could see better outside the airplane, and began to search the skies for 007, both visually and on radar, but was not able to spot his old friend.

As the Plaintiffs' Steering Committee went to work on discovery, KAL was ordered to produce the crew of KAL 015 in Washington for depositions in October 1984. The copilot and flight engineer appeared and were questioned by the PSC, but Captain Park did not show up. KAL's attorneys explained that Captain Park, having reached the age limit of 55, had been retired from flying duty and later had resigned from KAL. Since he was no longer a KAL employee, we could not force KAL to produce him for questioning. But given the lack of other useful witnesses, Don Madole and George Farrell decided to try to meet with Captain Park and determine if he could help our case.

Don Madole, then the partner in charge of our Washington office, was a former Navy and airline pilot and former chief of accident hearings for the Civil Aeronautics Board. He had represented the United States in many foreign accident investigations and thus was experienced in questioning foreign airline captains. But George Farrell had even stronger qualifications for dealing with Captain Park. George was a career U.S. Marine pilot who flew Corsair fighter planes in combat against the Japanese during World War II, and remained on active duty to fly through much of the Korean war before taking up his second career as a lawyer. Thus George was a comrade-in-arms of Captain Park, who had flown 170 combat missions against the North Koreans and had received 17 medals. It was decided that George Farrell would take the lead in interviewing Captain Park.

With some difficulty, George was able to meet Captain Park in Seoul in 1985. It seemed that Park was eager to tell his story, but had some fears about pressure that KAL and the Korean government might put on him if he testified. Park explained that he had been scheduled to go to Washington with his two crewmates to give his deposition in 1984, but he had balked at the instructions given to him by KAL's staff lawyer: He was not to try to remember too much that might help the lawsuits brought by the passengers' families, since they posed a huge financial threat to KAL. He felt that if he followed those instructions on his deposition, he would have to lie, and in his mind that would be "like killing all those 269 people all over again." The confrontation with KAL management over his unwillingness to slant his testimony led to his involuntary retirement and eventual resignation.

George Farrell had half a dozen meetings in Seoul with Captain Park, and finally gained his confidence. Park was comfortable talking to a fellow pilot, especially one who had helped his country during the long struggle against the North Korean communist forces. Finally George convinced Captain Park that he should come to Washington to have his deposition taken in September 1986. Park actually flew to the United States, but just a few days before the deposition was scheduled to begin in Washington, he notified George that he could not go ahead because he had received some communications that caused him to feel his life was in danger. The deposition had to be cancelled, and the plaintiffs were back at square one.

George Farrell then tried to convince Captain Park to give his deposition in Seoul. Park said that he would go ahead only if he were assured that the South Korean government approved of his testifying. The PSC undertook the complicated process of getting the necessary orders for the Park deposition to be taken in Seoul. It began with an order from Judge Robinson in Washington, which would not be effective itself without further action by the American and Korean governments. The PSC had to get the U.S. State Department to request the Korean government, through diplomatic channels, to issue a subpoena ordering Park to testify in Seoul. That diplomatic procedure ran into the wall of secrecy maintained by both the American and Korean governments from the outset of the 007 shootdown. The PSC struggled in vain for more than a year to get a simple one-page subpoena issued in Seoul. Finally, with the help of a Korean law firm, the subpoena was issued and served on Captain Park.

Captain Park appeared for his deposition in a conference room at the Hotel Lotte in Seoul on September 23, 1987. The videotape of the deposition shows a brightly painted oriental screen as the background, complete with hummingbirds and butterflies. There were real flowers on the table which had to be pushed aside to make room for all the official government documents as Don Madole began the questioning.

Don and George were aware that Captain Park still wanted some kind of official confirmation that the Korean government did not object to him testifying. At the start of the deposition, Don turned to Roberto Powers, a U.S. State Department official from the American embassy in Seoul, and began the process of reassuring Captain Park.

> MR. MADOLE: Mr. Powers, could you explain through the interpreter that this matter has been before the Korean Government, through their Ministry of Foreign Affairs, and the Ministry of Foreign Affairs has approved this deposition and has no objection to his testimony beginning today?

Powers explained that after receiving an order for the deposition from Judge Robinson of the U.S. District Court in Washington, the U.S. Embassy in Seoul had submitted a diplomatic note to the Korean Ministry of Foreign Affairs asking that the Korean courts order Captain Park's deposition to be taken in Seoul. After a delay of more than six months, the Korean Ministry of Foreign Affairs finally advised the U.S. Embassy that the Court of Seoul City had issued a subpoena to Captain Park calling for his deposition to be taken on this date. Then Don asked the question that Captain Park needed to have answered:

> MR. MADOLE: Mr. Powers, as the Second Secretary and Consul for the American Embassy in Korea, is it correct, sir, that the Korean government has approved of this deposition, based on your knowledge of these proceedings?
> MR. POWERS: I think that is correct.

That statement, plus the official Korean court subpeona that ordered him to testify, satisfied Captain Park. Then George Farrell took over to begin questioning him about Flights 007 and 015. Working through an interpreter even though Captain Park had a good command of English (as required of all airline pilots for communications in flight), George finally got to the heart of the case.

> Q.[by Mr. Farrell] You discussed with me times when crews dumped fuel and had problems. [The captains had been disciplined by KAL.] From your knowledge of Captain Chun, do you think he was afraid to dump fuel and go back because of fear of Korean Air Lines?
> A.[by Captain Park, through the interpreter] I would say a host of factors were involved in this particular case. First of all,

what I'd like to say is the prestige, dignity, things of that nature, which must have been entertained by Captain Chun, and his—number l, his credibility was at stake, and number 2, prestige and dignity, and number 3, Captain Chun was picked as a prestige pilot, so there again he must have taken into consideration his—what we call face, and the stigma, possible stigma which he couldn't possibly erase. So, all of these factors must have been involved.

Q. Was one of those factors a fear that the Korean Air Lines would take—give him punishment for dumping fuel and returning?

A. Of course, why, that—yes, the answer would be yes. In other words, Captain Chun must have been afraid of being put to sanction or punitive action by KAL, if he dumped the fuel.

Park's answers explained why the prestige pilot, Captain Chun, would go on with the flight after discovering that his INS had been misprogrammed. KAL's management was known to be very parsimonious, and they did not take kindly to the loss of thousands of gallons of expensive fuel. They had fined and reprimanded the other captains who had misprogrammed the coordinates of the takeoff airport. Captain Chun did not greatly fear the loss of 15 or 20 days pay that the other fuel-dumping captains had suffered. It was the reprimand, the public disgrace, that struck at the essence of the oriental man's honor, pride, dignity, self-respect: his *face*.

It was a good bet that most jurors would accept Captain Chun's desire to avoid loss of face as the reason why he intentionally refused to return to Anchorage. That did not mean that he intentionally flew on into Soviet territory to get himself and the 268 others on board shot down. It was more likely that he chose to rely on his exceptional piloting skills to navigate safely to Seoul without the INS. There were other sophisticated navigation devices at his command, which he had used successfully in the years before the INS was available. He would try to make it to Seoul without the INS, even though this required him to fly close to Soviet territory at night over water. The decision to fly on without the INS was an intentional act that put his plane in extraordinary danger which came to fruition over Sakhalin Island.

So Captain Park atoned as best he could for his wartime buddy's wilful misconduct. His deposition was played on videotape at the trial in Washington. Dignified and compelling in his presentation, Captain Park Yong Man could have been chosen from Hollywood central casting for the role of the senior pilot who best understood the state of mind of his friend and fellow pilot, Captain Chun Byung-in. The jury held Korean Air Lines responsible for wilful misconduct, thus eliminating the $75,000 Warsaw Convention limitation.

The airline's insurers appealed to the Circuit Court of Appeals in Washington, but the jury's wilful misconduct verdict was upheld unanimously by a three-judge panel consisting of Chief Judge Abner Mikva, a former liberal Democratic member of Congress; Judge James Buckley, brother of William F. Buckley Jr. and formerly a conservative Republican senator from New York; and Judge Clarence Thomas, who would go on to be appointed to the Supreme Court by President George Bush.

The staying power of the Plaintiffs' Steering Committee against KAL, its insurers, and the hostile governments of the United States, the Soviet Union, and the Republic of Korea, tells us much about what to expect from the Equalizers in the future. Even though Captain Park was intimidated and put in fear for his life when first scheduled to testify, the Washington jury finally heard his evidence and righted a wrong. In less than half a century, plaintiff's tort lawyers had moved from a helpless underdog position in the Jane Froman case to a force strong enough to overcome the efforts of superpower governments to obscure the facts surrounding an international disaster.

This progress is reflected in a more recent Warsaw Convention case that arose out of the 1989 crash of a Boeing 707 flown by a charter operator, Independent Air. It was carrying 137 Italian tourists from Italy to the Dominican Republic, with a scheduled refueling stop at Santa Maria in the Azores. While approaching to land at Santa Maria, the crew descended to an altitude of 2,000 feet despite their knowledge that they had to stay above 3,000 feet in order to safely clear the mountaintops in the approach area. This resulted in the plane crashing into the mountains east of the airport, which were clearly shown on the aeronautical charts and were the only mountains on the island.

Our firm was retained by the passengers' families, and we brought suit against the owner and operator, both of whom were American companies. We chose to sue in Florida because the company that owned the plane had its headquarters there. Since we did not have an office in Florida, we brought in as local counsel Aaron Podhurst, whom we consider to be Florida's leading aviation lawyer. Gerry Lear, who succeeded Don Madole as head of our Washington office, took charge of discovery. The last deposition he took was that of Captain Everett Terry, Independent Air's chief pilot at the time of the accident, who was designated as the defendants' expert witness for the trial. Gerry took Captain Terry through the steps leading up to the fatal descent, establishing that the crew members knew there was a mountain between them and the landing runway, and that they were required to maintain at least 3,000 feet of altitude until they knew they had cleared the mountains and were in position to land safely. Gerry went on with the questioning:

> Q.[by Mr. Lear] Is it further true that the crew should have been at an altitude of 3,000 feet? A. Yes.
>
> Q. And is it further true that if the crew descended below 3,000 feet they knew that they would come within 70-some feet of the mountain in question? A. They should have known that, yes.
>
> Q. Notwithstanding that knowledge, they did descend to 2,000 feet? A. Yes.
>
> Q. Captain, considering the knowledge the crew had, was it a knowing violation of the Federal Air Regulations to come that close to the mountain? A. Yes. They are not authorized to fly that close to the terrain.
>
> Q. Do you consider that knowing violation of the Federal Aviation Regulations to be a reckless violation? A. There's so many circumstances involved, sir, I am reluctant to answer something like that.
>
> Q. I am afraid you have to, though. That's your job. A. It's just flying that close to the terrain is a reckless maneuver, yes.

Thus the airline's own chief pilot and expert witness admitted that the crash was caused by a reckless maneuver, a "knowing violation" of the air safety regulations. Based on Captain Terry's admissions, Dade County Circuit Judge Richard Y. Feder granted summary judgment to the plaintiffs on the question of wilful misconduct, ruling that there were no longer any questions of fact relating to liability to be decided by the jury. The cases would go on from there to the question of compensation for each family. When I learned of that decision in the summer of 1992, I was reminded of our inability to win any compensation for Jane Froman despite Rod Sullivan's equally reckless maneuver.

The Equalizers in the 21st Century

My guess is that justice in American tort cases will continue to depend largely upon jury trials, contingent fees, and the Equalizers in the next century. Indeed, the role of the Equalizers in achieving compensation, accountability, and deterrence will be more important than ever, because the dizzying pace of technological innovations in medicine and communications redoubles the need for sophisticated legal specialists who have the know-how to make use of these innovations and the money to invest heavily in their clients' causes. (*In the final chapter, we will consider the pros and cons of the Equalizers, jury trials, contingent fees, punitive damages, and other controversial aspects of tort law. In this chapter I merely try to predict what tort practice will look like in the next century.*)

The millions who watched the William Kennedy Smith rape trial on television in 1991 were treated to a parade of expert witnesses, each one covering a minute portion of the case, such as weather, grass, sand, sound, house design, clothing fabrics, and sexual dysfunction. These highly developed forensic skills are even more likely to be used in high-stakes tort litigation than in criminal trials. In addition to courtroom experts, today's tort lawyers must consider such sophisticated tools as "community attitude studies" (scientific polling of local residents matching the demographic make-up of potential jurors, to determine which type of juror would be most favorably disposed to the client's claims, and which evidence they would find most compelling); computerized management of documents and other evidence; and computer-generated animated accident reconstructions, which can be played on the courtroom television monitor to demonstrate to jurors how and why the accident happened.

All of these innovations add dramatically to the cost of preparing tort cases. Defendants, backed by the multi-billion dollar treasuries of insurers and businesses, have little problem in financing such aids. On the plaintiff's side, usually it is the lawyer who pays all the bills, hoping to be reimbursed if the case is successful. Today it is not unusual for a plaintiff's lawyer to lay out $50,000 to $100,000 for expenses in a single case, and ten to fifteen times that amount in a mass disaster case. In the next century, I think the figures can only go higher.

The courtroom battle of experts reached new technical heights in the litigation arising out of the 1985 crash of Delta Air Lines Flight 191 at Dallas/Fort Worth Airport. The accident was caused by a "wind shear"—a sudden change in wind direction and speed—that deprived the crew of control as they were attempting to land. After several years of litigation, all the passenger injury and death cases were settled by Delta's insurers. The insurers then sued the United States, seeking to recover all the money paid in these settlements, plus the amount paid to Delta for loss of the aircraft (a total of more than $150 million), on the theory that government employees in the National Weather Service and in the FAA-operated air traffic control center had failed to provide the Delta crew with weather data that would have enabled them to avoid the effects of the wind shear. This lawsuit brought by Delta's insurers against the federal government was tried for 14 months in the Dallas federal court. For the first time, both sides used CGVG (computer generated video graphics) in their trial presentations.

In a scenario that would have warmed the heart of Walt Disney, the lawyers for each side produced animated three-dimensional reconstructions of the accident in color, accurate to the split second. The government's animation showed on the screen what the crew members would have seen on their airborne radar if they had used it properly. Another animation showed a model of the plane descending through its last 2,000 feet toward landing, with the audio replaying the conversations between the captain, the co-pilot, and the tower that had been captured on the cockpit voice recorder. Separate animations reproduced the readings of the airspeed indicator and other instruments, as the plane proceeded to lose too much airspeed in the last 500 feet when it flew into the wind shear. Judge David O. Belew Jr., sitting without a jury (none are permitted in suits against the USA), decided that the weather information given to the crew was sufficient to enable them to avoid the accident if they had used it properly. He found that the crew possessed substantially all the weather information available from government sources, and indeed were aware of some weather conditions that were unknown to the NWS and FAA personnel. So the defendant USA won the first courtroom animation contest.

It is estimated that the CGVGs cost the government over $500,000. Delta probably spent a comparable amount on their animations. Fortunately the cost of CGVG animations is coming down as the pioneering phase gives way to more general use. Animations are now widely used for training technical personnel and designing sophisticated products. Since the Delta Texas crash trial, they have been used in other aviation accident cases, as well as in cases involving motor vehicles, roller coasters, and medical malpractice. By the 21st century they will be commonplace, and jurors will expect to see the accident scenario unfold on the video screen instead of having to rely on pictures painted by lawyers' oratory. Eventually jurors will be able to use *virtual reality*, donning space-age computerized helmets that have tiny video monitors in front of each eye. Virtual reality systems today are being used to assist in the design of buildings and automobiles, and to instruct doctors in new surgical techniques. Since the helmets enable the viewer to "walk" through the scene— whether it be a building layout or an animation of a patient's anatomy—they will permit jurors to relive the accident experience right in the courtroom, with the ability to change the scenario by pressing buttons that animate the effects of taking proper action to avoid the accident. It is difficult to imagine anyone but the Equalizers providing this kind of presentation for accident victims—and even the Equalizers will not be able to afford such expenditures unless they continue to collect contingent fees on the winning cases that pay for the losers and provide the incentive for risky investments.

In addition to the wider use of expert courtroom witnesses, I think the Equalizers will continue to develop their own in-house expertise for use in preparing cases for trial. Often lawyers must have considerable technical mastery of the case to determine what kind of expert witness is needed, and what subjects the expert is competent to testify about. Our firm pioneered this concept by staffing with pilot-lawyers. As noted, when our firm consisted of eight lawyers, all of us were pilots. When we diversified into other tort cases, we added non-pilots, but the pilots still predominate. Other firms have met this need with such combinations as doctor-lawyer, engineer-lawyer, nurse-paralegal, and pharmacist-paralegal. In addition, some Equalizers make a practice of videotaping interviews with their expert witnesses (especially physicians) and sending the tapes to the defense lawyers, who then can make realistic settlement offers based on what they will be confronted with in court if they don't settle.

Traditionally, Equalizer firms have been small in size, built around a single leader who is business-getter, financier, manager, settlement-negotiator, and trial/appellate lawyer, with the other lawyers largely supporting his efforts. While their size remains small (usually 5 to 15 lawyers even in the leading firms), the functions are beginning to change. The practice has become too complex for one person to wear so many hats. Thanks to ATLA and other bar programs, there are now thousands of competent tort trial lawyers. Most leading firms have at least two or three lawyers who try important cases, and the team approach is being used to coordinate all the firm's activities. There is even a place for old hands with long experience to counsel on strategic decisions such as the choice of forum and the theories to be pursued in complicated cases.

Jury trials will continue to play a vital role in righting twenty-first century wrongs. The Seventh Amendment guarantees jury trials in civil cases brought in the federal courts, and there are similar provisions in state constitutions. Some people question the use of juries in civil cases, and we will consider their arguments in the final chapter. Here it is appropriate only for me to say that I can see no reason to anticipate that the jury trials which are as old as our nation will be written out of the Bill of Rights in the next century. For most Americans, jury duty is the most direct and satisfying opportunity to particpate in democratic government. The alternative to jury trial is trial by judges who are elected by the voters or appointed by elected officials. Very few Americans would like their own grievances to be decided by judges who inevitably are products of the highly distrusted political processes.

Critics of trial by jury often focus on sensational media stories of multi-million-dollar tort verdicts, in which the reporters usually give sketchy details (if any) of how the total was calculated. It is true that since the 1960s, tort awards have increased faster than the rate of inflation. The main reason is that prior to that time, as we have seen, the courts were not enforcing the right to recovery of the entire damage inflicted. Today, thanks to the self-education of the Equalizers, many accident victims are represented by lawyers who understand the full extent of physical and emotional injuries and are able to portray them clearly enough for judges and jurors to appreciate the burdens which the plaintiffs will be forced to carry every minute of their lives— burdens of financial hardship, pain, suffering, indignity, and loss of even the simplest pleasures of life that the victims previously enjoyed. There are hundreds of textbooks and videotapes demonstrating how to prove damages in tort cases, including a six-volume set on the causes, effects, and evaluation of pain, written by physicians who are experts on disability. At the same time, again thanks largely to the Equalizers, judges and jurors have come to realize that they can use the power of the state, through damage awards, to compensate fully, to force accountability, and to deter future wrongdoing—and so to equalize the positions of the great and the small.

Thus, the larger awards are not the result of new legal principles, but rather of enforcement of the long-standing principle that the wrongdoer must put the victim back in the pre-accident position, to the extent that money can do this. The awards have also grown because one of the biggest items in personal injury damages is the cost of ongoing health care, including surgery, rehabilitation, and nursing, which has skyrocketed beyond the rate of inflation. Another reason is that our modern wonder drugs and other medical advances have kept alive victims of devastating injuries (including paralysis) who in former times would have died of their injuries or ensuing infections. There are now more than 500,000 such victims who have survived crippling accidents. The least that the wrongdoers can do for them is to provide whatever comfort can be bought in the health-care market, expensive as that is today.

Let's look at some recent cases that demonstrate how multi-million dollar awards come about. In a 1981 Florida case, the plaintiff was severely injured in an auto accident, rendering him a permanent quadraplegic. The jury awarded $6 million in damages, which the defendant's lawyers attacked as being excessive. Both the trial judge and the appellate court judges held that the $6 million award was not excessive. The appellate court wrote a detailed opinion analyzing all the elements of damage that the jury considered. The court noted:

> The plaintiff was 24 at the time of the accident, married, intent on starting a family, atttractive, athletic, and an IBM salesman, earning in excess of $25,000 per annum, on the way up the corporate ladder. After some eight months in the hospital with endless hours of physical and occupational therapy, he has been left a permanent C5-6 quadraplegic. He is unable to walk or even sit upright and has only the most limited use of his upper extremities. He has no bowel or bladder control and is sexually impotent. He cannot even perspire below the neck. He is on continual medication, and prophylactic care is necessary to guard against respiratory or urinary tract infection and breakdown of skin tissue. He is unable to provide himself with the most elementary of daily care, such as bathing, shaving and other grooming, and cannot be left alone for any extended period of time. The future will be the same. There were introduced into evidence or described by various therapists and physicians who testified in this case a depressing array of mechanical paraphernalia that plaintiff must utilize in some grotesque approach at daily living, ranging from mechanical and pneumatic hand splints to catheters and diapers.

The appellate court also noted that the plaintiff "lives in fear that his wife will abandon him and is degraded by his need for her assistance in the most intimate of bodily care." Citing the

expert witnesses that the plaintiff's lawyer called to document
these devastating physical and emotional injuries, and compar-
ing the $6 million award to the amounts upheld by appellate
courts in similar cases, the appellate court found that $6 million
was not excessive. Thus, the case of the IBM salesman rendered
quadraplegic takes its place in the jurisprudence of injury, to be
consulted by future courts in their scientific evaluation of compensation. In the end, every award is the product of judges as
well as jurors, for any award that approaches adequacy is likely
to be challenged as excessive, and only those that are well documented will survive the *remittitur* process.

In a 1987 New York case, a 22-month-old girl suffered severe
brain damage resulting from lack of oxygen during surgery. The
trial judge directed the jurors to break down their award into
specific categories and quantify each one separately. Thus their
verdict read as follows:

Pain and suffering	$1,500,000.
Loss of future earnings	$1,302,928.
Future medical expenses	$2,000,000.
Custodial and nursing care	$5,603,309.
Rehabilitation services	$1,986,983.
TOTAL:	$12,390,130.

Despite the fact that the plaintiff's lawyer documented all
these items with expert testimony that was virtually unopposed,
and the girl was left spastic and unable to walk, think, or talk,
the trial judge reduced the award to $10,393,130, and the appel-
late court finally reduced it to $6,143,130. That was in 1987.
Given the steeply increased costs of health care since then, it
would probably require an award closer to the jury's $12 million
evaluation to assure lifetime care for the victim.

A 1990 Louisiana case tried in Tangipahoa Parish District
Court involved the claim of a five-year-old girl who had con-
tracted Reyes Syndrome because of a faulty medical prescrip-
tion. The illness caused severe permanent brain damage and
retardation to an IQ of 42. The case was tried without a jury
because neither side requested one. The trial judge found for the
plaintiff and awarded $9,324,964.31. Under Louisiana law,
awards are broken down into *special damages* and *general damages*.
Special damages include loss of earnings and costs of health care
and rehabilitation, while general damages cover items like pain
and suffering, disability, disfigurement, loss of enjoyment of life,
and emotional distress. The trial judge broke down his award

into $5,324,964.31 for special damages and $4 million for general damages. The appellate court affirmed the award for special damages, noting that it was fully documented by expert witnesses and hardly challenged by the defendant. But it reduced the $4 million general damages to $2.5 million, even though it too was documented by qualified experts in special education, speech, neurology, and psychology. Thus the final award, totalling $7,824,964.31, was the product of a trial judge and three appellate judges.

The same principles of judicially-supervised compensation we have seen in these three personal injury cases apply to wrongful death cases. While they do not involve the huge expenses of lifetime medical care, in many states they require compensation for the emotional as well as the financial losses caused by wrongfully taking another person's life. As we saw in Chapter 13, the shortchanging of widows and orphans is much more difficult today than it was before the coming of the Equalizers. Therefore, wrongful death awards have also climbed faster than the rate of inflation, but only because we are moving closer to enforcement of the victims' rights to adequate compensation.

Despite the progress in the last half of the twentieth century, we still have a long way to go before the American courts can be credited with giving as much protection to personal rights as to property rights. For example, the winner of a case involving contract or property rights is awarded interest from the date of the transaction that gave rise to the lawsuit, such as the breaching of a contract or the sale of a building. (This is known as "prejudgment interest," since it starts to run at the time of the transaction rather than when the plaintiff wins a court judgment.) But in most tort cases, the plaintiff's right to collect interest does not start to run until he wins the case and enters judgment, which might be four or five years after the accident.

This denial of prejudgment interest in tort cases is supposedly justified by differences in the nature of tort and property cases: In property cases the damages are "liquidated" (i.e. precisely fixed before the lawsuit) whereas in tort cases damages are "unliquidated" because they cannot be fixed precisely without a trial. If this is true, then courts throughout the world have wasted thousands of trials to determine the damages suffered in breach of contract cases. Where there is a dispute between the parties to a contract that requires a trial, the damages are no more liquidated or predetermined than they are in a tort case. Indeed, many times the *only* disputed issue in a breach of contract action is the amount of damage.

The specious distinction which robs tort victims of the right to recover interest from the date of injury encourages (and indeed subsidizes) defendants who wait until the eve of trial to make reasonable settlement offers. Why should they rush to settle cases—even those in which their liability is clear—when they can earn a healthy return on the money for several years while waiting out calendar delay? Interest imposed from the date of injury would give them a strong incentive to settle meritorious cases earlier.

Since animals are considered property, the old lawbooks are full of cases in which plaintiffs sued for the deaths of bulls, mules, horses, dogs, sheep, goats, and pigs, and collected interest from the date of the animals' deaths. Yet in many states plaintiffs who have lost relatives in fatal accidents do not have the same right to prejudgment interest. This is one of the remaining nineteenth-century injustices that the Equalizers have targeted for removal by the year 2000. At this writing, more than 20 states have partially or entirely discarded the old "unliquidated" concept and allowed prejudgment interest in tort cases.

As we have seen, advances in rights of action (types of lawsuits permitted) have developed much like the movement toward more adequate compensation: through the evolutionary process of equalizing personal rights with property rights. Publications like the *Wall Street Journal* periodically warn business executives that the courts are manufacturing new torts. But what really happens is that the single tort remedy—the righting of wrongs—is being enforced in an area where wrongdoers had enjoyed immunity in the past. Again, it is the kicking in of rotten doors rather than the construction of new edifices.

This advance is not always a steady march forward. Often there are backward steps as the Equalizers encounter judicial resistance to the stripping away of ancient immunities. A case in point is the wrongful death action brought by the family of the baseball immortal Roberto Clemente, who was killed near San Juan Airport on December 31, 1972, in the crash of a DC-7 airplane that he had chartered to fly relief supplies to the victims of an earthquake in Nicaragua.

Earlier that year, Clemente had led a group of Puerto Rican baseball players on a barnstorming tour of Nicaragua, which was enough to ignite a feeling of brotherhood in him. When the earthquake struck, he took it upon himself to mobilize the nonaffluent people of Puerto Rico to alleviate the suffering in Nicaragua. He spearheaded the drive that produced donations of food, clothing, and medical supplies, which he undertook to collect and transport to Nicaragua. He dispatched three full planeloads of relief supplies, and found that there was enough left over to require a fourth cargo plane. While at the airport on December 30, 1972, to supervise the loading for the third flight, Clemente was approached by one Arthur S. Rivera, who introduced himself as the president of the American Air Express Company, and offered to transport the remaining supplies in a fourth flight for $4,000. Clemente agreed, and told Rivera he would accompany the fourth planeload in order to make certain that the relief supplies were reaching the victims (rather than profiteers) in Nicaragua.

Our firm, representing the Clemente family, soon discovered that Roberto had signed his own death warrant by chartering a decrepit DC-7 that was hardly fit to taxi on the airport, much less to carry a full load of supplies to Nicaragua. The owner of the DC-7, Arthur Rivera, was a tramp operator with a long record of violations of the most basic FAA safety regulations. He was known to the FAA personnel at San Juan to be an outlaw, and the FAA inspectors knew that his DC-7 was not airworthy. He had hired an itinerant pilot, Jerry Hill, to captain the DC-7. Hill did not have adequate rest before the takeoff; he had no flight engineer; Rivera himself acted as co-pilot, although not qualified; there was no dispatcher or ground support; and the plane was overloaded by more than two tons. The engines were not in good enough condition to deliver the power needed for a safe takeoff, and one of them failed on the takeoff, causing the plane to crash in the ocean just beyond the airport. We had an open-and-shut case of negligence against Rivera. The only problem was that like all tramp operators, he had no liability insurance, and he had been killed in the accident, leaving no assets.

Our only hope of recovering damages for the Clemente family was to sue the United States government for negligence of the FAA. Here we were helped by an order adopted by the FAA in 1971, aimed at preventing accidents caused by tramp operators who ignored safety regulations. In 1970, 37 members of the Wichita State University football team were killed in the crash of an overloaded plane operated by unlicensed persons in violation of FAA regulations. At that point the FAA decided to take affirmative action to protect the public from such illegal charter operators instead of waiting for accidents to happen. The 1971 FAA order directed its safety inspectors to keep questionable operators under continuous surveillance, which was easy enough to do because they operated multiengine planes from large airports and had to file flight plans and get takeoff clearance from the

FAA tower before departure. The order required tower personnel to notify safety inspectors of impending takeoff, at which point the inspectors were to board the plane and check for safety compliance. If the inspection turned up any dangerous or illegal conditions, the persons chartering the service were to be notified immediately so that they could cancel the flight.

Among the dangerous conditions that the FAA inspectors were to look for were unairworthiness, overloading, and unqualified crew members. Rivera's DC-7 would have failed the inspection on all three counts. But the inspection was never made, even though Rivera was well known to the FAA officials at San Juan as an irresponsible scofflaw. Those FAA officials had simply ignored the surveillance order. They had not even bothered to set up the procedure (mandated in the order) through which the FAA tower personnel would notify safety inspectors of a request for takeoff clearance from a tramp operator. And while Roberto Clemente was rolling down the runway toward his death sentence, some of the FAA inspectors who could have saved his life were at a New Year's Eve party near the airport. They had never lifted a finger to implement the FAA's own life-saving order, which was specifically designed to prevent the type of avoidable accident that killed Clemente.

The case against the United States government was heard in San Juan by U.S. District Court Judge Juan R. Torruella in 1975. He sat without a jury because claims against the government must be decided by the judge alone. Chuck Krause, Don Madole, and Juanita Madole presented the case, which ended in a finding of liability by Judge Torruella. He permitted the government to take his ruling to the appellate court before getting into the question of damages. If they upheld the verdict, he would then hold another trial to fix compensation.

Appeals from the Puerto Rico federal court are heard by the U.S. Court of Appeals for the First Circuit, sitting in Boston. I took on the job of arguing the appeal for our side, and within a few minutes I knew we were in trouble. The three appellate judges brushed aside the main legal arguments and zeroed in on a policy question: If the government were held liable for the failure of the FAA safety inspectors to inspect Rivera's plane and report the dangers to Clemente, wouldn't this open the door to thousands of suits based on the failure of OSHA (Occupational Health and Safety Administration) inspectors to notify workers of safety violations discovered during factory inspections? They also questioned whether government agencies would undertake life-saving functions in the future if that might lead to tort liability.

I had prepared answers to these questions because the government lawyers had made these arguments in their appellate brief. I tried to distinguish the FAA surveillance order from ordinary OSHA inspections: The FAA itself recognized the emergency that existed after the Wichita State accident, and had taken the duty of affirmative action on itself to save passengers' lives. This affirmative action was the first, last, and only line of defense against illegal operators who could not be regulated in the usual way because (by definition) they made a practice of flouting government safety regulations. I argued that the fact situation in the Clemente case—government inspectors ignoring their own emergency safety order—was so bizarre that we were not likely to see its equivalent very often in the FAA, OSHA, or other agencies. In response to the judges' questions about the effects of Judge Torruella's decision holding the government liable for Clemente's death, I pointed out that in the months following that decision, the FAA had vigorously enforced the safety order by grounding 42 large aircraft and 30 pilots, wiping out an area at Miami International Airport known as Cockroach Corner where many tramp operators congregated.

I left the Boston courthouse hoping for the best but feeling uneasy about the judges' preoccupation with opening the floodgates to claims against OSHA. Sure enough, they unanimously reversed Judge Torruella, holding that the FAA had acted "entirely gratuitously" in issuing the emergency surveillance order. This was news to all those who understood the Federal Aviation Act to *require* the FAA to issue such orders when the safety of the travelling public is threatened. One can only wonder what the FAA inspectors are being paid for, if they are acting gratuitously in carrying out an order which their own superiors found necessary for the public's protection. The First Circuit, declaring that the life-saving surveillance order was gratuitous, decided that the government had no duty to warn Clemente, and therefore could not be held liable for his death.

Half a dozen lawyers in our firm worked on the Clemente case over a period of seven years, and we laid out thousands of dollars in expenses which we did not get back. We tried to get the U.S. Supreme Court to review the First Circuit's decision, but they refused to hear it. So the case ended in a total loss for the Clemente family and for us as their lawyers. Yet it was a great privilege to represent the Clementes, even in a losing cause. There was the further satisfaction of the salutary effects that

Judge Torruella's decision had on FAA enforcement of safety regulations against the tramp operators in Miami's Cockroach Corner and elsewhere. We accepted the financial loss as part of the cost of conducting a tort practice, which offsets the profits from contingent fees that appear overly lucrative to some who are not familiar with the capital investment and risks required to produce them.

Punitive Damages and Deterrence

One of the most controversial areas of tort law is punitive damages. Both sides of the argument will be aired in the final chapter. Here I predict that punitive damages will continue to play an important role as a deterrent to irresponsible and dangerous conduct, especially in product liability and environmental damage cases. I base this prediction on the assumptions that the drive for business profits will be as strong as ever; that business executives will continue to put profits ahead of safety when their companies have large investments in products that turn out to be unsafe or in factories that pollute the environment; that American business will continue to perform brilliantly in the field where it is the world leader: avoiding or neutralizing government regulation of safety and environmental policy; and that in many instances, the threat of punitive damages will continue to be the only sanction capable of protecting the public from this danger, because most businesses write off the costs of paying mere compensatory damages as a routine cost of operation.

The deterrent effect is clearly evident in product and environmental cases because the danger lingers on as thousands of defective products remain on the market (or pollutants continue to spew into the environment) and do their deadly damage year after year. The automobile driver who recklessly runs through a stop sign, or the airline pilot who makes a once-in-a-lifetime miscalculation, are less appropriate subjects for punitive damages because their conduct usually is not premeditated or in furtherance of a long-term profit-making strategy.

When I began law practice in 1948, the deterrent effect of tort suits was debatable, since there were no tort lawyers strong enough to recover punitive damages, and the awards for compensatory damages were usually well within the limits of liability insurance, which was so cheap that wrongdoers had no financial incentive to avoid injuring other people. But with the advent of the Equalizers, higher awards that approximated the real damage forced liability insurers to raise rates for habitual wrongdoers, and sometimes they would withdraw coverage entirely unless the wrongdoers could demonstrate that they had removed the dangers. Then came punitive damage verdicts, which in many states must be paid directly by the wrongdoers rather than the insurers—for it is not the insurers that the law seeks to punish and deter. Manufacturers began to learn that they would have to make their products safe or assume heavy financial risks that could not be covered by cheap insurance. Now the combination of adequate awards for compensatory damages and the threat of punitive damages in extreme cases produces a clear deterrent. Indeed, as we shall see in the final chapter, the only question raised by critics of punitive damages is whether the deterrent is so strong that it is harmful to the Golden Goose of American business.

To take one product group as an example of the deterrent effect, factory machinery sold without safeguards caused thousands of amputations each year up to the 1970s. But manufacturers of unsafe machinery began to have difficulty getting insurance coverage because the Equalizers, using the new strict liability weapon, created the industry's first strong deterrent: lawsuits that made it more expensive to sell dangerous machines than to make them safe. The National Safety Council took notice of the reasons for improved machine safety in the 1970s:

> Most machine manufacturers make point-of-operation and power transmission guarding "standard equipment" on all stock type machines, meaning the machine cannot be purchased without guards. This highly desirable state of affairs has in the main resulted from legal actions and legislation holding the manufacturer liable for accidents arising from unsafe design or manufacturing of his machines.

One would think that things would be different in the aviation industry, which had to be safety-conscious from its inception to overcome the public's fear of leaving the ground. There is extensive government regulation of virtually every phase of aviation, particularly safety. You would not expect that the highly motivated professionals who manage the airlines and fly the jumbo jets would need any further incentive to make their operations as safe as possible. But even in that field, the value of the tort deterrent is demonstrable. Consider the case of Captain Eddie Rickenbacker and the De Havilland Comet.

Rickenbacker, who was America's leading fighter ace in World War I and later developed Eastern Air Lines into one of the nation's premier air carriers, pioneered many advances in military and commercial aviation safety. In the early 1950s he was invited over to England for a preview of the first commercial jet airliner, the four-engine De Havilland Comet. In his autobiography, he told the story of his first and last flight in a Comet:

> I visited in the cockpit, then strolled back toward the tail. Halfway down the aisle, I suddenly stopped short. I couldn't believe what I was seeing. The sides of the plane seemed to be moving in and out like an accordion. I pushed my finger up against the side. I could feel it. It scared the living daylights out of me. Sooner or late that metal would fatigue and crack. At forty thousand feet, the pressurized cabin would explode like a toy balloon.

Captain Eddie quickly told his hosts that he was late for another appointment, and cut the flight short so that he could minimize the risk to himself. Once on the ground, he pointed out the dangers of the repeated expansion and contraction to De Havilland's engineers and executives, but they had faith in their design and refused to make any changes. As Eddie wrote:

> Three Comets crashed before the cause was determined. The fuselage had exploded, just as I feared it would. The Comet crashes were a great blow to British prestige. From my personal experience with the plane, I was able to warn American manufacturers about this accordion weakness, and steps were taken to prevent it.

This was a commendable service to the American manufacturers, but as a member of the exclusive club of aviation insiders, Captain Eddie was inhibited from making a public statement critical of an aviation manufacturer, even a foreign one. A public announcement with Rickenbacker's prestige behind it could have forced De Havilland to reveal the results of its own tests or to allow impartial observers aboard to check the effects of the accordion movements. This could have saved the lives of hundreds of people who died in the three Comet crashes. At the very least, if he had spoken out after the first crash, he could have saved those who were lost in the second and third crashes. And if the Comets had been subjected to American tort litigation, it is very likely that depositions taken by the plaintiffs' lawyers after the first crash would have uncovered correspondence with Rickenbacker and other evidence that could have forced De Havilland to ground the Comet until modifications made it safe to fly. It is no coincidence that the United States is the world leader in aviation safety and at the same time the only major nation that permits judges and juries to award damages which approach the amount of harm actually done.

The role of punitive damages as a much stronger deterrent than government regulation is illustrated by two disastrous products: the Ford Pinto automobile, and the Dalkon Shield birth control device manufactured by A.H. Robins Company. We'll discuss those products—and the lawsuits they spawned—in the final chapter. Hundreds of other products had to be modified or taken off the market because of dangers revealed in product liability lawsuits, including other automobiles, asbestos, breast implants, and many pharmaceuticals. This deterrent has also had some positive effects, as noted by the industry-financed Conference Board of New York in its 1987 report, "Product Liability: The Corporate Response." Based on its survey of 232 American companies with annual sales of at least $100 million, the board concluded:

> Where products liability has had a notable impact—where it has most significantly affected management decision-making—has been in the quality of the products themselves. Managers say products have become safer, manufacturing procedures have been improved, and labels and use instructions have become more explicit.

The fact that such deadly products were kept on the market by executives who knew of their dangers makes one wonder about the basic morality of American business management. It is tempting to speculate on whether the bad guys who'll do anything for a buck inevitably muscle their way to the top echelons of business. But I don't think that's the answer. As a group, the top executives of our large manufacturing enterprises are leading contributors to the nation's welfare, through their military service and their support of education, religion, and good works. Morally, they are as good a group as our nation can produce. But somewhere along the line, most of them develop a double standard which permits them to live with (indeed, to be comfortable with) practices in business that they would never use or condone in their personal lives. There is no evidence that those below them would be immune from this double standard if they were promoted to the top jobs. In large companies, there is often a form of team psychology that causes seemingly moral people to participate as a group in immoral business actions that few of them would take on their own. This team drive to succeed often turns corporate management into a steamroller that runs right over safety problems if they stand in the way of profits.

Consider our disgraceful record of exporting products that are banned from the domestic market because of their known danger to human life. Many of the household names of American business—e.g., Dow, Merck, Johnson & Johnson, Upjohn— have dumped dangerous products overseas (especially in Third World countries) after our government found them so hazardous that they could not be sold here. In the 1970s, with Jimmy Carter as president, there was a strong drive to prohibit this "toxic trade." After Congressional investigations revealed the shocking facts (including the exporting of millions of children's pajamas treated with cancer-causing chemicals after their sale was banned at home), President Carter signed an executive order on January 15, 1981, prohibiting the export of toxic drugs, pesticides, and other deadly products that had been banned domestically. But Carter's humane order lasted little more than a month, for Ronald Reagan took over and as one of his first presidential acts, he revoked the export ban because it put U.S. products "at a competitive disadvantage."

Since jobs and profits are involved, the grisly trade goes on. But how long would it last if the Third World victims were allowed to sue the American exporters in the American courts, with American Equalizers as their lawyers?

Even with its defects and horror stories, we Americans believe that the profit-driven free market system is the best we can devise to spread the good life to most of our people, and that it is the most hospitable to democratic principles. Most other nations have come to believe this as well, some after trying various forms of socialism that promised more egalitarian results but proved to be unworkable and sometimes undemocratic. So the answer does not lie in turning away from free-market capitalism, but in maintaining accountability of the company—and eventually individual accountability of its officers—for the immoral group actions of professedly moral individuals. Perhaps a better method of maintaining accountability will emerge, but for the foreseeable future we'll have to rely mainly on the deterrent effect of tort law—especially punitive damages—as wielded by the Equalizers. In that way, the Equalizers have become ombudsmen by default.

The sad truth is that few business managers would take the trouble to protect the public safety if it weren't for lawsuits. What else but the threat of lawsuits would induce motel owners to put strong locks on room doors, or provide security guards to prevent rape? It was only after singer Connie Francis won a multi-million dollar verdict for a motel rape that the owners began to take such precautions. By the time government regulators catch up with the worst offenders, they are willing to pay a slap-on-the-wrist fine, or they have wrung all the profits out of a dangerous product and are ready to move on to the next one. Certainly the code of business ethics will not inhibit them, for there is no such code. Business leaders have begun to debate whether to adopt such a code, but even if they do, you can bet that it will not have any enforcement machinery like the systems that govern doctors, lawyers, and other licensed professionals.

In a 1990 report on "Smoking and Health," U.S. Secretary of Health and Human Services Dr. Louis W. Sullivan said:

> Cigarette smoking is the chief preventable cause of death in our society. It is directly responsible for some 390,000 deaths each year in the United States, or more than one of every six deaths in our country. The number of Americans who die each year from diseases caused by smoking exceeds the number of Americans who died in all of World War II, and this toll is repeated year after year.

Yet the tobacco industry rolls along, uninhibited by government regulations restricting advertising and requiring warnings on every pack. The tobacco merchants continue to kill at least 390,000 Americans (and an estimated 2.5 million people worldwide) each year with impunity, for one reason: the Equalizers have not been able to win tort suits against them. The tobacco industry has fought tort cases as a group for decades, knowing that jury verdicts are the one force capable of putting them out of business. Now that the dangers of smoking are so well known and highly publicized, judges and jurors for the most part have turned away claims based on smoking because there is a choice involved—a choice, that is, if you disregard the addictive qualities of tobacco that hook many smokers for life.

I predict that by the end of this century, the Equalizers will catch up with the tobacco merchants. The first breach came in the 1992 U.S. Supreme Court decision that allowed victims to sue tobacco companies that allegedly misrepresented or fraudulently withheld information concerning the health effects of smoking. Further breakthroughs will probably come in claims arising from secondhand smoke cases: the passive exposure to toxic tobacco fumes that kill an estimated 53,000 *nonsmokers* each year. The defenses of contributory negligence and assumption of risk that shielded the tobacco manufacturers from smokers' suits will not help them in suits by nonsmokers. Also, the ancient tort of *nuisance* may be invoked, since it has been applied to illnesses and injuries caused by those responsible for fouling the air with noxious fumes. Now that government studies have documented the health threat that tobacco poses to nonsmokers, it is only a matter of time before the Equalizers put an end to this carnage. The tobacco giants, sensing that the roof may fall in at any time, have used their huge resources to diversify into other product lines that will keep them alive even if they lose their lucrative cigarette trade.

An important breakthrough came in a 1991 decision by the Federal Court of Australia, holding that advertisements by the Tobacco Institute of Australia claiming that there was no scientific evidence of tobacco's dangers to nonsmokers were misleading and deceptive. The claim was brought by the Australian Federation of Consumer Organizations, whose solicitor, Dr. Peter Cashman of Sydney, is an embryo Equalizer. Peter has pioneered product liability suits in Australia, and is dedicated to delivering the knockout blow to the tobacco industry through passive smoking suits.

In 1992, an Australian jury awarded $85,000 to another Peter Cashman client, Mrs. Liesel Scholem, an employee of the Health (!) Department of the State of New South Wales, who contracted emphysema and chronic asthma as a result of her 12-year exposure to tobacco smoke in her office environment. If upheld on appeal, this award will be paid by the employer rather than the tobacco manufacturers, but in the optimistic world of the Equalizers this is a long step toward the final kicking in of the rotten door that now shields the tobacco merchants from liability. Once that door is splintered away, cigarette manufacturers will face claims for compensatory and punitive damages that can drive up the cost of cigarettes to ridiculous heights and eventually accomplish that which attempts at government regulation cannot do: shut down the cigarette production lines.

Keeping the Courts Open in the 21st Century

My predictions about the continuing role of the Equalizers assume that the civil courts will remain open. As of 1992 this was by no means certain, as state after state encountered budget problems which threatened to curtail civil trials so that hard-pressed judges could keep up with the ever-growing caseload of criminal prosecutions that must be given first priority. I have suggested two methods of strengthening the funding of our civil courts: (1) Demonstrating that civil litigation is already an important source of revenue for the forum community, in order to build support for higher appropriations; and (2) Taxing the proceeds of successful lawsuits, and dedicating the tax funds to financing the court system.

A 1986 study by the Rand Corporation's Institute for Civil Justice found that in the typical state court tort case with average compensation of about $30,000, the cost to the forum community is less than 2 percent of the compensation, and fees paid to plaintiffs' and defendants' lawyers total 42 percent. Thus the average cost to the community is about $600, and the total legal fees for both sides are about $12,000. This means that for every dollar of cost to local government, $20 is recycled into the local economy through payments to lawyers.

What happens to that $12,000 in legal fees? If we calculate the law firms' overhead expense at the typical 50 percent, half of the $12,000 goes into salaries paid to those working in the law firms, and to local suppliers of goods and services used by law firms. Many of these expenditures generate state and local tax revenue in the form of levies on payrolls, income, real estate, and sales. Indeed, the other 50 percent of the lawyers' fees that goes to the law partners as profit also produces substantial tax revenues and local expenditures. Taxes, of course, build courthouses and pay salaries of judges and court personnel.

Thus, most of the $12,000 lawyers' revenue per tort case benefits the local economy by creating and sustaining jobs and commerce throughout the community, from the landlord who collects rent on the law office, to the student who delivers sandwiches and coffee to the law firm's lunchroom, to the dealer who sells and services the lawyers' personal automobiles.

Even more striking is the beneficial effect of mass disaster litigation on the forum's economy. Another Institute for Civil Justice study covers the amounts paid in compensation of aviation accident victims from 1970 to 1984 in state and federal courts. The study concludes that the average compensation in such cases was $363,000, with $72,000 being paid to plaintiffs' lawyers and $49,000 to defendants' lawyers for fees and expenses. Assuming there are 100 plaintiffs (not a large number for an airline crash) the total recovery would be $36.3 million; the total amount paid to plaintiffs' lawyers would be $7.2 million; and the total paid to defendants' lawyers would be $4.9 million. Thus the total amount paid to lawyers would be $12.1 million against a community cost of less than $14,000. Economists tell us that payments like the $12.1 million in legal fees circulate through the local economy with a force of at least 3.5 times the initial figure, so that the total favorable economic impact is $12.1 million times 3.5, or $43,750,000.

It is apparent that civil litigation produces billions of dollars worth of commerce, in the form of expenditures by those who benefit directly and indirectly from that litigation. And commerce is exactly what public officials desperately seek to attract to their communities. Consider some examples:

- Mayor David Dinkins of New York recently announced appropriation of $150 million for improvements to the National Tennis Center, which the city leases to the U.S. Tennis Association for the annual U.S. Open tournament. The main reason for this huge expenditure is to keep for the city the indirect benefits of the millions of dollars spent in New York hotels, restaurants, and shops by those attending the two-week U.S. Open tournament. Previously, New York City spent tens of millions of dollars to refurbish Yankee Stadium for the same reasons.
- In 1979, the Austrian government completed building a $500 million Vienna office complex for the United Nations. The complex is leased to the United Nations for one schilling a year, so there is no direct return to the government on this investment. But tiny Austria (population: 7.5 million) was willing to spend half a billion dollars to gain the indirect public benefits of the jobs created in Vienna and the local expenditures of the United Nations.
- In 1991, Indianapolis agreed to provide $300 million to United Airlines to induce that company to move its aircraft maintenance center there. United pledged that it would create 6,300 jobs in Indianapolis.

Today the construction of almost any new American factory or business facility that will create ongoing jobs is subsidized by federal, state, and local government grants and tax breaks. Often there are other large public expenditures required, such as road and sewer construction costs. Some grants from federal agencies for acquisition of land and relocation of residents have exceeded $100 million for a single new plant. Usually the only compensation to the government treasuries is in the form of the indirect benefits of local expenditures, payrolls, and commerce. Every state has an agency devoted to attracting such new facilities, and there are many city and county agencies as well.

From the standpoint of economic benefit to the community, is there any significant difference between the commerce created by the tennis matches, baseball games, United Nations activities, and factories in these examples, and the commerce created by civil litigation? If anything, civil litigation deserves a higher priority because it is designed to produce justice and is an integral part of our participatory democracy. And unlike many other forms of commerce, civil ligitation does not create pollution or other undesirable side effects.

I am not suggesting that any steps be taken to encourage or create more civil litigation even if it is profitable to the community. The demand for civil litigation is determined by free-market principles, more so in the United States than anywhere else, because there is greater access to qualified representation here. That is one of the big reasons why we have more lawyers per capita than other nations—we also have more justice per capita. If the consumers who constitute the free market didn't want it that way, there would be a lot of lawyers seeking other careers.

All of these points can be documented by financial impact studies which can produce stronger legislative support for the addition of new judges and court facilities. As a retirement project, I am trying to convince bar associations and others interested in preserving American justice to undertake such studies. Although profitability is limited to civil cases, the additional judges assigned to those cases would also reduce the criminal docket backlogs in the many courts where the same judges hear both civil and criminal cases.

Even if the suggested financial impact studies help to support the appropriations needed for court expansion, another step will probably be required: a small user charge (or tax) on the billions of dollars collected annually by successful civil litigants through verdicts or settlements. At the rate of only one percent, such a charge would yield very large sums, probably enough to pay for all the new judges and courtrooms that the system could use. In fairness, this charge should be earmarked for creation of new judgeships and the expansion of present court facilities, many of which are located in depressed urban neighborhoods.

This one percent charge also could be considered for the federal courts, which otherwise probably would not be in a position to benefit from increased local commerce in the way that state courts can, since the impact of expenditure of lawyers' income cannot be measured so readily in the federal court system. If each federal district court maintained a fund composed of such charges, it could be earmarked for creation of new

judgeships and courtrooms in the district. Again, this would relieve the presssures on both criminal and civil calendars, since
federal district judges hear both kinds of cases.

In many states today, civil trials are long delayed (and in
some places almost at a standstill) because of massive increases
in criminal prosecutions. If a nominal charge to those civil plaintiffs who are fortunate enough to get their cases tried or settled
will relieve this congestion, I believe it is well worth considering.
If contingent fees were based upon the net amount received by
the plaintiff after payment of this charge, then lawyers would
also be making a major contribution to keeping the wheels of
justice turning. Please note that I am not proposing an increase in
filing fees. The one percent charge would be payable only in
cases successfully concluded by trial or settlement.

The idea of taxing successful litigants has already made its
way onto the political stage. In his struggle to balance New York
State's 1992-1993 budget, Governor Mario Cuomo proposed a
$34 million cutback in the sum allocated to the court system. The
state's highest judicial officer, Court of Appeals Chief Judge Sol
Wachtler, refused to accept this, saying that it would result in the
shutting down of much of the court system, particularly on the
civil side, since priority had to be given to criminal trials. During
an impasse that lasted for several months, 470 court workers
were laid off; about a quarter of New York's civil trial system
was shut down; Judge Wachtler filed suit against Governor
Cuomo to void the budget cutbacks; and Governor Cuomo filed
a countersuit in federal court. During the negotiations to defuse
this constitutional crisis, Judge Wachtler proposed a one percent
tax on successful civil suits, to be dedicated to funding the court
system. Governor Cuomo agreed to the tax, but wanted the proceeds to flow into the general treasury instead of being dedicated
to the courts. Finally in January 1992 Cuomo and Wachtler
reached an agreement that wiped out the budget cutbacks and
enabled the court system to limp along for another year. The one
percent tax on successful civil suits was put aside for the moment, but a provision for New York State to receive 20 percent of
all punitive damage awards was enacted, the money to go into
the general treasury.

Thus it is apparent that desperate governors and state legislators will soon get around to taxing successful civil litigants.
The only question is whether lawyers will be perceptive enough
to realize that such taxes provide a natural reservoir of funds
needed to keep our court systems functioning reasonably well. I
have made it another retirement project to try to alert lawyers to

the opportunities provided by such taxes, and the dangers of allowing them to be imposed without dedication to the courts. I see such taxes in a double light: as a means of keeping our courts functioning for our own citizens, and for expanding them as needed to permit foreign citizens to bring suits here when they have claims that are legitimately related to American companies or transactions.

Excellence and Performance-Based Pay

We have seen that the Equalizers' quest for excellence has resulted in the attainment of the American Dream by many of the Equalizers and their clients. I believe that this attainment is also important as an inspiration to those seeking a better life through free-market capitalism within a democracy—a category which now includes most of the world.

The Equalizers have attained a degree of excellence and have made some dreams come true, without government or banking subsidies. They have had to make their way as independent, self-reliant entrepreneurs. They provide one of the few useful services that is available to everyone, even those who have no money. Indeed, the best of the tort lawyers are just as accessible to the poor as to the rich, because poor people suffer injuries which make them equally valuable clients. This happens less often in medicine, and it practically never happens in accounting, architecture, or other professions.

One of the long-standing problems of capitalism has been its unequal distribution of wealth and income which in turn leads to disparity of power—the "impunity" that Ambrose Bierce equated with wealth. Empowerment, especially of the poor, became a buzzword in the George Bush White House, as conservative Republicans sought ways of softening the impact of unequal wealth distribution and tried to produce at least the appearance of equal opportunity. The Equalizers make good on that promise by empowering the poor and the weak—the underdogs whom they represent. The Equalizers also nurture other values traditionally espoused by conservatives, Republicans, and many others: they help to keep families together, and they reduce dependency on government intervention.

The American tort lawyers who have become Equalizers have achieved a high degree of professional excellence. We must be excellent merely to survive, since we only get paid when we achieve good results for our clients, and we constantly face opposition from defense lawyers who are chosen for their excellence by the insurance companies that dwarf us and our clients in size and resources. We lead the world in achieving fair compensation for accident victims, and that is our job. This is a uniquely American accomplishment.

As we'll see in Chapter 16, there are no tort lawyers anywhere outside America who are able to become Equalizers in this way. Other countries have counterparts of our corporate and criminal lawyers, but not our Equalizers. This is not because their laws are so different from ours. It is their *lawyers* that are different, because their systems prohibit contingent fees, and thereby prevent lawyers from developing into Equalizers. The other legal systems protect property rights and the status quo more than they protect individual rights. Even in the old communist and socialist regimes, there were no Adequate Awards and no Equalizers, for the dictators and bureaucrats would never risk giving such power to independent outsiders like tort lawyers.

American tort lawyers achieved excellence—and thereby became Equalizers—by hard work, self-education, and the need to perform well in order to survive and prosper. As noted, it was not favorable provisions of American law that brought about this excellence, for the law itself was even more favorable during our first century when there was no requirement of proving fault. While the excellence of the Equalizers directly benefits only themselves and their accident-victim clients, the way that they have achieved excellence is of broader significance. Its principles can help us to achieve excellence in other fields, such as business, finance, social work, and even government. Wouldn't it be great if our auto manufacturers, pollution control specialists, drug enforcement agents, teachers, and bankers performed their jobs as well as tort lawyers?

One key to excellence is embodied in the much-maligned contingent fee, through which the tort lawyer profits to the extent that he accomplishes his mission by benefitting his client. In the maritime world, there has long been a practice of "No Cure, No Pay" agreements for tugboat operators who salvage ships that are in need of rescue at sea. The tugboat operator gets nothing if he does not rescue the troubled vessel, but if he is successful he gets an agreed percentage of the value of the ship and its cargo. This principle has been discovered recently by many of the experts who are seeking ways of recharging the batteries of American business. In their lingo, it is called Performance-Based Pay (PBP).

Performance-Based Pay is being tried at all levels of American business, from the lowest-paid unskilled workers to the chief executive officers. This is a long-standing practice in paying top management, but it is now being pushed down the ladder to the lower rungs of employment. PBP variable-pay plans covered more than 4 million employees in 1991, and nearly half the Fortune 500 companies are testing such schemes. Those who perform below reasonable expectation receive less-than-average pay for the job inovlved, while those who excel get higher pay and bonuses. Gauging performance is not as simple for them as the tort lawyer's percentage of the amount recovered for the client. But management consultants are hard at work developing appropriate standards for judging performance, so that eventually this incentive to achieve excellence will be available throughout American business.

Stockholders are awakening to the fact that their shares need not be cheapened by millions of dollars in salaries and bonuses being paid to corporate officers who produce losses rather than profits. In 1991, the average annual compensation of the chief executive officers of our major companies was $2.8 million, and many of them received tens of millions. Seven and eight figure compensation can be justified only if the CEO enriches the company proportionately. CEOs of Japanese and German companies were not nearly so well paid, even though their companies often outperformed American competitors. The spectacle of Chrysler Chairman Lee Iacocca (salary: $4.5 million) sitting next to Toyota Chairman Toyoda (salary: $690,000) at the 1991 Tokyo export-import conference focused public attention on the fact that the performance of their companies was inversely proportional to their compensation. The Securities & Exchange Commission, institutional investors, and legislators such as Senator Carl Levin (Democrat, Michigan) are beginning to think about ways of using their powers to peg executive pay more closely to performance.

Within the legal profession, whose leaders historically looked down upon the contingent fee and its practitioners, broad changes in fee structures are under way. Legal costs of large corporate clients have escalated rapidly, and their in-house legal departments are trying to cut these expenditures. More and more, they are demanding that outside law firms charge flat fees for specific tasks, and that contingent fees be used instead of the old standby, the billable hour. In a 1992 *Business Week* article, Catherine Yang noted that large corporations "are wrangling major concessions from their clock-obsessed lawyers" by insisting on "value billing" rather than hourly fees. A new industry has sprung up, devoted to auditing the hours billed to clients by law firms. As Chief Judge Richard Neely of West Virginia puts it, the charging of fees according to the number of hours worked "leads to mindless paper generation from which clients suffer economically, courts suffer logistically, and lawyers suffer in terms of their personal self-esteem." And James Robertson, partner in one of the largest firms in Washington, D.C., on assuming the presidency of the D.C. Bar for 1991-1992, titled his first message to the membership in *The Washington Lawyer*, "The Beginning of the End of the Billable Hour?"

The Federal Deposit Insurance Corporation (FDIC) is the single largest employer of law firms, since it uses outside lawyers to try to recover money lost by failed banks and S&Ls. FDIC legal costs for this activity ran over $700 million in 1991. To make this expenditure more efficient, the FDIC has begun to use contingent fees. In one of the largest FDIC cases, its attempt to recover billions of dollars from Drexel Burnham Lambert's former junk-bond guru Michael Milken, the agency retained a leading New York corporate firm, Cravath Swaine & Moore, on a modified contingent fee basis. The Cravath firm will receive a minimum of $300 per hour for its work, but that fee will be doubled if the FDIC recovers $200 million or more from the litigation.

Even liability insurer carriers—the traditional foes of contingent-fee plaintiff's lawyers—are seeking outside law firms that will defend accident claims on a contingent-fee basis. Again, this cannot be the simple percentage fee of the plaintiff's lawyer, but there are many ways in which these defense fees can be related to the results achieved rather than being billed by the hour regardless of the outcome.

Beyond business and law practice, Performance-Based Pay can be applied to one of our biggest national headaches: education. Paul Zane Pilzer, a successful real estate investor who served as an advisor to both the Reagan and Bush administrations, has proposed a PBP plan to halt the deterioration of our schools. His plan would allow public and private schools to compete for the education dollar. We currently spend about $5,000 annually per pupil in grades 1 through 12, a total of $292 billion per year. Instead of paying a flat fee and increasing it each year while the performance worsens, as we do now, why not put it on a contingent fee basis? Let the schools get paid between $2,500 and $7,500 per pupil, depending on how much each student actually learns in relation to the average level, as determined by a national test. This would keep our average payment at the $5,000 per year level, but the good schools would flourish and the bad ones would gradually drop out because those receiving only $2,500 per student would not have enough money to keep paying teachers for not teaching (which is what we are doing in many schools now).

Pilzer believes that the best teachers and school administrators would band together to form new schools, in association with investors seeking profits. This $292 billion industry would be our largest, fully six times the size of auto manufacturing. Thus it would attract our best and brightest entrepreneurs, managers, and financiers. The key is motivation to excel, which works for tort lawyers and can also work for teachers.

House Majority Leader Richard Gephardt (Democrat, Missouri) developed a similar principle for government expenditures, which he christened "rewards for results" in 1991. This principle of using government appropriations to pay only for programs that produce positive results can be applied to most government functions at the federal, state, and local level, including those performed by the 19,000 Congressional staff members who work on Capitol Hill. Again, not as simple as the tort lawyer's percentage fee, but certainly worth the trouble of developing standards for measuring and rewarding excellent performance.

In their 1991 book, *Reinventing Government*, David Osborne and Ted Gaebler describe many instances in which government agencies, from local school boards to huge bureaucracies like the Defense Department, have used entrepreneurial innovations to link pay to performance. They call upon all government agencies to "fund outcomes rather than inputs."

Along with the new emphasis on Peformance-Based Pay, American business has discovered that *quality* is a key ingredient in the competitive advantages that we have lost to Japan, Germany, and other nations. Business leaders now realize that maintaining high quality of products and services leads to lower costs and higher productivity, as well as customer satisfaction. Many articles and books stressing the need for higher quality appeared in 1990-1991. Jerry Bowles, a New York-based business consultant, and Joshua Hammond, president of the American Quality Foundation, published a 1991 book entitled *Beyond Quality*. They observed:

> Years of short-term management thinking, indifferent workers, outdated plants, low capital investment, and declining productivity had left America vulnerable to attack in virtually all of its basic industries. As we enter the second decade of quality

improvement in the United States, it is clearer than ever that continuous improvement is a fundamental survival issue.

Bowles and Hammond said that quality ranked so low in American business priorities that a 1985 survey of institutional investors listed the quality of a company's products last as a factor in stock selection. How did this happen? The authors say:

> The short answer is that American industry grew fat, lazy, and arrogant. It failed to invest in people, clung to outmoded methods of production, lost touch with its customers, and grossly— sometimes fatally—underestimated its foreign rivals. As a result, its products and services failed to meet the rising quality standards of international competition.

Bowles and Hammond also point out that American manufacturers have traditionally assumed that a certain number of products will always be defective, with this result:

> Because of this mind-set, which prevailed during the first two-thirds of this century, defective products became an unpleasant but common way of life in the age of planned obsolescence. So ingrained was the notion that perfection was impossible (or at least would cost too much) that suppliers were allowed to ship out parts at a one percent Acceptable Quality Level (AQL). That meant the purchaser had agreed to accept one percent defective parts.

In contrast, Japanese industry, faced with the need to demonstrate excellence in order to gain even a tentative foothold in the world market, aimed for—and largely achieved—total quality control, meaning zero defects.

Lloyd Dobyns and Clare Crawford-Mason collaborated on television programs that helped to spur interest in improving quality. In their 1991 book, *Quality or Else: The Revolution in World Business*, they teach many lessons to be learned from Japan, where even cocktail waitresses keep statistical charts to improve performance. Their teaching is not limited to business, for, as they say in their book:

> Quality is a system, and it is the one system that can solve America's economic problems. Quality can also improve education, streamline federal and state bureaucracies, help with growing social problems, and maybe even make airlines run on time.

Tom Peters established himself as the guru of *excellence* by writing two best-selling books on the subject during the 1980s. He warns that the American standard of living must fall unless we achieve excellence by raising the quality of our goods and services to the extent needed to regain many of our lost customers. He condemns the attempt to protect failing American industries by restricting imports of higher quality foreign products. He gives the example of U.S. Steel, which received a $6 billion subsidy through government-imposed steel import quotas. Did U.S. Steel use this windfall to raise the quality of steel products and regain competitiveness? No, they used the money to buy Marathon Oil Company.

Given this recognition of the need for quality, one would expect both government and business to make every effort to rid the market of defective American products and services. Here the Equalizers play an important role, through the product liability suits that make it expensive to injure people with defective products. The last thing our economy needs is for government to nurture and subsidize defective products. Yet, as we shall see in the final chapter, that is just what some business and government leaders are trying to do. In the process, they condemn the Equalizers as a cause of America's inability to compete with foreign manufacturers. This attempt to blame the tort lawyers obscures the fact that most of the foreign-made products which are taking our overseas markets, far from being defective, are of demonstrably higher quality than the American counterpart products. We have also lost large chunks of our domestic markets (automobiles, televisions, chips, textiles) to foreign manufacturers whose products must face the same liability risks as American manufacturers because they are subject to suits in American courts for defective products sold here.

When it comes to lawsuits that attack defective products, there are two choices: (1) We can have government intervene to protect the manufacturers of defective products by curtailing the right to sue; or (2) We can let the law take its course and then let the market decide whether defective products should be supported. One would suppose that the conservative free-market choice would be number 2. Indeed, the so-called Chicago School principles, espoused initially by conservative law and economics professors at the University of Chicago, would let the courts and the markets decide this question. Some commentators have criticized the Chicago School for equating efficiency with justice, claiming that this makes some of its attitudes on personal rights less than humanitarian. But in our field of interest, the Chicago

School holds that tort law, because of its deterrent effect on dangerous behavior, is a system for bringing about "an efficient allocation of resources to safety and care." So says one of the Chicago School's leading scholars, Richard A. Posner, who serves as a judge on the U.S. Court of Appeals for the Seventh Circuit as well as a senior lecturer at the University of Chicago Law School.

In their 1987 book, *The Economic Structure of Tort Law,* Judge Posner and his co-author, University of Chicago Economics Professor William M. Landes, apply truly conservative principles to the tort system:

> If we are right, tort law is a much simpler, more elegant, and more consistent body of law than most tort scholars have suspected.
>
> Although products liability is the area where the reader might expect us to express the most concern with the efficiency of common law rules, our analysis suggests that the rules of products liability make a good deal of economic sense. In making this assertion, we part company with much conservative thinking on tort law, which regards modern products liability law as an unmitigated disaster.

The "conservative thinking" referred to by Landes and Posner is actually more of a socialistic approach, since it proposes to substitute government intervention for the efficiency of the free market. Some judges and academics who consider themselves conservatives assume the knee-jerk attitude that in any contest between a consumer and a manufacturer, the manufacturer must win in order to protect American business, thereby preserving America's standard of living. This head-in-the-sand attitude is not true conservatism. When it is applied to cases involving defective products, it is harmful both to business and to our national living standards, because it removes the incentive to achieve the excellent quality that Landes and Posner find so important:

> Because the manufacturer aggregates the expected accident costs of all his present and future customers, an imperceptible cost to the individual consumer becomes a noticeable cost to the manufacturer, inducing him to look for ways of making long-run improvements in safety.

Those who seek to protect defective products sometimes charge that punitive damages are an every-day feature of product liability suits, and that this could ruin many businesses. Landes and Posner say this:

> But as a matter of fact punitive damages are not awarded routinely in products liability cases but only where there are circumstances of aggravation. These include reckless indifference to safety, gross negligence, and concealment by the manufacturer of the dangerousness of his product from consumers. The last is a form of fraud, which is an intentional tort.

Given the Equalizers' important role in the free-market approach to defective products, why are the Equalizers so often attacked in the media as the greedy cause of America's inability to compete in world markets? We'll try to answer that question in our final chapter, during the televised debate between Humphrey Bogart and Sydney Greenstreet.

CHAPTER 15

The Unpleasantness at the Players Club

Up to now our case stories have involved Equalizers who represented plaintiffs. Sometimes the shoe is on the other foot: the plaintiffs have wealth and power, and the defendant is the underdog who needs an Equalizer. Take the case that became known as "The Unpleasantness at the Players Club" (with apologies to Dorothy Sayers and Lord Peter Wimsey).

The Players Club, officially named The Players, was formed in 1888 to serve as a New York meeting place for professional actors and others connected with the theatre. The founder was Edwin Booth, the leading American actor of his time, whose 100-night run of *Hamlet* in 1864 was not equaled until John Barrymore's 101-performance run in 1921. Edwin Booth was the brother of Lincoln's assassin, John Wilkes Booth, a fact that interfered only temporarily with Edwin's career. As soon as it was learned that he had no connection with the assassination, he returned to the stage and went on to even greater prominence. Edwin served as the first president of The Players, and upon his death in 1893, his five-storey brownstone townhouse on Gramercy Park passed to The Players under his will. It became the official clubhouse, and has been preserved throughout the twentieth century in its 1890s decor. In 1913, Actors Equity, the performers' union, was founded in Edwin Booth's study overlooking Gramercy Park.

Our story is set in the early 1980s, by which time most of the great names of the American theatre were members, or, as they call themselves, Players. On any given day, one could expect to see people like James Cagney, Jason Robards, John Gielgud, and Alfred Lunt dining or having a drink there. I lunched there occasionally as the guest of my long-time close friend, John Connell, who for many years played the starring role of Dr. David Malone in the NBC television soap opera *Young Doctor Malone*. John later became a leader in voice-over television commercials, as the spokesman for such products as Getty Oil, Maxwell House Coffee, and H & R Block Tax Service. While the food was even less distinguished than most New York clubs (which is to say that it was pretty awful), I always enjoyed visiting The Players. It is a museum of the early American theatre and a musty relic of the gaslight era. That charm plus the prospect of seeing (and perhaps even meeting) legendary actors was irresistible to a show-business buff like me. Therefore, I was unhappy when John told me that we wouldn't be eating lunch at The Players any more. I was even more distressed when he explained the reasons.

I should tell you that John Connell is a very unusual person, something on the order of Ralph Nader in his sense of moral indignation. He is not one to blink at any injustice, no matter how remote from his personal life, and he will not hesitate to get involved in trying to right wrongs that most people would shrug off as inevitable defects in our permissive society. A long-time vice-president and member of the board of directors of the Screen Actors Guild, he fought relentlessly to have that organization place some limits on the portrayal of violence in films and on television. This campaign resulted in a unanimous resolution by the SAG board condemning excessive violence in television programming. Then he proposed that the Guild get some of its famous actor-members to do something about lack of health insurance, for the thousands of SAG members who work too infrequently to get coverage, and for the 35 million Americans who do not have any medical insurance. For this effort, which got many star entertainers interested in the national health insurance problem and thereby helped to make it a leading issue in the 1992 presidential election, he was honored by the SAG with a special award.

Knowing John's background, it did not surprise me that he became estranged from The Players because he refused—as a matter of principle — to ignore charges of possible corruption. On a January morning, John participated in a SAG negotiating session with management at a midtown hotel. After the meeting concluded, John was walking toward the subway to take the train to the Players for lunch, when The Players' former doorman tapped him on the shoulder. The doorman, who knew John's reputation for probity, unfolded to John detailed charges of corruption that he said he had witnessed while working at the club.

The most serious of these charges related to The Players' then manager, a full-time professional, whom we'll call Mr. Laurel; and the then chairman of the club's management committee, whom we'll call Mr. Hardy. The latter was a member of The Players elected by the club's board of directors from its own ranks. While this voluntary position carried no salary, Hardy was paid for acting as a security man at club parties, and also did some maintenance and construction contracting work at the club, for which he was paid. The arrangements for these payments to Hardy were known to and approved by the club's executive committee, and so they would not be improper if Hardy rendered accurate bills. But the former doorman told John that he had witnessed the passing of money from manager Laurel to club official Hardy, under circumstances which led the doorman to believe that the payments were kickbacks or bribes. The doorman also charged that outside organizations, which were permitted to rent the club's facilities for their own functions, paid gratuities that amounted to about 15 or 20 percent of the total bill. The doorman understood that these gratuities were supposed to be paid to the waiters, bartenders, and doormen who worked at these functions, and he questioned whether these employees ever received the full amounts due to them.

The former doorman's charges rang a bell with John, since he had previously heard similar allegations of financial irregularities from the treasurer of The Players, who resigned entirely from the club after its executive committee refused to take remedial action that he had recommended. John had met with the executive committee to ask them to reconsider the treasurer's charges, but they had turned this suggestion down.

On the day of his encounter with the ex-doorman, John had dinner with his close friend and fellow Player, Richard Kiley, another public-spirited citizen who was unwilling to shut his eyes to allegations of corruption even if the charges involved only stealing tips from waiters and doormen. Kiley, a bright star of stage, screen, and television, was most famous for his performance in the title role of *Man of La Mancha.* John told Richard about the disturbing charges made by the ex-doorman, and both agreed that they should talk to a lawyer about these allegations. John made an appointment to meet with his personal lawyer, an entertainment specialist named Nahum Bernstein, who, like several other prominent show-business lawyers, was also a member of The Players. Richard Kiley came along.

Nahum Bernstein, in addition to being a senior eminence of the New York bar, had special qualifications for determining the credibility of the doorman's charges. Nahum served as a U.S. Army intelligence officer during World War II. After distinguished field service for which he was decorated, he was made an instructor at a secret Office of Strategic Services (OSS) school in California. Returning to civilian life, he was recruited in 1947 by the fledgling state of Israel (then still called Palestine) to head up the training of its intelligence personnel, known as the Shoo-Shoo boys (the Hebrew slang for secret agents). During the critical years of 1947-1949, he was the trusted lawyer and troubleshooter for Israel in the United States, in which position he helped that nation to raise funds, recruit volunteers, and obtain supplies needed in the conflict with its Arab neighbors.

Nahum, of course, had no way of determining whether the doorman was telling the truth, but he concluded that the charges were serious enough to warrant investigation by The Players. As a lawyer, he was mindful of the fact that the acts reported by the doorman, if they happened, amounted to felonies. This required him and his clients to report these charges to the club, for the failure to do so might leave them open to charges of compounding a felony. He advised John Connell and Richard Kiley that it would be best to write a confidential letter to the club's president, detailing the charges made by the doorman. John and Richard agreed, and so Nahum wrote a three-page letter, as a Player himself and as lawyer for John and Richard, to Players President Roland Winters, who had played detective Charlie Chan in films.

Nahum Bernstein's letter was not cordially received. Pressure was put on him to drop the request for an investigation as being unworthy of a Player, and it was suggested that he consider resigning from the club. But he and John Connell and Richard Kiley felt strongly that the charges should be investigated, especially since they were not satisfied with the executive committee's handling of the changes previously requested by the club's treasurer. Bernstein, Connell, and Kiley persisted. John called a closed-door meeting of about 25 other Players whom he thought would also demand investigation of the doorman's charges. This developed enough support to convince Players President Winters that the question would be raised from the floor at the upcoming annual membership meeting if he did not act. Only then did he agree to appoint a select committee of seven Players to look into the charges and report its findings to the board of directors. Throughout this entire hassle, Bernstein, Connell, and Kiley took no position on the truth or falsity of the doorman's charges, but merely sought to have them properly investigated.

The select committee took five months to do its job. While it required sworn statements from Bernstein, Connell, and the doorman, its questioning of Manager Laurel and Management

Committee Chairman Hardy was not conducted under oath, according to the record of their depositions. During those depositions, Laurel and Hardy were questioned only about the charge that Laurel had passed kickback money to Hardy, which both men denied. They were not questioned about the alleged siphoning of gratuities that were intended for the waiters, bartenders, and doormen.

Finally the select committee unanimously concluded that there was no substance to the doorman's charges. They sent the club's board of directors a report to that effect, at the end of which they went on to castigate Bernstein and Connell for bringing up such groundless charges without verifying their truth. The report did not explain how Bernstein or Connell could have conducted such an investigation when they had no authority over Laurel, Hardy, or other prospective witnesses. It did not mention the fact that the doorman offered to take a lie detector test, or that he had gone on to a managerial position with a fast-food chain. The report closed with the pronouncement that any member who did not accept the select committee's conclusions had "a very simple and honorable alternative—to submit his resignation."

Two weeks after the select committee filed its report, Bernstein and Connell were summoned to a private meeting with Players' officials. Richard Kiley decided to come along. They were told that the board of directors demanded that Bernstein and Connell resign from the club immediately or face expulsion. They refused to resign, and Bernstein warned that if they were expelled, they would go to court to seek reinstatement.

Four days later, Bernstein and Connell each received a letter of suspension from membership pending a hearing before the board of directors on a motion to expel them from the club. No suspension letter was sent to Richard Kiley. Apparently The Players were not interested in taking on Don Quixote.

Finally Bernstein and Connell were summoned to appear before the board of directors for the hearing on their expulsion. The main ground for expulsion was the charge that the doorman's allegations which Bernstein recounted in his letter to Players' President Roland Winters were false and were *known* by Bernstein and Connell to be false. This was also cited as a violation of House Rule 11 which proclaimed that everything seen or heard in the clubhouse was confidential, and no report of any such actions or conversations could be published or circulated by any member.

As the hearing got under way it became apparent that the "evidence" against them would consist solely of Bernstein's letter to Winters and the report of the select committee. There would be no witnesses testifying against Bernstein or Connell to substantiate the charges that they had known the doorman's allegations to be false—no accusers whom they could confront, nor anybody whom they could cross-examine. They were given the courtesy of addressing the meeting, but that was to be the extent of their "hearing" on charges that they had behaved so dishonorably as to warrant expulsion.

In his statement, Nahum Bernstein recalled that he had been a member of the New York bar for 50 years; a Player for 19 years; and that his marriage ceremony had taken place in the club, under the John Singer Sargent portrait of Edwin Booth. He said that he had advised Connell and Kiley that as loyal Players, they had no choice but to submit the allegations of serious wrongdoing to the club president. All three of them had hoped that the charges were unfounded, but they had no way of determining that, and no authority to do anything but call the charges to the president's attention. They all accepted the select committee's finding that the charges were unfounded, as they had agreed to do when the committee was appointed. Nahum then read the charge that he and Connell had known the doorman's allegations to be false, and asked Winters to present proof of this, so that he could refute it. Winters's response was, "Just proceed, sir." Every time Nahum asked what the evidence or proof was, he was simply told to keep talking until he had completed his statement. Nobody was going to submit any proof. The expulsion vote was going to be decided on the charges, not on the evidence.

In his statement, John Connell read aloud a letter that had been sent to the board of directors:

> I believe there are three types of behavior in this world. One, to see the wrong and do what you feel is right. Two, to see the wrong and do nothing. Three, to see the wrong and attempt to cover it up. I believe John Connell and Nahum Bernstein have adhered to the first rule and I continue to stand squarely with them. If they are expelled, my resignation from The Players will be in the first mail. Sincerely, Richard Kiley.

The hearing ended as it had begun. The directors listened in silence as Bernstein and Connell attempted to defend themselves against invisible witnesses and nonexistent evidence. They were called upon to prove their innocence without a word being spoken against them to their faces.

As soon as Bernstein and Connell left the meeting room, the board voted to expel them permanently. Thus, in the stately Gramercy Park home of Edwin Booth, new meaning was given to the terms *Star Chamber, kangaroo court*, and *Kafkaesque*.

When the expulsions were announced to the membership of The Players, Richard Kiley promptly resigned in protest. He was followed by other prominent Players who could not stomach the board's actions. In his letter of resignation, Jason Robards expressed his shame in being associated with those "who would attempt to destroy and malign the character and reputation of these two exemplary human beings." He signed off with "Gentlemen, adieu."

Nahum Bernstein made good his promise to sue if expelled. Neither he nor John was actually interested in resuming membership in the club that had treated them so shabbily. They planned to seek reinstatement through the courts just to clear their names, and then resign immediately. Nahum brought an action on behalf of himself and John Connell to set aside their expulsion and reinstate them to membership. But in New York, as in most states, the courts are reluctant to intercede in the internal affairs of a private club. Members up for expulsion do not have the right to a due-process hearing or trial if the club rules provide otherwise. The Players' constitution required only that members be given two weeks notice of the hearing, written charges, and an opportunity to be heard. It did not require the board to produce evidence, or allow Nahum and John to confront their accusers, or do anything more than sit and listen to their statements. The court found that The Players had followed its internal procedures in limiting the explusion hearing, and refused to intervene. That was the end of membership in The Players for Bernstein and Connell. But it was not the end of the unpleasantness.

Just before expiration of the one-year statute of limitations on defamation (libel and slander), Nahum and John were served with legal papers informing them that Laurel and Hardy were suing each of them for defamation, based on their having published false charges by repeating the allegations of the doorman to Players President Winters and to other Players. Laurel and Hardy each claimed $5 million in compensatory damages and $5 million punitive damages, making a total of $10 million each, and $20 million overall.

Since Nahum was being sued himself, he was not in a position to act as John Connell's lawyer. In fact, because Nahum was being sued for having written a letter as a lawyer, his malpractice insurance company retained a law firm to defend him. That firm could not defend John, and so John asked me to look at the complaint and advise him how he should proceed.

As I read the complaint, the whole lawsuit smelled very fishy to me. One of the main purposes of legitimate defamation suits is to stop the circulation of false statements, even if the defendant cannot afford to pay a substantial judgment. Yet Laurel and Hardy did not even bother to sue the doorman, leaving him free to continue circulating the charges that they had engaged in financial shenanigans. While claiming that these charges damaged their reputations to the tune of $20 million, they sued only Bernstein and Connell, who had never made such charges but had merely asked that the Players investigate the doorman's allegations. Furthermore, the lawyers for Laurel and Hardy were a prominent corporate firm that would not normally be representing people of their economic strata. I was pretty sure that neither Laurel nor Hardy could afford to pay the hourly rates of such a firm. It didn't seem likely that they had taken the case on a contingent fee, because they were not the type of firm to do so ordinarily, and this case was hardly a potential bonanza that would justify an exception. When I discussed my feelings with John, we both concluded that the lawsuit was probably another step in the campaign of The Players' ruling clique to send a message that the management of their fiefdom was not to be questioned by the members. Thus John was the underdog, being sued by nominal parties who were probably fronting for The Players' power elite.

Regardless of who else—if anyone—might be behind the lawsuit, we had to treat it as a serious attempt to collect $20 million from John Connell for caring enough about his club to report to the president charges of serious misconduct by two management officials. Technically, defamation suits can be brought against those who merely repeat or pass along a false statement originally made by someone else. But as a member of The Players, John had the right to pass along the doorman's charges to the president in order to protect the club and his interest in it. This gave him what the law calls a "qualified privilege," meaning that he could not be sued for libel or slander unless he repeated the statements in bad faith, or with malice. To overcome this qualified privilege, the plaintiffs would have to prove that John knew the doorman's statements were false, and that he spread these false charges with the intention of injuring Laurel and Hardy.

The complaint alleged malice, so it could not be thrown out without a trial. Indeed, it alleged that John caused the doorman's charges to be sent to the club president for "selfish, self-aggrandizing purposes," as part of an attempt to gain influence, office, or standing in The Players. To anyone who knew John Connell this charge would be patently ridiculous, since he had actually turned down an invitation to be named to The Players' board of directors. All of the actions he sought to take as a member of The Players were clearly designed to benefit the club rather than himself.

I told John that I would be happy to defend him. In fact, I thought the suit was so outrageous that I offered to represent him free of charge, but he insisted on paying. Although the case was a terrible ordeal for John and his family, I found myself eagerly looking forward to every step. Perhaps it was because I thought I was in a position to help a dear friend and a noble person. It was partly that, but I also felt that as a long-time plaintiff's tort lawyer, I had a special obligation to torpedo what I saw as a preposterous tort suit that did not belong in the courts. I believe that every unfounded tort suit makes it more difficult for victims who have actually been wronged to get proper redress of their claims.

The first problem in defending the defamation case was to avoid any side effects from the unsuccessful effort that Nahum Bernstein had made to get the courts to reinstate John and himself to membership. I knew that Laurel and Hardy's lawyers would try to claim that the judge's ruling in that prior case had determined that Bernstein and Connell had acted with malice to spread false charges, for the expulsion by The Players' board of directors was purportedly based on such a finding. If the first judge had decided that question, Laurel and Hardy would not have to prove malice again. They would be entitled to summary judgment—a ruling in their favor without a trial—on the issue of liability, leaving only the amount of damages to be fixed by a jury. As expected, the plaintiffs' lawyers asked the court to grant summary judgment. I opposed on the ground that the prior case determined only that The Players had followed its own internal rules for expelling members, and that the court had made no finding as to the truth or falsity of the doorman's charges, or malice on the part of Bernstein and Connell. The judge agreed with my position, ruling that the prior decision "has no bearing on the issue of whether the alleged defamatory remarks were false and made with actual malice."

Round One had necessarily been a defensive maneuver. Now it was time to take the offensive, where I felt more at home. The central irony of this case was that while John was being sued for $20 million for having done his duty by asking his lawyer to write a confidential letter to one person—Players President Roland Winters—the club itself and the seven-man select committee had spread the allegedly false charges throughout much of the membership. If John was to pay damages for informing one person, then The Players itself and the select committee should be in the same boat. Accordingly, I filed a third-party complaint against the club and the members of the select committee, which brought them into the case so they could share the fun of getting sued for $20 million for having done their duty. They did not take kindly to this maneuver. They had to retain lawyers, who immediately moved to dismiss the third-party complaint. But the court denied this motion, and so The Players and its seven-man select committee remained aboard as third-party defendants, facing our claim that if John Connell were held liable, they should be required to pay whatever damages were assessed.

Now it was time for discovery. I served notices for taking the depositions of Laurel and Hardy, and listed the documents they were to produce. Laurel and Hardy each alleged in the complaint that he "has been greatly injured in his business, employment, and status, and...has suffered grave impairment of his good name, business reputation and social standing, has lost or may lose the esteem and respect of his friends, acquaintances, and business associates, has suffered great pain and mental anguish, and is in danger of being further seriously injured in his business and employment opportunities, all to his damage in the sum of $5 million." These standard allegations in defamation cases leave the plaintiffs open to searching examination. If their good names and reputations were so badly damaged, what were their reputations before the defamatory remarks were made? Were they spotless, as the allegation of $5 million worth of compensatory damages would imply? Or did they already have shady reputations, which therefore could not have been badly damaged even if defamatory statements were made with malice? To answer these questions, one would have to know practically the whole life stories of Laurel and Hardy. That was what I set out to discover.

The deposition of Laurel, the club manager, came first. He had to bring with him all his income tax returns, bank statements, cancelled checks, and records of securities accounts for the preceding ten years. These documents would help me to determine whether he had received any money on the side which was not part of his agreed salary from The Players. Receipt of under-the-table income would tend to support the doorman's charges. Since truth is a complete defense to charges of defamation, the question of Laurel's income was a crucial point in the case.

With so much ground to cover, we set aside three days for Laurel's deposition. On the first day he produced tax and bank records going back about six years. I made copies of them for study that night, and proceeded to question him about his entire career, going back to his high school days. At every stage I asked for the names and addresses of people whom he had encountered and who would be familiar with his reputation and social standing. When his lawyer objected, I reminded him that $5 million worth of compensatory damage to that reputation was being alleged. As the day wore on, I got the feeling that Laurel had been talked into bringing this suit without fully understanding its implications for him, and that he was losing his enthusiasm for carrying it on. We adjourned for the day, with the understanding that he would return for further questioning the next morning.

The following morning, about ten minutes before the scheduled resumption of Laurel's deposition, his lawyer phoned. "I have some startling news," he said. "My client just now reported to me by phone that he is unable to carry on with the deposition because of—in his words—uncontrollable diarrhea!" That was a first for me. Since the deposition was being conducted in my office, I quickly agreed to postpone it until Laurel got the problem under control. In the meantime, I requested that we go ahead with Hardy's deposition. The lawyer said he would see what he could do about producing Hardy.

I was looking forward with great anticipation to questioning Mr. Hardy. You will recall that he served as chairman of the club's management committee without compensation other than the agreed payments for construction jobs and for acting as a security operative at club parties. Prior to the depositions, both plaintiffs were required to submit written bills of particulars, and one of the questions they had to answer under oath dealt with the amounts and sources of their incomes. Laurel had answered this question straightforwardly, listing his weekly salary and other agreed payments from the club. But Hardy's reply was rather vague, to put it mildly. He claimed to have been self-employed for the past 15 years, but did not name any job title, business, or profession as the source of income, nor did he give any income figures. He too would have to produce his tax returns and all financial records for the past 10 years, including the records of all construction and maintenance work done for The Players, and the club's approvals of payment for that work. I planned to take the deposition of The Players later as a third-party defendant, and require its officers to produce all its records of payments to Hardy, to verify their correctness.

A few days after the interruption of Laurel's deposition, his lawyer phoned back to tell me that Hardy was spending the entire summer in St. Louis and so would not be available until the fall (it then being early June). I have always thought that St. Louis is a fine city, but its climate does not commend it as a likely summer resort. When I pressed for resumption of Laurel's deposition and indicated that I might have to go to court to force Hardy to interrupt his St. Louis summer, the lawyer told me that there was a good chance that his clients would be disposed to drop the case. He did not ask whether John Connell would pay anything to get rid of the case, because I had made it clear at the outset that not a cent would ever be offered in settlement. A few days later, the lawyer confirmed that his clients wished to drop the case without any payment by Connell or the Bernstein estate (Nahum having died of cancer at age 76 soon after the defamation action was started).

When I relayed this news to John Connell, he was elated that the burden of this $20 million claim had finally been lifted. But he also felt a sense of emptiness and continuing outrage. Could Laurel and Hardy put him and his family through this hell, and then just walk away from it when it came time for them to produce their evidence?

Lawsuits usually are terminated by payment of an agreed settlement or the amount fixed by a trial, or by a trial verdict in favor of the defendant. In those rare instances where the plaintiffs drop the case without receiving any payment, usually the persons being sued are happy to agree to the termination. But if the defendants do not agree, the plaintiffs must apply to the court for permission to drop the case. The court has discretion to impose terms and conditions on the plaintiffs in cases where termination of the action might be prejudicial to the defendants. These terms and conditions can include the payment of the defendants' legal fees, where it can be shown that the action was "frivolous" or was brought for improper purposes. This power to impose sanctions is rarely used, since the American rule on legal fees is that each side pays its own lawyers regardless of the outcome. The winner of a lawsuit is awarded "costs," but this refers only to out-of-pocket litigation expenses such as court filing fees, and does not include legal fees. This differs from the English "fee-shifting" rule of costs, which automatically requires the losing party to pay the winner's legal fees as well as its own in all cases, regardless of merit or motive.

I told John that I would oppose the application of Laurel and Hardy to terminate the case, and would request the court to order a hearing on the question of the real motives behind this lawsuit, as a prelude to ordering the plaintiffs to pay John's legal fees. I warned John that most New York judges were happy to have cases terminated without trial, and usually would not inquire into motives. Indeed, most judges would probably think we were ingrates for prolonging the litigation instead of being content to walk away from a $20 million lawsuit without having to pay anything. On the rare occasions when judges ordered payment of sanctions, it was usually in extreme cases, such as those involving outright harassment, with a plaintiff repeatedly filing the same claim that had previously been dismissed or dropped.

The judge considered our documentation of the ordeal that John had suffered, but in the end he did the expected by allowing Laurel and Hardy to terminate their case without holding a hearing as to their motives for suing. The customary American rule was applied: each side would pay its own legal fees.

So ended The Unpleasantness at the Players Club. If you're wondering whether John Connell would have fared better in the English courts, the answer is "no." Two factors caused the self-destruction of the Laurel and Hardy lawsuit. First, we were able to bring in The Players and the seven-man select committee as third-party defendants, so that Laurel and Hardy wound up pressing a claim that might have to be paid by their own employer. Second, we were able to conduct searching discovery which neither Laurel nor Hardy had the stomach to endure. Neither of these weapons would have been available to Connell in the English courts. He could not have risked bringing The Players and the select committee into such a suit in England, for if the jury held him responsible for even a nominal amount of damages, he would have had to pay the huge legal fees of the eight third-party defendants, in addition to the fees of Laurel and Hardy. And we could not have taken the deposition of Laurel or Hardy under the very narrow English discovery rules. Therefore, once Laurel and Hardy commenced the action, they could have stayed the course in England, and probably could have forced Connell to make some kind of settlement to avoid the risk of financial ruin.

It is possible that if we had the English rule in the United States, Laurel and Hardy might have been deterred from filing the suit by the threat that if they did not win, they would have to pay Connell's legal fees. However, if someone else put them up to bringing the suit, presumably that person would have assumed the risk of paying Connell's fees as well as the fees for Laurel and Hardy's own lawyers. For example, the British world-class swindler Robert Maxwell avoided disclosure of his financial manipulations during his lifetime by suing—or threatening to sue—anyone who made such charges. He had enough money to intimidate those in a position to reveal his crimes. He brought 21 libel actions against those who published two biographies of him. Maxwell was sheltered by Britain's severe libel laws, which put the burden on the defendant to prove the truth of the statements in question, and also restrict the discovery needed for adequate defense. But even without the extraordinary protection of the English libel laws, a Robert Maxwell intent on using the legal system to harass a John Connell could accomplish this by using his wealth, without worrying about the possibility that Connell would survive the litigation and collect a large sum for his legal expenses.

Even if Laurel and Hardy were suing on their own rather than fronting for The Players' power elite, it is doubtful that they would have been inhibited by the English fee-shifting rule, since neither had the kind of wealth or income that would make this prospect a realistic threat. In any event, even if one assumes that American adoption of the English fee-shifting rule might generally inhibit irresponsible lawsuits, the cost is far too high in relation to the possible benefits. For every groundless lawsuit that might be avoided by fee-shifting, there would probably be thousands of meritorious claims that would die aborning because of the extreme financial burden of losing. Thus the precious accessibility of American justice would be sacrificed if we adopted the English rule that all losing parties must pay the other side's legal fees.

Since the time of The Players case, many of our courts have broadened the use of sanctions to discourage frivolous and unprincipled litigation. Today, Laurel and Hardy would have a harder time finding a reputable law firm to take on such a case. And if they dropped it without going on to trial, they might well face an order to pay the defendants' legal fees. (We'll return to the English rule on legal fees in the next two chapters.)

After the court permitted Laurel and Hardy to terminate their lawsuit, there was a final decision for John Connell to make. Where a civil suit has been brought without probable cause or for an ulterior purpose, and has been terminated in favor of the person who was sued, that person may sue the former plaintiffs for the tort of *wrongful civil proceedings*. This tort is sometimes called "malicious prosecution," but that term really applies to actions arising out of improper criminal prosecutions rather than civil suits. John could have brought an action against Laurel and Hardy for wrongful civil proceedings, because their dropping of the defamation suit amounted to a termination in favor of John. But this would have involved him in years of reliving an ugly chapter in his life. It would have been difficult for us to prove the motivation behind the defamation suit, because we would have had to delve into Laurel and Hardy's discussions with their lawyers before they filed suit. They would have claimed that we should not have access to those discussions because they were covered by the attorney-client privilege, which might have been upheld. And even if we won, neither Laurel nor Hardy had enough money to pay the likely judgment. In the end, John followed my advice and decided not to pursue a suit for wrongful civil proceedings.

Among the many decorations that John Connell received for his service as an Air Force gunner during World War II was the Purple Heart. An Oak Leaf Cluster should have been added to that Purple Heart for his suffering at the hands of his clubmates. But he, Richard Kiley, Jason Robards, and others who resigned have gotten along very well without The Players. John has gone on with his exemplary career and public service work, which includes continuing his efforts to involve leading entertainers in the quest for national health insurance. One of his major ideas has been the creation of a national lottery to finance health care for those who cannot afford insurance. Nor has his bitter experience at The Players caused him to shy away from speaking out against injustice or stupidity on the part of those in authority. John had been both a master of ceremonies and an honored presidential guest at the White House. But when President Ronald Reagan saw fit to salute Hitler's SS troops by making an official visit to their cemetery at Bitburg, West Germany, John was a leader in the public protest.

Sometimes I think about The Players case when I read uninformed articles to the effect that our insurance companies and manufacturers are being held hostage by unscrupulous plaintiff's lawyers who file unfounded suits in the hope of extorting settlements. These stories never explain that it is far cheaper in the long run to fight these cases to the hilt rather than settle for even as little as ten cents on the dollar. Fighting them sends a message that will deter the filing of future suits. And if an individual like John Connell could successfully resist an unfounded $20 million claim, why can't the insurers and manufacturers, with their large treasuries and batteries of skilled litigators, do the same?

I assure you that their defense lawyers would relish to opportunity to blow such cases out of the water. Many would be happy to modify their usual fee arrangements, if necessary, to make it easier to resist unfounded claims. By definition, such cases are relatively easy to defend because they are likely to be brought, if at all, by plaintiff's lawyers who are inexperienced, short on resources, or both. The experienced, successful plaintiff's lawyers are too busy with serious claims to take on such garbage, even if one assumes that they would not recognize the ethical obligation to reject unmeritorious cases.

CHAPTER 16

The Law of the Yukon

Jim Robertson (name changed to protect family privacy) was living the American Dream. A leading St. Louis orthodontist at age 35, with an income of over $200,000 a year, Jim had patients including the children of many prominent politicians, business leaders, and famous professional athletes. He was married to a lovely woman, was the father of three delightful children, and was only a month away from the birth of his fourth, when he decided to indulge in his only passion apart from his work and his family: big game hunting in Northwest Canada. So it was that in September 1982 he arrived in Whitehorse, Yukon Territory, where he would board the seaplane that was the only means of access to the wilderness camp where he would spend his 10-day hunting vacation.

The plane he had chartered was a rugged, single-engine high-wing DeHavilland Beaver, mounted on twin floats for bush operations. The weather was sunny and warm as Jim walked on to the lakeside loading dock, shook hands with the pilot, and put his camping gear into the Beaver's baggage compartment. The takeoff from the lake appeared normal from the ground, but just after takeoff, with the Beaver only about 200 feet in the air, the engine conked out. Although there was a river bed and a small pond ahead of the plane, the pilot chose to turn back and try to land on the lake. That decision was a mistake. Heavily loaded for takeoff and now without power, the Beaver was unable to maintain sufficient airspeed for the turn. It stalled (lost flying speed) and plunged into the timber below. Jim Robertson and the pilot were killed instantly.

I first heard this sad tale from the St. Louis estate lawyer who represented Jim's widow and children. He called and asked if I would take on the case against the operator of the Beaver and anyone else who might have been responsible. I told him that I would look into the cause of the accident and let him know if I thought we could help recover compensation for Jim's family.

The Canadian aviation authorities took this type of accident seriously since single-engine floatplane operations are vital to communications in the bush regions that comprise much of Canada's territory. They recovered the wreckage and made a thorough investigation which revealed that the cause of the engine failure was the fracture of a piston pin that attached one of the engine's nine pistons to its connecting rod. When that pin cracked, the connecting rod became misaligned and then broke, which in turn caused the engine to stop.

The engine was a Pratt & Whitney R985 Wasp Junior, one of the all-time classic piston engines. I had flown many hours behind Wasps in Air Force training planes, and later in crop-dusting aircraft that used military surplus Wasps as the engine of choice. Although it was designed and first built in the 1930s, it was still in extensive use half a century later. When properly overhauled (every 1,000 hours) and maintained, it was the most reliable engine for demanding operations such as crop-dusting and bush flying.

By 1980, when this particular Wasp was last overhauled, there was one company that dominated the rebuilding of Wasps: Aero Engines, Inc., of Los Angeles. I knew the company well, and had once visited their overhaul shop, which was close by Dodger Stadium in Chavez Ravine. Sure enough, the Wasp that failed in the 1982 Yukon accident had last been overhauled by Aero Engines.

In the mid-1950s, Pratt & Whitney, although no longer manufacturing the Wasp, was still supplying parts to operators and overhaul contractors. Their long experience revealed that some Wasps engaged in demanding operations experienced piston pin failures. To overcome this problem, Pratt & Whitney offered as an option a piston pin with a thicker wall than the original pins. Many Canadian bush operators had the thick-walled piston pins installed in their Wasps during overhaul, but the operators of the Yukon Beaver apparently were not aware of this problem. When they sent this Wasp to Aero Engines for overhaul, it came back with the same thin-walled piston pins that had been installed originally.

On top of that, examination by the Canadian authorities after the accident revealed that the fatal crack in the piston pin began at the site of corrosion on the inside of the pin. The government investigators determined that the corrosion must have existed at the time the engine was overhauled. Yet the original thin-walled, corroded pin was reinstalled by Aero Engines in Los Angeles. Either they did not spot the corrosion during their inspection, or they considered it insignificant.

When we studied the accident investigation file, it looked like a good case for our California office to file against Aero Engines. The operator was also legally responsible, but most bush operators have low insurance coverage and few tangible assets. Furthermore, we would have had to go to Whitehorse in the Yukon Territory to sue the operator, taking on all the extra baggage of a Canadian lawsuit that would probably not produce the kind of seven-figure award that was needed to properly compensate Jim Robertson's family. I told the St. Louis lawyer that we would be happy to take the case on, and introduced him to Tim Cook, head of our California office, who would be in charge of the litigation.

Tim filed suit against Aero Engines in Los Angeles, and quickly was confronted by a motion to dismiss the case on the grounds of *forum non conveniens*, which means what it sounds like: "this is not a convenient forum." Historically, the plaintiff always had the right to choose the forum for the lawsuit, but the courts would intervene to protect a defendant from the burdens of producing witnesses and documents a long way from home. We scoffed at the idea that Aero Engines could claim that its home city of Los Angeles would be an inconvenient place to produce their witnesses and documents. Besides, in order to win such a motion, the defendant must convince the court that there is another forum where the defendant can be sued which is more convenient. The lawyers for Aero Engines were up to this challenge. Even though Aero Engines could not be sued in the Yukon Territory or anyplace else in Canada because the company had no office there, their lawyers told the court that they would agree to be sued in the Yukon Territory court. They argued, in effect, that it would be more convenient for them to produce their evidence in Whitehorse, 2,000 miles north of Los Angeles, than to make the half-hour drive from their overhaul shop near Chavez Ravine to the Los Angeles County courthouse.

We thought it would be ridiculous to send American plaintiffs like the Robertsons all the way to the Yukon Territory to sue an American defendant, when they had already sued that American defendant in its home town. But we had to take the motion seriously because in recent years, courts that were overwhelmed by drug cases and other criminal prosecutions were finding novel ways to reduce their civil caseloads. Thus the "convenience" factor in *forum non conveniens* motions was modified to include the convenience of the court. Even though it was obviously most convenient for the defendant to produce its evidence in its home town, if the case involved some out-of-state factor, such as an accident happening elsewhere, the judge might decide that it was more convenient *for the court* if the case were sent to another jurisdiction.

To make a long story short, that's what happened to Tim Cook's effort to sue Aero Engines in Los Angeles, where it had its only place of business. The trial court judge dismissed the case on condition that Aero Engines submit to Canadian jurisdiction at Whitehorse, capital of the Yukon Territory, which their lawyers happily agreed to do. We appealed to the intermediate appellate court and finally to the California Supreme Court, to no avail. Therefore, in the fall of 1985, three years after the accident, we found ourselves ousted from the American courts, forced to decide what to do about suing in Canada.

If we had been sent to Toronto, or Montreal, or any other large Canadian city, we might have simply told the Robertsons that it would be best for us to help them select a competent Canadian law firm and let that firm take the case on from there. But being tossed out of Los Angeles and told to file in the Yukon Territory was, somehow, a more personal challenge. Besides, I've always been an easy mark for sentimental journeys, and the Yukon is a legendary place. The travel brochures extol its great natural beauty, with "snow-fed lakes backed by perpetually white-capped mountains, and forests and streams abounding with wildlife." But for me the lure of the Yukon is the memory of the 1890s Klondike gold rush, as enshrined in the stories of Jack London and the poems of Robert Service. While my favorite is Service's "The Shooting of Dan McGrew," on this occasion I recalled his more relevant poem, "The Law of the Yukon," which opens with these lines:

This is the law of the Yukon, and ever she makes it plain:
"Send not your foolish and feeble; send me your strong and your sane—
Strong for the red rage of battle; sane, for I harry them sore;
Send me men girt for the combat, men who are grit to the core;
Swift as the panther in triumph, fierce as the bear in defeat,
Sired of a bulldog parent, steeled in the furnace heat.
Send me the best of your breeding, lend me your chosen ones;
Them I will take to my bosom, them I will call my sons;
Them I will gild with my treasure, them will I glut with my meat;
But the others—the misfits, the failures—I trample under my feet."

Service goes on to record the hazards facing those who challenge the Law of the Yukon, including being "Left for the wind to make music through ribs that are glittering white." While our

Yukon adventure fortunately did not involve such physical in-dignities, the legal obstacles that faced us were almost as daunt-ing.

First, there was the problem of proving liability to a Cana-dian judge who would be sitting without a jury. He might con-clude that the operator had been victimized by Aero Engines, the overhaul contractor. Even if he held the operator liable, it did not carry enough insurance to pay the kind of compensation that the Robertsons deserved. Holding Aero Engines responsible was a special problem since Yukon law required us to prove specific negligence. Had we been able to try the case in California or any other American state, we could have won the case against Aero Engines by simply showing that they supplied a defective en-gine. They would be strictly liable for this defective product, even if we could not prove how or why the defect (the corroded piston pin) came about.

If we got over the liability hurdle, there were even more difficult questions on damages. Under American law, whether in California or Missouri (where the Robertsons lived), the dam-ages would total several million dollars. Multiplying Jim's earn-ings of $200,000 per year by his work expectancy of 30 years (65 minus his age, 35) gives you a total of $6 million. That's not the way its done, however, since damages are based on loss of sup-port suffered by the widow and children. Deducting about $100,000 per year for taxes and Jim's personal expenditures, money that the widow and children would not have received if he had lived, you still come up with about $3 million for loss of support. That amount would first be "reduced to present value" because it would be paid in a lump sum instead of periodically over 30 years, and then it would be increased by allowing for inflation. These two adjustments pretty well cancel each other out, so that the rough estimate of $3 million for loss of support would be close to the mark. It might be higher if we could show that Jim's income would have increased even more than the rate of inflation. There would also be substantial damages for the loss of love, affection, training, advice, and education that was suf-fered because of the death of Jim Robertson, the husband and father. Altogether, a good American jury verdict in 1985 would have been about $4 million, and a good settlement would have been anything above $2.5 million, given the uncertainties of in-surance coverage.

In the Supreme Court of the Yukon Territory, and in all of Canada, there had never been an award approaching those fig-ures. Indeed, there had never been an award of as much as $1 million American, and only a handful of $1 million Canadian awards. Canadian judges, steeped in the English tradition, generally awarded much smaller sums than American juries. That was the main reason why Aero Engines' insurers went to the trouble of having the case moved from Los Angeles to Whitehorse. And just to throw in another Robert Service-type zinger, Canadian courts considered the likelihood of remarriage by the widow and reduced their awards proportionately. Not only was Jim Robertson's widow young and atttractive—she had actually remarried by the time the case was sent to Whitehorse.

I regarded this case as a personal challenge because I was rankled by the injustice of the *forum non conveniens* ruling that shunted this fine American family from L.A. law to Yukon law. I sympathized with the Los Angeles judges who were swamped by criminal cases, but I could not accept the closing of the California courts to claims against a local manufacturer whose insurer was allowed to select for the claims of this widow and four young childen the most remote and unfavorable forum imaginable. Along with my partners, I decided that regardless of the cost of handling a single claim thousands of miles away from our nearest office, we should try to make this a test case: a model for turning a forum dismissal into a victory for the plaintiffs and a demonstration of American-type justice that might help Canadian accident victims to achieve more just compensation in their own courts.

I wish I could tell you that I then took charge of the case in the Yukon court. But I was nearing retirement, and given the stern warnings of Robert Service, I decided that the only lawyer in our firm who was sired of a bulldog parent and made of grit to the core was Tim Cook, a graduate of the U.S. Naval Academy and holder of the Distinguished Flying Cross for his exploits as a Navy combat pilot in Vietnam. Tim was also an experienced aviation lawyer and from his base in our California office he could gather the evidence needed to pursue the liability of Aero Engines.

I'd have to write another book to describe all that Tim Cook went through in the four years that it took to prepare and try the case in the Yukon Territory. There is space here only for a few highlights. Needing to team up with Canadian lawyers, Tim recruited old colleagues at Edwards Kenny & Bray in Vancouver, British Columbia. Working with Stephen Gill, Brian McLean, and Peter Larlee of that firm, Tim succeeded in counteracting the effects of the widow's remarriage by producing a post-nuptial agreement with the new husband that kept their finances separate, so that she received no support or other financial benefit from her remarriage. After a trial lasting more than three weeks, the team won a verdict of $3.7 million Canadian, which ran well over $4 million after prejudgment interest was added—a result we would have been very happy to achieve at the end of a jury trial in Los Angeles. The verdict reflected the testimony at the trial of several American expert witnesses, including economists, actuaries, and consultants on the value of American dental practices. It required a second lawsuit to force the insurers to pay the amount awarded by the court, as they tried to disclaim coverage for a large part of the judgment. Interest was added in the second suit as well, so that we finally collected $4,820,000, a sum that reflected the actual losses suffered by the Robertson family.

Justice Harry Maddison of the Yukon Supreme Court, who presided over the trial, was in a position to dispense strictly Canadian justice by awarding something less than $1.5 million. But by blending American and Canadian justice in this case, he sent a message to the insurers who had cynically claimed it was not convenient to try the case at the defendant's home office in California, and he established a new norm for compensation that is bound to help thousands of Canadian accident victims for years to come. Thus was a part of the American Dream—equal justice under law—transplanted to the supposedly remote wilds of the Yukon Territory.

The Yukon case was unusual in that the claim of an American plaintiff against a local American company was sent to a foreign country. More often in our practice we have encountered cases brought by *foreign* citizens arising out of foreign accidents, where the cause of injury or death was a product (usually an airplane) manufactured in the United States. If these claims are filed at the place where the defective airplane was manufactured—the place where all the witnesses and documents relating to the defect are located—can the manufacturer claim that it is "inconvenient" for those claims to be tried at its home base?

The prototype was the litigation arising out of the 1974 Turkish Airlines DC-10 accident. That first crash of a fully loaded jumbo jet, carrying 333 passengers and a crew of 13, occurred on a beautiful spring Sunday in the forest of Ermemonville, near Paris. The plane had just taken off from Paris's Orly Airport and was still in its initial climb, when it suddenly plunged to the ground, killing all aboard. The cause was traced to the faulty design of the rear cargo door, which blew open when the plane reached 10,000 feet altitude. This in turn caused the cabin floor to collapse, resulting in severance of control cables and a deadly nosedive. Although the passengers came from 24 different nations, we were able to defeat a *forum non conveniens* motion and hold all the cases in the Los Angeles federal court, in whose district the Long Beach McDonnell Douglas DC-10 factory was located. While Turkish Airlines was protected by the Warsaw Convention damage limitations, the limitations applied only to the air carrier, not to manufacturers. Eventually all the cases were settled according to Los Angeles damage standards. Senior Federal Judge Peirson Hall, in charge of the cases, made certain of that by appointing panels of retired Los Angeles judges to determine what a Los Angeles jury would award in each case. Those figures were then used as the basis for final settlement negotiations.

We achieved similar results in the cases arising out of the 1973 Varig Airlines Boeing 707 crash near Paris, which arose out of a small fire (probably from a cigarette placed in a trash bin) in one of the rear passenger lavatories. The fire caused the lavatory's plastic wall coverings and other materials to smoulder and smoke, circulating a poisonous mixture of carbon monoxide and cyanide throughout the plane. The deceased passengers came from 14 foreign nations, the largest groups coming from Brazil and France. Although there were no Americans aboard, several American manufacturers were involved. We kept the cases in the New York state court, and finally all were settled. The Varig case resulted in important safety steps to prevent such accidents, including NO SMOKING signs in lavatories and changes in the materials used for cabin upholstery.

Sometimes foreign citizens get the benefit of American compensation standards without ever filing suit in the U.S. So it was in the cases of the Dutch families whose relatives were killed in the world's worst air disaster, the March 1977 collision at Tenerife in the Canary Islands between Boeing 747s operated by Pan Am and KLM, the Dutch airline. We had been retained to file suit in New York for a large group of the Dutch families, along with American families who suffered casualties on the Pan Am plane. In December 1977, KLM's insurers, faced with the threat of New York lawsuits, agreed to settle with each Dutch family at American compensation levels, which meant that in many cases they would be paying ten to fifteen times more than the claimants would be awarded in the Dutch courts. Thus the American tort system sent a Christmas gift to the bereaved Dutch families. (Further details on the Turkish DC-10, Varig Boeing 707, and Tenerife collision cases, as well as the *forum non conveniens* aspects of the litigation arising out of the Israeli Entebbe raid of

1976, will be found in my 1980 book, *Lawsuit*.)

London Law: The Equalizers are Coming

As we have seen, compensation of accident victims in Great Britain has historically been niggardly by American standards. From the beginning, the basic stance of the British civil courts was to protect property interests, at the expense of personal rights if necessary. Courts in America, modeled after the English system, continued on the same track even after the colonies broke away. While we have not yet completely abandoned that stance, we have come much further away from it than have the British courts. Their reluctance to award full compensation has been nurtured by several important differences from the American legal system. Civil jury trials generally are restricted to libel cases, so that accident compensation is decided by judges who are expected to follow established guidelines that severely limit the amounts to be awarded. There is a more extensive welfare state in Britain, including socialized medicine. Until very recently, it was considered to be illegal for British lawyers to charge contingent fees. And, for the most part, British accident victims are represented by lawyers who, when it comes to accident cases, do not function as entrepreneurs or Equalizers in the style of McKenzie Brackman or its real-life American counterparts.

Two British lawyers—actually English "solicitors"—who are doing a lot to change this picture are Rodger Pannone and Michael Napier. As you probably know, solicitors perform all the functions of American lawyers, except that in major litigation they usually bring in barristers to conduct trials and appeals. Since solicitors deal with the clients and handle everything up to the trial itself, they are the principal actors in British accident compensation, because most cases are settled without trial, as in American practice.

Rodger Pannone began practice in 1965, and joined Britain's largest firm of labor union solicitors in 1970. There he represented injured claimants and learned about the deficiences of English compensation. Later he joined a general practice firm in Manchester, and began to spend most of his time on complex accident cases.

I first encountered Rodger during the Turkish Airlines DC-10 litigation, where he played an important role in the international team effort that established a successful pattern for obtaining American-type justice for foreign claimants injured by American companies. That experience, and others arising out of his representation of Thalidomide and asbestos victims, convinced him that the United Kingdom needed a specialized task force to deal with the unique demands of mass disaster litigation. By that time Rodger was senior partner of his Manchester general practice firm, which eventually became known as Pannone March Pearson.

Michael Napier, a colleague of Rodger Pannone in their early practice days, became senior partner of a prestigious Sheffield firm of general practice solicitors, Irwin Mitchell. Like Rodger, Michael had pioneered pharmaceutical product liability in the 1970s, particularly as the leader in the many claims against Imperial Chemical Industries (ICI) for victims of the beta-blocker heart drug Practolol (Eraldin). To this day the ICI voluntary points-based Practolol Compensation Scheme remains a model for such litigation. Michael was the first solicitor advocate before the European Court of Human Rights, and has written and lectured widely on torts and forensic psychiatry.

Rodger and Michael collaborated in the British Opren litigation, an experience that crystallized their separate visions that a specialist firm was needed to deal with such cases. So it was that in 1985 they launched Pannone Napier, Britain's first disaster law firm. Pannone Napier is actually a joint venture of the two general practice firms (Pannone March Pearson and Irwin Mitchell), and has its own London office headed by Mark Mildred.

Pannone Napier's earliest projects were pharmaceutical product liability claims such as those arising out of the notorious Dalkon Shield intra-uterine contraceptive device that caused so much suffering among women all over the world, including Britain. They were able to join the British cases with the thousands of American cases pending in our courts, and were part of the group that eventually forced the manufacturer, A.H. Robins, into bankruptcy. Dalkon Shield was a monumental long-running disaster that Pannone Napier handled skillfully, but it was in the field of transportation disasters that the firm was to establish its unique reputation.

On August 22, 1985, a Boeing 737 operated by British Air Tours (a subsidiary of British Airways) suffered an engine explosion during its takeoff run at Manchester Airport. The pilot jammed on the brakes and aborted the takeoff, but flames from the exploded engine spread to the fuel tanks and quickly engulfed the cabin. 82 occupants were fortunate enough to escape, although most suffered serious injuries. But the other 55 died in the fire.

Since Britain has adopted a form of the Warsaw Convention, called the Carriage by Air Act, to minimize the liability of its domestic airlines, ordinarily the claims of the Manchester disaster victims would have been limited to £75,000 each. But Rodger Pannone knew that the exploded engine had been manufactured by good old Pratt & Whitney in Hartford, Connecticut, U.S.A., and that the Carriage by Air Act, like the Warsaw Convention, protected only carriers, not manufacturers. An aircraft engine that explodes on takeoff is a defective product, unless the manufacturer can show that the explosion was caused by faulty maintenance, which was not the case in the Manchester accident. A defective product made in the United States means that a product liability claim can be prosecuted in the American courts. Pannone Napier moved swiftly to organize the Manchester Air Disaster Group, and formed a Steering Committee of solicitors to direct the Group. For the first time, victims of a domestic British airline accident had a chance to win compensation that was measured by their real losses rather than by the artificial £75,000 barrier.

Pannone Napier quickly mobilized all of the victims' solicitors into the Group, and began an unprecedented campaign on television and in newspapers, designed to bolster the staying power of the victims and to bring the insurance underwriters to the negotiating table. Although the insurers were accustomed to making cheap, quick settlements with victims who had no other alternatives, they soon found themselves surrounded by Pannone Napier and the fledgling Group of accident victims. Reluctantly the insurers entered into negotiations which from the beginning were based upon the threat of American product liability litigation. Nothing else could have produced any offers beyond the arbitrary £75,000 statutory ceiling. Investigation revealed that the materials used by Boeing for the linings and upholstery of the cabin walls made the effects of the fire more devastating to the occupants, and so Boeing was brought in as a potential defendant.

The negotiations went on for months, when finally an overall settlement agreement was announced. It was the first to bear the Pannone-inspired title of "Mid-Atlantic Settlement," based on the principle that each claimant would receive a sum that was about halfway between the probable awards in the English and American courts. By agreement, the amounts paid in settlement must remain secret, but it is common knowledge that the final settlement formula consisted of a multiple of the probable English award. For example, if the negotiators agreed that the American award in a particular case would probably be about six times as much as the English award, then a Mid-Atlantic Settlement would require the insurers to pay three times the amount of the English award.

I was privileged to act as advisor to Pannone Napier on the prospects for compensation in the American courts. My contribution was more symbolic than substantive, since it was the specter of facing an American jury that forced the insurers to settle. As in the case of the Dutch Tenerife victims, the American legal system presented a gift to the Manchester claimants that they could not have achieved in their own courts. But they could not have made the threat of American litigation credible without the unique services of the mass disaster specialists, Pannone Napier.

The Manchester settlement was also an important demonstration of Pannone Napier's integrity. As the cases were settled in England, their fees and those of all the victims' solicitors were calculated under the English system, which requires the defendants to pay the plaintiffs' legal fees as part of the settlement. The amount of the fee was not expressed as a percentage of the settlement, since percentage fees were not permitted in the U.K. In each case, the solicitors' fees under the English system were much less than what they would have received through even a minority share of an American contingent fee. Therefore, in advising their clients to accept the Mid-Atlantic Settlement negotiated in England, Pannone Napier and each of the victims' solicitors were giving up the chance of collecting a much higher fee through litigation in the United States.

Sometimes it is necessary to pursue claims in the American courts before a Mid-Atlantic Settlement offer is forthcoming. So it was in the next Pannone Napier aviation disaster case, this one arising in Scotland.

The exploration for oil in the North Sea is conducted from drilling platforms that are like floating hotels. The oil drilling workers do their jobs on the platforms and remain aboard to eat and sleep there. Usually they work for two-week stretches and then return to shore for two weeks off. This commuting is handled by fleets of large helicopters, which became the busses, trucks, and ferries of the North Sea. The largest of these is the Boeing Vertol "Chinook," the commercial version of a widely-used military helicopter which can carry more than 40 passengers. Shortly before noon on November 6, 1986, a Chinook operated by British International Helicopters, Ltd. (a company owned by tycoon Robert Maxwell) was approaching the landing pad at Sumburgh in the Shetland Isles of Scotland, carrying 44 oil-platform workers as passengers and a crew of three. When it was about two-and-a-half miles from landing, the pilots heard a roaring noise, followed by a loud "bang." The helicopter suddenly went out of control and dove into the sea, killing all but the captain and one passenger.

Investigators of the U.K.'s Air Accidents Investigation Branch quickly determined that the direct cause of the crash of the twin-rotor Chinook had been a catastrophic failure of the forward transmission which in turn led to de-synchronization of the rotors followed by collision of the forward and rear rotor blades. This destroyed the systems that kept the helicopter aloft, and it dropped like a rock into the sea. Why did the forward transmission fail? The answer was to be found in the history of the commercial Chinook.

The transmission of power from the engines to the rotors has always been a problem in helicopter operations, due to vibration that leads to loosening and excessive wear of vital parts. In the Chinook this caused loosening of the bolts which held together joints of the transmission. As this problem became known, the transmissions had to be inspected frequently to assure that the bolts did not become so loose as to cause a detachment that would lead to the kind of failure that brought on the Shetland Isles disaster. These inspections required considerable teardown, so that the Chinooks had to be taken out of service every 300 hours and laid up for several days. This operating penalty put Boeing at a competitive disadvantage against other manufacturers whose helicopters were not required to be taken out of service that frequently.

Boeing engineers at its Vertol helicopter plant near Philadelphia decided to overcome this competitive drawback by modifying the transmission so that it would not require the 300-hour teardown inspection for loose bolts. The new transmission, called the -6 (dash six), differed from its predecessor, the -5, mainly in that it used larger bolts that could be more tightly secured. The change from -5 to -6 transmission had to be submitted to the Federal Aviation Administration. Based on test data submitted by Boeing, the FAA approved the change to the -6 in 1985. Using the same Boeing data, the U.K.'s Civil Aviation Authority (CAA) also approved, and BIH's North Sea Chinooks were changed over to the -6 transmission. Both the U.S. and the U.K. agencies accepted Boeing's claim that the -6 eliminated the bolt-loosening problem, so that the 300-hour teardown inspection for loose bolts would no longer be required. So it was that the BIH Chinook that crashed in the Shetland Isles was equipped with -6 transmissions.

As Britain's Air Accidents Investigation Branch (AAIB) investigators recovered the wreckage, they made a chilling discovery. The failure of the transmission gear that led to de-synchronization and disintegration of the Chinook began with a fatigue crack, which in turn was caused by the design of the new -6 transmission. Unlike the old -5 model, the new transmission permitted fretting and corrosion which formed a trench that provided a site for fatigue cracks. Thus, the very modification that was supposed to make the Chinook safer caused the loss of 45 lives in history's worst civilian helicopter crash. Quickly the FAA and the U.K.'s CAA, realizing that approval of the -6 modification had been a mistake, ordered the new transmissions removed from all Chinooks, to be replaced by the old -5 model which would again require the 300-hour teardown inspection.

All the victims were U.K. citizens, most of them residents of the Aberdeen area. When their surviving relatives consulted their family solicitors, most of them were told initially that compensation would probably be limited to no more than £75,000 under the Carriage by Air Act, Britain's domestic version of the Warsaw Convention. That was the most that the operator, British International Helicopters, could be forced to pay in the Scottish or English courts. But some of the family solicitors were aware of the results achieved for British victims of the 1974 Turkish Airlines DC-10 Paris crash, and the Mid-Atlantic Settlement that Pannone Napier had negotiated in the 1985 British Air Tours Manchester accident. Both of those cases involved American aircraft manufacturers, as did the Shetland Isles Chinook disaster. The family solicitors decided to form a group to investigate their clients' legal rights, especially the possibility of obtaining adequate compensation by suing Boeing, the Chinook's manufacturer.

A few weeks after the accident, the Chinook Disaster Legal Group held a meeting in Aberdeen and selected four Scottish solicitors as the Steering Committee: Patrick Davies, David Burnside, and Sandy Kemp of Aberdeen, and Fred Tyler of Edinburgh. The Group engaged Rodger Pannone as a consultant, assisted by his partner, Geraldine McCool. Rodger then asked me to look into the possibility of suing Boeing in the United States. So it was that on a February evening in 1987, I met with Rodger, the Steering Committee, and the entire Group of solicitors in a cold solicitor's office in Aberdeen.

At the meeting I outlined a plan of action. Our firm would undertake to represent the Chinook victims in the United States, filing suit in Philadelphia, where Boeing's helicopter division was located and where all the Chinooks were designed and manufactured. Since we did not have an office in Pennsylvania, we would retain as local counsel Arthur Raynes, whom I considered to be Philadelphia's leading tort lawyer and an ideal choice for the Chinook case because his firm had the depth and experience to deal with the demands of complicated litigation. One of Arthur's major victories was the American Thalidomide litigation, which he was able to keep in the United States (and settle favorably) despite the fact that his clients were Canadians and the drug was never licensed in this country. I outlined the prospects as well as the problems of suing Boeing in Philadelphia. Their lawyers would, of course, try to get the cases dismissed on the grounds of *forum non conveniens* by arguing that since the accident happened in Scotland and the claimants lived there, Scotland would be a more convenient forum that Philadelphia. If we could keep the case in Philadelphia, we would have a much better chance of winning on our claims of product liability, since the U.K. did not have a strict liability provision at that time. Also, the compensation would be several times higher than in the U.K., where the judges used archaic formulas that were guaranteed to send widows and orphans away with much less money than they needed to carry on the lives they were leading before the accident.

After a couple of hours of discussion, I was asked to leave the room so that the Group solicitors could take a vote. I walked around the unheated office briskly, trying to keep warm while they deliberated. Finally they called me back in and Patrick Davies, the chairman, announced that they had unanimously decided to retain our firm to sue Boeing in Philadelphia. Among their main reasons was the inability of these claimants to take on a giant like Boeing in the U.K., where contingent fees were not permitted and the widows would be ordered to pay Boeing's huge legal fees if they lost the case. No victims had ever taken on an aircraft manufacturer in such a case in the U.K. courts. Thus, it was clear to the Group's solicitors that their clients had much to gain and little to lose by launching the case in Philadelphia.

After we filed the claims of the 44 Group members in the Philadelphia Court of Common Pleas (the local state court), Boeing made the anticipated *forum con conveniens* motion. In addition to the usual arguments, Boeing claimed that the accident had been caused by negligence of two British contractors whom BIH had called in to modify BIH's Chinook transmissions from the -5 to the -6 model. Both these contractors were small companies that had offices only the U.K. and thus could not be sued in Philadelphia. Therefore, Boeing argued, it would be unfair to hold the trial in Philadelphia because Boeing would not be able to bring the two British contractors or BIH into the case to assume their rightful share of the blame. On the other hand, if the Philadelphia court granted Boeing's *forum* motion, the two contractors and the operator, BIH, could be sued in the U.K., and all the responsible parties would be before the court there.

This was a strong argument if one assumed that BIH and/or the two contractors had anything to do with causing the accident. After consulting with helicopter engineers, we were convinced that the faulty design of the -6 transmission was the sole cause, and that the way it was installed by BIH and its contractors had nothing to do with its failure. As we prepared our response to Boeing's *forum* motion, Stewart Edward Bell QC (Queen's Counsel), Sheriff Principal of Grampian, Highland and Islands, announced that he would convene a Fatal Accident Inquiry into the Chinook disaster in his court at Aberdeen, starting May 11, 1987. This would be a formal court hearing, complete with Scottish barristers (who are called advocates there), to determine the causes of the 45 deaths. We had to prepare for this Fatal Accident Inquiry (FAI) as though it were a trial of our clients' claims, for if the Sheriff Principal decided that BIH or its two contractors had contributed to causing the accident, Boeing would have strong support for its *forum* motion and we might be thrown out of the Philadelphia court.

The court proceedings at the Aberdeen FAI had to be conducted by the Scottish advocates and solicitors, but it was up to us to supply them with the ammunition to destroy Boeing's claim that others were at fault. The Steering Committee was able to engage Lord Morton of Shuna QC, one of Scotland's leading advocates, to represent the Group. Members of the Steering Committee and Pannone Napier supported Lord Morton and his assistant, Richard Keen. Jim Crouse of our firm, a lieutenant-colonel in the U.S. Army Reserve and a qualified helicopter pilot, coordinated the technical evidence. Jim brought over with him a leading American expert on helicopter design, who remained in Scotland throughout the Inquiry. Arthur Raynes and his partner, Harry Roth, attended the entire Inquiry, and were very helpful in opposing Boeing's attempt to blame others. Our firm laid out all the expenses of the plaintiffs' FAI team, including the Scottish advocates' fees.

The Inquiry ran for five full court days. Boeing withdrew its contentions against one of the contractors, but insisted that BIH and the other contractor had not followed Boeing's instructions for installation of the -6 transmission. Lord Morton did a masterful job of shooting down these contentions, so that when the Sheriff Principal issued his determination on June 30, 1987, he found no fault on the part of BIH or the contractor. He determined that the crash was caused by the failure of the -6 transmission following the fretting and corrosion which brought on the rapidly spreading fatigue cracks.

The Sheriff Principal's determination deprived Boeing of official support for its theories, but a second test was to follow quickly. The AAIB, the U.K. agency charged with investigating major aircraft accidents, circulated a draft of its report to the interested parties, including Boeing. The AAIB report reached the same conclusions as had Sheriff Principal Bell, which was bad news for Boeing. But under U.K. law, those mentioned in the draft report had the right to challenge any findings by requesting appointment of a Review Board to reconsider the AAIB's findings. This had been done only once before in U.K. history, but in the Chinook case Boeing's lawyers were determined to do everything possible to keep alive their accusations against BIH and the contractor in support of their *forum* motion. They requested and were granted a review in Scotland's highest trial court, the Court of Session in Edinburgh. This held up public release of the AAIB report, and we would not be able to use it to oppose Boeing's *forum* motion unless and until the Review Board upheld it.

The AAIB Review Board was even more important to the plaintiffs than the Sheriff Principal's Fatal Accident Inquiry. While Boeing could claim that the FAI was short on technical expertise and was not designed to fix the scientific cause of the crash, the AAIB Report was much more detailed and would be accepted as authoritative throughout the aviation industry. Boeing brought over a team of engineers and helicopter experts in an effort to convince the AAIB Review Board that BIH and the contractor who modified the -5 transmission to -6 were at least partly responsible for the accident. To counter Boeing's formidable efforts, we reassembled much of the team we had used at the Sheriff Principal's FAI. Jim Crouse and our helicopter engineer supplied the technical expertise; the members of the Chinook Disaster Legal Group's Steering Committee were the solicitors; and, since Lord Morton had moved on to assume one of the highest judicial offices in Scotland, our advocate was Colin N.

McEachran QC. Arthur Raynes and Harry Roth came over from Philadelphia and again worked with the team.

The Review Board, chaired by Sheriff P.G.B. McNeill QC, assisted by Professor P. Hancock and Mr. K.V. Kellaway as Assessors, sat for 21 days in the Court of Session in Edinburgh. After hearing much more detailed evidence than had been presented at the FAI, the Review Board ruled in our favor. In their report they said that BIH did nothing improper in the maintenance or operation of the Chinook. Since Boeing had been forced to withdraw its charges against the English -6 modification contractor, this left Boeing as the sole culprit.

The Review Board noted that Boeing had failed to call three witnesses who had relevant knowledge, and that Boeing had not conducted any tests to support its claims. The Review Board also concluded that the record could support the inference that Boeing's actions in the U.K. investigation were taken merely to support its strategy of seeking a *forum non conveniens* dismissal of the Philadelphia lawsuits. For these reasons, Boeing was taxed for the entire public expense of the Review Board hearings and deliberations. Unfortunately this did not include the considerable expenses of the plaintiffs' Group, which our firm again had to lay out as part of the cost of supporting the Philadelphia litigation.

Thus a small group of oil workers' widows were able to defeat the world's largest aircraft manufacturer at its own game of blueprints and engineers in a public trial before its peers in the technical world of aircraft engineering. To many of the widows, this victory, which held Boeing publicly accountable, was as important as seeking adequate financial compensation.

The two trials in Scottish courts deprived Boeing of its strongest argument for a forum dismissal: the claim that BIH or the English contractors should share their liability. The forum non conveniens motion was denied, and the Chinook litigation went ahead in Philadelphia.

As the scene shifted from the picturesque courtrooms of Aberdeen and Edinburgh to the dilapidated City Hall building that housed the Philadelphia Court of Common Pleas, we began discovery, which enabled us to examine Boeing's records and question its employees. While the FAI and AAIB proceedings in Scotland had produced a record of about 3000 pages of documents, we went into much greater detail, forcing Boeing to produce more than 15,000 pages of records. We took the depositions of 17 Boeing employees who had worked on the Chinook project, some of whom we had to track down to their retirement homes.

As a result of this exhaustive discovery, most of which was conducted by Jim Crouse, we found that Boeing had not applied the lessons learned from problems of its military Chinooks to those that were sold to commercial operators. A "smoking gun" document unearthed by Jim Crouse was a 1981 article published by two of Boeing's Chinook designers in the *Journal of the American Helicopter Society*. More than five years before the Shetland Isles disaster, these Boeing engineers described a one-piece gear and shaft that "eliminates a potential fretting site as well as several hundred pieces of fastening hardware" in the Chinook transmissions, "resulting in a simpler, lighter, and more reliable assembly." Boeing adopted the one-piece assembly for the hundreds of Chinooks it had sold to military forces, but did not bother to make this life-saving modification to the handful of civilian Chinooks, probably because they felt that the small civilian market did not justify the cost of obtaining FAA approval. The fretting that caused the fatigue cracks in the BIH Chinook transmission could not have occurred in any of the military Chinooks because the assembly where the fretting occurred was eliminated by the one-piece gear.

From the one-piece gear (which had not been mentioned in the FAI or AAIB Review Board hearings) we moved to another vital area of discovery: Boeing's records of transmission failures and problems of the military Chinooks before they were fitted with the one-piece gear. FAA regulations required that Boeing report these problems to the FAA when it applied for civilian licensing of the Chinook. But our discovery—which included forced production of Boeing's own records as well as our own search of U.S. Army records at the Army overhaul depot at Corpus Christi, Texas—revealed that Boeing had received hundreds of reports of military Chinook transmission problems and failures which it did not report to the FAA.

Finally Jim Crouse took the deposition of the FAA official in charge of approving the -6 modification which had caused the Shetland Isles disaster. During that deposition, Jim placed on record the documents showing Boeing's failure to report military transmission failures and problems. The FAA official testified that he had never seen these documents; that they had never been filed with the FAA despite the FAA regulations requiring such filing; and that if Boeing had filed them, the FAA would have required much more extensive testing before approving the -6 modification.

All this evidence added up to a strong case of liability, possibly strong enough to support punitive as well as compensatory damages against Boeing. When we completed discovery, the cases were assigned to Common Pleas Judge Armand Della Porta for trial. He brought both sides together and finally all the cases were settled without trial. By agreement, the amounts must remain confidential, but it is public knowledge that the compensation formula yielded the victims' families much more than they could have collected in U.K. courts. Indeed, without the Chinook Disaster Legal Group and its Scottish solicitors and advocates, English solicitors, and American lawyers, Boeing would have been in a position to avoid payment of any compensation and to escape public accountability for its mistakes which caused the BIH Chinook disaster.

The Chinook Disaster Legal Group functioned smoothly despite having to break new ground in many areas. It has served as a model for cooperation among representatives of the victims of such disasters. It demonstrated the need for steering committees composed of experienced litigation solicitors. No matter how skilled the American lawyers may be, there are many problems in international litigation that simply cannot be dealt with from across the ocean. There are media statements affecting the clients' peace of mind that must be made on very short notice. There are explanations of American law and procedure that must be translated into terms that can be understood by the solicitors for each family, and the families themselves. There are times when British clients simply do not feel comfortable taking the word of American lawyers without the advice of local experts on the steering committees, on vital questions such as whether there is any need to sue in America in view of the offers being made in Britain. There are government investigations, public enquiries, and protective actions, the handling of which can be crucial to success of the American litigation. Our firm had maintained a London office since 1976, but after experiencing the team approach in the Chinook case we closed that office and decided to function through the steering committees.

The lessons of Chinook were to be put into effect again even before the Chinook cases were settled, for the people of Aberdeen were hit by a second and even worse North Sea disaster less than two years after the BIH Chinook crashed in the Shetland Isles. At 10 p.m. on July 6, 1988, an explosion rocked the Piper Alpha offshore drilling platform in the North Sea, setting off a chain of fires and further explosions that destroyed it. Of 226 persons aboard, 165 were killed, as well as two rescue workers. Most of the 61 survivors saved their lives by diving into the sea, some of them from positions as high as 175 feet above the water.

The initial explosion occurred in Module C, where the gas from the producing oil wells was compressed. After that explosion, caused by an operating error, the fires and other explosions were fed by continued flow of oil and gas to the platform from the pipelines connected to it. The explosions caused loss of electrical power and knocked out most of the control and communication facilities. As a result, all six safety systems that were designed to minimize the damage from explosions and to facilitate escape in time of emergency—sprinklers, shutoff valves, emergency lights, alarms, life rafts—were disabled and failed to work. Most of the workers were in the sleeping quarters (called the "accommodation") when the explosions occurred. Since the accommodation was located on top of the gas compression module, most of its occupants were trapped and died in the dense black smoke and flames.

The Piper Alpha platform was owned by a consortium of four oil companies: Occidental, International Thomson, Texaco, and Union Texas. The registered owner and main operator was Occidental. But—significantly for legal purposes—it was not the the American company, Occidental Petroleum Corporation. Ownership was in the name of Occidental Petroleum (Caledonia) Ltd., a subsidiary of Occidental Petroleum (Great Britain) Ltd., which in turn was a subsidiary of the Los Angeles-based parent Occidental company. Thus there were two layers of corporate armor plate separating the American Occidental company from legal responsibility. The same was true of the other three owners, which were English subsidiaries of foreign companies.

While most of the victims were from the Aberdeen area, there were some from other parts of the U.K. As the bereaved families and the injured survivors consulted their family or labor union solicitors about compensation, it became apparent that another Chinook-type group effort was needed, on an even larger scale since there were more than 200 claims involved. The members of the Chinook Group Steering Committee—Patrick Davies, David Burnside, and Sandy Kemp of Aberdeen, and Fred Tyler of Edinburgh—were pressed into service again, with Patrick and Sandy reprising their roles as chairman and secretary respectively. Four more members were added: Jimmy Roxburgh and Peter Watson of Glasgow, David Short of Edinburgh, and Alan Goldsmith of Liverpool. The Pannone Napier team was represented by Rodger Pannone, Mike Napier, and Geraldine McCool. Eventually the Piper Disaster Group included the families of 136 deceased workers and 49 injured survivors. The remaining claimants were represented by trade union lawyers who formed their own group and cooperated closely with the Piper Disaster Group.

Since our firm had successfully represented groups of plaintiffs in the two previous oil platform disaster cases litigated in the United States—the 1982 Ocean Ranger collapse off Newfoundland, and the 1983 disappearance of the Glomar Java Sea in the South China Sea—the Piper Disaster Group called me in a few days after the accident. The U.K. solicitors had to know very quickly what their chances were of suing in the United States. If they sued in Scotland or England, the compensation would be below the level needed to sustain the families at their pre-accident standards of living. Their only hope for adequate compensation was to sue in the United States (as in Chinook) or to force the insurers to make a Mid-Atlantic Settlement in order to avoid American lawsuits (as in British Air Tours/Manchester). In those prior cases, it was clear that we could sue those responsible in the United States, since American-made aircraft and engines were directly involved. But in Piper Alpha much of the fault for the fatal explosions and fires fell upon British companies that owned and operated the platform and were responsible for the safety systems that failed when they were needed.

The main culprit was Occidental—but legally it was Occidental Petroleum (Caledonia) Ltd., an English company that had no office in the United States. Our main hope of successfully suing Occidental of Caledonia in the U.S. was to prove that it was the *alter ego* of the Los Angeles-based parent Occidental company. Ordinarily that is a difficult burden, because the corporate lawyers who organize subsidiaries take great pains to create the appearance of separate legal entities, by maintaining different slates of officers and directors and operating independently of the parent. But in this case the gods of litigation smiled upon us, because the chief executive officer of the parent Los Angeles company, Occidental Petroleum Corporation, was Dr. Armand Hammer.

It was well known to one and all in the oil business that Armand Hammer ran his own show, regardless of whether he was seeking an asbestos franchise from Lenin, or oil concessions from the King of Libya or the Prime Minister of the United Kingdom. The word "ego" fitted Hammer like a glove, for he was the personification of all the Occidental companies no matter where they were incorporated. Lest there be any doubt about who was responsible for each important step in building the obscure Occidental into the 8th largest American oil company and the 12th largest American industrial concern, Hammer confirmed it in his 1987 autobiography, titled (inevitably) *Hammer*. Throughout this 526-page tribute to himself, Hammer used the word "I" in place of Occidental dozens of times, particularly in the long chapter on his North Sea oil adventure and the building of the Piper Alpha platform. From the formation of the consortium of companies that operated Piper Alpha, to the negotiations with the prime ministers and lesser lights of the British government, to the design and operation of the platform, it was Hammer, not Occidental/Caledonia, who took every important action. Indeed, he perceived other chief executives as the *alter egos* of their huge companies, as in this description of one of the major contracts he awarded for the building of Piper Alpha: "Steve Bechtel came in to lay a thirty-inch pipe on the seabed from Piper to the isle of Flotta." Referring to Occidental's takeover of Cities Service Company, he said it was "unquestionably the most important acquisition I ever made."

Hammer's egocentric business style made it likely that we could get jurisdiction in the United States over all the Occidental companies by serving the lawsuit papers on him. There were also several American companies involved in the design and building of Piper Alpha, using some facilities and personnel located in Texas and Louisiana. I decided to recommend to the Piper Disaster Group that suit be filed in Texas, which (as we saw in Chapter 13) had humanized its wrongful death law so that the taking of human life was an expensive proposition for those responsible. I thought it would be necessary to file suit in Texas to force the defendants to enter into serious settlement negotiations. This was a very complicated case involving more than a dozen large companies and their insurers. It would not be easy to fix responsibility or to move those insurers quickly toward an agreement to contribute to overall settlements, and that alone would delay settlement negotiations until a massive public inquiry was completed, followed by months (if not years) of detailed discovery. But I was mistaken about the time factor, largely because I had never dealt with Armand Hammer.

On July 22, 1988—less than three weeks after the Piper Alpha explosion—the Piper Disaster Group Steering Committee met with representatives of Occidental in Aberdeen. The meeting was requested by Occidental, whose team was headed by Gene Silva of the Houston law firm Vinson & Elkins, and included an assistant general counsel from Occidental's Los Angeles headquarters. From the outset, Gene Silva made it clear that Occidental wanted to settle these claims without ligitation, and that they were willing to consider the "American buyout factor" as part of the settlement package. In other words, Occidental would accept the Group's ability to mount litigation in the United States, and would negotiate for a Mid-Atlantic Settlement formula that would include consideration of the likelihood of keeping the case in the U.S., as well as the probable awards in American courts. Silva and the Scottish lawyers for Occidental proposed that their team try to reach agreement with the Group's Steering Committee on the probable awards of the Scottish courts for half a dozen typical cases, and then try to negotiate a multiplier of the Scottish awards as the American buyout factor in the Mid-Atlantic Settlement formula.

Nothing like this had ever happened so quickly in a major disaster case. As soon as I was informed of the Aberdeen meeting with Silva, I guessed that Armand Hammer was behind this approach. While this has never been officially confirmed, I believe that only a person with his drive and brass could force Lloyd's of London and other large insurers to move so quickly toward such a landmark settlement—for it was clear from the beginning that a Mid-Atlantic Settlement would require payment of least $200 million in compensation. There were special reasons why Armand Hammer—almost a caricature of the Daddy Warbucks type of international financier—would involve himself personally in these negotiations that were really the business of Occidental's insurers.

You will recall that the Piper Alpha accommodation, in which most of the deaths occurred, was located above the gas compressor module, the most likely place for a major explosion. It didn't have to be that way. Other drilling platforms had their sleeping quarters located at a safe distance from the compressors. Some North Sea operators, especially the Norwegians, placed the sleeping quarters on separate structures, taking the trouble to ferry the workers to and from the working platform to assure that they would not be trapped in their beds by a compressor explosion. These two options were more expensive than the choice made by Occidental for Piper Alpha: putting the accommodation over the compressor to save space and money. For Occidental, read Dr. Armand Hammer. If you watched Hammer's face in the newscasts of his condolence visit to Aberdeen with Prime Minister Thatcher, you would not doubt that he felt personal responsibility for this appalling disaster.

Piper Alpha kept me busy through the summer months of 1988. In addition to briefing the Steering Committee on the prospects for maintaining the litigation in the United States, I now had to prepare them for negotiating the American buyout factor, by calculating the amounts that the Texas courts would award in the model cases and backing up these calculations with convincing authorities. I knew that Gene Silva would be doing his job by producing lower appraisals of Texas awards. Finally a date was fixed for a London meeting of the Steering Committee with the defense lawyers, to try to agree on a Mid-Atlantic Settlement formula for the death cases, which lent themselves more readily to appraisal than the claims of the injured survivors, many of whom were still undergoing medical treatment. I was asked to come over to London to attend the meeting and conduct our side of the debate with Gene Silva on the Texas damage levels.

The London meeting took place on October 14, 1988, barely three months after the disaster. Sitting at our side of the table, flanked by Rodger Pannone and Michael Napier, facing more than a dozen leading insurance and oil company lawyers, I could feel the power of the American tort system lifting the bereaved Aberdeen families from the poverty that would have been their lot under Scottish law—indeed, under the laws of practically all countries outside of the United States.

Later that day, when the debate was over and the defense team presented their final formula for the Mid-Atlantic Settlement, my pride jumped up several notches. The much-maligned American compensation circus, skillfully deployed by Pannone Napier and the Steering Committee as a hammer over the heads of the insurers, had produced a settlement that would have been difficult to top in the American courts without years of risky litigation. Again I must respect the agreement to keep the formula and the figures confidential, but numerous reports published in Britain have put the total compensation over $250 million. As University of Texas law professor Hans W. Baade put it, the Mid-Atlantic Settlement Formula in the Piper Alpha case produced "United States-level recoveries, discounted by the factors of time, uncertainty, and expense of litigation in that country."

The death case settlements were based upon statistics like ages, earnings, and number of relatives, that could readily be agreed upon. But the injury cases involved more subjective factors and therefore did not lend themselves so readily to an overall settlement forumula. One of the major items of damages was the post-traumatic shock disorder (PTSD) suffered by many of the survivors because of their involvement in the Piper Alpha holocaust. Some of them had their shoes or clothing catch fire before jumping into the sea. Nearly all would be haunted by the screams they heard coming from the accommodation, where their friends were trapped in an inferno. Scottish doctors and lawyers were not as familiar with PTSD as were the Americans. To help on that aspect, Chuck Krause (now head of our Texas office) and I brought in Bob Chaffin, a leading Houston tort lawyer, who did a fine job in assembling the medical-legal data needed to push through an appropriate settlement formula for the injury cases. He was assisted by his lovely wife and law partner, Ana Arrango Chaffin, who once had practiced with our firm in New York. Ana and Bob met during our collaboration on the litigation arising out of the 1982 Ocean Ranger drilling platform disaster off Newfoundland, and they decided to make the arrangement permanent.

When the defense team made their final settlement offer at the London meeting, the Piper Disaster Group asked me to appraise it. Chuck Krause, Bob Chaffin, Ana Arrango and I went over each case, and decided that the figures were high enough so that we would have to recommend acceptance. While we might have gotten higher settlements or verdicts in Texas, that would have taken years of litigation, and in the end we could not be certain that the courts would sustain our efforts to sue the Occidental group and the other owners in Texas in view of the legally separate roles of the U.K. subsidiaries that operated Piper Alpha. There was also the possibility of a *forum non conveniens* dismissal, although the Texas and Louisiana state courts usually do not grant such dismissals. Before leaving London, I recommended to the Steering Committee that the offers be accepted. I did so with some reluctance because acceptance would cut the American lawyers out of a contingent fee that would probably have run into many millions of dollars. I was paid for my work with the Steering Committee, but not on the basis of a percentage of the settlements.

The Steering Committee voted to recommend acceptance. They called a meeting of all the solicitors in the Group, to be held in the Advocates Hall, Aberdeen, for October 24th. They asked me to attend and to explain the reasons for the recommendation that the settlement offers be accepted. So it was that I addressed an audience of more than 100 solicitors and talked myself out of what probably would have been the largest legal fee ever paid in an accident case.

Armand Hammer, 90 years old when the Piper Alpha platform exploded, lived another two years. When he died at 92 in 1990, his obituary covered a full page in the *New York Times*. The *Times* also noted his passing on the editorial page, concluding with this statement:

Armand Hammer was a flawed buccaneer, a bragging impresario. But his efforts for peace were formidable, his gifts to charity extraordinary. Few private citizens can claim to have equaled them. His life spanned the entire history of Communism, and he was probably the only American who could have told Mr. Gorbachev what Lenin was really like. Which he probably did.

I would add that in my opinion, he was one of the major forces behind the most sensible settlement of any major disaster case. While he probably acted out of a need to expiate his own guilt, the point is that he got the job done. And in the end I think it proved to be a good business decision for Occidental and its insurers, who were saved years of expensive litigation that probably would have wound up with the same overall result at much greater financial and emotional cost to all concerned. Instead, the bereaved North Sea families were spared litigation and received adequate compensation before the first Christmas following the disaster.

I was scheduled to retire as a partner of our firm at the end of 1988, moving up to "of counsel" status, meaning that I would be available as a consultant on specific cases but would no longer have the responsibility of managing the firm. That chore was taken over by Chuck Krause, working from the Texas office. In the New York office Ken Nolan became the resident managing partner. Ken, a former writer and editor for the *New York Times*, has worked on many aviation cases, but is best known for trying cases involving catastrophic injuries to children. With the Piper Alpha settlement serving as an appropriate swan song, I jumped the gun on my retirement by repairing to Florida at Thanksgiving time. But my respite did not even last through the holiday season, for on December 21st, Pan Am Flight 103 was blown out of the skies over Lockerbie, Scotland. Rodger Pannone was on the phone again, and my trans-Atlantic commuting would soon resume.

The U.K. solicitors who represented most of the ground victims in Lockerbie and most of the British passengers formed the Lockerbie Air Disaster Group, again modeled on the Chinook Group. This was a joint Scottish-English project, since all the ground victims were Scottish and most of the U.K. passengers were English. Rodger Pannone and Geraldine McCool joined the Steering Committee for Pannone Napier, along with Fred Tyler of Edinburgh (a veteran of both Chinook and Piper Alpha); Peter Watson of Glasgow, who had also served in Piper Alpha, and became secretary of the Lockerbie Group; Anne Rafferty and

Jimmy Stevenson of Lockerbie; Lyall Moodie of Dumfries; and two London solicitors, Chris Erving and David Greene.

I was called in as the American attorney for the Group. There was no move by Pan Am's insurers to negotiate a Mid-Atlantic Settlement, and so it was clear that the British victims would have to sue in America. There was a choice between New York, where Pan Am had its headquarters, and Florida, where the airline also had extensive operations and where its two subsidiaries responsible for security were based. I recommended Florida, and chose as our local counsel Aaron Podhurst of Miami, with whose firm I had collaborated in Florida's first successful aviation accident cases back in the 1950s. Our respective firms had worked together on many aviation cases over a period of more than 35 years, and we still considered Aaron to be Florida's leading aviation tort lawyer.

The Group accepted my recommendation, and we filed suits in the Florida state court in Miami for most of the British passengers' families and most of the Lockerbie residents who had suffered physical injuries or had lost relatives. When the Boeing 747 *Maid of the Seas* exploded and disintegrated, it rained fire and destruction on the little town of Lockerbie, directly causing 11 deaths and many serious injuries. Aaron Podhurst brought the ground cases on first, and they were set down for trial in September of 1990. Unlike the passenger cases, the ground claims did not involve the Warsaw Convention, and thus the plaintiffs needed to prove only ordinary negligence rather than wilful misconduct. On the eve of trial, Pan Am's insurers agreed to settle all those ground claims. Again, we have agreed to keep the amounts confidential in order to protect the privacy of our clients.

The Fatal Accident Inquiry (FAI) was an extraordinary challenge for the Lockerbie Air Disaster Group Steering Committee, since its 270 deaths constituted the largest mass murder in history. To accommodate the many parties, witnesses, journalists and spectators, John S. Mowat QC, Sheriff Principal of South Strathclyde, Dumfries and Galloway, conducted the FAI in a converted hospital in Dumfries. He heard evidence from 131 witnesses over 55 days of court hearings. The Lockerbie Group Steering Committee arranged for two of Scotland's leading advocates to represent the Group's families: Brian Gill QC and Colin Campbell QC. Members of the Steering Committee took turns in attending the FAI and assisting the two advocates. For our firm, the major work on Lockerbie was done by the father-and-son team of Frank Granito Jr. (a former Navy pilot and FAA attorney who joined our firm in 1967) and Frank Granito III.

That is all I can tell you about Lockerbie, because at this writing the passenger claims are still pending in the American courts and as one of the lawyers representing families of American and British passengers, I cannot comment now.

Along with Chinook, Piper Alpha, and Lockerbie, Pannone Napier organized successful claimants' groups in domestic British disasters, including the 1987 P&O ferry sinking at Zeebrugge, Belgium (which I call "domestic" because it did not involve the threat of American litigation); the 1987 King's Cross London Underground fire; the 1988 British Rail train crash at Clapham; and the 1989 *Marchioness—Bowbelle* ship collision on the Thames. Meanwhile they continued successful representation of British victims of long-running pharmaceutical disasters, some of which, like Dalkon Shield, involved litigation against the manufacturers in American courts.

Rodger Pannone personally has built a strong following among English solicitors for his dedicated service on the Council of the Law Society, England's counterpart of the American Bar Association. His drive to modernize English solicitors' practice helped to broaden the right of solicitors to conduct more court proceedings without barristers, and to enlarge the public's access to justice. These accomplishments helped to elect him Deputy Vice-President of the Law Society for 1991-1992, which means that according to past practice he will become Vice-President in 1992 and President in 1993. Michael Napier has built an equally solid reputation as a litigator, organizer, and manager. He has been especially prominent in organizing a British counterpart of ATLA (called APIL, for Association of Personal Injury Lawyers) and in promoting the Centre of Advanced Litigation (COAL) at Nottingham Law School, where he serves as a visiting professor, the first to occupy the Stuart Speiser Chair of Disaster Law.

Through their personal triumphs, Rodger Pannone and Michael Napier have shown that English solicitors, even though shackled by Dickensian rules, can become entrepreneur-lawyers and Equalizers in tort cases. As the British Sunday newspaper, *The Observer*, said in a 1991 profile of Rodger, "His recent career is a spectacular example of what a strong-minded individualist can accomplish by applying reason to an archaic tradition." In fact, from his lofty position Rodger now has some advantages over American Equalizers. Great Britain is a much tighter society than the United States, so that with a single nationally-televised press conference, Rodger can get the "disaster group" message across to most of the British people immediately. The media will give him this platform because they have learned to trust and respect him. He has developed effective methods of coordination with all British solicitors through the Law Societies of England, Scotland, and Northern Ireland. And his past deeds have won him the continuing support of consumer and public service organizations which can be very helpful in strengthening claimants' groups. In our more diverse society, no American lawyer has that much clout.

Yet, even though other brave solicitors are following in the footsteps of Pannone Napier, I don't think the British people can gain the degree of access to their legal system enjoyed by Americans unless there are basic changes. In my opinion, the key to transplanting that part of the American Dream to Britain is to allow solicitors (and barristers when involved) to be compensated in proportion to the benefits they gain for their clients. That, I think, will open the way for the second necessary reform: bringing British damage awards into line with the actual losses suffered by tort victims, either by permitting jury trials or changing the methods by which judges are required to compute damages.

Contingent fees, which most people think of as the American percentage fee of about one-third of the amount recovered in tort cases, historically were officially prohibited in the U.K. (They are usually called "contingency fees" in the U.K., but we shall stick with the American form of "contingent.") Neither solicitors nor barristers were permitted to take on claims without charging a fee, even if they lost the case. Supposedly, the amount of their fee was not related to the amount collected if they won. Yet, Order 62 of the Supreme Court, the official rule under which English solicitors' fees are fixed by court officials, requires consideration of the amount of money involved in the case; its complexity; the skill and specialized knowledge required; and the importance of the case to the client. Therefore, a solicitor who won or settled such a case was always supposed to be compensated in proportion to the amount involved. The only non-contingent aspect of such a fee was the fact that the solicitor was to be paid something regardless of winning or losing. The *amount* of the fee was always supposed to be at least partially dependent on the amount involved in the case. And since "skill and specialized knowledge" must be considered, logic would seem to dictate that the fee be higher for the skill demonstrated in winning and lower in the case of a loss.

The ban on contingent fees dates back to the beginnings of the British legal system. Supposedly it was a matter of principle.

Historically, British lawyers considered it "unprofessional" to be paid solely on the basis of the result achieved, or to forego any fees in a losing case. Yet, English solicitors have long been permitted to take a percentage of the debts they collect for clients without litigation. And Scottish solicitors for many years have been allowed to take a percentage of "extra-judicial settlements," meaning any kind of claim that is settled before suit has been filed. The allowable percentages in Scotland start with 25 percent of the first £1,000, and slide down to 2.5 percent on the excess over £10,000. Furthermore, it was common knowledge that many British solicitors would take on cases without expecting to be paid if they lost, the English solicitors doing this unofficially and the Scottish solicitors doing so openly under their approved "speculative litigation" system.

It is difficult for an American lawyer to perceive any ethical grounds for distinguishing between claims collected without suit and those requiring suit, or between claims for personal injuries and those for unpaid debts. As an outsider, these differences appear to me to be based upon custom rather than principle.

Claimants who cannot afford to pay lawyers are not completely powerless in the U.K., since it has a system of legal aid that includes civil as well as criminal cases. But in order to qualify for legal aid in civil cases, the applicant must first satisfy the local Legal Aid office that he has reasonable grounds for suing. This can be a complicated process, and it requires considerable evidence of a viable claim at a stage when there may be little available to the claimant's lawyer. If this hurdle is cleared, the applicant then must submit to an examination of his financial means by an assessor of the Department of Health and Social Security. Only those whose annual disposable income is below £7,500 and whose disposable capital (not including home ownership) is less than £8,560, will receive meaningful amounts of legal aid for personal injury cases. Depending on the financial position, legal aid may be only partial, so that the applicant will be required to contribute to the payment of legal fees. Apart from these restrictions, legal aid is considered a welfare benefit that must be kept under tight control, especially under Conservative governments. Therefore, in tort cases, it can never provide the same degree of access to the courts as does the contingent fee.

In a 1989 Green Paper the Lord Chancellor's Department lists the arguments for and against allowing contingent fees in Britain. One of the challenges to contingent fees is that they "may result in a conflict of interest between lawyer and client," since the "lawyer will have a direct financial interest in the outcome of the case and will be unable to give the client impartial advice." If I had to hire a lawyer to represent me in a suit, I would prefer that he give me partisan advice on how we could achieve the best result, and I would feel very secure about him getting paid in exact proportion to the results he achieved rather than billing me for an hourly or lump sum fee no matter how badly he butchered the case.

The 1989 Lord Chancellor's Department Green Paper lists some of the potential side-effects of this "conflict of interest": (1) the lawyer might be tempted to encourage the client to settle early to avoid the effort involved in fighting the case; (2) the lawyer might be tempted to enhance the client's chances of success, by coaching witnesses or withholding evidence; (3) the lawyer might concentrate on cases with high nuisance value where the defendant is more likely to "be forced into making an offer to settle;" and (4) the lawyer might concentrate on cases that are most likely to succeed.

The first two contradict each other, but even if we assume that each applies to a different set of lawyers, they don't make much sense to me. Why would a lawyer force an early settlement if he shared handsomely in the fruits of further effort? Furthermore, most clients are interested in an early settlement rather than prolonged litigation. As a client, I would be very uneasy about a fee system that rewards the lawyers for dragging the case on as long as possible to create more billable hours or services. As to coaching witnesses and withholding evidence, this happens quite often in cases where lawyers are being paid by the hour. It is a question of the lawyer's ethics rather than the form of his payment.

As to side-effect number 3, any contingent-fee lawyer who concentrates on cases with "high nuisance value" will find himself looking for another livelihood, since these cases are vigorously opposed by insurers and corporate defendants because they provide opportunities for the defense lawyers to chalk up easy victories and for the defendants to set an example for deterrence of future nuisance suits. Number 4, while inconsistent with number 3 in that it portrays a lawyer who is taking only perfect cases and also engaging in nuisance practice based on unmeritorious cases, is actually desirable. The more selective lawyers become in taking on litigation, the more likely it is that the most meritorious cases will dominate the legal system and the nuisance-value cases will be weeded out. Only by paying lawyers to take on nuisance cases regardless of their merit can the legal system be polluted.

The Green Paper also says that experience in the United States suggests that contingent fees encourage juries to award excessively high damages, and encourage litigants to bring cases with very little merit, leading to a litigation explosion. Not mentioned is the fact that trial and appellate judges review jury awards and reduce those that are excessive. Nor is it explained how lawyers can make a living from "cases with very little merit" if they are not paid for losing them.

Despite these negative images of contingent fees, the Green Paper listed some arguments in favor of trying them in Britain: the opportunity for many claimants who do not qualify for legal aid to have their day in court; "a greater level of commitment on the part of the lawyer;" and competition among lawyers. It also noted that the then current (Thatcher) government policy favored deregulation, which meant removal of restrictions and widening of choice for consumers (clients) and suppliers (lawyers) unless clearly contrary to the public interest. Apparently these arguments carried some weight, because the door to British contingent fees was opened slightly by Parliament's enactment of the Courts and Legal Services Act 1990, which permits "conditional fee agreements" that provide for fees to be increased according to the results achieved, subject to limits imposed by the Lord Chancellor. At this writing, it appears that the Lord Chancellor will limit the increase to 10 percent of the agreed fee.

It is tempting for American lawyers to dismiss the British ban on contingent fees with a single question: Unless this is supposed to be a game for lawyers only, why not let the consumers decide which type of fee they want to pay? But there are some practical barriers in Britain that do not exist in the United States. If British judges are to continue fixing damages under the stereotyped schedules, contingent fees won't do the claimants much good since they will not receive any more money merely because the basis of the fee is changed. Indeed, if awards remain at the same level and the fees are paid from those awards, the claimants will receive less money in those cases where even the best professional efforts cannot increase compensation. Perhaps the coming of contingent fees will in itself make plaintiff's lawyers more effective. But the simplest cure is to permit jury trials in all civil cases, not only in defamation cases. Jury trials were permitted in all English tort cases prior to World War II, when the shortage of jurors led to the present restrictions. Jury trials are permitted in Scottish tort cases. Allowing the citizenry to participate as jurors would be an important step toward democratizing what is now widely perceived as an elitist legal system.

Judges could retain the power to curb excessive verdicts by ordering new trials, as in the United States. Or, if unlimited jury
trials are not practical, the method by which judges assess damages could be brought up to date by legislation or directive from
the Lord Chancellor.

Another practical obstacle to effective contingent fees in Britain is the rule that the losing party must pay the winner's legal
fees—the fee-shifting that we discussed in the preceding chapter.
This would inhibit some claimants from going to court even if
they didn't have to pay fixed fees to their own lawyers. However, the deterrent effect of fee-shifting is minimized in British
tort cases by the fact that more than 90 percent of them are
settled before verdicts are rendered. Also, it seems safe to assume
that if British solicitors are able to develop into Equalizers, tort
plaintiffs will lose fewer cases and the risk of financial losses
from fee-shifting will be considerably diminished.

As an outsider, I don't pretend to have authoritative answers
to the questions about use of the contingent fee in Great Britain.
I believe, however, that I qualify as an expert on the needs and
desires of British claimants in accident cases, since I have represented hundreds of them in contingent fee situations. From that
experience, I have observed the consumers' reaction to the contingent fee. To them it is a godsend, for they know that without
it they could not match the litigation power of McDonnell
Douglas, Boeing, Occidental Oil, the makers of the Dalkon
Shield, or any insurance company. They would have to follow
the age-old custom of absorbing much of the financial burden of
someone else's negligence, on top of their own crippling injuries
or the emotional loss caused by the death of a loved one. And
they would have to let these powerful wrongdoers bury their
mistakes without the public disclosure, accountability, and future deterrence that can be forced only by an Equalizer.

I'll never forget a meeting I had with an Englishman who
had lost his son, an only child, in an accident that was caused by
a large American company. As he told me how he had worked to
raise the son, the first in the family to attend a university, and
how callous the American company had been in covering up the
causes of the fatal accident, there was no hint of tremor in his
voice. I wondered how he had the strength to tell that story
without breaking down. But when I told him that I would represent him on a contingent-fee basis and sue the company at no
cost to him, I noticed that tears formed in his eyes.

There is no doubt that consumers throughout the world
would choose the contingent fee if they could hire an Equalizer.

This would give them real access to justice, most of them for the first time. But it is not possible for Equalizers to develop outside the United States unless they can find ways to raise the artificially suppressed levels of compensation. The Englishman who lost his son showed tears of gratitude because I agreed to pursue his case in the United States, not in Britain.

The Global Perspective

The foregoing discussion of the inadequacy of British tort compensation applies to practically all other nations except the United States. This may surprise legal scholars who are accustomed to dividing the world's major legal systems into two groups: the *common law* nations (Great Britain and its present and former colonies, including the United States), and *civil law* nations, comprising most of the rest of the world. The civil law, so titled to distinguish it from ecclesiastical or canon law, is based upon the compilations of Roman jurists under the auspices of the Emperor Justinian. The modern Roman law is embodied in the famous Napoleonic Code of 1804, now called the Civil Code. While there are many important differences between the common law system used in the Anglo-American countries and the civil codes in force elsewhere, these differences do not govern the development of Equalizers. For example, France, the leading civil law nation, does not follow the English common law system, but it excludes contingent fees and civil jury trials just as the U.K. does. Thus, most of the world is united in denying the ordinary citizen the effective court access enjoyed by Americans since the Equalizers developed.

Yet, no radical changes in basic law are required to open the way for Equalizers to develop throughout the world. Tort claims under the French Civil Code are governed by a remarkably concise rule that is stated in one sentence, unchanged since the time of Napoleon: "Any act by which a person causes damages to another makes the person by whose fault the damage occurred liable to make reparation for such damage." That sentence would serve just as well if the procedures were altered to permit French lawyers (and their counterparts throughout the world) to develop into Equalizers by allowing them to use contingent fees and to try their cases to juries or to judges who are under direction to repair the damage by awarding adequate compensation. Virtually every legal system in the world pays lip service to the principle of reparation by fair and adequate compensation for wrongs. To enforce that principle, no new structures need be built. All that is needed is to kick in the rotten doors barring most victims from meaningful access to the courts, as was done in the United States.

French legal officials appear to be satisfied with the inadequate compensation available to most French accident victims. But when the French government itself is the claimant, and there is a chance to sue in America, the attitude changes. A case in point is the litigation that followed the 1978 breakup of the supertanker *Amoco Cadiz* that spewed 220,000 tons of crude oil into the seas off Brittany, blackening 180 miles of coastline in one of France's most important tourist and fishing regions.

Our firm was retained by privately-owned businesses in Brittany that had suffered losses: operators of fishing boats, restaurants, and hotels, whose 1978 seasons were wiped out by what was then the world's worst oil spill. Our French colleague, Paris *avocat* Jean-Marc Gernigon, who had worked with us on the two major Paris air crashes (Varig Airlines in 1973 and Turkish Airlines in 1974), advised that our clients could not hope to recoup their losses in the French courts. Therefore, the clients retained us on a contingent-fee basis to sue in America. We filed suit against Amoco in Chicago, since it was from their Chicago headquarters that Amoco executives had directed the voyage of the *Amoco Cadiz*, even to the point of keeping the desperate captain waiting on the radiotelephone while they debated the terms of salvage proposed by a German tugboat operator. (By the time the Chicago Amoco executives accepted, it was too late to tow the supertanker to safety.) While our clients' loss-of-business claims added up to millions of dollars, by far the largest damages were suffered by the French government, which had kept thousands of soldiers and sailors in Brittany for more than six months to clean up the water and land damage from the tons of oily waste that was the color and consistency of chocolate mousse.

The Republic of France could have enjoyed the home team advantage by suing Amoco in the French courts. Instead, its lawyers chose to follow our lead and sue Amoco in Chicago. Indeed, they went us one better: they also sued Astilleros Espanoles S.A., builders of the *Amoco Cadiz*, who had earlier built the ships in which Columbus sailed to the New World. After trials on liability and damages, more than $200 million was awarded to the plaintiffs in the Chicago federal court. Most of the award went to the Republic of France, whose American and French lawyers saw their choice of forum vindicated by collecting much more compensation than they would have received from a French judge.

Japan is a civil law nation that supposedly requires wrong-doers to "make reparation" to their injured victims, as per the Napoleonic Code. But enforcement of this right has been blocked by centuries of cultural opposition to the public airing of dis-putes. One would have thought that the democratization of Ja-pan after World War II would have given its citizens real access to the courts. But Japan's democracy is run by a unique alliance of business and government that is credited with nurturing spec-tacular economic growth—and militates against empowerment of loose cannons like the Equalizers who might upset the cozy establishment. The Japanese legal system prohibits contingent fees and civil jury trials, and requires would-be plaintiffs to pay their own lawyers up-front fees totalling up to 8 percent of the claimed damages. There is also a nonrefundable court filing fee of one-half of 1 percent of the damages claimed. Moreover, the government limits the number of judges and litigation lawyers, so that less than 1,000 law graduates are permitted to take the bar exam each year. This creates such heavy caseloads that trials often drag along at the snail's pace of one court session per month. No wonder, then, that in 1987, after 15 years of inconclu-sive litigation, the exhausted families of the victims of Japan's worst coal mining disaster were forced to settle their claims for a fraction of their real damages. These barriers reflect the contin-ued official disapproval of those who would disturb Japan's cul-tural harmony by daring to bring disputes to court.

I have had the privilege of representing Japanese families who lost relatives in airline crashes caused by defective Ameri-can products. I can testify that their attitude is no different from those of American, British, French, or Chinese families who suf-fered such losses. They want fair compensation, as well as public accountability on the part of those who caused the damage.

There are signs that the inequity and corruption nurtured by the Japanese policy of blocking access to the courts may create public pressure for reform. Some interesting insights were pro-vided in "Japan's Rigged Casino," a 1992 *New York Times Maga-zine* article written by *Times* Tokyo correspondent James Sterngold. He describes some of the frauds practiced by Japanese stockbrokers with the tacit approval of the government/industry establishment:

> An official of the Daiwa Securities Company, Japan's second-largest brokerage house, had approached a prominent corpora-tion, Tokyu Department Store, and proposed that Tokyu pay 90.5 billion yen (about $675 million) for securities whose mar-

ket value was only 30 billion yen. According to Tokyu, Daiwa promised it would repurchase the securities later, at a price that would guarantee Tokyu a small profit.

This blatant market-rigging game is reserved for privileged customers. It is known as *tobashi* ("flying"). Brokers keep these overvalued shares flying from account to account until the market price rises high enough to make the rigging unnecessary. Then the game stops, with all the insiders having profited from these fraudulent transactions. But in 1991 the Tokyo stock market was caught in a continuing downward spiral that made the shares Tokyu bought worth even less than 30 billion yen. As Sterngold reports:

> Faced with the prospect of a loss in the hundreds of millions of dollars, Daiwa refused to repurchase the securities at the promised value. That prompted a desperate Tokyu to do something all but unheard of in a society where financial dealings are generally kept out of the public eye. It went to court.

Thus, it appears that when the effects of secret manipulations are oppressive enough to business interests, even the "non-litigious" Japanese may go to court. It was the lawsuit brought by Tokyu that finally exposed the "flying" scheme to public light and started a strong push for reform of the stock market.

Sterngold also describes how Japanese organized-crime groups (call *yakuza*) serve as substitutes for lawyers and courts:

> For their part, the yakuza have been able to work their way into legitimate society by offering their services for resolving disputes where no other efficient means exists. While Americans enjoy access to the courts to resolve disputes, in Japan litigation is almost unheard of because it is so expensive, time-consuming (cases can take 10 years and more) and rarely produces results that challenge the status quo. Therefore, to collect on an overdue loan, you can hire a member of a yakuza group to stand outside the home of the debtor and hurl obscenities and insults until the debtor caves in. Disputed traffic accidents are handled at times by one party hiring a mobster to intimidate the other into agreeing to a resolution.

Little wonder, then, that "Japan Inc." clings to its anti-litigation stance, under the guise of preventing its culture from becoming adulterated by Western (particularly American) notions of justice. But there are encouraging signs of change. At this writing, the Japanese legislature, responding to consumer pressure, is considering enactment of the nation's first strict product liability statute. During the 1980s, a few consumers braved the rigged legal system to press suits for injuries caused by defective products. An article in the March 9, 1992 edition of *Business Week* told the story of Chisao Kaji, a resident of Osaka, whose Sharp television set caught fire and burned down his house. His daughter was overcome by the fumes and died. Mr. Kaji sued Sharp for $176,000, claiming that the faulty design of the TV caused the fatal fire. Sharp declined comment, but it recalled 48,000 TVs after receiving 18 more reports of fires. While Mr. Kaji may have to tough it out on the obstacle course that is the Japanese legal system, his bravery has already saved other consumers from the tragic fate of his daughter.

A Job for the American Equalizers

How can American lawyers help to spread the equal justice part of the American Dream to Japan and the rest of the world?

First, by continuing to set the humanitarian example in American courts. There is evidence that American principles of compensation eventually spread to other civilized nations. For example, in 1985 the Council of the European Communities issued a directive ordering each member nation to adopt a statute establishing strict liability for product defects, following the American principles that we discussed in Chapter 12. Prior to this directive, it was a herculean task to prove fault on the part of a manufacturer in any British or European court. Great Britain adopted the directive in the Consumer Protection Act of 1987, and most of the other EC members have put it into effect as well. Thus, in addition to Britain, the consumers of Belgium, Denmark, France, Germany, Greece, Ireland, Italy, Luxembourg, the Netherlands, Portugal, and Spain will soon be protected by strict product liability. Since at least 12 other nations are pressing to join the EC, it is likely that strict product liability will extend to all of European civilization before long. Other American innovations, such as specialization in tort practice and expertise in the psychological aftermath of injuries, are slowly but surely making their way into foreign legal systems, so that there has been a general world-wide rise in accident compensation beyond the basic rate of inflation. But much more needs to be done before there is real enforcement of the Adequate Award principle that is embodied in the laws of all civilized nations.

The importance of the American example was pointed out by University of Wisconsin Law Professor Marc Galanter in a 1992 article:

> America is a highly legalized society that relies on law and courts to do many things that other industrial democracies do differently. But it is worth recalling that one realm in which the United States has remained the leading exporter is what we might call the technology of doing law—constitutionalism, judicial enforcement of rights, the organization of law firms, alternative dispute resolution, public interest law. For all their admitted flaws, American legal institutions provide influential (and sometimes inspiring) models for governance of business transactions, the processing of disputes, and the protection of citizens.

Second, in addition to providing examples, we can try to actively assist the Pannone Napiers and potential Equalizers in other countries to establish contingent fees and jury trials, or to find other ways to gain real access to justice for the great majority of their people who have never had that privilege. As Rodger Pannone is fond of saying, "The English system of justice, like the Ritz Hotel, is open to everyone." We need not press for carbon copies of the American system. Our "no-win, no-pay" percentage fee is not the only way. What is needed is a fee system that gives lawyers the opportunity to be paid in proportion to the benefits they obtain for their clients, and thus provides the basis for accumulation of the resources needed to become entrepreneurs and Equalizers. Likewise, trial by jury is not required if another way can be found to raise awards to the level of real compensation, although juries are preferable because they also provide the opportunity for citizens to participate in democracy in a way that is sometimes more meaningful than voting for one or another of the established political parties.

Third, we can press our American courts to keep jurisdiction of cases in which foreign victims seek compensation from American companies for injuries inflicted by defective American products or services. There is an understandable tendency on the part of overworked judges to reduce their calendars by granting *forum non conveniens* dismissals in cases with foreign aspects, even when the plaintiffs are Americans, as we saw in the Yukon case. Given the crushing burden of criminal trials and budget shortages, it will not be easy to convince our judges that they should make extra efforts to keep our courts open to foreigners—even those who have legitimate reasons for suing in America. While allowing foreigners to participate has always been a part of the American Dream, many judges feel that they have their hands full just keeping the courts going for local citizens, leaving no time for esoteric notions such as fulfilment of the American Dream. More tangible reasons for keeping the cases here can be furnished by the two projects that we discussed in Chapter 14: Demonstrating that civil litigation is already an important source of revenue for the forum community, and working for enactment of taxes on successful lawsuits that will be dedicated to financing the court system. While these projects are needed to keep American courts functioning properly for our own citizens, they can also furnish increased revenue for the forum court in cases brought here by foreign citizens.

Finally, in cases where American judges turn their backs on justice and the American Dream by finding that it is more convenient for American companies to be sued in foreign countries, we can follow the example of Tim Cook and the Law of the Yukon. We can stay with those cases and conduct discovery against the American companies here, because the orders granting forum dismissals often condition such transfers on the defendants' agreement to submit to American-type discovery even after the case is refiled in the foreign country. Then we can work with the foreign lawyers to achieve the best possible result in their courts, hoping that the example of American discovery and the potential application of other aspects of American law to the American defendants will produce more just awards than would occur in an ordinary case that has no American dimension.

After all, why should British (or French or Japanese) victims of American companies receive less compensation from their own courts than American victims would receive in American courts, especially since the same liability insurance policies cover the claims of both the American and foreign victims? Why shouldn't damages be assessed according to the law of the place where the wrongdoing occurred, in order to deter such conduct in the future? Why shouldn't the American level of damages be the world standard, since it alone is high enough to provide compensation and deterrence? And why shouldn't other democracies place the same high value on life and limb as Americans do? Indeed, why shouldn't they enforce their own law, which mandates full reparation for accident victims?

Access to Justice in the New World Order

Eventually, the empowerment of Frank Capra's "little pushed-around guy" through the American Equalizers, as seen on television and in other media, will create a demand for similar access to justice throughout the world. As noted, the European Community has taken a long step in that direction with its imposition of strict product liability. The emergence of the EC, the internationalization of business through interlocking ownerships and global marketing, the toppling of the Berlin Wall, and the collapse of communism, herald the coming of a New World Order based upon a democratic, market-oriented socio-political system. In a 1992 article, George Washington University Professor William Halal observed:

> The biggest event of our time is that unprecedented advances in computerization, telecommunications, and other forms of information technology are integrating the entire globe into a single, highly sophisticated economic-political system. Lech Walesa grasped intuitively the underlying force that powered the revolution he merely guided in Poland: "How did all these reforms appear?" he asked rhetorically, "The result of computers, communication satellites, television."

New York Times commentator R.W. Apple Jr. described the August 1991 coup attempt that Boris Yeltsin thwarted as "a vivid demonstration of the power of global communications to shape the world." Apple wrote that the moral support Russia received from the United States, Great Britain, and Germany

> ...was reinforced by the image of Russian Republic President Boris Yeltsin spouting defiance from the top of a Soviet tank— one of those emblematic moments that television can burn into the world's consciousness. In addition, modern communications obviously played a major part over the past six years in planting the seeds of democracy, much more deeply than many had thought possible before this week, in the hitherto stony soil of Russia, with its long history of tyranny. When the test came, Soviet citizens in the hundreds of thousands exposed themselves to danger to defend abstract ideals many had learned of by radio and television.

At the same time, the editorial page of the *Wall Street Journal* spoke of a New World Order that would lead to a well-integrated world:

The significance of what the world just watched in Moscow is immense. It is in all likelihood the most important thing that has happened in the world since 1945. Indeed, it is probably the end of an era that started with the assassination of Archduke Ferdinand at Sarajevo in 1914. This will mark the end of attempts to remake the world through military power; instead, ballots won. Now mankind is at last free to construct a new world order.

Following dissolution of the Soviet Union, Yeltsin soon found that Russia and the other republics were in urgent need of a legal system that was compatible with democracy. No such framework was left by the Soviet Union, which was built upon the rule of tyrants rather than the rule of law. Along with shortages of food and technology, the Russians had no more than 10 percent of the lawyers and judges they now needed. Quickly they turned to the United States for help. The American Bar Association, American judges and lawyers responded enthusiastically. As ABA President Sandy D'Alemberte reported in 1992:

> In Moscow, our delegation found an eagerness among Russian officials for technical cooperation in virtually every aspect of their emerging legal system. This technical-assistance challenge would overwhelm the legal profession of any single nation except the United States. Our 750,000 lawyers, 175 accredited law schools, extensive court system, numerous bar and other legal organizations are an immense source of technical assistance to Russian reformers.

The New World Order will increase the importance and power of the business enterprise, which will create the need for new safeguards against the well-known proclivity of business to trample on individual rights. These safeguards may take the form of bureaucracies, as in the collectivist systems, or empowerment of the individual, as in the United States. Since collectivist solutions have been found wanting, it appears likely that individual empowerment will become more prevalent. Ultimately, if the New World Order is to remain democratic and true to free-market principles, it will require forces like the Equalizers all over the world to assure individual empowerment through equal access to justice. Just as the television-inspired Russian people turned back the KGB thugs, so will the Japanese people some day throw off the Yakuza thugs who serve as a substitute for access to Japanese courts.

There are many critics of America's "litigious society," both at home and abroad. The Equalizers are prominent symbols of that society, especially targeted because they profit by (relieving) other peoples' misery. But in the end the critics are unable to suggest any better method of balancing the scales of justice in a free-market society than by providing enough financial incentives for lawyers to make themselves into Equalizers. ABA President Sandy D'Alemberte, in a 1992 speech responding to lawyer-bashing by Dan Quayle and business interests, said:

> If U.S. lawyers are the problem, then why are the emerging democracies in Central and Eastern Europe clamoring for our help to establish their new legal systems? After generations of living under the thumb of government, with no redress in courts, they are seeking a better way to protect the rights of individuals against harmful actions by government and business. They are seeking enforceable rights, with independent courts as the last line of defense.

D'Alemberte might have added that the World Bank has begun to condition development loans to poor nations on the presence of sufficient private lawyers to assure the proper functioning of a free-market economic system.

The global demand for Equalizers is building right now. For better or worse, the world is awash in American pop culture. *L.A. Law* is popular throughout the world, translated into a dozen languages and showing in more than 30 countries. The real-life McKenzie Brackmans in those countries, whether called Pannone Napier or D'Artagnan Zola, are not far behind.

CHAPTER 17

The Faulty Falcon

Up to this point I have tried to tell the story of how the Equal-izers changed things in the courts, and how this relates to the American Dream. You are probably aware that these changes have not been received warmly by all sectors of our society. Rather than cluttering up the running story with ideological wrangles about the pros and cons of these changes, I have left them for this last chapter. Here we will consider the charges made by various groups and individuals that the "liability explosion" is harmful to the country and should be curbed by the legislatures and the courts. Because I have been involved in some of these events, I do not feel that I can discuss them dispassionately, and so I have appointed a spokesman for each side.

Representing the Equalizers will be Humphrey Bogart. His opponent, by far the heavyweight of the two, will be Sydney Greenstreet. Our moderator will be John Huston, who directed Bogart and Greenstreet in the filming of Dashiell Hammett's *The Maltese Falcon*.

That 1941 Warner Brothers film marked Huston's debut as a director and Greenstreet's first movie role after a long stage ca-reer during which he performed most notably in the Shakespear-ean theatre and in plays with Alfred Lunt and Lynn Fontanne. For Bogart, it was his first major role as a sympathetic character after playing assorted criminals in dozens of films. It was in the Sam Spade role that Bogart found the screen image he would use for the rest of his career: a tough, world-weary loner with a personal code of honor. It was the third movie version of the *Falcon* story, the first two being disastrous flops in which teams of Hollywood screenwriters managed to mutilate Hammett's classic novel beyond recognition. John Huston wrote the screen-play for the 1941 version. When he read the Hammett book he decided that it was almost a perfect screenplay in itself—not only the plot, but the style and dialogue as well. By following Hammett's star, he created a film masterpiece out of what Warner Brothers thought would be just another detective story B-movie.

Let us assume that Sydney Greenstreet has been hired as a spokeman for the insurance companies, manufacturers, and other business interests who are pushing "tort reform," meaning intervention by Congress and the state legislatures to change the rules on how the courts handle tort cases; and that Humphrey Bogart is speaking for the plaintiff's tort lawyers of America, as well as the consumer and labor organizations that are opposed to legislation that would restrict access to the courts or change the rules on how damages are assessed. (If anything about this choice of spokesmen bothers you, feel free to reverse their roles or pencil in your own spokespersons.)

Greenstreet and Bogart are seated at a circular table facing John Huston, the moderator, as he begins the televised discussion.

MODERATOR HUSTON: Good afternoon, gentlemen. We are here to discuss the American system of tort law—that is, the way in which our courts determine whether there is legal responsibility for injuries, and if so, how much should be paid in compensation. When I say "injuries" I include fatalities as well. We have all seen in the media charges that our tort system is suffering from a "liability explosion," perhaps as part of a larger "litigation explosion" or as a by-product of an overly litigious society. There are charges that the courts are allowing too many people to recover too much money in personal injury and wrongful death cases, and that among other bad economic effects, this is putting American manufacturers at a competitive disadvantage against foreign manufacturers whose home court systems are not so liberal in handing out compensation. We are told that this imbalance is caused by greedy plaintiff's lawyers who are out to collect huge contingent fees—that is, fat percentages of the amounts awarded for compensation, and that the situation has become serious enough to require legislative restrictions. Mr. Greenstreet, since you are representing the people making these charges, would you please begin by explaining what they are based on?

MR. GREENSTREET (opening brief case and putting four books on the table): Most assuredly, sir, I shall be happy to do so. These findings that our tort system is in need of reform are based on detailed professional studies, such as those contained in these very well known and authoritative books. This one, for example, published in 1991, is entitled *The Litigation Explosion: What Happened when America Unleashed the Lawsuit.* It was written by a well-known expert, Walter K. Olson. And this one, *Liability: The*

Legal Revolution and its Consequences, written in 1988 by another renowned authority, Peter W. Huber. These books—

MR. BOGART: Just a minute, Sydney. Don't both of those writers work for the Manhattan Institute?

MR. GREENSTREET: Most assuredly they do, sir. That information appears right on the cover of each book.

MR. BOGART (*picking up the two books*): Yes, it does, Sydney, but neither book says what the Manhattan Institute is. They don't tell us that the Manhattan Institute for Policy Research is a right-wing think tank outfit, founded by Reagan's CIA director, William Casey, and that it's financed by business and insurance people who want to reduce the cost of liability insurance by limiting the amounts that victims can recover for their injuries. They even want to protect manufacturers of defective products—

MODERATOR HUSTON: Hold on, Mr. Bogart. Are you saying that just because these two authors—Walter Olson and Peter Huber—are employed by the Manhattan Institute, that their statements are not worthy of discussion?

MR. BOGART: No, John, don't get me wrong—I'm not saying that. But Sydney here is trying to pass off these two writers as disinterested professionals who have made some kind of impartial studies in the public interest, without telling us that their paychecks come from a think-tank that's supported by the companies that would benefit by making the taxpayers or the victims of accidents bear more of the costs.

MR. GREENSTREET (*picking up third book*): By gad, sir, I admire a man who comes right to the point! But I am speaking in the public interest, and to avoid any question of partiality, I put aside these two books that disturb you so much, and I move on to this one that I'm certain you'll accept as impartial.

MR. BOGART: What's this one, Sydney?

MR. GREENSTREET: This, sir, is the famous book, *Straight Shooting: What's Wrong with America and How to Fix It*, authored by the renowned president of Boston University, Dr. John Silber. He has held that lofty position since 1970, and is one of the highest paid and most admired of our university presidents. And in 1990, he won the primary election to become the candidate of the Democratic Party for governor of Massachusetts. I take it, sir, you will concede that such a man is not beholden to the insurance or business interests that you mention, and that he can hardly be tainted with conservative political credentials?

MR. BOGART: Oh, all right, Sydney, I'll concede that. And what bright ideas does he have about the tort system?

MR. GREENSTREET: In point of fact, sir, much of what Dr. Silber says in his chapter on "The Litigious Society" coincides precisely with the views of the two experts from the Manhattan Institute whose books you do not care to discuss. Let me read you just a few pertinent lines:

> ...the high costs of defending against a product liability suit—costs often measurable in millions of dollars and hundreds of man-years—force many companies to succumb to legalized extortion. Though clearly in the right, a company may offer a plaintiff a large out-of-court settlement—choosing to make a legalized payoff rather than face the staggering costs of winning its case. In contrast, many of our strongest international competitors are protected in their own country by severe legal limits placed on product liability. Many of them—the Japanese in particular—have resisted becoming lawyer-driven societies like our own. American firms, burdened with the increasing costs of product liability, are finding it more and more difficult to compete effectively in the international marketplace.

MR. BOGART: Sydney, when you read rattle-brained stuff like that, I begin to understand how Silber managed to lose the election for governor as the Democratic candidate in an overwhelmingly Democratic state. Yes, he did swallow the line put out by the Manhattan Institute boys, but he didn't understand the gibberish he was parroting. Some political advisor probably told him he could gain votes by attacking lawyers, because most voters trust lawyers about as much as used car salesmen.

MODERATOR HUSTON: That's a pretty strong denunciation, Mr. Bogart. Do you have some facts to back it up?

MR. BOGART: I certainly do, John. Silber says that the high costs of defending lawsuits force many companies to succumb to "legalized extortion." Everything about that charge is ridiculous. First of all, strict product liability applies only to *defective* products. In fact, the major cases are based on products so defective that they had to be recalled by the manufacturer. Second, the manufacturers do not defend product liability cases. They carry liability insurance, and it's the insurance companies that defend in court and decide when and if to settle, and how much to pay in settlement. They're in the business of defending claims, and their annual profit is based on how little they pay out for settlements and verdicts. If they decide to settle, they're making an expert business judgment that a jury and a series of reviewing judges will find the product defective. They settle only at levels that make business sense. If the claimants won't settle for a reasonable fraction of the probable court award, the insurance companies will force them to go to trial. It doesn't take a university president to figure out who has the most muscle when it comes to a court battle: the individual claimant, who might be anything from a school kid to an old widow, or the multi-billion dollar insurance company with its full-time staff of high-powered defense lawyers.

MR. GREENSTREET: You amaze me, sir. Don't you agree that it is legalized extortion when a company pays a large out-of-court settlement even though clearly in the right?

MR. BOGART: No, it's not extortion, Sydney, it's insanity. If an insurance company makes a settlement on behalf of a manufacturer who is "clearly in the right," the insurance company's management should be fired. If the manufacturer is in the right, it means the product is not defective. If the insurer settles one claim for a product that is not defective, that payment will attract many more such claims—maybe thousands of them. It's much cheaper to fight the first few claims, and show the world that the plaintiffs can't prove the product is defective. The legal expenses of fighting a few unfounded claims will be far lower than paying out hundreds or thousands of unjustified settlements for products that are not defective. The plaintiff's lawyers don't get paid for losing cases. They're not going to take on cases in which they can't prove that the product was defective. By the way, Sydney, does Silber give any examples of settlements paid when the manufacturer was "clearly in the right?"

MR. GREENSTREET: Dr. Silber is a renowned philosopher who has been compared to the immortal Sir Thomas More. He lays down basic principles in his book, and is not concerned with minute details.

MODERATOR HUSTON (picking up the Silber book): I notice, Mr. Greenstreet, that Dr. Silber's book contains many technical notes giving sources for various statements, but none regarding any settlements paid for products made by companies that were "clearly in the right." But let's get back to Dr. Silber's charge that the burden of product liability suits has made it more difficult for American manufacturers to compete in the international marketplace. How do you respond to that, Mr. Bogart?

MR. BOGART: Again, Silber is all wet. If he was right, then consumers in Japan, Germany, and other countries would enjoy many useful products that are not available here—but he doesn't mention one, because there are none. And he doesn't name a single American company that is unable to compete internationally because of product liability costs. First of all, Japanese manufacturers who sell their products in the United States by the millions are subject to the same product liability laws as American companies. Some of them, like Toyota, have set up plants right in the United States. But whether the Toyota is made in Japan or in Kentucky, Toyota can be sued here under American law for any damages caused by a defective product. Yet the foreign manufacturers are selling so many of their products here that we have a trade imbalance of over $100 billion a year. They have to carry the same insurance as American companies to protect against product liability suits. If their insurance premiums are lower, it's because their products don't have as many defects as American products do.

MODERATOR HUSTON: Then how do you explain our loss of markets, Mr. Bogart?

MR. BOGART: In a nutshell? American manufacturers are losing out because their products are lousy. Just look at the markets for television sets and microchips. Those products don't cause injuries and so they don't even involve product liability claims, but American manufacturers have lost the market to foreign companies who simply make the products better at lower prices. In the competition to sell TVs, VCRs, and microchips, our manufacturers have not only lost out in overseas markets, but they've lost most of our own domestic sales as well. Ever tried to buy a TV set that was made in America?

MR. GREENSTREET: Well, sir, are you aware that no less an authority than President George Bush's Council on Competitiveness blames product liability cases and other litigation expenses for our competitive disadvantage in world markets? Indeed, sir, in their 1991 report, the president's council concludes, "In a survey of over 250 American companies, more than three-quarters of the executives said they believe that the United States will be increasingly disadvantaged in world markets unless modifications are made in the liability system."

MR. BOGART (laughing): You're good—you're very good! You're passing off that report as George Bush's work, but you know very well that the so-called "President's Council on Competitiveness" is headed up by that great legal authority, Vice-President J. Danforth Quayle! That means the business and insurance lobbyists can write anything they want into the Council's reports.

MR. GREENSTREET: By gad, sir, you are a character! Surely you are aware that Mr. Quayle is himself a lawyer?

MR. BOGART: Oh, yes, Sydney, Dan Quayle certainly is a lawyer. Nobody can challenge his dedication to the law. He even gave up the chance to serve in Viet Nam so he could go to law school!

MODERATOR HUSTON: Gentlemen, it seems immaterial whether Dan Quayle is a lawyer. The important point is that the Council that he heads is making the claim that liability suits are hurting America's competitiveness. What proof does his Council submit on that point?

MR. BOGART: They submit no proof, because there is none. For the great majority of American manufacturers, liability insurance costs amount to less than one percent of total expenses. If a particular company has a product liability problem, it's because they put out a defective product that injures people. Does Quayle really expect Americans to throw away their legal rights in order to protect the manufacturers of defective American products? Does he really think that these defective American products will then sweep the world's markets, in competition with the higher quality products made by foreign manufacturers? The whole competitiveness issue is a phony, a setup if I ever saw one.

MR. GREENSTREET: And who, sir, is being set up? Could you possibly be upset because your benefactors may lose out on some juicy legal fees if the laws are changed to restore American competitiveness?

MR. BOGART: The people who lose their legs, or their eyesight—the parents whose children suffer brain damage, the women whose husbands are killed, because a manufacturer is greedy and irresponsible enough to keep a defective product on the market—that who's being set up! I wonder if Quayle and his Council have thought about the loss of competitiveness that these victims suffer. They can't even compete for menial jobs if they're crippled by defective products. But instead of trying to make their products safe, our manufacturers are spending time and money to lobby Quayle's Council, as well as Congress and the state legislatures, for laws that will subsidize their defective products. If they spent some of that time and money making good products, their competition problems could be solved. Instead, they want their injured victims to bear the cost of their lousy defective products—and then, before you know it, the taxpayers will be picking up the tab for the victims' medical and welfare expenses!

[John Huston's father, Walter Huston, enters the scene, dressed as a merchant ship's captain. He is carrying a small package wrapped in newspapers and string. He staggers over to the table and puts the

package down in front of Humphrey Bogart. Then he tap-dances his way out of the scene.]

MODERATOR HUSTON: Sorry, gentlemen, he's always trying to build up his part.

MR. GREENSTREET: Pray tell, Mr. Bogart, what have you got there?

MR. BOGART (opening the package to reveal a foot-high statue of a bird): If you'll stop salivating, Sydney, you'll recognize this as the Mark III Falcon, manufactured by Filmland Falcons of Hollywood, California. It sells for $20,000, and is supposed to be gold-plated and encrusted with jewels from head to foot. You'll notice that the cheap imitation gold plating is peeling off, and many of the "jewels" have fallen out of their holes. The jewels that managed to stay in place are nothing but glass. Suppose, Sydney, that you paid $20,000 for this Mark III, relying on the ad that said it was gold-plated and encrusted with jewels. If your lawyer told you that you could get your 20 grand back because this bird is defective, what would you do?

MR. GREENSTREET: Really, sir, I don't see what this cheap little trick has to do with our serious discussion!

MR. BOGART: Sorry to bring back painful memories, Sydney, but I am making a serious point here. I'll assume that you and many other people who bought this faulty falcon would demand their money back, and their lawyers would collect it for them if the manufacturer, Filmland Falcons, refused to refund it. This would cause heavy legal expenses for the manufacturer. There is a company in Malta called Trusty Falcons, Ltd., that puts out a similar model which *is* gold-plated and encrusted with real jewels that don't fall out. Their falcon also sells for $20,000. Now, Filmland Falcons has its Washington lobbyist get in touch with Dan Quayle's Council. As you know, Quayle's Council works in secret and is accessible to business lobbyists through the back door. It's not hampered by the red tape you find in other government agencies, such as public hearings and the need to listen to both sides. They don't even disclose the names of any people or organizations whom they spoke to. So Filmland's lobbyist privately tells Quayle's Council that Filmland Falcons can't compete with Trusty Falcons of Malta because the "defect" claims of American buyers are causing intolerable legal costs which the Malta company does not have to face. Now, what should Quayle tell this lobbyist? Should he have the Council support legislation that would prevent the American buyers from suing to get their money back if they bought defective Mark III's? Or should Quayle tell the lobbyist that his client had better try to compete by taking their lousy defective falcon off the market and replacing it with a product that delivers as advertised?

MR. GREENSTREET *(chuckling):* Really, sir, your little fairy tale has nothing whatever to do with the need to curb runaway liability suits!

MR. BOGART: Oh, yes, it does, Sydney! Suppose we put aside the falcon and replace it with products that were the subject of real-life lawsuits: say, contaminated surgical bandages, or the birth control device that destroys women's insides, or the construction material that fills homes with formaldehyde. These are defective products that not only cheat the buyers when they don't perform as advertised—they also cause injuries and deaths. Are you saying that Quayle should step in and try to protect the markets for those defective products that are *more dangerous* than the Mark III Falcon, by making the injured victims give up their legal rights?

MR. GREENSTREET: By gad, sir, you persist in mixing apples with oranges!

MR. BOGART: Get this straight, Sydney: I'm mixing your right to get back the $20,000 you paid for a defective product, which is a property right, with the personal rights of people to be compensated for injuries caused by a defective product. If a defective airliner crashed into this building, you wouldn't hesitate a minute to make the manufacturer pay $300 million to replace the building. Suppose 300 passengers were killed in the crash. Are you telling me that our economy can't afford the $300 million it would take to compensate their families? Sooner or later, our legal system has to give personal rights the same protection as property rights.

MR. GREENSTREET: You speak as if the Council is advocating that all rights to sue for product liability be extinguished. In point of fact, sir, the Council is only concerned with bringing product liability costs of American manufacturers down to the lower level of costs enjoyed by foreign competitors.

MR. BOGART: The only way they can do that is by cutting down the compensation paid to victims of defective American products. Take this family *(showing photograph)* that lost its breadwinner when the husband was killed in a plane crash caused by a defective engine. That left a widow and four young children on their own. Now, let's say that you cut back their compensation by half. Which two children would you allow to go to college? And here's another victim of the same crash *(picking up another photograph)*. This fellow survived but was badly burned. Both of his ears were burned off. Now, Sydney, which—

MODERATOR HUSTON: I think you've made your point, Mr. Bogart. Do you know of any authoritative reports that contradict the Quayle Council's conclusions about the impact of liability costs on our competitiveness?

MR. BOGART: I sure do, John. There are dozens of detailed reports about the reasons for our loss of competitiveness, but none of them mention liability suits. For example, there's the federal government's own 1990 study, *Making Things Better*, conducted by the non-partisan Congressional Office of Technology Assessment. There's the widely-read Tom Peters books on the *excellence* that we need to become competitive again. There are studies of leading American companies that are competitive— 1991 books like *Quality or Else*, by Lloyd Dobyns and Clare Crawford-Mason, and *Beyond Quality*, by Jerry Bowles and Joshua Hammond. There's the 1991 study of "The Quality Imperative" by *Business Week* magazine. They say that the key to competitiveness is quality. Unlike Dan Quayle's group, they don't find any connection between legislation protecting defective products and the regaining of American competitiveness.

MR. GREENSTREET: Of course, sir, you can find books written by individuals who will take almost any point of view, no matter how ridiculous. Surely you would not equate these individual writings to the findings of a large group of experts like the President's Council on Competitiveness?

MR. BOGART: Well, Sydney, since you asked, let me give you two groups of qualified experts who found no connection between liability for defective products and competitiveness. Long before Quayle got into the act, Ronald Reagan appointed the President's Commission on Industrial Competitiveness, headed by John Young, the chief executive of Hewlett-Packard, one of America's most competitive manufacturers. There were 30 people on that commission—business leaders, government officials, university presidents. They looked at competitiveness from every angle, including the legal system. They made some suggestions about the patent and anti-trust laws, but nobody mentioned product liability.

MODERATOR HUSTON: When did they report to President Reagan, and what did they recommend to improve competitiveness?

MR. BOGART: They issued a two-volume report, *Global Competition*, in 1985. They said we needed to create and apply new technologies; develop a more skilled, flexible, and motivated work force; reduce the cost of capital; and make trade a national priority. Then a few years later, Massachusetts Institute of Technology set up its own commission that reached pretty much the same conclusions. The 16 MIT professors said in their 1989 report, *Made in America*, that the problem "is manifested by sluggish productivity growth and shortcomings in the quality and innovativeness of the nation's products." They looked into the underlying causes for two years, and not one of them even mentioned product liability.

MR. GREENSTREET: But you will concede, sir, that the United States has the strictest product liability laws in the world?

MR. BOGART: I will concede that our strict liability for defective products is the bellwether for the world, and is now being copied by other countries. For example, the European Community adopted a regulation that requires all of its 12 countries to install strict liability for defective products. The main purpose of the European Community is to improve the economic competitiveness of the member countries. So, unlike Dan Quayle, they don't see any connection between strict liability for defective products and loss of competitiveness. And remember that two vital ingredients are needed for strict product liability: number one, a defective product; and number two, injury caused by that product.

MODERATOR HUSTON: You've said that several times, Mr. Bogart.

MR. BOGART: I have to keep repeating it because Sydney—and his friends, Silber and Quayle—never use either word, "defective" or "injury." They try to make product liability look like some kind of a game that lawyers play for their own good. It's a different picture when you include those two little words.

MR. GREENSTREET: By gad, sir, I'd like to see you try to wriggle out of this one! Are you aware that product liability suits have virtually destroyed the American small airplane industry? American manufacturers shipped only 608 single-engine piston-powered planes in 1990, compared to over 14,000 shipped in 1978. Cessna stopped making small planes in 1986. Piper went into bankruptcy in 1991. And all this happened for one reason: product liability costs jumped from $24 million for the whole industry in 1977, to a colossal $210 million in 1985. Today, the cost of liability insurance for each airplane manufactured far exceeds the costs of all the labor and materials that go into the building of the plane. Do you deny any of these facts, sir?

MR. BOGART: For once, Sydney, all your figures are right. But again, all those costs are caused by products that have been found defective by juries. Each jury's finding is reviewed by the trial judge, who will throw it out if it isn't supported by legal evidence. Many of these cases go on to the appeals courts, and anywhere from three to ten more judges review the findings of defects. So here you have a whole industry that was turning out defective products. Unlike television sets, defective airplanes cause terrible injuries. You don't always walk away from airplane accidents—you could get killed. This is also a field in which very few products were sold even in the good years— 14,000 planes compared with millions of TV sets. When you have a small output that's capable of doing a lot of damage, you're going to have high insurance costs for defective products.

MODERATOR HUSTON: Do you mean to say that the entire industry is incapable of turning out small airplanes that are not defective?

MR. BOGART: That's what they seem to be telling us, because they're demanding legislation that will take away the right to sue them for the damage done by defective products. I'm sure that American ingenuity will revive this industry sooner or later. There's still a large potential market here, and it's not going to be filled by foreign manufacturers because they're subject to the same strict liability for defective airplanes that they sell in the United States. We've had problems like this before. During World War II, our sources of natural rubber were cut off, but we developed synthetic rubber which is even better than the natural kind, and now most of the market is supplied by synthetic rubber even though natural rubber is available again. And our auto manufacturers were pressed to improve gas mileage in the 1970s, so they replaced $300 carburetors with $25 computerized fuel injectors, and they doubled the gas mileage. This is part of what the experts call the "technology gap" that drives us to improve standards of living and safety. The automobile manufacturers screamed that safety rules would hurt their sales, but now they're competing to see who can spend the most money advertising safety features like airbags to *boost* their sales. Sydney's people claim that product liability suits stifle innovation, but here the lawsuits have created a huge demand for innovative airplanes, which will bring new factories, new jobs, and legitimate new fortunes for American entrepreneurs.

MODERATOR HUSTON: How can the small plane manufacturers close their technology gap?

MR. BOGART: They could start by going all-out to investigate potential breakthroughs. For example, our military forces have pushed parachute technology to the point where they can drop trucks and even tanks by parachute. This technology can be adapted to installing parachutes on light planes that will allow the whole plane to come down safely in an emergency. There are airplane chutes on the market that weigh only 25 pounds and cost only $3,000, and have already saved dozens of pilots who paid to have them installed in their own planes. But apparently the lightplane manufacturers would rather sulk about the legal system than take advantage of this opportunity for innovation.

MR. GREENSTREET: And while we're waiting for this parachute fantasy of yours to float out of the sky, sir, you will note that thousands of jobs have been destroyed in Kansas, Pennsylvania, and Florida, where we used to have thriving factories turning out light planes.

MR. BOGART: Yes, that's regrettable. But many of those skilled workers were in demand for other jobs, and thousands of new jobs will be created when the light-plane manufacturers wise up and close the technology gap.

MODERATOR HUSTON: I remember that when Vice-President Quayle presented the report of the President's Council on Competitiveness at the 1991 American Bar Association convention, he got a lot of public support for his position that we had too many lawyers and too many lawsuits. In fact, it's the first issue that he seemed to get public support on. Can you explain that, Mr. Bogart?

MR. BOGART: You and I both have had unpleasant times with mouthpieces, John, in our divorce cases. Most people hate lawyers because the lawyers who oppose them have the power to hurt them financially, or take their children away, or put them in jail. In the process, lawyers are always questioning whatever people say, trying to make them look like liars because that's the lawyers' job under the adversary system. Any politician can get a cheap laugh or a standing ovation by bashing lawyers in general. But you'll notice that fictional lawyers who can't hurt us, like the characters in L.A. Law and other TV shows, have become our folk heroes.

MODERATOR HUSTON: Do you think that dislike of real-life lawyers will ever change, Mr. Bogart?

MR. BOGART: No, John, I think it's human nature to hate lawyers. Litigation is an unpleasant experience and an unwelcome expense, even for the winners. And every case has a loser who's likely to blame both lawyers—his own and the other guy's. Business people especially hate tort lawyers because they provide what Ralph Nader calls "citizen oversight" of business operations. They resent this intrusion into the business power structure by mouthpieces for outsiders. But you won't find many accident victims who hate their lawyers, because those lawyers usually produce compensation without any outlay by the victims. Quayle spoke in generalities about the lawyers who file 18 million new lawsuits every year. But that 18 million total is mainly composed of cases like landlord squabbles with tenants, family fights over child custody and support payments, small claims, social security disputes, and that kind of stuff. Less than five percent of the 18 million new cases are tort claims, and that even includes minor fender-bender claims. Quayle didn't give any data showing that we had too many tort cases or too many tort lawyers. Actually the number of new tort cases filed increases only in proportion to the growth of our population.

MR. GREENSTREET: Well, sir, Mr. Quayle also pointed out that the United States, which has only five percent of the world's population, has over 70 percent of the world's lawyers. Do we really need 70 percent of the world's lawyers?

MR. BOGART: That 70 percent figure is right out of the Dan Quayle School of Jurisprudence. It's another phony that can't stand the light of day. As a matter of fact, the United States ranks 35th on the list of lawyers per 10,000 population, if you include all the people in other countries who hold law degrees and do legal work even if they are not licensed to appear in court. Most other countries do not require lawyers to pass bar exams like we do, but most of them have far more lawyers per capita. Besides, most American lawyers spend their time prosecuting or defending criminal cases, or enforcing government regulations, or helping business try to avoid taxes or government regulation, rather than handling tort cases.

MR. GREENSTREET: Are you actually claiming that Japan has as many lawyers per capita as the United States?

MR. BOGART: They have *more*, Sydney—31.71 per 10,000 to our 28.45 per 10,000, to be exact. I know that your friend Silber describes Japan as a society that is not "lawyer-driven," but as usual he hasn't done his homework. Right now, in fact, Japan has far more law students than we do—about 159,000 to our 120,000—even though their population is less than half of ours. Most of these law students go into legal jobs with corporations and the government, but the Japanese don't call them lawyers. Japan is crawling with people doing the work of lawyers, but only a handful of them are allowed to represent people in court.

MR. GREENSTREET: Very agile, sir! You've dodged my question by talking about bureaucrats and paper-pushers instead of lawyers who sue people. Why do we need such a high percentage of the world's lawyers who are licensed to sue?

MR. BOGART: We do need a healthy percentage of those who can represent people in court, Sydney, because our brand of freedom puts much more demand on our legal system than you get in other countries. We have a long tradition of access to the courts by everyone, and we believe in settling our disputes fairly. The Soviet Union didn't need many lawyers because there wasn't much for them to do. Their people had no access to justice. Let me read you this from the English news magazine *The Economist:* "Americans spend much time suing each other partly because their society, more than others, emphasizes individual rights and allows its citizens to test them in courts; people in many countries would die for the chance to be so litigious."

MODERATOR HUSTON: Do the ordinary people in other democracies have less access to the courts than Americans do?

MR. BOGART: Yes, John. Even in democratic countries, they rely more on social legislation which reduces everyone to the lowest common denominator. Here we believe in the free market, and the right of everyone to go to court if necessary to protect their rights. You do believe in the free market, don't you, Sydney?

MR. GREENSTREET: I most assuredly do, sir. But I fail to see the connection with the question of our having 70 percent of the world's lawyers. Are you aware, sir, that a 1991 poll in Michigan showed that 73 percent of the people felt we had too many lawyers, and that we didn't need anything like 70 percent of the world's lawyers?

MR. BOGART: Yes, that's one of those loaded questions that'll get you only one answer. The real question should be, "Are you willing to give up any of your legal rights in order to reduce the number of lawyers we have in America?" How many people would give you a "yes" answer to that one? If you're really a free-market man like you claim, you'll let the free market continue to decide how many lawyers we need. Nobody subsidizes our lawyers. They can't stay in business unless there's a real need for their services.

MR. GREENSTREET: But surely, sir, you have heard the story of the town that had only one lawyer, who barely eked out a living until a second lawyer moved there. Then both of them prospered handsomely, because they were able to stir up disputes that required legal services for both sides!

MR. BOGART: Yes, Sydney, I've heard that one. You don't happen to know the name of the town, do you? It must be called Stupidville, since it has a lot of people who can be talked into starting expensive lawsuits that they don't really need.

MODERATOR HUSTON: While we're on the subject of the free market, Mr. Greenstreet, how do you reconcile your support of tort reform—that is, government intervention to protect business interests—with your free-market principles?

MR. GREENSTREET: Even the strongest advocates of freedom from government intervention draw the line at extortion. Since the litigation explosion has reached the point of legalized extortion, government must step in because business is powerless to resist.

MR. BOGART: Oh, so we're back to Silber's heart-rending tale of extortion? The helpless insurance companies at the mercy of the powerful plaintiffs—

MODERATOR HUSTON: I think we've covered that, Mr. Bogart. While we're talking about Dr. Silber, is there anything else in his book that supports your position, Mr. Greenstreet?

MR. GREENSTREET: There most assuredly is, sir. He goes right to the heart of the matter by attacking contingent legal fees and the greedy lawyers who collect them. He writes:

> The argument is made—most often by the legal profession—
> that contingency fees are designed to help those who would
> otherwise be unable to afford the services of a lawyer. For the
> most part, however, the beneficiaries are not the needy but the
> lawyers and the greedy.

MR. BOGART: I don't even have to ask you, Sydney, whether Silber quotes any authority for that asinine statement. More than 9 million Americans suffer disabling injuries in accidents every year, and over 94,000 are killed in accidents. Silber brands most of them as greedy, without knowing the first thing about their injuries, their loss of income, their suffering, or how much compensation they actually receive. Apparently he thinks they are automatically greedy because they take advantage of the greatest bargain available in any market: the contingent fee which gives them the services of the best tort lawyers in the world without them laying out a cent of their own money. Would they be less greedy if they insisted on paying their lawyers by the hour, win or lose? Obviously, Silber doesn't have the slightest idea how few of them could afford to make claims if they couldn't get good lawyers to take their cases on contingent fees. Maybe he'd like it better if we had a system like the British Legal Aid, where the taxpayers foot the bill for civil cases brought by people who can't afford legal fees, and the lawyers get paid by the government whether they win or lose. Imagine how that would play out in the American political system!

MODERATOR HUSTON: I notice, Mr. Greenstreet, that Dr. Silber mentions "the greed of attorneys, especially underemployed attorneys who take their cases on contingency." Do you happen to know how he arrived at the conclusion that the attorneys who take contingent fees are "underemployed"?

MR. GREENSTREET: Perfectly simple logic, sir. It is apparent that the better class of lawyers, the real professionals, command regular fees regardless of the outcome, and do not become financial partners with their clients. Those who work on contingency must be desperate for work, and therefore are underemployed.

MR. BOGART (laughing): Oh, yes, Sydney, you're very good! First Silber says the plaintiff's lawyers are greedy, which means that they make more money than they need. How can they be greedy and underemployed at the same time? These poor, underemployed slobs are the same lawyers who Silber says are holding the giant manufacturers and insurance companies as hostages. And Quayle says these underemployed stiffs are keeping American industry from competing in world markets!

MODERATOR HUSTON: The word "greedy" seems to get quite a workout in these discussions. My dictionary defines it as "desiring more than one needs or deserves." How would you apply that definition to the controversy over the tort system, Mr. Bogart?

MR. BOGART: How much money does the accident victim need to put him back to where he was before the accident, as far as money can bring him back? That's up to the jury. If he asks for more than he deserves, he might lose the whole case and get nothing. The amount that the jury awards will be reviewed by the trial judge and by judges in the appeals courts, according to standards the courts have developed from handling millions of cases. In the end, the accident victim gets no more than he deserves, and often he's lucky to get that.

MODERATOR HUSTON: And the victim's lawyer?

MR. BOGART: Like just about everything else in this country that works, John, the tort lawyer's practice is driven by self-interest. He gets a percentage of what he recovers for the victim, usually about 33 percent. There's a free market for those services, and the victims can shop around for lower fees or even for non-contingent hourly fees if they would rather pay that way. Overhead expenses take up a good 50 percent of legal fees, and the lawyers have to lay out thousands of dollars for case expenses like investigation, expert witnesses' fees, and depositions. Close to half the cases that go to trial are won by the defendants, so the lawyers get no fees and usually they also lose the thousands they have invested in the case. So the lawyers get what they deserve too. If they were greedy—if they were getting more than they deserved—you'd see thousands of other lawyers use our free market to go into competition with them.

MR. GREENSTREET: Do you mean to say, sir, that if an injured person is awarded three million dollars, and the lawyer's take is one million dollars, that the lawyer is not being greedy?

MR. BOGART: That's exactly what I mean, Sydney. The injured person would not be "awarded" three million dollars without the lawyer. If the insurance companies paid out that kind of money without being forced to, they could put all the tort lawyers out of business overnight. To get that three million dollars requires education, skill, years of experience, and a big investment in the kind of legal clout that is strong enough to fight the giant insurers and their staffs of well-trained defense experts. If anybody's greedy or selfish here, it's the perpetrators who kill or maim the victims—the companies that collect money from the public for a service or a product that's shoddy or defective, and the reckless drivers who think only of themselves.

MR. GREENSTREET: Well, sir, pray tell us, if the glowing picture you paint for the contingent fee is accurate, why is it constantly under attack?

MR. BOGART: It's constantly being attacked by the insurance and business interests who would like to have accident victims at their mercy. They know that if they could somehow knock out the contingent fee, they could go about their business as they did in the nineteenth century, maiming and killing people without any cost. Sometimes the contingent fee is attacked by academics like Silber, who don't take the trouble to understand how crucial it is to equal justice under law. But you'll never see it attacked by the people who pay it: the victims who gladly give up a percentage of their compensation to get the best legal services available. Have you ever heard anybody squawk about paying a million dollar fee to a lawyer who won them a three million dollar settlement or verdict? And when foreigners are injured by an American company, they line up quickly to pay American contingent fees instead of the hourly fees that their local lawyers charge, because they know they'll do far better under the contingent fee system.

MR. GREENSTREET: I put it to you, sir, that the contingent-fee lawyer is no better than a bounty hunter!

MR. BOGART: I'm trying to keep this discussion on a high plane, Sydney, but I can't do that if you describe your own sponsors as criminals on the lam that have bounty hunters chasing after them.

MODERATOR HUSTON: Dr. Silber also writes, "An underemployed lawyer has every reason to pursue a case, for he puts at risk only his time, which by virtue of his underemployment has no commercial value. That is a risk insufficient to ensure sound judgment." Would both of you gentlemen please comment on that?

MR. BOGART: That makes as much sense as Silber's other rantings. Anybody who knows anything about tort law realizes that the effective plaintiff's lawyers are not underemployed. Even the newcomers and the lesser lights who have time on their hands can hardly afford to take on losing cases, because they get paid nothing and on top of that, they're out of pocket for hefty expenses. They'd soon be out of business unless they could actually intimidate the insurance companies into paying them for worthless cases. Don't you think the insurance lawyers can spot the underemployed stiffs with lousy cases? And why would the insurance companies settle worthless cases, when they have thousands of defense lawyers bidding for their business? For a few thousand dollars in legal fees, they can take those cases to trial and win them. They actually win about half the cases that go to trial, and that includes lots of legitimate claims that are just too hard for individuals to prove against big companies.

MR. GREENSTREET: Actually, Mr. Moderator, the statement you just read appears in the section of Dr. Silber's book in which he suggests that America should adopt the English rule of fee-shifting. That is, the loser should pay the winner's legal fees. As you know, sir, the American rule is that each side pays its own lawyers, win or lose. The English rule would restore some balance to our legal system by weeding out groundless suits which can be brought with impunity under the American rule. This is especially applicable to cases in which the plaintiff's lawyer acts on a contingent fee, so that the plaintiff has absolutely nothing to lose by pressing a groundless suit. Dr. Silber is joined in this position by the President's Council on Competitiveness, which concluded in 1991 that fee-shifting should be tried in certain federal court cases as an experiment that might lead to clearing up much of our court congestion.

MR. BOGART: Again comes the flim-flam, Sydney! The real purpose of fee-shifting is to limit access to the courts to those who can afford to pay whopping fees if the judgment goes against them. The English system came in handy for Captain Bob Maxwell, the world-class swindler, who automatically sued anyone who questioned his financial manipulations. Lots of people knew what he was up to years before his phony empire self-destructed, but they were afraid to speak out because he had enough of the public's money in his till to finesse the loser-pays rule and intimidate anyone who challenged him. Quayle simply wants to keep the courthouse doors closed to all but those who are rich enough to shrug off the fees of big-time law firms—like $200 to $400 an hour.

MODERATOR HUSTON: What about the claim that the English fee-shifting rule would clear up our court congestion problems, Mr. Bogart?

MR. BOGART: That's another phony argument, John. At least 95 percent of all tort cases are settled without trial now, so the loser-pays rule could only apply to the five percent of cases that are tried, because that's the only way you get a loser. It couldn't make any sizable dent in our civil court calendars. But the real problem is the 81 million criminal cases filed in our state courts each year. Less than a million tort cases were filed in 1990, and their total is expanding only in proportion to population growth. Besides, we already have the most reliable device for screening out frivolous claims: the contingent fee. Prosecuting frivolous claims on a contingent fee is the lawyer's quickest route to the poorhouse. And our courts already have the power to make the loser pay the winner's legal fees in irresponsible lawsuits that are designed for harassment. The English rule that would make the loser pay in every case is another Quayle-Silber red herring.

MR. GREENSTREET: A red herring, indeed, sir? Then how do you explain the fact that virtually every civilized nation has the loser-pays rule, so that the winner of the case is made financially whole when his legal position is vindicated?

MR. BOGART: Again, Sydney, only in America do we want our courts to be open to everyone who has been injured by someone else. Other countries are content to restrict litigation to the wealthy, but the people who built America didn't see it that way. Our Supreme Court rejected the loser-pays rule way back in 1796, and we've tried to keep our courts open to everyone since then.

MODERATOR HUSTON: Do you have anything more recent than 1796?

MR. BOGART: Sure, John. It comes up every 10 or 15 years, and the Supreme Court has always refused to go for it. The last time was in 1975, and the court stuck to its guns, saying that the American rule was deeply rooted in our history and in the congressional policy of keeping the courts open to everyone.

MODERATOR HUSTON: I think I interrupted you, Mr. Bogart.

MR. BOGART: Let me just finish off the English loser-pays rule by saying that it would keep millions of people from collecting valid claims. We'd wind up with some of the socialism that Britain had to substitute for access to the courts. The Consumers Union, which represents the broadest cross-section of Americans, said that Quayle's fee-shifting plan would produce "more uncompensated victims and few incentives to make safer products." Take asbestos as an example. The first few cases brought against the asbestos manufacturers were lost by the plaintiffs, because it took the plaintiffs' lawyers a long time to dig up the proof needed to win. After the first few losing cases, the plaintiffs' lawyers were able to prove that the manufacturers had known asbestos was dangerous for more than 30 years. If we had the English rule, those early losing plaintiffs would have been socked for the manufacturers' legal fees—millions of dollars— and nobody would have taken the chance of filing the second wave of suits which finally got the smoking-gun documents produced and took that killer product off the market. Furthermore, fee-shifting would bring millions of relatively trivial claims into our courts—claims where the liability is clear but the amount involved is too small to make it worthwhile to pay your own lawyer. You'd get a free ride if the other side has to pay, so why not sue? And once you sue, why should you settle at a reasonable discount if the other guy will be paying all the trial expenses?

MODERATOR HUSTON: Gentlemen, let's move on to another controversial subject: punitive damages. As I understand it, there are two types of damages in tort cases. Compensatory damages are designed to put the injured person back where he or she had been before the accident, to the extent that money can do this. They compensate for medical expenses, loss of bodily functions, lost income, physical and mental pain and suffering, and the like. Punitive damages, on the other hand, go beyond compensation to punish the defendant—to make an example of the defendant, which is why punitives are also known as exemplary damages. How do you justify this rather drastic remedy, Mr. Bogart?

MR. BOGART: Punitive damages are justified only in extreme cases, where the defendant's conduct is intentional or reckless, rather than merely negligent. Throughout our history, the courts have found that punitive damages are sometimes necessary to deter irresponsible conduct by the company being sued, and by others who will learn from the example.

MR. GREENSTREET: Punitive damages are nothing more than a windfall that is tacked on to the compensatory damages voted by the jury. Even in extreme cases, why should the plaintiff be the one to collect the punishment?

MR. BOGART: Because the plaintiff is the only one with the incentive and the resources to prove the case and collect punitive damages. The government has its hands full with criminal prosecutions and the uphill battle it is fighting to keep business on the level. Government agencies have little incentive and practically no resources for trying to collect punitive damages that arise out of tort cases. This was recognized way back in 1890, when the Sherman Antitrust Act was passed. Even though the government was given the power to send monopolists to jail and to hit them with heavy financial penalties, the Sherman Act also gave private citizens who were damaged by monopolists the right to sue for triple damages. There have been thousands of successful private antitrust suits. If we need private punitive suits to deter damage to businesses, imagine how much more we need them for damage to life and limb.

MODERATOR HUSTON: I understand some states now require that plaintiffs who collect punitive damages must share them with the state. For example, Florida provides that 40 percent of any punitive damage judgment be paid to a state agency. If all states adopted that principle, would that satisfy you as to the fairness of allowing private citizens to sue for punitive damages, Mr. Greenstreet?

MR. GREENSTREET: Certainly not, sir. It still amounts to a punishment without a crime. If the state charged a company with committing a crime, it would have to prove this beyond a reasonable doubt. But private citizens are allowed to exact these penalties under the standard for civil cases, a mere preponderance of the evidence, which can be as close as 51-to-49 percent.

MR. BOGART: History has shown us that this kind of punishment is needed to deter business from deliberately risking the lives and well-being of its victims. It's almost impossible to convict a company of a crime, and even if you do that, they usually get off with a small fine because the company is faceless and there is really no individual accountability. Many companies are willing to pay compensatory damages as a cost of doing business. Usually they can insure against compensatory damages cheaply enough so that they don't have to give a second thought to consumer safety—*unless* they have to worry about paying whopping punitive damages.

MR. GREENSTREET: How can you expect our businesses to operate when the standards for punitive damages are so vague? Do you realize that our 50 states have many different punitive damage standards, such as malice, reckless disregard of safety, fraud, spite, oppression, and despicable behavior?

MR. BOGART: All those standards are clear enough, Sydney. Business people know when they are deliberately putting the public at risk, no matter what label you put on it. Nobody whose motives are pure gets stuck for punitive damages. If a jury hangs a bad punitive damage rap on the defendant, the trial judge or the appeals judges will knock out that verdict.

MR. GREENSTREET: This is the only country in which jurors have unlimited power to punish businesses. They can, and often do, award millions of dollars in punitive damages, when the actual damage to the plaintiff may only be a few thousand dollars. Surely, sir, you cannot defend the placing of this unrestricted power in the hands of ordinary jurors?

MR. BOGART: The jury's award must be based on the facts of the case. They can't just sit there and write in whatever amount they'd like to sock the company for. The amount has to be an appropriate punishment for the irresponsible conduct involved. The jury is instructed to consider the degree of wantonness, the motives, and the other common sense factors that reasonable people would use to mete out fair punishment.

MR. GREENSTREET: Including the wealth of the defendant?

MR. BOGART: Of course, Sydney! How can you figure out how much to punish them unless you know how much they're worth? If a company is worth only a few hundred thousand dollars, a punishment of twenty thousand or so would be serious for them. It would get their attention and make them change the practices that they're being punished for. But what if the defendant is a billion dollar company? They'd laugh off a $20,000 punishment. The whole purpose of punitive damages is to make the punishment sting the defendant into changing his ways.

MR. GREENSTREET: "Sting the defendant," sir? Use the civil courts to administer a sting? It sounds un-American to me!

MR. BOGART: Well, Sydney, there was a case in Illinois about 150 years ago, in which the plaintiff's lawyer went even further. Seems the defendant had taken advantage of the widow of a Revolutionary war veteran, and swindled her out of some of her pension money. The plaintiff's lawyer made some notes for his final argument to the jury: "Money retained by defendant—not given by plaintiff. Revolutionary War. Describe Valley Forge privations. Ice. Soldiers' bleeding feet. Plaintiff's husband. Soldier leaving home for army. SKIN DEFENDANT. Close." The lawyer who asked that Illinois jury to skin the defendant for his dishonesty was a fella named Abraham Lincoln.

MR. GREENSTREET: Well, sir, can you honestly call it "due process of law" when a jury is empowered to take the property of a company's stockholders, and maybe even throw a company's employees out of work, by rendering a huge punitive damage verdict based on nothing more than a mistake by a low-level employee?

MR. BOGART: The U.S. Supreme Court considered the due process question in 1991, and found nothing wrong with the state courts allowing juries to assess punitive damages against companies for the misdeeds of employees, provided that the jury members are given instructions on the proper elements to consider in reaching their verdicts. The Supreme Court—loaded with conservative judges appointed by Nixon, Reagan, and Bush, by the way—said that punitive damages have always been an important part of the state law system for deterring wrongdoers. The court said that letting the jury assess punitive damages against a corporation for intentional acts committed by employees "creates a strong incentive for vigilance by those in a position to guard substantially against the evil to be prevented." In other words, we need to force the higher-ups to keep their employees from intentionally injuring people, and the only way to send that message is to have the jury bill the company for enough money to make a big difference on the bottom line.

MR. GREENSTREET: Obviously, sir, you are not a businessman yourself. You do not have the responsibility of running a great corporation which provides jobs for thousands of people and supplies the products and services that give us such a high standard of living. If you were in that position, you would realize that American businesses face a veritable army of government bureaucrats who regulate their every move and penalize them when they make the slightest mistake. On top of that weighty burden, you insist on the right of your buccaneers-for-hire to assess multi-million dollar fines by way of punitive damages. For shame, sir!

MR. BOGART: Sydney, I'm touched by your concern about over-regulation of business, especially after Reagan and Bush pulled the teeth out of so many government agencies. Maybe you like what deregulation did for our Savings and Loan industry. But we all know that companies hire armies of lawyers, lobbyists, and public relations operators who are very handy at fouling up the government regulators. The company lawyers are especially good at contesting regulations that the agencies propose. Sometimes these regulations are delayed as much as 15 to 20 years. Usually, all that business has to do is tie up the bureaucracy for a few years while they keep selling a defective product. By the time the creaky government machinery gets around to doing anything about the product, its useful life is over and the company has moved on to its next gyp. Businessmen laugh off regulation. It has no sting. Often the government agency isn't even told about a product problem until some tort lawyer tracks it down in the company records, as in the Dow Corning breast implant case. Even when government agencies know the facts, they can't skin the defendant like Abe Lincoln did to the guy who cheated the Illinois widow!

MR. GREENSTREET: By gad, sir, you are brazen! Do you honestly believe that plaintiff's contingent-fee lawyers should be allowed to decide whether breast implants are safe? Aren't you shocked by the fact that it was these money-mad lawyers who forced the FDA to suspend sales of the Dow Corning breast implants?

MR. BOGART: Yes, Sydney, I am shocked that the FDA had to learn of the dangers from a lawsuit because Dow Corning covered up serious complaints they had received from surgeons for as much as 20 years. But the problem here is not that the FDA finally learned of the hazards through the work of tort lawyers. The FDA might have learned about it from a garbage man who picked up records that Dow Corning was trying to trash. I wouldn't be ashamed of the garbage man for calling these dangers to the FDA's attention; again, I'd be ashamed of Dow Corning. And it wouldn't matter to me whether the garbage man was being paid a flat monthly rate or if his pay was contingent on the actual amount of garbage he hauled away. In either case, the fault and the shame belong to Dow Corning, and in the end the FDA decides whether these breast implants or any other medical devices are safe and effective enough to remain on the market.

MR. GREENSTREET: Why shouldn't the FDA collect the fines or punitive damages? Why should this be left up to self-interested lawyers, and why shouldn't the money be shared by the public through the FDA?

MR. BOGART: Oh, your sponsors would love that, wouldn't they, Sydney? They could use their lobbying clout to inject politics into every FDA decision to seek punitive damages. We'd be dependent on a bureaucracy that can't even force the manufacturers to file honest test reports, much less go to court against the giant legal firms that defend these cases. Your sponsors don't like having this power in the hands of plaintiff's lawyers who can't be lobbied or intimidated. But the very fact that the manufacturers want the FDA to have the exclusive power to seek punitive damages shows that they don't consider the FDA—or any government agency, for that matter—the kind of threat that the independent plaintiff's lawyers pose to the covering up of product defects.

MODERATOR HUSTON: Mr. Bogart, can you give us an example of a defective product that eluded government regulation but was forced off the market by punitive damages?

MR. BOGART: There are dozens, John. Probably the most famous example is asbestos. The manufacturers knew that asbestos was deadly way back in the 1930s, but they kept selling it because no government agency could stop them, and the plaintiff's lawyers didn't have much clout then. In the 1970s, plaintiff's lawyers discovered evidence that the manufacturers had known for 30 years that they were condemning the workers who handled asbestos, and then juries started socking them all over the country. The juries forced asbestos off the market, and only then did government agencies ban its use.

MODERATOR HUSTON: Did all that happen because of punitive damages?

MR. BOGART: It was a combination of thousands of compensatory damage claims for which the manufacturers didn't have a lot of insurance coverage, plus punitive damages that they also had to pay. Their insurance coverage was light because the beginnings of the asbestos disaster went back to the 1940s, when there were practically no product liability cases.

MODERATOR HUSTON: Can you give us an example of a major defective product that was forced off the market purely by punitive damages?

MR. BOGART: Sure, John—the Ford Pinto. Ford's designers put the Pinto fuel tank behind the rear axle, where an impact as slight as 20 miles an hour would make the axle act like a can opener, splitting the fuel tank and spraying gasoline into the passenger compartment, where a spark or heat would ignite the gasoline and incinerate the people in the car. The federal agency wanted to require more protection for the gas tank, which would have cost Ford less than $10 per car, but Ford tied them up in knots for more than five years while they kept selling the Pinto firetraps. Finally a California jury socked Ford with a $125 million punitive damage verdict, and that got their attention. Only after that verdict in 1978 did Ford recall the Pinto to make the gas tanks safe.

MR. GREENSTREET: How many jobs would be left in America if juries were permitted to assess punitive damages of $125 million against one company for one accident?

MR. BOGART: In the Pinto case, the trial judge reduced the punitive damages from $125 million to $3.5 million. Without the punitive damages, Ford's cheap liability insurance would have covered the verdict, and they would have left a million and a half firetrap Pintos on the road. The jurors, all residents of the conservative Orange County area, didn't pull the $125 million figure out of a hat. The evidence showed that Ford saved more than $100 million by flaunting the government safety regulators even though Ford's engineers were aware of the likelihood of burning people to a crisp after the slightest rear-end collision.

MR. GREENSTREET: Do you hold, sir, that juries should have the power to drive our great companies into bankruptcy through punitive damage verdicts?

MR. BOGART: As a champion of the free market, Sydney, I'm sure you'll agree that any company that keeps a life-threatening product on the market after learning of the dangers is not entitled to financial protection of that product, especially not through government intervention. If their conduct is outrageous enough to ruin the lives of thousands of victims—like the Dalkon Shield people—then bankruptcy is the proper free-market result.

MODERATOR HUSTON: Can you tell us briefly about the Dalkon Shield?

MR. BOGART: Sure. The A.H. Robins Company of Richmond, Virginia, makers of Robitussin and Chap Stick, decided to go into the birth control business. They bought an IUD—intra-uterine device—from the Dalkon Corporation, and put it on the market in 1971 with practically no testing. Using false and inadequate test reports, they plugged the Dalkon Shield as being safer than oral contraceptive pills, and they convinced over 4 million women to have it installed. It turned out that the Shield didn't work very well for birth control. But worse than that, it caused hundreds of thousands of women to suffer pelvic infection, sterility, miscarriage, deformed births, or septic abortions. Some women even died from the diseases produced by the Shield. Even though Robins continued to deceive doctors and the public, they finally had to suspend U.S. sales in 1974—although they continued to peddle their deadly Shield in third world countries for another year. Even then, it took another five years before Robins—under pressure of lawsuits that threatened its solvency—agreed to notify the millions of victims that they should have the device removed. There were punitive damage verdicts all over the country, and finally Robins filed for bankruptcy in 1985. Couldn't happen to nicer people!

MODERATOR HUSTON: How many product liability suits result in punitive damage verdicts, Mr. Bogart?

MR. BOGART: Very few—a lot less than one percent of the cases filed. Usually it happens only in cases where the manufacturers kept the product on the market even after they knew it was dangerous, like the Dalkon Shield crowd did. Even when juries award punitive damages, the trial and appeals judges look those cases over very carefully to make sure the proof is there. If it isn't a very strong case, the judges take the punitive damages away.

MODERATOR HUSTON: Mr. Greenstreet, I gather from your remarks that you are not enamored of trial by jury in tort cases. Can you tell us why?

MR. GREENSTREET: Most assuredly, sir. Life has become very complicated since the horse-and-buggy days when we started using juries in tort cases. Jurors are chosen at random from the population, without regard to their lack of capacity to grasp the technicalities of birth control devices, airplanes, and even the design of today's automobiles. Furthermore, jury trials are longer and more expensive than trial by judges, which is the sane system used by practically all other nations.

MR. BOGART: Sydney, you're assuming that judges have much greater technical knowledge than jurors. If you walk into any courtroom you'll see that it's just the opposite. The judge has been a lawyer all his adult life, and isn't trained in anything else. The jurors may be anything from accountants to rocket scientists, and collectively they have far more diversified experience and knowledge than the judge. Besides, if you gave American judges the job of deciding civil cases, you'd put tremendous political pressure on them. First thing you know, political hacks all over the country would pose as middlemen and would try to collect money under the table for influencing judges.

MODERATOR HUSTON: How do you respond to Mr. Greenstreet's point about other nations using judges rather than juries to decide civil cases?

MR. BOGART: The right to jury trials in civil cases as well as criminal cases is an important part of our history. The Brits took this right away during Colonial times, and this was one of the main grievances mentioned in the Declaration of Independence.

The Seventh Amendment, which is part of the Bill of Rights, guarantees trial by jury in civil cases. Thomas Jefferson said that the right to jury trial was "the only anchor yet imagined by man, by which a government can be held to the principles of its constitution." Sitting on a jury is the closest that most of us come to actually participating in our government. It gives us much more direct power than the votes we cast for candidates who look pretty much the same no matter what their party label is.

MR. GREENSTREET: Surely you will concede, sir, that jurors are biased in favor of the individual, the "little guy" whose station in life is similar to theirs, when an individual is suing a large company or someone whom they expect to carry liability insurance?

MR. BOGART: You've put your finger on the heart of the jury system, Sydney. Juries have diversity. They are six or twelve people from different walks of life, usually selected from the voting lists. Each side has the right to question them, to learn about their work and their home lives, and to search out bias. If the lawyers on either side are suspicious of bias, or if they just don't like the way a juror looks at them, they have plenty of challenges which they can use to dump them. But you can't dump a judge. You can't even question him to search for bias.

MR. GREENSTREET: Well, sir, I'm sure you are aware that even in America, judges sometimes sit without juries in tort cases, such as claims against the United States government, and other trials in which neither party has requested a jury. How do you account for the well-known fact that juries award much more money in tort cases than judges do?

MR. BOGART: That's completely unpredictable, Sydney. Many times judges have awarded more than jurors might have given in the same case. Anyway, every jury verdict is subject to reduction by the trial judge and appeals judges if it is excessive, so your argument is meaningless. Any experienced trial judge will tell you that juries are right most of the time, because they apply what the sociologists call "community values".

MR. GREENSTREET: Community values indeed, sir! And what are we to think about the community values of the Philadelphia jury that heard the case of the woman who claimed she had psychic powers? She testified that she lost these mysterious powers when she went to a hospital and the staff injected her with a dye that was needed for a CAT scan. The jury went for her story hook, line, and sinker. They awarded her *one million dollars* for the loss of her psychic powers! This was such an outrageous miscarriage of justice that President Ronald Reagan told the story to the nation on television.

MR. BOGART: Yes, Sydney, Ronnie was great with the punchlines, but sometimes he forgot some of the facts. Like the fact that the trial judge in that Philadelphia case threw the jury's verdict out the window, and the psychic lady got nothing. Ronnie told a few other concocted horror stories that your sponsors palmed off on him, but they were all debunked by Ed Bradley on a *60 Minutes* segment in 1988.

MODERATOR HUSTON: What about Mr. Greenstreet's point that jury trials take longer and are more expensive—isn't the cost of the legal system a great concern of our local, state, and federal governments?

MR. BOGART: Jury trials take slightly longer, but the mere existence of the jury helps to settle lots of cases that would otherwise go to trial. John, you're talking about a bulwark against tyranny and corruption, a part of our Bill of Rights that Jefferson considered more important than the right to vote. It's priceless.

MODERATOR HUSTON: Our time is getting short, gentlemen. Let's get back to our original topic: tort reform. What is it, Mr. Greenstreet, and why do we need it?

MR. GREENSTREET: Well, sir, as you know, since the 1970s there has been an ongoing liability explosion that has brought our insurance companies and businesses to the brink of disaster. Soft-hearted jurors and soft-headed judges have disregarded centuries of legal precedent, and have turned our courts into casinos where the plaintiff's lawyers enrich themselves at the expense of the rest of us. They have not only conjured up many new torts that can be sued for—they have also multiplied the amounts collected, often by a factor of 5 to 10 times the existing compensation level, even after adjusting for inflation. That's why we need reform immediately.

MR. BOGART: Sydney, those so-called new torts are nothing more than enforcements of the basic law that has been with us since we became a nation. Your sponsors squawk about strict liability for defective products, but they know that we had strict liability for all kinds of injuries, whether caused by a product or a horse or a human being, way back when George Washington was president. The requirement of proving fault came later, to protect business during the Industrial Revolution. We've always used tort law to right wrongs. Our law is what everybody's ever thought about justice, about right and wrong. It's the conscience of humanity.

MODERATOR HUSTON: If memory serves, those last two sentences were spoken by Dana Andrews in *The Ox-Bow Incident*. In any event, Mr. Bogart, what about Mr. Greenstreet's charge that the amounts collected by accident victims soared way beyond the rate of inflation during the 1970s and 1980s?

MR. BOGART: For the second time Sydney is right, John. But what he didn't tell you is that before the 1970s, accident victims were badly shortchanged—and often got no money at all—because their lawyers weren't strong enough to enforce the existing rights to compensation. In the old days, the amounts collected were compromises rather than compensation. That's why the recent rise looks so dramatic, but it's nothing more than a catching-up to bring the adding machine up to the "zero" starting point by including fair compensation for all the items the law allows, like loss of future earning power, physical and mental pain and suffering, and loss of enjoyment of life. And nobody's ever figured up how many billions we save every year in tax dollars that would have to be spent for medical care and welfare entitlements of accident victims if they were not compensated through the tort system.

MODERATOR HUSTON: Mr. Greenstreet, please tell us what steps have been taken toward what you call tort reform.

MR. GREENSTREET: There has been a groundswell, sir, a grass-roots movement to reform tort law in virtually every state. Progressive statutes have been passed by the state legislatures to limit damages for pain and suffering; to revise the methods of calculating punitive damages; to limit contingent legal fees; and to enact other badly-needed reforms.

MR. BOGART: That groundswell, Sydney, was manufactured by lobbyists for insurance and business people who want to go back to having their victims subsidize shoddy products and services. They should spend that money on the tort reform we really need: eliminating the torts by encouraging excellent products and services. Instead, they pay lobbyists to operate in the smoke-filled rooms of the state legislative committees. They push through laws that stifle excellence and protect incompetent and dishonest people from enforcement of the laws we have lived by since Colonial days. That's why a lot of courts have thrown out these so-called tort reform laws as unconstitutional.

MR. GREENSTREET: Pray tell, sir, what would happen to American business, and all the jobs and benefits it creates, if liability insurance was not available at affordable rates?

MR. BOGART: As you know very well, Sydney, liability insurance companies are really investment managers today. A lot of them use what they call cash-flow underwriting. They collect whatever premiums they can and invest them at high returns. They hang on to this premium money for years, even if there are large claims, because they're able to stall lawsuits in the courts until they wring out every last dollar of investment profit. If the claims payments total up to more than the investment profits, the insurers then have an incentive to demand that defective products be designed safely, or that shoddy operators install safeguards against injuries. The insurers could quickly reform the people who commit the torts by insisting on excellence before agreeing to write the insurance. If they call themselves insurance companies, they ought to do more than shuffle paper investments. Besides, there is no evidence that tort reform will reduce insurance rates. The National Association of Insurance Commissioners, who regulate the industry, told Congress that insurers' losses were caused by their underwriting practices rather than the condition of tort law.

MODERATOR HUSTON: Apart from the fact that tort reform laws originate with those who are called upon to pay tort damages, why do you object to them, Mr. Bogart?

MR. BOGART: My objection is really based on that simple old right-or-wrong test that Dana Andrews spoke about. If a manufacturer sells a defective product that maims a consumer, is it right for the state legislatures to make the consumer victim bear the economic costs of his injuries, on top of having his life devastated by the injuries? Tort reform is an attempt to substitute socialistic government intervention for the free-market system that has produced the fairest and most accessible legal system the world has ever known. I object to the buying up of legislative votes when these questions have always been decided in our courts, according to the conscience of the community. In this country, the courts are the great levelers. In our courts, all men are truly created equal.

MODERATOR HUSTON: Hmm. "The great levelers." "Truly created equal." Gregory Peck as Atticus Finch in *To Kill a Mockingbird*, if I'm not mistaken?

MR. BOGART: Right again, John. *Mockingbird* became a classic because it was based on the great American theme of equal justice under law. But not even Greg Peck could make a winner out of tort reform. The courts *are* our great levelers, but without a special breed of lawyers—the Equalizers—that leveling wouldn't mean much because most people wouldn't have access to the courts.

MR. GREENSTREET: The *equalizers*, sir?

MR. BOGART: Yes, Sydney—but not the kind of equalizers you and I packed in our holsters. These Equalizers are the tort lawyers who lift their clients onto their shoulders by putting their talent and their money on the line. Without them and their contingent legal fees, the little guy that you spoke of couldn't sue the big company that maimed him with a defective product or a shoddy service. In fact, practically nobody could stand up to the giant insurance companies without the Equalizers. Your sponsors wouldn't bother with their tort reform lobbying because it wouldn't matter what the law was. Nobody could enforce that law without the Equalizers.

MR. GREENSTREET: So you consider tort reform undesirable because the tort system works perfectly well now, Mr. Bogart?

MR. BOGART: It's far from perfect, Sydney. It's messy and noisy, just like the human nature and democracy that it springs from. But if the needs of human nature and democracy count for anything, it's head and shoulders above any other country's system. And it's constantly being updated and reformed by unbiased people: the judges who are elected, or who are appointed by elected officials, and the jurors who directly apply changing community values. Your so-called tort reform is undesirable because it would would turn the clock back to the kind of justice that Jane Froman received: $8,300 to compensate her for the pain of 27 operations, plus millions of dollars in medical expenses and lost income.

MR. GREENSTREET: Do you honestly believe, sir, that one or two aberrations like the Jane Froman case require us to be become a lawyer-driven society?

MR. BOGART: The alternative to the Equalizers is either the Jane Froman type of shortchanging powerless victims, or—you'll love this, Sydney—the Japanese legal system that shuts victims out of court so that they have to hire hoodlums called *yakuza,* who arrange compensation by strong-arming the people who caused the accident.

MODERATOR HUSTON: You've emphasized the *ombudsman* role of the Equalizers, and you've told us how they go about policing the business community. It seems to me that you're justifying the crude remedies of the tort system on the ground that they lead to social justice, aren't you?

MR. BOGART: Nothing that fancy, John. We could argue all day about what "social justice" means. Tort law is about simple justice, the righting of wrongs. It's about compensation, accountability, and deterrence.

MR. GREENSTREET: Mr. Bogart, your public has come to look upon you as a symbol of rugged individualism, an unsentimental loner. Yet you seem to be advocating a risk-free society, a world that is made completely safe for you by others. Aren't you a bit out of character today, sir?

MR. BOGART: No, Sydney, I feel very comfortable in this role. I'm not looking for a risk-free society, but I would like to live in one where people can't profit by injuring innocent victims. Just make the big shots and the crooks accountable for their sins and mistakes like the rest of us, and I'll take my chances with life's hazards. Besides, I like representing the Equalizers because they're my kind of guys. They play out the American Dream.

MR. GREENSTREET: How so, sir?

MR. BOGART: In a lot of ways, Sydney. They fight for the underdog. They're damned good at what they do, and they got there on their own. Nobody subsidizes them or passes laws to protect them from the market or the conscience of the community. They live well, but for every dollar they take in, two dollars goes to an underdog who would be helpless without their clout. They have a lot to do with equal justice under law.

MR. GREENSTREET: You make them sound like Knights of the Round Table, sir.

MR. BOGART: No, Sydney, they're just ordinary guys and gals in the morals department. It just happens that the tort system casts them in the role of Equalizers. If they perform well, if they make a success of it, they can't help but fulfill the American Dream, happy ending and all.

MR. GREENSTREET: When it comes to solving practical problems, Mr. Bogart, what good is a dream?

MR. BOGART: Oh, come on, Sydney! The three of us worked in the Dream Factory. Was it all a waste of time, or did we help people make their dreams come true? One of the things wrong with this country is that we're losing the American Dream. It's a big part of what made us great, and we've got to get it back. We can't let greed take over. People can still get rich, but they've got to earn it, like the Equalizers do.

MODERATOR HUSTON: Gentlemen, we've earned our stipends today because our time is up. Thank you for coming back to dramatize these important issues.

As the lights go down, Greenstreet, Huston, and Bogart clear the table and prepare to leave. Greenstreet notices that Bogart is holding a battered textbook covered in faded red leatherette. The

title: *Handbook of the Law of Torts*, First Edition, 1941, by William
L. Prosser, Professor of Law, University of Minnesota.

"What's that, Bogie?" asks Greenstreet.

"This? Why, it's—er—the stuff that dreams are made of."

Notes

Following are citations of major cases, books, and articles mentioned in the text, as well as others that may be of interest. Case citations always begin with the volume number. Thus "71 U.S. 2 (1886)" refers to a decision of the United States Supreme Court in 1886, appearing at page 2 of volume 71 of the official *United States Reports*. Names of publishers of legal textbooks are not customarily given, since they are available in law libraries.

Chapter 1

Page 1: W. Safire, *Safire's Political Dictionary* 18-19 (New York: Ballantine, 1978).
J. Adams, *The Epic of America* (Boston: Little Brown, 1931).

Page 2: J. Guimond, *American Photography and the American Dream* 12 (Chapel Hill: Univ. of North Carolina Press, 1991).

Page 5: D. Brown, *You Gotta Believe!* (New York: Morrow, 1991).
S. Terkel, *American Dreams: Lost & Found* (New York: Pantheon, 1980).

Page 9: E. Long, *The American Dream and the Popular Novel* (Boston: Routledge & Kegan Paul, 1985).

Page 10: D. Madden, ed. *American Dreams, American Nightmares* (Carbondale: Southern Illinois Univ. Press, 1970).

Page 11: J. Patterson and P. Kim, *The Day America Told the Truth* (New York: Prentice Hall, 1991).
M. Seligman, *Learned Optimism* (New York: Knopf, 1990).

Page 15: F. Capra, *The Name Above the Title* (New York: Macmillan, 1971).

Page 17: R. Sklar, *Movie-Made America* (New York: Random House, 1975).

Chapter 2

Page 37:   *Lincoln Savings & Loan Assoc. v. Wall*, 743 F.Supp. 901 (1990).

Page 38:   M. Mayer, *The Greatest-Ever Bank Robbery* (New York: Scribner, 1990).

Chapter 3

Page 44:   M. Bender and S. Altschul, *The Chosen Instrument* (New York: Simon & Schuster, 1982).

Page 45:   R. Davies, *Pan Am: An Airline and its Aircraft* (New York: Orion, 1987).

Page 51:   O. Allen, *The Airline Builders* 168-69 (Alexandria, VA: Time-Life Books, 1981).
K. Follett, *Night Over Water* (New York: Morrow, 1991).

Chapter 5

Page 86:   The decision of the New York Court of Appeals holding that Jane Froman's ticket was properly delivered is reported at *Ross v. Pan American Airways*, 299 N.Y. 88 (1949).

Chapter 6

Page 98:   R. McLarty, *Res Ipsa Loquitur in Airline Passenger Litigation*, 37 Va. L.Rev. 55 (1951). See also S. Speiser, 1 *Res Ipsa Loquitur*, Chapter 10 (1972).

Chapter 10

Page 182:   The decision of the U.S. Supreme Court in the *Titanic* litigation is reported at *Ocean Steam Navigation Company Ltd. v. Mellor et al*, 233 U.S. 718 (1914).

Page 186:   A. Steuer, *Max D. Steuer*, Trial Lawyer 277 (New York: Random House, 1950).

Page 188: The decision placing property ahead of life and liberty is *Children's Hospital v. Adkins*, 284 F. 613 (1922), affirmed by the U.S. Supreme Court in *Adkins v. Children's Hospital*, 261 U.S. 525 (1923).
F. Hare, *My Learned Friends* 7-8 (1976).

Page 191: R. Nader, *Unsafe at Any Speed: The Designed-In Dangers of the American Automobile* (New York: Grossman, 1965).

Page 200: The Appellate Division's affirmance of the finding that there was no collusion is reported at *Nader v. General Motors Corp.*, 292 N.Y.S.2d 345 (App. Div. 1968).

Page 202: Justice Brust's decision on the constitutional right of privacy is reported at *Nader v. General Motors Corp.*, 292 N.Y.S.2d 514 (Sup.Ct., Special Term 1968).
The Appellate Division decision is reported at *Nader v. General Motors Corp.*, 298 N.Y.S.2d 137 (App. Div. 1969).

Page 203: The Court of Appeals decision is reported at *Nader v. General Motors Corp.*, 25 N.Y.2d 560 (1970).

Page 204: W. Prosser, *Handbook of the Law of Torts* 816 (4th ed. 1971).

Chapter 11

Page 214: G. McKnight, *Gucci: A House Divided* (New York: Donald I. Fine, 1987).

Page 218: Judge Conner's decision on use of the Gucci name is reported at *Paolo Gucci v. Gucci Shops, Inc.*, 688 F.Supp. 916 (1988).

Chapter 12

Page 222: M. Belli, *The Adequate Award*, 39 Cal.L.Rev. 1 (1951).

Page 237: *Winterbottom v. Wright*, 152 Eng. Rep. 402 (1842).
MacPherson v. Buick Motor Co., 217 N.Y. 382 (1916).

Page 238: The annotation on the privity rule written by Al Gans in 1946 is "Manufacturer's liability for negligence causing injury to person or damage to property of ultimate consumer or user," 164 A.L.R. 569.
The New Jersey Plymouth auto case is *Henningsen v. Bloomfield Motors, Inc.*, 32 N.J. 358 (1960).

The California Shopsmith power tool case is *Greenman v. Yuba Power Products, Inc.,* 59 Cal.2d 57 (1963)

Page 239: *Escola v. Coca-Cola,* 24 Cal.2d 453 (1944).

Page 240: Prosser's major law review articles on the privity question were: W. Prosser, *The Assault Upon the Citadel (Strict Liability to the Consumer),* 69 Yale L.J. 1099 (1960); and W. Prosser, *The Fall of the Citadel (Strict Liability to the Consumer),* 50 Minn. L. Rev. 791 (1966).

Page 243: The decision of the New York Court of Appeals in the American Airlines drum-type altimeter case is reported at *Goldberg v. Kollsman Instrument Corp. and Lockheed Aircraft Corp.,* 12 N.Y.2d 432 (1963).

Page 244: G. Priest, *The Invention of Enterprise Liability: A Critical History of the Intellectual Foundations of Modern Tort Law,* 14 Journal of Legal Studies 461 (1985). The three aviation case "possibles" mentioned by Professor Priest are: *Middleton v. United Aircraft Corp.,* 204 F.Supp. 856 (1960), decided under the federal Death on the High Seas Act; *Siegel v. Braniff Airways, Inc.,* 204 F.Supp. 861 (1960), decided under Texas law; and *Conlon v. Republic Aviation Corp.,* 204 F.Supp. 865 (1960), decided under Michigan law.

Chapter 13

Page 249: *Baker v. Bolton,* 170 Eng. Rep. 1033 (1808). The case that first construed Lord Campbell's Act to limit damages to pecuniary loss was *Blake v. Midland Railway Co.,* 18 Q.B. 93, 118 Eng. Rep. 35 (1852).

Page 251: R. Bork, *The Tempting of America* 2 (New York: Simon & Schuster, 1990).

Page 254: *Kilberg v. Northeast Airlines,* 9 N.Y.2d 34 (1961).

Page 256: The Second Circuit's *en banc* decision is reported at *Pearson v. Northeast Airlines,* 309 F.2d 553 (1962).

Page 259: The Second Circuit's decision in the Gordon Dean case is reported at *Gore v. Northeast Airlines,* 373 F.2d 717 (1967).

Page 262: *Blake v. Midland Railway Co.,* 18 Q.B. 93, 118 Eng. Rep. 35 (1852).

Page 263: The Scottish case is reported at *Brown v. MacGregor*, 17 F.D. 232 (1813).

Page 265: The case of the two nuns from Oregon is reported at *Goheen v. General Motors Corp.*, 263 Or. 145 (1972).

Page 267: The substitute mother case is reported at *Zaninovich v. American Airlines*, 271 N.Y.S.2d 866 (App. Div. 1966).

Page 269: The U.S. Supreme Court decision on loss of society and mental anguish of surviving relatives is reported at *Sea-Land Services v. Gaudet*, 414 U.S. 573 (1974).

Page 271: The Texas Supreme Court decision is reported at *Sanchez v. Schindler*, 651 S.W.2d 249 (Tex. 1983). The Tulane article cited by the Texas Supreme Court is S. Speiser and S. Malawer, *An American Tragedy: Damages for Mental Anguish of Bereaved Relatives in Wrongful Death Actions*, 51 Tulane L.Rev. 1 (1976).
The other Texas Supreme Court decisions are: *Cavnar v. Quality Control Parking, Inc.* 696 S.W.2d 549 (Tex. 1985); and *Clifton v. Southern Pacific Transportation Co.*, 709 S.W.2d 636 (Tex. 1986).

Page 274: Prosser's evaluation of *Recovery for Wrongful Death* will be found in W. Prosser, *Handbook of the Law of Torts* (4th ed. 1971) at page 902.

Chapter 14

Page 281: S. Hersh, *The Target is Destroyed* (New York: Random House, 1986).

Page 287: The decision of the Court of Appeals for the District of Columbia Circuit is reported at *In Re Korean Air Lines Disaster of September 1, 1983*, 932 F.2d 1475 (1991).

Page 290: The Delta Air Lines Flight 191 decision is reported at *In Re Air Crash at Dallas/Fort Worth Airport on August 2, 1985*, 720 F.Supp. 1258 (1989).

Page 292: The Seventh Amendment reads as follows: *In suits at common law, where the value in controversy shall exceed twenty dollars, the right of trial by jury shall be preserved, and no fact tried by a jury shall be otherwise re-examined in any court of the United States, than according to the rules of the common law.*

Page 294: The Florida case of the injured IBM salesman is reported at *Tamarac v. Garchar*, 398 So.2d 889 (Fla App D4, 1981).
The New York case of the brain-damaged girl is reported at Merrill v. Albany Medical Center Hospital, 512 N.Y.S.2d 519 (App. Div. 1987).

Page 295: The Louisiana Reyes Syndrome case, *Sharkey v. Sterling Drugs, Inc.*, was decided by the Louisiana Court of Appeal, First Circuit, on April 23, 1992. At this writing there is no official lawbook citation available. The Docket Number in the Court of Appeal is CA/91/0890.

Page 298: Judge Torruella's decision is reported at *Clemente v. United States*, 422 F.Supp. 564 (1976).

Page 299: The First Circuit's decision is reported at *Clemente v. United States*, 567 F.2d 1140 (1977).

Page 301: The quotation on improved machine safety is from National Safety Council, *Accident Prevention Manual* 796 (7th ed.).
The De Havilland Comet story is quoted from E. Rickenbacker, *Rickenbacker: An Autobiography* 414 (Englewood Cliffs: Prentice-Hall, 1967).

Page 306: The Australian Federal Court decision on misleading and deceptive advertising is reported at *Australian Federation of Consumer Organizations v. The Tobacco Institute of Australia Ltd.* (1991) ATPR 41-079.

Page 307: The 1986 Rand study of the cost of litigation to the forum community is J.S. Kakalik et al., *Costs and Compensation Paid in Tort Litigation*, Rand/ICJ publication no. R-3391-ICJ, 1986.
The Rand study on aviation accident litigation is J.S. Kakalik et al., *Costs and Compensation Paid in Aviation Accident Litigation*, Rand/ICJ publication no. R-3421-ICJ, 1988.

Page 314: C. Yang, "Lawyers Start to Stop the Clock" (*Business Week*, August 17, 1992).
J. Robertson, "The Beginning of the End of the Billable Hour?" (*The Washington Lawyer*, July/August 1991).

Page 315: P. Pilzer, *Unlimited Wealth* (New York: Crown, 1990).
D. Osborne and T. Gaebler, *Reinventing Government* (New York: Addison Wesley, 1992).

Page 316: J. Bowles and J. Hammond, *Beyond Quality* 12-26 (New York: Putnam, 1991).
L. Dobyns and C. Crawford-Mason, *Quality or Else: The Revolution in World Business* 1 (Boston: Houghton Mifflin, 1991).

Page 317: T. Peters and R. Waterman, *In Search of Excellence* (New York: Harper & Row, 1982).
T. Peters and N. Austin, *A Passion for Excellence* (New York: Random House, 1985).

Chapter 16

Page 352: The AAIB Review Board decision, along with the original AAIB report, were published together in *Aircraft Accident Report 2/88*, Air Accidents Investigation Branch, Department of Transport (London: Her Majesty's Stationery Office, 1988).

Page 358: A. Hammer, *Hammer* (New York: Putnam, 1987).

Page 360: H. Baade, *Foreign Oil Disaster Litigation Prospects in the United States and the "Mid-Atlantic Settlement Formula,"* 1989 Journ. Energy & Natural Resources Law 125.

Page 366: The 1989 Green Paper is entitled *Lord Chancellor's Department: Contingency Fees*, Cm 571 (London: Her Majesty's Stationery Office, 1989).

Page 372: J. Sterngold, "Japan's Rigged Casino" (*New York Times Magazine*, April 26, 1992).

Page 374: T. Holden, "Consumers Start Telling it to the Judge" (*Business Week*, March 9, 1992).

Page 375: M. Galanter, "Public View of Lawyers" (*Trial* , April 1992).

Page 377: W. Halal, "East is East, West is West" (*Business in the Contemporary World*, Spring 1992).

Chapter 17

Page 381: W. Olson, *The Litigation Explosion: What Happened when America Unleashed the Lawsuit* (New York: Truman Talley-Dutton, 1991).

P. Huber, *Liability: The Legal Revolution and its Conse-quences* (New York: Basic Books, 1988).

Page 382: J. Silber, *Straight Shooting: What's Wrong with America and How to Fix It* (New York: Harper & Row, 1989).

Page 385: President's Council on Competitiveness, *Agenda for Civil Justice Reform in America* (Washington DC: Office of the Vice President, August 1991).

Page 389: U.S. Congress, Office of Technology Assessment, *Making Things Better: Competing in Manufacturing*, OTA-ITE-443 (Washington DC: U.S. Government Printing Of-fice, February 1990).
J. Bowles and J. Hammond, *Beyond Quality* (New York: Putnam, 1991).
L. Dobyns and C. Crawford-Mason, *Quality or Else* (Bos-ton: Houghton Mifflin, 1991).
T. Peters and R. Waterman, *In Search of Excellence* (New York: Harper & Row, 1982).
T. Peters and N. Austin, *A Passion for Excellence* (New York: Random House, 1985).

Page 390: President's Commission on Industrial Competitiveness, *Global Competition: The New Reality* (Washington, DC: U.S. Government Printing Office, January 1985, two volumes).
M.I.T. Commission on Industrial Productivity, *Made in America: Regaining the Productive Edge* (Cambridge, MA: M.I.T. Press, 1989).

Page 393: On the number of lawyers per 10,000 population in the United States and 99 other nations, see R. August, "The Mythical Kingdom of Lawyers" (American Bar Association Journal, September 1992). A later study questioned the ability of Professor August or anyone else to draw firm conclusions from the very limited data available on the number of "law providers" out-side the United States; see M. Galanter, "Re-entering the Mythical Kingdom" (American Bar Association Journal, November 1992).
On the number of law students in Japan compared to the United States, see M. Kato, *The Role of Law and Lawyers in Japan and the United States*, 1987 B.Y.U. L.Rev. 627, 661.
On the Japanese legal system, see T. Kitawaki and R. August, "The Myth of Japan as a Land Without Lawyers" (International Bar News, March 1987); R. Miller, *Apples*

v. Persimmons: The Legal Profession in Japan and the United States, 39 Journ. Legal Education 27 (1989); and "The Japanese Solution: Kill All the Lawsuits" (*Business Week*, April 13, 1992).

Page 399: The first U.S. Supreme Court decision to reject the loser-pays rule was *Arcambel v. Wiseman*, 3 Dall. 306 (1796). The most recent reaffirmation of that position by the Supreme Court was in *Fleischmann Distilling Corp. v. Maier Brewing Co.*, 386 U.S. 714 (1975).

Page 402: Abraham Lincoln's "SKIN DEFENDANT" note is reproduced in F. Hill, *Lincoln the Lawyer* 215-16 (New York: Century, 1906).

Page 403: The U.S. Supreme Court decision upholding punitive damages is *Mutual Life Insurance Co. v. Haslip*, 111 S.Ct. 1032 (1991).

Page 411: The testimony of the National Association of Insurance Commissioners that "tort reform" legislation would not reduce insurance rates was given before the House of Representatives Subcommittee on Commerce, Consumer Protection, and Competitiveness in December 1987.

Index